Common Grace and the Gospel

COMMON GRACE AND THE GOSPEL

CORNELIUS
VAN TIL

SECOND EDITION,

INCLUDING THE COMPLETE TEXT OF
THE ORIGINAL, 1972 EDITION

EDITED BY K. SCOTT OLIPHINT

PUBLISHING
P.O. BOX 817 • PHILLIPSBURG • NEW JERSEY 08865-0817

ISBN: 978-1-59638-583-2 (pbk)
ISBN: 978-1-59638-584-9 (ePub)
ISBN: 978-1-59638-585-6 (Mobi)

Page design by Lakeside Design Plus

Printed in the United States of America

Library of Congress Cataloging-in-Publication Data

Van Til, Cornelius, 1895-1987.
  Common grace and the gospel / Cornelius Van Til ; edited by K. Scott Oliphint. – Second
Edition, including the complete text of the original, 1972 edition.
      pages cm
  Includes bibliographical references and index.
  ISBN 978-1-59638-583-2 (pbk.)
  1. Grace (Theology) 2. Reformed Church–Doctrines. I. Oliphint, K. Scott, 1955-
editor. II. Title.
  BT761.3.V34 2015
  234–dc23
                              2014037805

CONTENTS

FOREWORD
BY K. SCOTT OLIPHINT

W hen I first began reading Van Til's works, the only category I had for him was something like "Christian philosopher." The reason for that was that his terms, concepts, mode of argument, etc., were beyond any theology I had read in my nascent Christian experience. I was aware of such terminology and concepts only because of the philosophy classes I was then taking in college.

As I have come to appreciate over the years, however, the foundation for everything Van Til sets forth is his thoroughly biblical and Reformed theology. Part of the problem in understanding Van Til's writings is that, in his works, he was assuming that the rest of us would read him with that same theology in mind. If we do read him with an eye for his biblical and Reformed foundation, virtually every term, concept, mode of argument, etc., will find its home in that foundation. This is unquestionably the case in this volume.

As Van Til notes in the beginning, this book is a collection of essays. These essays were written over a period of roughly twenty-five years. Given the different time and context of each of the essays, we can expect that there will be differing emphases in them as well. But even with differing emphases, there is similarity of content and concepts in them all.

My comments throughout this volume attempt to clarify and explain Van Til's arguments, so we need not detail those here. An initial, general point is in order, however, and then we will discuss three overriding themes that are found throughout this work and that should guide our reading through each essay.

First, the more general comment. Throughout this collection of essays, Van Til wants to provide a "third way" to think about "the common grace problem": "Going off to the right by denying common grace [as with Hoeksema] or going off to the left by affirming a theory of common grace patterned after the natural theology of Rome [as in some of Kuyper's formulations] is to fail, to this extent, to challenge the wisdom of the world" (p. 168).

The "third way" that Van Til proposes is a way that goes neither to the left nor to the right. Unwilling to move "to the right," Van Til will not deny common grace. Such a denial, as he will make clear, is unbiblical, and it presupposes an improper application of the rules of thinking. Those who deny common grace think "abstractly" and "deductively," so that certain truths of Scripture are squeezed out because they cannot fit within the constraints of abstract reasoning.

The primary point to keep in mind, therefore, with respect to the *rejection* of the doctrine of common grace (a rejection that Van Til opposes), is that it is based on a *fallacious logical deduction* from the truth of God's eternal decree, a decree both to elect a people and to pass over others. Such deductions deal with "abstractions" and thus fail to be biblically concrete.[1] Not only so, but they undermine a biblical philosophy of history. It is this practice of drawing fallacious deductions that Van Til is concerned to address, and he addresses it with deep biblical content in each of these essays (though his terms may not, on the surface, betray that content).

So Van Til cannot move to the right. Neither, however, will his "third way" move "to the left"; it will not allow for a notion of neutral concepts or activities (as in the "theology of Rome") in which there can be no Christian challenge because there is thought to be, in such concepts or activities, no real rebellion against God. There can be no view of common grace in which the Christian and the non-Christian, it is supposed, have certain concepts and ideas that are, at root, in common. This kind of commonality can be no part of common grace, according to Van Til, because, in part, if such commonality existed, there could be no challenge to the non-Christian in those areas of his life and thinking. More importantly, such thinking does not give due credit to the biblical and Reformed notion of the antithesis between believer and unbeliever.

1. In the preface, Van Til summarizes for us "the point of view that binds the several chapters of this book together." The "point of view" of which Van Til speaks is that, due to the Christian notion of a "limiting concept," "there is an intelligible, though not an exhaustive, intellectually penetrable basis for human experience" (p. xlix).

Because Van Til will not move to the right or to the left in his articulation
of the doctrine of common grace, some revision is necessary. That revision
focuses on three fundamental and interconnected themes that are central
to Van Til's doctrine of common grace. Thus, it is crucial to understand
these themes and to recognize their presence throughout this book.

There are myriad theological and philosophical issues that these essays
on common grace touch upon; all of them could be pursued with profit
and edification. However, in light of Van Til's assessment of that which
binds these essays together, and in order to provide a more general over-
view of them, I want to highlight three main and overriding themes that
are more or less assumed in each chapter in this work and that provide
an interpretive grid through which to read them all. These themes are not
necessarily terms that Van Til repeats often, nor are they the only themes
that could have been chosen; rather, they are dominant concepts that help
us understand the substance of Van Til's arguments and his development of
the doctrine of common grace throughout each essay. Using Van Til's own
language, then, these three themes are: (1) **fearless anthropomorphism**,
(2) **concrete thinking**, and (3) **limiting concepts**.

Although these three themes may sound a bit abstract, they should be
seen, as I hope to show, as terms that invariably point us to the biblical
truths of the Reformed faith. Not only so, but these three interrelated themes
are best seen as entailing each other. That is, we are not being fearlessly
anthropomorphic unless we are thinking concretely and articulating our
theological doctrines (with respect to these issues) as limiting concepts.
These themes are not enumerated here in the order of their appearance
in the essays, nor are they chosen because of the number of times they
appear in this collection of essays. Rather, they seem to me to be the central, controlling themes for everything Van Til wants to emphasize about
common grace and its related theological concepts. Indeed, in some ways
they are central to everything Van Til wrote. That should not be surprising,
given that these essays span so much of his teaching career.

Before we set out to explain these three themes, it is crucial to remember
where, theologically, Van Til begins his thinking about common grace—and
about everything else. He begins with the ontological Trinity. To "**begin
with**" the ontological Trinity means, at least, that the reality of God *as God*
must be the assumption and controlling reality behind everything else that
is said. Specifically, as we will note below, the three themes themselves
are what they are only in light of the fact that the triune God is absolutely
independent, in and of himself. That is, he is *essentially* independent;

there is no sense in which God needs anything in order to be who he is, in and of himself. This truth begins to inform the mystery that is part and parcel of the three themes below. Apart from this truth, there is little to no mystery in the Christian faith. Not only so, but apart from this truth, God is in some essential way in need of something outside of himself in order to be who he is as God. That cannot be the case. The Bible begins with the ontological Trinity in its first four words. Since only God *was* in the beginning, he cannot need anything in order to be who he is.

Not only so, but because the God who alone is independent is triune, the oneness of God that we confess as Christians must be affirmed in its triune diversity as well. That is, God is three in one, not simply one. His three-in-oneness is the foundation for the interplay in creation of the one (universal categories) and the many (particular things). The triunity of God is indeed a mystery, and that mystery has its analog in all of creation as his creatures recognize both unity and diversity in the world God has made. Creation, then, is mysteriously analogous to the triune God's character. In this way, Van Til takes seriously, and rigorously applies, Herman Bavinck's dictum that the lifeblood of theology is mystery.[2]

It is only in the context of God's triune aseity (that is, his absolute self-existence and independence, in and of himself), which is the bedrock foundation for everything Van Til argues in this work (and in all of his works), that the three themes below take their proper place.

(1) FEARLESS ANTHROPOMORPHISM

Van Til does not use the phrase *fearless anthropomorphism* that often in these essays, but everything that he says about common grace, including its relationship to God's decree and to our total depravity, as well as the knotty problems surrounding God's will of decree and his will of command, includes and presupposes this idea.

The Reformed faith holds that the relation between God's will of decree and his will of command cannot be exhaustively understood by man. Any relation between what God does in eternity and what he does in history is clothed in mystery. That is, God decrees and controls whatsoever comes to pass. Embedded in that sovereign, unconditional, and all-encompassing decree, however, are God's commands, which may or may not be fol-

2. Herman Bavinck, *Reformed Dogmatics*, ed. John Bolt, trans. John Vriend, 4 vols. (Grand Rapids: Baker Academic, 2003–2008), 2:29.

lowed. How can both things be compatible? How can it be that God decrees *all things*, and at the same time sets forth his commands, which can be transgressed? How do these two "wills" cohere? The answer to this question highlights the mystery through which biblical truth flows. As Van Til develops his notion of common grace (and as he interacts with William Masselink), there are contrasts and comparisons made between "Amsterdam" and "Old Princeton." So, says Van Til:

> Amsterdam and Old Princeton agree that the relation between the will of decree and will of command cannot be exhaustively understood by man. Therefore every point of doctrine is a "difficult problem." As men we must think analogically. God is the original and man is derivative. We must not determine what can or cannot be by argument that starts from the will of decree apart from its relation to the will of command. In particular we must not say that God cannot display any attitude of favor to the generality of mankind because we know that He intends that ultimately some are "vessels of wrath." On the other hand we must not argue from the revealed will of God with respect to man's responsibility to the denial of man's ultimate determination by the will of decree. We need therefore at this point, *which is all-inclusive,* to be "fearlessly anthropomorphic." (p. 215, emphasis added)

As we noted above, the first thing that must be understood in any discussion of common grace is the *mystery* that obtains by virtue of God's character and his relationship to creation. To put it simply, there is no mystery when there is no creation. God exhaustively knows himself and all things. Mystery ensues (for the Reformed) at the point of creation, specifically, the creation of man (male and female). When God created man, he determined to create man in his image. That determination included the fact that man would be responsible for and in history, due to his covenant relationship to God. Man would make choices, and those choices would influence, for better or for worse, the flow of history and his relationship to God. Indeed, those choices would influence God's attitude toward man. God would, in a *real but penultimate* sense, *react* according to man's choices.[3]

3. This "reaction" of God, in a Reformed context, presupposes his exhaustive, unconditional decree. In a semi-Pelagian or Arminian context, God's reaction presupposes man's autonomy; not so for the Reformed.

Not only so, but as God chose to make man in his image, he also determined that Adam would be the covenant head of all mankind. As such, Adam was the representative of every person who would ever exist. Thus, Adam's choices were not just his, but also, by virtue of his representation, all of ours.[4]

None of this, however, can be understood as denying, subverting, undermining, or eliminating in any way the fact of God's unconditional and eternal decree, by which he determines and exhaustively controls "whatsoever comes to pass." God "works all things according to the counsel of his will" (Eph. 1:11), and there is nothing on which God depends in order to determine and carry out his sovereign plan.[5] That plan ultimately and immutably determines every detail of history and of eternity.

To reiterate our point above, when Van Til encourages *fearless anthropomorphism*, he is not using that phrase in a vacuum. The notion itself, as he reminds us, must be understood within the context of a Reformed doctrine of God and of his covenant with man: **"A fearless anthropomorphism based on the doctrine of the ontological trinity, rather than abstract reasoning on the basis of a metaphysical and epistemological correlativism, should control our concepts all along the line"** (p. 111).

The "fearless anthropomorphism" of which Van Til speaks has its foundation in the ontological Trinity. In other words, we can be properly anthropomorphic only if we first understand the aseity of the triune God. That is, our notion of the ontological Trinity must include the fact that God—Father, Son, and Holy Spirit—is altogether independent, in and of himself; he is not in need of anything. Before there was creation, there was the triune God, and he was not constrained by time, by space, or by anything at all in order to be, eternally and immutably, who he is.

This truth is monumentally important to grasp, and it is the central focus of anything else that we say or believe, about common grace or anything else, as Reformed Christians. It is this view of God that distinguishes Reformed Christianity from Arminianism. Roger Olson, in his book on Arminian theology says as much:

Contrary to popular belief, then, the true divide at the heart of the Calvinist-Arminian split is not predestination versus free will but the

---

4. For an exegetical analysis of Adam's covenant headship and its implications for us, see John Murray, "The Imputation of Adam's Sin," in *Justified in Christ*, ed. K. Scott Oliphint (Fearn, Ross-shire, UK: Christian Focus Publications, 2007).

5. It is worth noting Psalm 50 at this point. God comes to judge his people because they have denied his Word, and have convinced themselves that God is in need of them and their sacrifices. God reserves strong language of judgment for such sins.

guiding picture of God: *he is primarily viewed as either (1) majestic, powerful, and controlling or (2) loving good, and merciful. Once the picture . . . is established, seemingly contrary aspects fade into the background, are set aside as "obscure" or are artificially made to fit the system.*[6]

The difficulty with Olson's assessment is that he sets up a false dichotomy, a disjunction between God's majesty *or* his mercy, for example, which the notion of fearless anthropomorphism is well suited to address. Thus, as will become evident in some of these essays, a Reformed notion of fearless anthropomorphism shows the invalidity of Arminian assessments, such as Olson's. Before elaborating on what a fearless anthropomorphism is, however, we need to acknowledge why Olson might (to some extent, rightly) make this assessment of the "Calvinist" picture of God.

In a right and proper zeal to uphold the sovereign majesty of the triune God, many Reformed (or Augustinian) theologians have not, at the same time, been intent on being fearlessly anthropomorphic. The perhaps unintended result has been a view of God that is much too abstract (thus, *unbiblical*, according to Van Til) and aloof, too far removed from man and his world to interact, really and truly, with us in time. A few examples of this tendency might be instructive; many more could be provided. For example, at the beginning of his work on the Trinity, Augustine says this: "[Scripture] has borrowed many things from the spiritual creature, whereby to signify *that which indeed is not so*, but must needs so be said: as, for instance, 'I the Lord thy God am a jealous God;' (Ex. 20:5) [see also Ex. 34:14; Deut. 4:24, 5:9, 6:15; Josh. 24:19; Ez. 36:6; Nah. 1:2] 'It repenteth me that I have made man,' (Gen. 6:7)."[7]

We need to think carefully about what is said here. Is it proper and biblically warranted to say that what Scripture says is *"not so,* but must needs so be said"? Do we really want to affirm that Scripture teaches that which is *really not so,* or not in conformity with the way things *really* are, or not the case, after all? Would this way of thinking not lean toward a wrong view of Scripture? If we think in the way Augustine encourages, can we consistently take Scripture seriously when it speaks about God?

6. Roger E. Olson, *Arminian Theology: Myths and Realities* (Downers Grove, IL: IVP Academic, 2006), 73 (emphasis added).

7. Augustine, *On the Trinity*, trans. Arthur West Haddan (Edinburgh: T. & T. Clark, 1873), I.1.2 (emphasis added).

How, for example, might one go about preaching, to use Augustine's example, Exodus 20:5? Would the minister stand up before his congregation and say, " 'Thus saith the Lord, 'I the LORD your God am a jealous God.' Brothers and sisters in Christ, Scripture must needs speak this way, but it is not so. The Lord is not a jealous God. He is simply borrowing something from the creature." Surely, a minister who uttered such things would have his credentials rightly called into question.

Thomas Aquinas, whose doctrine of God can, in places, be consistent with that which was emphasized at the time of the Reformation, nevertheless stumbled as his mentor, Augustine, had done.[8] So, he says:

> Since therefore God is outside the whole order of creation, and all creatures are ordered to Him, and not conversely, it is manifest that creatures are really related to God Himself; whereas in God there is no real relation to creatures, but a relation only in idea, inasmuch as creatures are referred to Him. *Thus there is nothing to prevent these names which import relation to the creature from being predicated of God temporally, not by reason of any change in Him, but by reason of the change of the creature; as a column is on the right of an animal, without change in itself, but by change in the animal.*[9]

Without detailing the medieval notion of a "real relation" (which notion is more complicated than it appears on the surface), we can see that in the illustration Thomas gives we have the central focus of his assertion. The relationship that creatures have to God, and God to us, is analogous to the relationship that a column has to an animal. The column is on the right of the animal because of movement or change in the animal, not by virtue of any change in the column. In other words, because God is immutable (which he is), his relationship to creatures, according to Thomas, needs qualification such that the creature is "really" related to God, but not God to the creature; the latter relationship can only be "ideal."

The question asked above can be broached here as well. What might we think of a preacher who stands before his congregation and says, "Dear

8. My own conviction is that, since Aquinas, too many have adopted his ideas and language uncritically, especially with respect to his doctrine of God, and thus have had no clear and cogent way to affirm much, if not most, of what Scripture says about God and his dealings with, and activity in, creation.

9. Thomas Aquinas, *The Summa Theologica of St. Thomas Aquinas*, trans. Fathers of the English Dominican Province, 2nd ed. (London: Burns, Oates, and Washburne, 1920–1942), 1.13.7 (emphasis added). Available online at home.newadvent.org/summa/1013.html.

friends, we know that God is not really, but only *ideally*, related to us. But fear not, we are *really* related to him." This view, too, is plagued with abstraction, and fails to be fearlessly anthropomorphic.

Abstract and misleading views like this could be multiplied. Here is how Paul Helm describes what he takes to be Calvin's view of a similar matter. In discussing the atonement and its relationship to God's disposition toward us, Helm notes:

> So the truth about atonement, about reconciliation to God, has to be represented to us as if it implied a change in God, and so an inconsistency, an apparent contradiction, in his actions towards us. But in fact there is no change in God; he loves us from eternity. There is however, a change in us, a change that occurs as by faith Christ's work is appropriated. *The change is not from wrath to grace, but from our belief that we are under wrath to our belief that we are under grace.*[10]

Calvin's view, according to Helm, is that we move from wrath to grace merely in what we believe about our standing with God, since there can be no change in God. That is, we move from *our belief* that we are under wrath to *our belief* that we are under grace, but those beliefs do not comport with the way things *really* are.

Imagine, then, a preacher preaching on Ephesians 2:1–8: "Yes, says Paul, you were children of wrath. And yes, dear friends, God has, by grace, made you alive in Christ. But surely you must recognize that, if you are one of God's elect, you were not *really* under God's wrath. What Scripture is teaching you here is not the way things *really* are with respect to God; it is teaching you what you must *believe*. And, in spite of the way things *really* are, you must *believe* that, if you are in Christ, you have moved from wrath to grace. But, make no mistake, you *really* have not. Since God cannot change, his disposition toward you has not *really* changed; only your beliefs have changed. And those beliefs, which Scripture itself encourages, were not true to the way God *really* is toward you." How long might such a preacher last in a theologically orthodox church? Any congregation, session, or presbytery worth its salt would see to it that this preacher found another calling.

Two more examples should suffice. Stephen Charnock seems to have taken the bad with the good from Aquinas in his explanation of God's

10. Paul Helm, *John Calvin's Ideas* (Oxford: Oxford University Press, 2004), 395.

disposition toward us: "God is not changed, when of loving to any creatures he becomes angry with them, or of angry he becomes appeased. The change in these cases is in the creatures; according to the alteration in the creature, it stands in a various relation to God."[11]

So, at the risk of repetition, when Scripture says that God is angry with us, does it *really* mean that the change is "in the creatures"? This strains the clear meaning of language beyond recognition.

Lastly, it seems even Bavinck was reluctant to be fearlessly anthropomorphic with respect to his understanding of God: "We can almost never tell why God willed one thing rather than another, and are therefore compelled to believe that he could just as well have willed one thing as another. *But in God there is actually no such thing as choice inasmuch as it always presupposes uncertainty, doubt, and deliberation.*"[12]

This point, too, utterly skews the clear teaching of Scripture. Are we meant to think that when Scripture says that God chose us before the foundation of the world, what it really means is that there was no such choice? Or, to use another example, is it the case, as Bavinck (and others) goes on to say, that God's willing of himself is *identical* to his willing of his creatures?[13] How can we make sense of such an idea, biblically speaking? It will not do simply to appeal to "mystery" here, since the biblical view of mystery does in no way include a denial of what Scripture clearly teaches.

These select quotations get to the heart of Van Til's concern in this volume. How, exactly, are we to think about the "apparent contradictions" that face us in Scripture, especially as they relate to God's character and to his general grace to all mankind? Concerning the examples above, we must ask why we have these aberrations with respect to the doctrine of God from solid, orthodox, and brilliant theologians. The reason, at least in part, is that, in each of the examples cited, these theologians were not fearlessly anthropomorphic. They rightly affirm God's aseity and the attributes that follow from his aseity (e.g., his eternity, infinity, and immutability). They are right to hold to these, and to resist any temptation to let them go. But then they begin systematically and "abstractly" (as Van Til would say) to make logical deductions from the principle, say, of aseity, without being controlled, first of all, by the data of Scripture. And this becomes their downfall as they begin to express things about God that are not the case.

11. Stephen Charnock, *The Existence and Attributes of God*, 2 vols. (Grand Rapids: Baker Book House, 1979), 1:345.
12. Bavinck, *Reformed Dogmatics*, 2:239–40 (emphasis added).
13. Ibid., 2:240.

To deduce from God's aseity or simplicity that he does not make choices, or that his will to create is identical to his willing of himself, or that he does not really relate to us, is to prefer abstract (unbiblical) deduction over clear biblical teaching. Because the doctrine of common grace entails the mystery of God's dealings with man, this is, in part, the burden of Van Til's discussion throughout this collection of essays: "Applying this to the case in hand, we would say that we are entitled and compelled to use anthropomorphism not apologetically but fearlessly. *We need not fear to say that God's attitude has changed with respect to mankind.* We know well enough that God in himself is changeless" (p. 89, emphasis added). Van Til affirms biblical truth, and does so in the context of what Scripture has to say, rather than as a deduction from (what turns out to be) an abstract principle.

It may help us at this point to advance beyond the details of Van Til's insistence on fearless anthropomorphism and to suggest how one can affirm, as Van Til does, *both* that "God's attitude has changed with respect to mankind" *and* that "God in himself is changeless." A proper assessment of this dilemma could occupy us for some time, but we can at least provide here the basic structure within which an answer can be given.[14]

How, then, does God remain altogether independent and immutable, while also interacting meaningfully with creation and with us? The one-word answer to the question is, "Covenant." When it comes to the subject of God's covenant with man, the Westminster Confession of Faith, chapter 7, section 1, says:

> The distance between God and the creature is so great, that although reasonable creatures do owe obedience unto Him as their Creator, yet they could never have any fruition of Him as their blessedness and reward, but by some voluntary condescension on God's part, which He hath been pleased to express by way of covenant.

What the Confession asserts in this section has massive and profound implications, first for theology proper, and then for our understanding of God's activity in history (and the order of these is crucial), including

14. For an extended, book-length answer to this question, see K. Scott Oliphint, *God with Us: Divine Condescension and the Attributes of God* (Wheaton, IL: Crossway Books, 2012). What follows below is *not* attributable to Van Til, but flows inexorably from the emphases that are present in this volume and elsewhere in his writings.

the doctrine of common grace. This confessional statement deserves the meditative attention of every serious Christian. To understand covenant, there are two things worth noting in this majestic section:

(1) In a chapter that summarizes God's covenant with man, the first thing that the Confession expresses is the infinite distance between God and man. But just what is this distance? Surely the notion of "distance" must be a metaphor, since in reality there never was, nor will there ever be, a spatial distance between God and man. God is present, fully and completely, in all places and at all times, into eternity, both in the new heaven and new earth and in hell. So the distance cannot be a spatial distance.

This "distance" focuses on the *being* of God in comparison to the *being* of his creatures. That is, it is an *ontological* distance. God is, as the Confession has already affirmed, "infinite in being and perfection, a most pure spirit, invisible, without body, parts, or passions; immutable, immense, eternal, incomprehensible" (2.1). As infinite in being, and as immutable, immense, and eternal, God is wholly other; he is beyond anything that mere creatures can think or experience. We cannot conceive of what God's infinity is; our minds cannot grasp or contain what God's eternity is. He is not limited by anything—not by space and not by time. So, there is a distance, a separation of being, between God and his creatures. God, and he alone, is independent (*a se*).[15] Everything else is dependent on him.

This is no philosophical idea or mere human speculation. It is rather a necessary implication of the first words of the Bible: "In the beginning, God . . ." These words affirm that at the beginning of creation (including the creation of time), God *was*. Given that truth, we confess that God alone is independent; what could God have needed when there was nothing existing but him alone? He existed before creation, and nothing else did. His existence was not dependent on anyone or anything else; it *could not* be dependent, since there was nothing in existence but the triune God. Before there was creation, there was only God—Father, Son, and Holy Spirit. There was no time, and there was no space; there was no "when" of God's existence, and there was no "where." There was only the triune God. He and he alone existed; he did not exist at a time or in a place. He simply *was*.

It is incumbent on the Christian to recognize this before, and in the context of, thinking about God's covenant relationship to creation. This

15. To see what the Westminster Assembly had in mind in WCF 7.1, note that added Scripture references at the end of this section (Isa. 40:13–17, Job 9:32–33, 1 Sam. 2:25, Ps. 113:5–6, Ps. 100:2–3, Job 22:2–3, Job 35:7–8, Luke 17:10, Acts 17:24–25, cited in the order given in this section) refer exclusively to this "distance" of God and the impossibility of our "fruition" of him.

is why the Confession begins where it does. The problem with any theology that will not confess the absolute independence and sovereignty of God is that it does not adequately account for God's majestic character, including his existence and independence prior to his act of creation. A theology that begins with "God-in-relationship" is a theology that will inevitably veer from the truth of Scripture and from a true confession of God's character, as well as of his covenant with man.

(2) It is worth noting, then, and it is a masterstroke of theological genius, that the Confession begins its section on covenant, as it must, with the majestic and incomprehensible character of God. This must be the starting place for all thinking about God and his relationship to creation. Any theology that goes wrong in its assessment of God inevitably goes wrong because it begins its theologizing with "God-in-relationship" rather than with the independent and immutable triune God. This is why, in the quotation from Olson above, there is such a vast difference between the Reformed and Arminian notions of God. The Arminian begins his thinking about God in terms of God-in-relationship; there is, therefore, an inevitable and essential dependence of God on his creation. God, for the Arminian, is one who can determine man's destiny only according to man's own independent choice, not God's.

The Westminster Confession is clear and explicit about God's essential independence in chapter 2 ("Of God, and of the Holy Trinity"). Now one might have thought that since the Confession already affirmed God's aseity in chapter 2, there would be no need to introduce such things again in chapter 7. But the genius of chapter 7 is that it was recognized that unless this distance between God and his creatures be first affirmed, any notion of covenant could be seen to be anemic, because it would be tied to a dependent God, as is the Arminian notion of God.

Once we recognize the ontological distance between God and creatures, which includes the fact, as section 1 says, that even though we owe obedience to him, we could have no "fruition of him as [our] blessedness and reward," we are then in a position to affirm just what it is that brought about God's relationship to his creatures.

Here is where we can begin to understand why and how we are to be fearlessly anthropomorphic. Two monumentally pregnant words—"voluntary condescension"—in this first section of chapter 7 affirm the initiation of God's relationship to his creatures, and we need to focus briefly on each of those words.

What does the Confession mean by "voluntary" with respect to God? In theology proper, we make a distinction between God's necessary knowledge and will and his free knowledge and will. This distinction is not tangential to our understanding of God; it is crucial to a proper grasp of his incomprehensible character. Given these two categories, it is perhaps more obvious that God's knowledge and will are necessary. As one who cannot but exist, and who is independent, God knows all things, just by virtue of who he is, and whatever he wills *with respect to himself* is, like him, necessary. Why, then, do we need to confess that God's knowledge and will are, with respect to some things, free?

We confess this, in part, because the contrary is impossible, given who God is. Since he is independent and in need of nothing, there was no necessity that he create anything at all. If creation were necessary, then God would be dependent on it in order to be who he is. But (contrary to Arminians, Molinists, Barthians, et al.) there is no such essential dependence in God. So, God's determination to create, and to relate to that creation, is a *free* decision. Two things are important to keep in mind about God's free knowledge and will.

First, the free knowledge and will of God have their focus in what God *determines*. That which God determines is surely something that he knows (for how could God determine that which was unknown, and what, for God, *could be* unknown?). That which God knows and determines is that which he carries out. In other words, to put it simply, there is no free knowledge of God that is not also a free determination (or act of will) of God. The two are inextricably linked.

God's knowledge is a *directing* knowledge; it has an object in view. His will enjoins some of that which he knows, and his power executes that which his will enjoins. What God freely knows is what he freely wills. We can see now that with the notion of "voluntary condescension" we have moved from a discussion of God's essential nature, involving his ontological distance from his creation, to an affirmation of his free determination to create *and to condescend*. This is something that God did not have to do; so, we move from a discussion of God's essential nature to a discussion of his free activity and those things that follow from that activity.

Second (and significant in our discussion of common grace), the free will of God is tied to his eternal decree. This is important for a number of reasons, not the least of which is that it reminds us that God's free will does not simply and only coincide with his activity in and through creation, but is active prior to creation. So God's free will includes his activity in and through creation, but is not limited to that activity. God's free determination is an activity of the triune God, even before the foundation of the world. Once he determined "whatsoever comes to pass," he freely bound himself (covenantally) to his creation for eternity.

So the initiation of the relationship of God to his creatures was a "voluntary" initiation. It was a free determination of God, and it was a free determination that took place "before the foundation of the world," that is, in eternity. This free determination included an agreement between the Father, the Son, and the Holy Spirit, an agreement sometimes called the *pactum salutis*, or covenant of salvation. The Father, the Son, and the Holy Spirit agreed, before the foundation of the world, to create and to redeem a people. They committed themselves to a certain relationship in, with, and for creation. This in itself was a free decision; it was "voluntary," and it was a decision of "condescension." But what does the word *condescension* mean in this context?

The word itself means "a coming down," and, like the word *distance*, is a spatial metaphor. As with the word *distance*, *condescension* is used metaphorically to communicate something that is much deeper and more glorious than might initially be realized. Just as there is no spatial distance between God and his creatures, so also can there be no "coming down" or "condescension" of God such that he begins to occupy a space that he did not otherwise occupy. In other words, because God is present everywhere, there is no place where he is not, and thus no place that he begins to occupy by coming down. He always and everywhere occupies all places, fully and completely.

So what does *condescension* mean? The best way to begin to grasp this glorious and gracious truth is to look to that supreme and ultimate example of condescension in Holy Scripture—the incarnation of the Son of God. In the incarnation, the second person of the Trinity "came down" in order to be *with us*, so that he might live an obedient life and die an obedient death on behalf of his people, rise from the dead, and ascend into heaven to reign. What did this condescension entail for him?

It did not mean that he began to occupy a place that he did not otherwise occupy. As the Son of God, thus fully and completely God, he was, is, and remains omnipresent. What it means is that the Son took on a human nature so that he might fulfill the plan of redemption that was decreed by him, together with the Father and the Spirit, before the foundation of the world. He took on, in other words, characteristics, properties, and attributes—call them *covenantal* characteristics—in order that he might relate to us in a way that he did not otherwise. His condescension was his taking on of a human nature in order properly, according to what the triune God had decreed, to relate to creation generally and to his people more specifically.

When the Confession affirms God's voluntary condescension, then, this is, in the main, what is meant. It means that God took on characteristics, properties, and attributes that he did not have to take on (remember this condescension was voluntary) in order that he might relate, even *bind himself*, to the creation and to his creatures. His commitment to that which is other than himself—his creation—included, by definition, a condescension. He freely bound himself to his creation, including his creatures, such that there would, from that point into eternity, be characteristics, attributes, and properties that he would take on, all by the sheer freedom of his will. These characteristics are such that God (the Son) could walk in the garden with Adam and Eve, meet and negotiate with Abraham concerning Sodom, meet with Moses on Mount Horeb and in the Tent of Meeting, wrestle with Jacob, confront and rebuke Joshua as the divine warrior, etc.—and, preeminently and climactically, come to save a people for himself.[16]

Perhaps we can now begin to see that to be "fearlessly anthropomorphic" is to recognize that God is able *both* to be infinite, eternal, unchangeable, etc., *and* to be angry, be gracious, love a people, hate the reprobate, be jealous, etc. Olson's false disjunction above can now be seen to have its resolution in a biblical view of covenant, a view in which God freely determines to condescend. Not only so, but Augustine's "it is not so," Helm's "no transition from wrath to grace," and Thomas's only "ideal relationship" of God to creation need not be affirmed. Rather, God's voluntary condescension requires that we affirm him to be both independent and in relationship to his creation—both immutable and able to move from a disposition of wrath toward us to a disposition of grace. By God condescending, eternity and time are united (as they are in Christ) without in any way separating, denying, or confusing one side or the other.

16. Given the influence of Geerhardus Vos on Van Til (on which, see below), it is worth noting here, with respect to God's condescension, that Vos calls it a "sacramental" condescension. Throughout redemptive history, sacramental condescensions on God's part include his appearing in human/visible form. Behind this visible form is the impression that God is altogether invisible. "Behind the Angel speaking as God, and who embodied in Himself all the condescension of God to meet the frailty and limitations of man, there existed at the same time another aspect of God, in which he could not be seen and materially received after such a fashion, the very God of whom the Angel spoke in the third person. . . . In the incarnation of our Lord we have the supreme expression of this fundamental arrangement." Geerhardus Vos, *Biblical Theology: Old and New Testaments* (1948; reset, Grand Rapids: Eerdmans, 1975), 74.

But there is a priority in our understanding of this great mystery. As the Confession makes clear in the first section of chapter 7, we must first recognize the infinite distance that there is between God and his creatures. In beginning with that ontological distance, we note that in God's character there is a priority to who he is quite apart from creation. That is, whatever else we affirm about God, we cannot in any way imply that his being-in-relation is symmetrical to his being-in-himself. The latter is necessary and could not be otherwise; God is who he is. The former, on the other hand, is free, and did not have to be at all.

Our fearlessly anthropomorphic understanding of God, therefore, has behind it the clear teaching of Scripture and also the free determination of God to commit himself to creation, and in that commitment to relate to us *really and truly* (not *ideally*). Such relationships, however, require no change in his essential character (since, by definition, that nature cannot change).

This, after all, is what God has done, and who he is, supremely in Christ. Van Til has this in mind as well. Just after encouraging us to be fearlessly anthropomorphic, he says: "**The Council of Chalcedon excluded logical deductions based on anything short of a combination of all the factors of revelation with respect to the God-man. So in the problem of common grace we must not argue for differences without qualification or for identities without qualification**" (p. 216).

In other words, that which points us clearly to fearless anthropomorphism is the biblical content contained in the Chalcedonian Creed. That creed affirmed that the person of the Son of God, who is, in the flesh, the Lord Jesus Christ, is to be "acknowledged in two natures, inconfusedly (ἀσυγχύτως), unchangeably (ἀρέπτως), indivisibly (ἀδιαιρέτως), and inseparably (ἀχωρίστως)." The two natures of Christ are not confused, changed, divided, or separated. Of course, the human nature is his only by virtue of the free determination of the triune God to save a people; the divine nature is his of necessity. But once he takes on that human nature, there must be no confusion, change, division, or separation of the two natures. We can affirm, then, that Christ is, as God, infinite, eternal, unchangeable, etc. But we can also "**fearlessly**" affirm that he was located in time and space, that he grew tired and hungry, that he grew in wisdom and in favor with God, etc. To deny one of those natures for the sake of the other is to do an injustice to the truth of Scripture, to deny the means of the salvation of men, and to detract from the inexhaustible glory of God!

So it is with God in history.[17] He came down (see, for example, Ex. 3:8), and in that condescension he did not cease to be God, for he cannot deny himself. But he did take on, really and truly, those characteristics that he deemed requisite for the carrying out of his eternal plan in history.[18]

It is this covenantal condescension that Van Til has in mind when he reminds us, throughout this collection of essays, that it is not possible for us to reason deductively about God's relationship to creation, generally, or about the relationship of God's decree to his common grace, more specifically. As we noted in the quote, above, from Van Til:

> We must not say that God cannot display any attitude of favor to the generality of mankind because we know that He intends that ultimately some are "vessels of wrath." On the other hand we must not argue from the revealed will of God with respect to man's responsibility to the denial of man's ultimate determination by the will of decree. We need therefore at this point, which is all-inclusive, to be "fearlessly anthropomorphic." (p. 215)

The reason we cannot work through a process of deduction from either of these two wills of God is that they refer both to God in eternity (will of decree) and to God's acts in history (will of command); in other words, they are both covenantally qualified. They presuppose that God is who he is, and that he has covenanted with his creatures. As Van Til makes clear in his first essay:

> But then, to say this is not to say that the "solution" offered on these questions is a "systematic" one, in the sense that it is logically penetrable by the intellect of man. The biblical "system of truth" is not a "deductive system." The various teachings of Scripture are not related to one another in the way

17. The controlling emphasis of the entirety of Van Til's discussion on common grace is his emphasis on covenant *history*. Though we do not have the space to pursue it here, it should be obvious to the reader that the influence of Geerhardus Vos, one of Van Til's most revered mentors and friends, is on every page of this volume. Much of Van Til's work has Vos's imprint on it.

18. Speaking of the Angel of the Lord in the Old Testament, Vos notes: "The form in which the Angel appeared was a form *assumed* for the moment, laid aside again as soon as the purpose of its assumption had been served." Vos, *Biblical Theology, Old and New Testaments*, 75. This temporary "assumption" in the Old Testament looks forward to the permanent assumption, "when the time had fully come," of a human nature by this same Angel of the Lord.

that syllogisms of a series are related. The "system of truth" of Scripture presupposes the existence of the internally, eternally, self-coherent, triune God who reveals Himself to man with unqualified authority. (p. xlviii)

So, it is illegitimate, biblically and theologically, to reason from the truth of God's eternal decree to a denial of a favorable attitude of God toward the reprobate in history. It is just as illegitimate to argue from God's mercy and grace toward all mankind that there could be no particular, sovereign election in eternity.

In sum, to be "fearlessly anthropomorphic" is to say that the God who can bring together two distinct natures—the divine and the human—in one person without confusing, changing, dividing, or separating each nature can surely bring together the "nature" of the eternal (decree) and the "nature" of the historical without violating any of the essential characteristics of each one. In the case of the incarnation, and of all of God's dealings in history, we cannot figure out *how* such things can be; but *that* they are and can be is without question, and it is the substance of our relationship to the God who made us and is redeeming a people for himself.

Only by being fearlessly anthropomorphic, therefore, are we able to reason *concretely* rather than abstractly, which brings us to our second point.

(2) CONCRETE THINKING

Since the next two themes follow from the first, much of the conceptual arsenal needed to explain this theme (and the next) is already contained in the first theme. It will be necessary to keep the first theme in mind as we think together about the second and third. Keep the notion of fearless anthropomorphism in mind, then, as we discuss the two remaining controlling ideas in Van Til's overall analysis of common grace.

The first thing we need to say is a reiteration of a point made earlier, but which must be repeated due to its almost total neglect in other analyses of Van Til. When Van Til urges "concrete thinking," he is, in effect, urging *biblical* thinking; conversely, abstract thinking is thinking that is inconsistent with the emphases and teaching of Scripture.[19] And Scripture,

19. The biblical impetus behind Van Til's notion of concrete thinking can best be seen, in the present volume, in the section entitled, "The Positive Line of Concrete Thinking" (pp. 79–113).

we should remember, is fearlessly anthropomorphic. So, says Van Til: "To think analogically, to be *fearlessly anthropomorphic*, is to think *concretely*, for it is to take all the factors of revelation into consideration simultaneously" (p. 216, emphasis added).

Implied in a method that takes revelation as epistemologically foundational is a proper view of thinking. So, the first general principle with respect to Van Til's emphasis on "concrete thinking" is that it requires a proper *view* and *use* of the laws of thought. In his critique of Herman Hoeksema's denial of common grace, Van Til says:

> It may perhaps be said that much of the abstract reasoning of Hoeksema comes from his failure to distinguish between Christian and non-Christian logic. We do not mean, of course, that the rules of the syllogism are different for Christians and non-Christians. . . . But when he says or assumes that God's revelation in Scripture may be expected to reveal nothing which will be apparently self-contradictory, we demur. (p. 36)

What Van Til says here is significant theologically (which means it is significant apologetically as well), in that it will enable us to think biblically about common grace. With respect to the fundamental and basic truths of Scripture, we must affirm that our beliefs are not able adequately to be reconciled with, or subsumed under, our typical patterns and laws of thinking. That is to say, our laws of thought must be used to *serve*, rather than to *determine*, how we think, especially how we think about Christian truth.

This is the case, as noted above, in one of the church's earliest creeds—the Chalcedonian Creed (451 A.D.). Had the writers of that creed been beholden to a standard pattern of syllogistic reasoning, they would have had no way to declare that Christ is one person with two distinct natures.[20] The truth that Christ is fully God and fully man would lead inexorably either to a one-nature or a two-person Christology. But, as Chalcedon affirmed, this would be to deny the biblical teaching on the second person of the

20. There are those who have sought to conform all biblical teaching to logical laws, and have introduced aberrant theology in the process. Gordon Clark, in a biting critique of the entirety of historic, orthodox Christology, both Catholic and Protestant, and in order to make Christology fit his (non-Christian) application of logic, argued that Christ is indeed two persons. Given his awkward definition of a person, however (viz., a collection of propositions), any definition including the word *person* cannot in this case be taken seriously. See Gordon H. Clark, *The Incarnation* (Jefferson, MD: Trinity Foundation, 1988), esp. 75–78.

Trinity. The truths of Scripture trump the standard syllogism, and should not be made to conform to it.

This is one central area in which "abstract" thinking is dangerous, even deadly, with respect to theological orthodoxy. Van Til's primary concern in this regard, especially as it touches on the issues surrounding the doctrine of common grace, has to do with the denial of the *historical* that ensues when abstract thinking is dominant:

> It is well to observe in this connection that a natural concomitant of the failure to distinguish between a Christian and a non-Christian foundation for true logic is the denial of the genuine significance of the historical. Given the belief in a self-sufficient God, the idea of temporal creation and genuine historical development is absurd. So says the non-believer. And so says the Arminian, using the neutral application of the syllogism. Calvinism, we are told, makes history to be a puppet dance. The Arminian has not seen the necessity of challenging the idea of a neutral logic. He reasons abstractly, as all non-believing philosophy does. The Arminian therefore also rejects the Reformed conception of history. He thinks of it as he thinks of philosophical determinism. (p. 38)

To reason abstractly is, for example, to take one truth—e.g., the truth of God's unconditional election—and to deduce from it that history is meaningless because it is predetermined. Or, to use another example, abstract reasoning would deduce that God's unconditional decree negates real, human responsibility. Abstract reasoning is inherently *nonhistorical*, and thus nonbiblical. It moves the Arminian, as it does the unbeliever (as well as the denier of common grace), toward a conclusion that negates Scripture's view of man and of history. And this is just to say that *concrete* thinking takes seriously the self-sufficiency (and meticulous sovereignty) of God, even while, at the same time, it affirms the meaningful progress of history and the real, meaningful, contingent, responsible choices of man.

We can see how the notion of fearless anthropomorphism is entailed in the plea for concrete thinking and for taking history seriously. Since God has come down in history, and has himself interacted meaningfully and significantly (even exhaustively) with and in the contingent progress of history, we must avoid any reasoning that moves deductively from God's sovereign decree and activity in eternity to a conclusion that denies or otherwise undermines the significance of historical progress and contingency. In this case, the standard syllogism simply will not lead us to the truth of Scripture.

There is one particular pair of terms in Van Til's discussion of concrete thinking that could lead (and has led) to some confusion. In the section on concrete thinking in this volume, Van Til argues for a notion of "earlier" and of "later" with respect to our understanding of common grace. The idea of "earlier" and "later" may, on the surface, seem to refer simply to history, such that "earlier" refers to an earlier date on the calendar and "later" refers to a later date. But there is much more in view in Van Til's use of those terms than a simple dateline. Not only so, but the notions of "earlier" and "later" could, if improperly construed, sound more like abstract thinking than like concrete thinking, so it may be useful to attempt to bring clarity to his use of these two ideas.

Van Til uses the terms *earlier* and *later* in the context of the debates on whether or not there is such a thing as common grace. In those debates, the differing parties are in agreement about the doctrine of eternal election. In other words, those who affirm the reality of common grace (as does Van Til) and those who deny the reality of it (as does Hoeksema) agree that God's eternal counsel is behind whatsoever comes to pass. At issue for both sides, then, is not the nature of the decree, but the way in which we are to think about the historical manifestation of that decree. Is God's electing purpose such that he can display no favor toward the nonelect in history (as Hoeksema believed), or is there a (perhaps incomprehensible) harmony between God's electing purposes in eternity and his disposition(s) toward mankind in history? In attempting to address this conundrum, Van Til employs the ideas of "earlier" and "later."

For Van Til, the "earlier" of common grace begins with Adam. Because Adam is the representative of all mankind, God's favorable attitude toward Adam in the garden entails his favorable attitude, representatively, toward all mankind. Thus, Van Til sees "commonness" itself as having its roots in the creation of Adam, not simply as an individual man, but as our covenant head. When Adam sinned, the attitude of favor that God had toward Adam, and toward mankind as represented by Adam, changed (note the "fearlessly anthropomorphic" language here) to an attitude of wrath toward Adam and of common wrath toward all men in Adam. Van Til says that, given the fall, "the elect and the reprobate are under a *common wrath*. If there is meaning in this—and who denies it?—there may and must, with equal right, be said to be an earlier attitude of common favor. Indeed, the reality of the 'common wrath' depends upon the fact of the earlier 'common grace'" (p. 90).

Note that Van Til puts the phrases *common wrath* and *common grace* in quotation marks here. He does that, in part, to highlight that the commonness in each case has its locus and focus in Adam as our covenant head, and not, at this point, in each person individually.

Van Til's biblical logic here is this: If it is the case that when Adam sinned, we all sinned, and thus when Adam sinned we all came under the wrath of God, then must it not also be the case that when God's attitude was favorable toward Adam in the garden, and when God *graciously* offered Adam the opportunity of eternal life, God was also favorable toward mankind generally and graciously offered eternal life to mankind in Adam? If so, then the wrath of God that comes to us individually, in history, presupposes the wrath that has come to us representatively by way of our common covenant head, Adam.

In other words, each of us individually is "dead in [our] trespasses and sins" because we are "by nature children of wrath, *like the rest of mankind*" (Eph. 2:1, 3). The wrath that is ours individually is what it is because of the wrath that is ours corporately. The "**earlier**," corporate wrath delimits, defines, and determines the "**later**," individual wrath that rests on each one of us "by nature," since the fall.

So also it is with the common grace of God. God's attitude of favor toward Adam, and his gracious offer of eternal life to him, includes, given Adam's covenant headship, God's attitude of favor toward all mankind and his gracious offer of eternal life to all mankind.

Once the fall occurs, however, Adam (and mankind with him) incurs the wrath of God, but Adam continues to live and breathe. He will continue, with Eve, to be fruitful and multiply. With the sweat of his brow, he will continue to subdue the earth. The wrath of God toward Adam is now initiated in the context of, and presupposes, God's common grace toward him as well. Not only so, but that common grace, as "earlier" grace, is the context in which the wrath of God, as well as the "special grace" covering of Adam and Eve, is given (Gen. 3:21–24). Thus, the "later" differentiating, special grace of God is what it is because of God's "earlier" common grace toward Adam, a common grace that allows for the incursion of God's wrath upon Adam.

A couple more points should be made with respect to the *earlier* and the *later*, as Van Til uses these terms. First, he says that "*after the common, in each case, comes the conditional*" (p. 90, emphasis original). So whatever the commonness is with respect to us, it is *prior to* that which is conditional (i.e., "early"). In the case of Adam, for example, Van Til is making the point that God's attitude was favorable to Adam in the garden, and, representatively, to us, but his favor was to be seen as the context within which God's conditional requirement ("Do not eat from that tree") would be given. In other words, it was *as* he was favorable toward Adam that God (conditionally) said Adam and Eve would live eternally, should they not eat from the tree of the knowledge of good and evil. So "common grace" was *earlier* because it was the context within which eternal life was promised to our first parents on the condition of continued obedience. (This will also apply to the free offer of the gospel, in which God's common grace is the background for the conditionality of that gospel offer.)

Second, with this in view, Van Til makes the further point that "**history is a process of differentiation**" (p. 90). By "**differentiation**," Van Til means that God's eternal decree of predestination and reprobation works itself out *for individuals, in history*. The common wrath of God has its meaning and application within the individual wrath that is ours "by nature." But it is a wrath that can only have its meaning and application within the context of God giving to *all men* life and breath and all things, of his rain and sunshine falling on both the elect and the reprobate. So also, the common grace of God has its meaning and application within the individual grace that is given to the elect.

As Van Til is sometimes wont to explain these truths using philosophical terms, this movement from "common" to "individual" is an example of the mutual relation of the one and the many, the universal and the particular, each finding its proper place, each entailing the other, with no primacy given to either.[21] The one, "commonness," has to be understood in light of its coherence with the many, "individuals," to whom the "commonness" is already (earlier) applied. Each without the other is vacuous; both together are meaningful.[22] As with fearless anthropomorphism, so also now with concrete thinking, the concern is to give full and due weight, biblically, to

21. This refers us again to the presupposition of the ontological Trinity, in whom there is no primacy given to the one (God) or the three (persons).

22. The late South African Christian philosopher Hendrik Stoker speaks of these two concepts as a "coherential contrapolar contrast." Though technical, the phrase aptly (and alliteratively!) expresses the true relationship of the one and the many, or the universal and the particular, as that relationship is grounded in the "three-in-one" of God's character. See H. G. Stoker, "On the Contingent and Present-Day Western Man," in *The Idea of a Christian Philosophy: Essays in Honour of D. H. Th. Vollenhoven*, ed. K. A. Bril, H. Hart, and J. Klapwijk (Toronto: Wedge Publishing Foundation, 1973).

the crucial importance of history, and God's redemptive plan for history, in light of God's electing purposes.

In light of this discussion, Van Til takes up, as he says, "the most perplexing aspect of the perplexing problem of common grace," which he sees to be the problem of the "conditional" (p. 91). This "most perplexing problem" can be summarized in a question: how can it be that God's attitude toward all men could be one of wrath, when, in eternity, he already determined graciously to save some and to pass over others? Or, to put it another way, when Christ says to the crowds, "Come to me, all who labor and are heavy laden" (Matt. 11:28), does that condition—to come to Christ—mean that all are under wrath until and unless they come? If so, what is the meaning of God's election? Not only so, but how can Christ offer this to all, when their eternal status with respect to Christ has already been determined, *by Christ himself* (together with the Father and the Spirit), before the foundation of the world?

Van Til proposes that if any progress is to be made in solving this "most perplexing problem," then "we shall need, in our humble opinion, to stress, as we have tried to do throughout, the idea of the earlier and the later, *that is to say, the historical correlativity of universal and particular*" (p. 91, emphasis added). The "idea of the earlier and the later," in other words, should be understood in the context of "the historical correlativity of universal and particular."

We need to remind ourselves at this point that all of this comes under the section entitled "The Positive Line of Concrete Thinking." So, what Van Til proposes here is not that we begin to think of the "universal" and the "particular" as abstract philosophical concepts. Rather, as he says, we need to see these two as historically, conceptually, and biblically-theologically correlative. In putting these terms into their proper, historical context, we avoid thinking of them in terms of "brute fact [i.e., particular] and abstract law [i.e., universal]" (p. 91). Instead, as we locate the universal and the particular in history, and as correlative, we see that God's (universal) common grace to all mankind can take its proper place only within the context of the (particular) application of special grace to the elect, as well as his passing over other individuals (particular) who are reprobate. There will be more on this in the next section.

In order to clarify his emphasis on the earlier and the later, as themselves an integral aspect of concrete thinking, Van Til takes an example from Valentijn Hepp. Van Til is concerned that Hepp seems to imply that it is possible for us to know, in a given group of people, who is elect and who is not. For example, Hepp says, "Let us not look at the lot of the non-elect in the congregation from the view-point of judgment only" (p. 91). Statements like this illustrate what happens when we think abstractly and not concretely; we may begin to think that it is possible for us to know God's eternal choice. When we think this way, not only do we presume to know the mind of God, but, with respect to the earlier and the later, we undermine a proper understanding of the process of historical differentiation.

Such presumed determinations of who is elect and who is not are impossible, from the perspective of history, and thus they confuse the earlier and the later. So Van Til says that Hepp's view forgets "the difference between the earlier and the later. The general presentation [of the gospel] comes to a generality [of people]. It comes to 'sinners,' differentiated, to be sure, as elect and reprobate in the mind of God, but yet, *prior to their act of acceptance or rejection*, regarded as a generality. To forget this is to *move the calendar of God ahead*" (p. 92, emphases added).

To "move the calendar of God ahead" means, for Van Til, that we presume differentiation prematurely, in that we presume who is elect and who is reprobate. This presumption affirms the later, that is, the differentiation that takes place with individuals, without giving due credit to the earlier, that is, the gospel call that goes out to "a generality" (common grace). This shows, it seems to me, that Van Til's reference to "the calendar" has less to do with the historical progression of the calendar and more to do with God's application of his eternal decree to individuals in history. In other words, Van Til's concern is not about days or months, with respect to history, but about the application of God's plan in the days and months of history. The context for that application is the "earlier" common grace, which is the background for the "later," conditional, special grace that comes to God's elect and the passing over that comes to the reprobate. The terms *earlier* and *later*, then, refer not simply to the progress of history, but to the conditionality of special grace that presupposes common grace.

With respect to that which is earlier, Van Til follows Calvin's argument against Pighius, and affirms that, prior to the fall, mankind, in Adam, was offered eternal life. As long as man, in Adam, continued in obedience, God would, in the future, finally and completely, give Adam, and thus all mankind, eternal life.[23] This offer of life could not have been anything

---

23. Much of Van Til's discussion in this volume utilizes and presupposes Calvin's terminology and arguments against Pighius. Note, for example, what Calvin says with respect to the offer of eternal life before the fall: "The truth of the matter is, that salvation was not

other than "common," and it was certainly "gracious." It was not gracious in the context of sin, but rather in the context of God's free determination to give the gift of eternal life to man—something that God did not have to do.[24] Thus, there is a kind of "common grace" before the fall, which sets the stage both for "common wrath" at and after the fall and for the common grace that is presupposed in God's universal wrath toward man. All of this is the foundation for the differentiation that takes place throughout history—as the call of the gospel goes out indiscriminately and sincerely to all (universal) and the elect are brought in (individually), while the reprobate (individually) reject the call of the gospel and remain in their sins (particular).

So, continues Van Til, following Calvin, the universality of the gospel promise "comes to sinful mankind, to mankind that has once before, when 'placed in a way of salvation,' been offered salvation. It comes to a generality that has once in common, in one moment, in one man, rejected the offer of eternal life through Adam. Mankind is now, to use words corresponding to the earlier stage, *placed in a way of death*" (pp. 93–94). That which corresponds to the earlier stage is not, we should note, simply that which is historically earlier. Van Til's point is that what corresponds to the earlier stage is that which is common to all mankind (both common wrath and common grace). So, the offer of life in the garden was an offer to Adam and, in him, an offer to all mankind. So also, when that offer was rejected by virtue of Adam's disobedience,

---

offered to all men on any other ground than on the condition of their remaining in their original innocence." John Calvin, *A Treatise on the Eternal Predestination of God*, in *Calvin's Calvinism*, trans. Henry Cole (Grand Rapids: Eerdmans, 1950), 92. It seems, as well, that Van Til's notion of conditionality harks back to Calvin's arguments.

24. This refers us back to our previous discussion of God's covenant as voluntary condescension. The notion that the covenant that God made with man had its foundation in his unmerited favor, or grace (though not grace as a response to sin), is nothing new in Reformed thought; neither does it undermine or in any way negate man's responsibility to be obedient to God's commands. According to Muller, "Divine grace, as indicated both in the doctrine of the divine attributes and in the developing Reformed covenant theology of the seventeenth century, is not merely the outward favor of God toward the elect, evident only in the postlapsarian dispensation of salvation; rather is it one of the perfections of the divine nature. It is a characteristic of God's relations to the finite order apart from sin, in the act of divine condescension to relate to finite creatures. . . . There is, both in the orthodox Reformed doctrine of God and in the orthodox Reformed covenant theology of the seventeenth century, a consistent identification of *grace as fundamental to all of God's relationships with the world and especially with human beings, to the point of the consistent assertion that the covenant of nature or works is itself gracious.*" Richard A. Muller, *Post-Reformation Reformed Dogmatics: The Rise and Development of Reformed Orthodoxy, ca. 1520 to ca. 1725*, vol. 3: *The Divine Essence and Attributes* (Grand Rapids: Baker Books, 2003), 570 (emphasis added).

mankind was "placed in a way of death." The "earlier" of which Van Til speaks, then, is directly related to that which is common in history. So, it has its focus in history, but is not simply an historical timeline.

Further on, Van Til asks a question directly relevant to our discussion above of fearless anthropomorphism: "Must we say that the wrath of God under which they rest, according to the revealed will of God, does not tell us of the real attitude of God to them?" (p. 95). In other words, how properly and biblically ought we to think about God's attitude toward the elect and the nonelect? To answer this, Van Til moves again to mankind before the fall.

With respect to men before the fall, "It was not some abstraction like creatureliness in them that was the object of God's favor. As concrete beings, eventually to be haters of God but not yet in history haters of God, rather, as yet in Adam good before God, the reprobate are the objects of God's favor" (p. 96). That is, Adam is not the covenant head of an abstraction like "creatureliness"; rather, he is the covenant head of real people—of every one of us—and God's disposition toward him is identical to his disposition toward us. In affirming this, Van Til also warns, "We are, therefore, to steer clear of Platonic abstractions. We are not to use the general offer of the gospel as an abstract idea" (p. 97). The general offer of the gospel has its genesis in Genesis; after the fall, it comes to Adam particularly, and to all mankind generally, in Adam. It then, as history progresses, comes to individual people, even as they themselves are each represented in the first man, Adam. There is the universal (mankind) and the particular (Adam), and to focus on one at the expense of the other is to think in abstraction, not concretely.

A close reading of this volume will help flesh out the points we are making here, but there is one concluding and crucial point with respect to "concrete thinking" that needs to be broached here. In speaking of "earlier" and "later," Van Til says, "All common grace is earlier grace. Its commonness lies in its earliness" (p. 99). By this, as we have seen, he means to point out that commonness was a function of Adam's covenantal headship, such that there was an attitude of favor toward all mankind, in Adam, originally, and there was an attitude of both common grace and common wrath toward all mankind, in Adam, at and after the fall. These attitudes provide the background and context in which God's electing purposes are carried out in redemptive history. To use Van Til's terminology, the "universal" of commonness has to be seen in the context of the "particular" of salvation for the elect and condemnation for the reprobate, and vice versa. To isolate one at the expense of the other is to do an injustice to both.

It should be seen as well that Van Til helps us to think concretely, that is, *historically*, as we contemplate the antithesis between believer and unbeliever in the context of God's common grace. He says:

> So while we seek with all our power to hasten the process of differentiation in every dimension we are yet thankful, on the other hand, for "the day of grace," the day of undeveloped differentiation. Such tolerance as we receive on the part of the world is due to this fact that we live in the earlier, rather than the later, stage of history. And such influence on the public situation as we can effect, whether in society or in state, presupposes this undifferentiated stage of development. (pp. 102–3)

Two comments here may help to clarify Van Til's points. First, Van Til says that we are to "hasten the process of differentiation in every dimension." What does he mean by that? Generally speaking, he means that we are to preach the gospel to all men, both believer and unbeliever, and to make that gospel known in our cultural activity as well. He mentions, in this context, the necessity for Christian schools. Such schools are (or should be) one attempt, among many, to show forth the radical and distinct differences that obtain between believer and unbeliever. They are meant to make clear that there is no neutral territory—not counting, not weighing, not measuring or anything—to which Christians can appeal. Common grace does not mean common education; the commonness of common grace can never imply neutrality.

In this "hastening," the world, at various times and in various ways, remains tolerant. Its tolerance varies with time and place, but no situation is as bad as depravity demands. This tolerance, notes Van Til, "is due to this fact that we live in the earlier, rather than the later, stage of history."

The point to be made in this last comment is that, again, Van Til is not simply thinking here of a historical timeline, such that tolerance means only that we have not reached the end of history. It does mean, of course, that when the end of history comes, historical differentiation will be complete. The sheep will be finally, completely, and eternally separated from the goats. But we should also remember that "*all* common grace is earlier grace." We live in the "earlier" stage of history whenever and wherever, in any particular context, the differentiation of elect and reprobate has yet to obtain.

An example here may help. In the library of Westminster Theological Seminary in Philadelphia there is a picture of Van Til on Wall Street in New York, Bible in hand, preaching to a crowd of listeners. That event itself shows forth an "earlier" stage in history; the "undifferentiated" crowd that is there, is there only by virtue of God's common grace. If, by God's special grace, someone came to know and believe on Christ in that crowd, there is evidence of both an earlier and a later aspect of God's grace. The "conditional" of the (later) gospel presupposes the common grace (earlier) of the crowd. So also with those who reject the gospel. The (earlier) common grace that allowed for the preaching of the gospel to that crowd, includes as well the (later) individual responses to that preaching. Differentiation takes place; the earlier (common grace) is correlative to the later of conditional differentiation.

This is "concrete" thinking; it embeds the reality of God's disposition toward mankind squarely in the historical process of differentiation. That differentiation is itself concrete, in that it is God's application of election, and his passing over of reprobation, that is taking place each day in history. The earlier and the later, the universal and the particular, the common and the individual, are historically correlative; they explain and delimit each other in the historical process, by virtue of God providentially—both commonly and individually—working out his eternal decree in history.[25]

In sum, then, "if we reason *concretely* about God and his relation to the world, we simply *listen to what God has told us in his Word* on the matter" (p. 191, emphases added). This brings us to our third and final theme.

(3) LIMITING CONCEPTS

We will remember that Van Til sees the notion of a *limiting concept* (as it is understood in a Christian way) as the glue that binds together the essays collected in this book. So understanding what he means by a "limiting concept" is central to understanding the book as a whole. But we could not move to an explanation of this term without first fleshing

25. In support of Van Til's analysis here, see G. C. Berkouwer, *The Providence of God* (Grand Rapids: Eerdmans, 1952), 76.

out our previous two themes, since *limiting concept* entails both *fearless anthropomorphism* and *concrete thinking*, and thus it was necessary to spend some time on those terms in order to understand this last controlling idea properly. Now that we have the first two in mind, we may be able to see why this third theme is, in Van Til's estimation, central to his arguments in these essays.

We need initially to recognize what a Christian "limiting concept" is, according to Van Til. In the first essay in this volume, he says:

> It is over against this post-Kantian view of the "limiting concept" that the writer speaks of a Christian limiting concept. This enables him, he thinks, to set off a truly biblical concept of mystery based on the God of Scripture, who is light and in whom is no darkness at all, from the non-Christian, in particular from the modern philosophical, concept of mystery. In the former case there is an intelligible, though not an exhaustive, intellectually penetrable basis for human experience. In the latter case man has no intelligible basis for his experience and, what is worse, insults the Christ who came to bring him light and life. (p. xlviii–xlix)

The term *limiting concept*, as used by Van Til, is a term that helps him to explain a "biblical concept of mystery based on the God of Scripture." Not only so, but to employ the non-Christian notion of a "limiting concept" and, thus, of mystery, destroys any basis at all for understanding human experience.

As we will see throughout this book, mystery is at the root of all Christian theology. When we affirm the ontological Trinity, the incarnation, the covenant of God with man, etc., we are articulating the truth of the matter, according to Scripture, but we are also affirming that our minds are not able to put the truth of the matter together in a way that is completely amenable to our usual ways of thinking. Perhaps the best word to denominate a teaching that requires us to affirm that which cannot be delimited by our laws of thought is "hyperdox," that is, a teaching of Scripture that must be affirmed, though it does not conform to, but rather transcends, standard rules of thought.[26] That is, these are teachings (*dox*) that are above (*hyper*) our typical (and proper) ways of thinking.

26. This term is from H. G. Stoker and may be preferable to the term *paradox*. A paradox refers to two mutually implied teachings that are set side by side; a hyperdox includes

Van Til refers to these teachings as "apparent contradictions." By that, he does not mean that they are explicit and obvious violations of the law of noncontradiction or some other canon of formal logic. That is, we do not affirm, for example, that God's attitude toward all men is gracious in the same way that God's attitude toward all men is not gracious. Similarly, we do not affirm that God is three in the same way that he is one. Nor do we affirm that Christ is God in the same way that he is man. There are deep and abiding issues in these truths of compatibility, but incompatibilities are not, per se, contradictions.

Van Til's notion of "apparent contradiction" is shorthand for recognizing that we are not able completely to subsume much of biblical teaching under our standard laws of thought. Our laws of thinking are not able exhaustively to demarcate the meaning of what we affirm to be true in Scripture. The problem is not, we should note, with our standard ways of thinking. God has created us so that we are not meant both to affirm and to deny the same thing at the same time and in the same way. He has created us so that we distinguish one thing from another (i.e., diversity). He has also created us to see and affirm the myriad relationships of differing things (i.e., unity). This is all part of "thinking God's thoughts after him."

The issue with respect to "hyperdoxes," then, is that an understanding of the character of God and his activity in the world will always transcend the typical ways we are meant to understand and know the world. Furthermore, and more importantly, the mystery of biblical teaching, the hyperdoxes given to us in Scripture, should form the foundation and basis for our typical ways of thinking. That is, we are not meant to apply our laws of thinking as far as we possibly can and then refer the remainder to "mystery." Rather, we *begin* with mystery, because we *begin* with the triune God himself. In that way, at minimum, we recognize that our typical ways of thinking are limited, are in need of their own foundation, and have their own God-given boundaries.

The controlling principle embedded in the Christian notion of a limiting concept, as Van Til uses it, is that God's revelation gives us truths—essential and basic truths—that the Christian will not be able to produce or affirm by using our basic rules of thought. We affirm what we believe and do

---

those two (or more) teachings, but affirms that they are above and beyond our human ability to understand. See Hendrik G. Stoker, "Reconnoitering the Theory of Knowledge of Professor Dr. Cornelius Van Til," in *Jerusalem and Athens: Critical Discussions on the Philosophy and Apologetics of Cornelius Van Til*, ed. E. R. Geehan (Nutley, NJ: Presbyterian and Reformed, 1977), 30.

through God's infallible and inerrant revelation to us. As Van Til says, "The various teachings of Scripture are not related to one another in the way that syllogisms of a series are related. The 'system of truth' of Scripture presupposes the existence of the internally, eternally, self-coherent, triune God who reveals Himself to man with unqualified authority" (p. xlviii).[27]

As Van Til will make clear, especially as he has in mind Calvin's response to Pighius, the Arminian objection to much of Reformed theology can be easily stated in a syllogism. "Pighius knows how to employ a well-turned syllogism. There is no escaping the force of his objection. If God is the ultimate cause back of whatsoever comes to pass, Pighius can, on his basis, rightly insist that God is the cause of sin" (p. 81). Moreover, says Van Til, "from the point of view of a non-Christian logic the Reformed Faith can be bowled over by means of a single syllogism" (p. 89).

The crucial point to be recognized here, however, is that the application of the syllogism, as well as other rules of thinking, to the Christian faith will have the effect of bringing God down from his majestic heights, and lifting man up to a presumed place of utter autonomy. God becomes less than sovereign, while man becomes the only and ultimate interpreter of his would-be autonomous experience.

This is, as Van Til makes clear, exactly the point that Paul is making in Romans 9:20. Paul recognizes, as he lays out the reality of unconditional election, that some in the church will be reasoning according to the very syllogism that Pighius uses against Calvin; they will not be inclined to submit their laws of thought to biblical truth. How does Paul address this problem?

We will recognize that the objections that Paul anticipated and addressed in this chapter are, nevertheless, objections that still flourish in many Christian circles. They flourish, however, not because God has failed to address them, but rather because there is a sinful tendency to ignore or otherwise mute Paul's responses.

First, Paul responds to the charge that election is unfair: "What shall we say then? Is there injustice on God's part? By no means! For he says

27. Since this point can be misunderstood, we should make clear here that, in all of this, we still do and must *use* our reason. To affirm "this and then that" is to make use of our cognitive faculties. This is why we have confined our discussion in this section to "our typical (or standard) rules of thought." Those rules, while used by our cognitive faculties, are not identical to those faculties.

to Moses, 'I will have mercy on whom I have mercy, and I will have compassion on whom I have compassion'" (Rom. 9:14–15). How could it be the case that God is unfair when his very choice of Jacob over Esau is grounded in his wholly good, sovereign, and independent character? God would be unfair if his choice of Jacob over Esau (and the elect over the reprobate) were arbitrary. But to be arbitrary would mean, for God, that there is some standard outside of him to which he is duty bound to adhere. God is his own wholly good standard. So Paul reminds us that God's own character is itself the absolute standard: "I will have mercy on whom I have mercy." Because God's choice is grounded in his character, it is a choice with the highest and most absolute rationale. The fact that we may not know that rationale is no argument against it (see Deut. 29:29). His judgments are, and remain, unsearchable to us (Rom. 11:33).

Paul then responds to the objection that if God determines who are his and who are not, even prior to their birth, simply on the basis of his sovereign choice, then surely he cannot blame anyone but himself for the outcome. How could he blame the reprobate, whose destiny was determined before the foundation of the world? To answer this objection, Paul refers again to God's sovereign character and sovereign right to do as he pleases:

> You will say to me then, "Why does he still find fault? For who can resist his will?" But who are you, O man, to answer back to God? Will what is molded say to its molder, "Why have you made me like this?" Has the potter no right over the clay, to make out of the same lump one vessel for honorable use and another for dishonorable use? (Rom. 9:19–21)

The main objections that have been incessantly lodged against the biblical view of God's electing purposes were already anticipated by God himself, through his apostle, and were answered. To aver that the answers are not satisfactory is to complain that God's own character is insufficient to ground his eternal actions. It is, in effect, to complain about the character of God himself. That is Paul's point.

Given this biblical teaching, it should be obvious that Reformed theology, confessing as it does God's absolute independence and sovereignty, requires the notion of limiting concepts. A theology that maps the teachings of Scripture according to standard laws of thought will have no puzzle to solve. The mind of man is fully capable, so it is thought, of putting all these apparent conundrums neatly together. In piecing together all the pieces of the puzzle by way of reason, however, the sovereign majesty of God is negated and the mind of man is exalted to the point of idolatry. So, says Van Til:

> Only those who are seriously concerned with interpreting the whole of history in terms of the counsel of God can be puzzled by the question of that which is "common" between believer and unbeliever. For both the Roman Catholic and the Arminian it is a foregone conclusion that there are large areas of life on which the believer and the unbeliever agree without any difference. Only he who is committed to the basic absolute of God's counsel can, and will, be puzzled by the meaning of the relative. (p. 18)

For Arminianism, there is no absolute counsel of God. All is relative to man's free and autonomous decision. But for Reformed theology, the absolute counsel of God is a limiting concept, requiring, as it does, the "relative" of the historical process. And this is an all-important point: limiting concepts, in order properly and biblically to be understood, *require* each other. They are not properly understood in isolation.[28]

So also for common grace. If one thinks that, given God's eternal and unconditional decree of election and reprobation, there is no room for common grace, then one is attempting to understand God's activity in history only in terms that logically flow from that eternal decree. In that case, there are no limiting concepts because God's decree in eternity is the only determiner of what happens in history. There can be no wrath (in history) for those chosen (in eternity), and no grace (in history) for those not chosen (in eternity).

But Scripture clearly urges us otherwise. Those who were by nature children of wrath, Paul says, were the very ones whom God made alive in Christ (Eph. 2:1–10). Thus, they were both under wrath and elect. So the electing purposes of God are themselves a limiting concept, entailing, as they do, the transition of God's disposition toward the elect from wrath

28. To say that these concepts *require* each other does not necessarily imply that they are conceptually or ontologically equivalent. There would be ontological equivalence for example, in our understanding of God as one (in essence) and three (in persons), but there would not be ontological equivalence in our affirmation of Christ as God (essentially) and man (covenantally).

to grace in history. So also God's decree of reprobation from before the foundation of the world requires the limiting concept of his goodness to all (Ps. 145:9) and the good gifts of rain and sunshine for all (Matt. 5:45), even as they reject the gospel and thus further the final differentiation of history.

Although Van Til does not explicitly bring together his notion of limiting concepts in the context of our two previous themes, we can begin to see how and why the ideas of "concrete thinking" and "fearless anthropomorphism" are inextricably linked to it. As we discussed, the quintessential culmination of fearless anthropomorphism is given to us in the person of Christ himself. In Christ, we have the limiting concept of the divine nature (which is eternal and essential to who he is as Son) entailing his human nature (which is "relative," in that it depends on God's free decision to redeem). The absolute (divine nature) and the relative (human nature), assuming, in the latter, God's free decision, entail each other. One without the other is meaningless with respect to his incarnate person. Not only so, but these two natures are not in conflict, but are brought together in the union of the person himself. So, in the end, there is no real conflict between the two, but rather unity—even though we are unable to bring the concepts together in our own minds.

This also demonstrates the importance of concrete thinking. We might be tempted to reason that the divine person of the Son could never *really* unite himself to anything created; that would undermine his deity and bring him down to the level of creation. But such thinking is only abstract. It is the kind of thinking that one would see in Islam, for example, beholden as it is to the dictates of reason.[29] To think concretely, however, is to affirm that God has come down to the level of creation. But in no way did that condescension detract from his full and majestic deity. The Son did not give up his deity in order to be man. The glorious truth of the gospel is that he remained who he is even while he became man for us and for our salvation. Without the notion of a limiting concept, in other words, not only is common grace not given its proper biblical weight, but the gospel itself loses its glory and grace. So, says Van Til: "So far from being a system of philosophical determinism that stultifies human knowledge and responsibility, the Reformed faith, being unreservedly based on biblical exegesis, is alone able to deliver

29. To see how this rational principle of Islam is worked out and addressed, see K. Scott Oliphint, *Covenantal Apologetics: Principles and Practice in Defense of Our Faith* (Wheaton, IL: Crossway Books, 2013).

to men the unadulterated joy of the gospel as it is in the Christ of the Scriptures" (p. xlix).

* * *

This discussion should suffice as a thematic and theological introduction to Van Til's consistent concerns as he addressed the doctrine of common grace throughout most of his career. The initial essay in this book dates to 1947, and it is likely that the last chapter of this book, written in 1972 and unpublished until this book was first put together, was the last thing that Van Til published in his career. The seamless character of these essays shows the consistency of Van Til's approach to the subject of common grace over the decades of his teaching ministry.

One other point is worthy of mention, and could easily have occupied this entire foreword, in that it deserves an extended essay. Of considerable interest in the last chapter is the following: "We join Schilder in rejecting Kuyper's distinction between Christ as the mediator of creation and as the mediator of redemption. We must unite the idea of creation in Christ with that of His redemption of all things" (p. 260).

The notion of uniting "the idea of creation in Christ with that of His redemption" certainly implies that the goal of Christ's mediatorial work is not twofold, as if he is the mediator of creation with one goal and the mediator of redemption with another. Rather, the goal of Christ as mediator is one, namely, to make known to us "the mystery of his will, according to his purpose, which he set forth in Christ as a plan for the fullness of time, to unite (ἀνακεφαλαιώσασθαι) all things in him, things in heaven and things on earth" (Eph. 1:9–10). "All things," therefore, are not meant to be placed in two different realms—one of common grace and one of special grace—but rather are to be brought together under one head, united in the *one* covenant of grace. History is moving inexorably toward the destruction of all Christ's enemies, as they are, by virtue of the gospel, made a footstool for his feet (see Col. 1:20; Rom. 11:36). This truth deserves much more attention than we have space to give it here, and it deserves much more study and attention than it currently receives in Reformed circles; but Van Til is clear in this last publication that the covenant of grace, including as it does the antithesis between believer and unbeliever, must be the presupposition of common grace, and thus there is meant to be now, as there will certainly be in the future, a universal demonstration of the lordship of Christ over all of life.

* * *

For this annotated second edition, I have provided translations where needed. I have also tried to include some historical detail and biography on most of the people mentioned herein and to explain some of the possibly confusing terminology that Van Til employs. Except for some augmentation of Van Til's source references, the additions (mainly here and in the notes) appear in the typeface you are now reading. Van Til's material, appearing in a more traditional text font, is otherwise virtually untouched.

I want to thank P&R Publishing for their commitment to republishing this important and central work in Van Til's corpus. It is impossible to understand Van Til's thought rightly without grasping the depth of his career-long exposition of common grace.

Finally, I want to thank Paul Maxwell for his energetic and tireless efforts and help in pulling many of the details of this work together.

AUTHOR'S NOTE

The first three chapters of this little book first appeared in 1947 as a pamphlet entitled *Common Grace*.[1] Chapter four, "Particularism and Common Grace," appeared under the same title in 1951.[2] The fifth chapter, "Common Grace and Witness-bearing," first appeared in the *Torch and Trumpet*, December, 1954–January, 1955, and was later published as a separate booklet.[3] Chapter six likewise appeared in booklet form, under the same title, "A Letter on Common Grace."[4] Chapter seven originally appeared as an appendix to my class syllabus on *Systematic Theology*.[5] The eighth chapter is a book review which appeared in *The Westminster Theological Journal* in November, 1968.[6] The ninth and final chapter has not appeared in publication before.

The reader is asked to bear in mind that these chapters do not form one unified whole, nor are they a collection of unrelated remarks. They are separate attempts to deal with particular aspects of the one theme—that of Common Grace and its relevance to the gospel.

1. Cornelius Van Til, *Common Grace* (Philadelphia: Presbyterian and Reformed, 1947).
2. Cornelius Van Til, *Particularism and Common Grace* (Phillipsburg, NJ: L. J. Grotenhuis, n.d.).
3. Cornelius Van Til, *Common Grace and Witness-Bearing* (Phillipsburg, NJ: L. J. Grotenhuis, 1955).
4. Cornelius Van Til, *A Letter on Common Grace* (Phillipsburg, NJ: L. J. Grotenhuis, n.d.).
5. Cornelius Van Til, *An Introduction to Systematic Theology* (Philadelphia: Westminster Theological Seminary, 1966).
6. Cornelius Van Til, review of *Reformed Dogmatics*, by Herman Hoeksema, *Westminster Theological Journal* 31 (1968): 83–94.

PREFACE

The present writer has from time to time been engaged in a study of the subject of *Common Grace*. The various brief studies published on this subject over a period of years are now brought together in the present volume.

The subject of Common Grace was originally of interest to the present writer because it seemed to him to have basic significance for the subject of Christian Apologetics. Anyone holding to the Reformed faith is constantly required to explain how he can do justice to the "universalism" of the gospel as presented in Scripture. How can he hold to election, especially "double election," without doing violence to the "whosoever will" aspect of biblical teaching?[1] How can he hold to "total depravity" and yet find a "point of contact" for the gospel among men in general?[2]

There is no way of discussing these problems adequately except by way of setting forth the entire "philosophy of history" as the

---

1. There is thought to be tension between the Reformed faith and the "universalism" of the gospel because of the Reformed view of God's eternal decree, including election. If it is true, as the Westminster Confession of Faith says, that "By the decree of God, for the manifestation of His glory, some men and angels are predestinated unto everlasting life; and others foreordained to everlasting death" (3.3), then it might be supposed that this same God, who ordains and decrees who will be saved and who will not, cannot sincerely call all men to repentance. Thus, the "universalism" (calling all men to repent) of the gospel is in tension with the particular election and reprobation of God's eternal decree.

2. The tension between a Reformed notion of total depravity and an apologetic "point of contact" is different from the tension mentioned in the previous footnote. If all men are totally depraved, in that they are truly dead in their trespasses and sins, how could the truth of Scripture ever really "connect" with that depravity? To use an analogy, what could be said to a person who is truly dead that would cause him to respond? If the condition of man is spiritual death, then, it is thought, nothing we say to him could ever really reach him. And yet, we are commanded to preach the Word, so that people might be saved.

Reformed confessions teach it. When the Reformed view of the philosophy of history is set forth on a frankly biblical basis it appears that the questions pertaining to "human responsibility" and to "the point of contact" find their "solution" in the Reformed faith and nowhere else.

But then, to say this is not to say that the "solution" offered on these questions is a "systematic" one, in the sense that it is logically penetrable by the intellect of man. The biblical "system of truth" is not a "deductive system." The various teachings of Scripture are not related to one another in the way that syllogisms of a series are related. The "system of truth" of Scripture presupposes the existence of the internally, eternally, self-coherent, triune God who reveals Himself to man with unqualified authority.[3]

On the surface, and by the sound of words, all this might seem to indicate a neo-orthodox approach to the question of God and His relation to man. The opposite is the case. The neo-orthodox view of the relation of God to man is based on the idea that since man cannot have a "systematic," i.e., purely rationalist knowledge of God, he must, in purely irrationalist fashion, fall back on the notion that any "systematic" interpretation of God's "revelation" is nothing more than a "pointer" toward something of which man knows nothing. That is to say, the neo-orthodox view of God's relation to man is based on the modern, particularly the post-Kantian, philosophical notion of truth as being nothing but a limiting concept. Man is surrounded by an ultimate void and he must direct the "flashlight" of his intellect into impenetrable mist.[4] It is over

3. This is a monumentally important point, as it serves to set Scripture in its proper, foundational place in theology. Reformed theology is a *system* of theology. It confesses biblical doctrines that entail and imply each other, and that cohere and are consistent. But this does not mean that the doctrines are comprehensively understood, or that they are confessed because our minds have penetrated to their depths, so that we know exactly how they all relate. Following from the paragraphs above, Van Til is making explicit the fact that biblical teaching cannot simply be arrived at by a simple syllogism (deductively). One might infer, for example, that since God chose his own people in eternity, and all those chosen will necessarily be saved, that there can be no sincere offer of the gospel to all men or legitimate command from God that all repent. But this kind of reasoning, no matter how logically valid, will not stand the scrutiny of Scripture. We derive our doctrines from Scripture, and the dictates of reason are meant to serve, rather than rule, in our systematizing of those doctrines. See K. Scott Oliphint, *Reasons for Faith: Philosophy in the Service of Theology* (Phillipsburg, NJ: P&R Publishing, 2006).

4. Here Van Til assumes that the relationship of Kantian philosophy to neoorthodox theology is grasped. A "limiting concept," for Immanuel Kant, was something posited by him so that we would recognize the limits of our understanding. Kant posited a "noumenal"

against this post-Kantian view of the "limiting concept" that the writer speaks of a Christian limiting concept. This enables him, he thinks, to set off a truly biblical concept of mystery based on the God of Scripture, who is light and in whom is no darkness at all, from the non-Christian, in particular from the modern philosophical, concept of mystery. In the former case there is an intelligible, though not an exhaustive, intellectually penetrable basis for human experience. In the latter case man has no intelligible basis for his experience and, what is worse, insults the Christ who came to bring him light and life.[5]

This is the point of view that binds the several chapters of this book together. So far from being a system of philosophical determinism that stultifies human knowledge and responsibility, the Reformed faith, being unreservedly based on biblical exegesis, is alone able to deliver to men the unadulterated joy of the gospel as it is in the Christ of the Scriptures.

---

realm as a limiting concept, since our understanding of the "phenomenal" realm could never extend to things as they are in themselves. Thus, the noumenal was the "limiting concept" of the phenomenal.

Much of Kant's philosophical structure and content was taken over by neoorthodox theology. Put simply, neoorthodoxy set forth a "wholly other" (i.e., noumenal) God, who is "known" (to the extent that he is) only in a revelatory Event. The "truth" of that revelation-Event is strictly experiential; it comes, not through Scripture, but directly from above. Even so, it has its origin in a God who is "wholly other" and thus ultimately unknowable. So what is known in the revelation-Event is a limiting concept, directing us to the "impenetrable mist" of a wholly other, and unknowable, God. What Van Til is saying is the opposite of neoorthodoxy because (1) he takes the truth of Scripture seriously, as the Word of God, and thus (2) God's incomprehensibility is predicated on the basis of that truth, not in spite of it.

5. That is to say, the Christian view of mystery is that mystery *is not* ultimate, in that God is light; there is nothing mysterious or unknown to him. The non-Christian view of mystery is that mystery *is* ultimate, in that it serves only to "limit" what we know.

PART ONE

CHAPTER 1

THE CHRISTIAN PHILOSOPHY OF HISTORY

The question of where he may find a point of contact with the world for the message that he brings is a matter of grave concern to every Christian minister and teacher.[1] The doctrine of common grace seeks, in some measure at least, to supply this answer. But to give the answer desired the concept of common grace must be set in its proper theological context. In discussing the problem, the present paper accordingly deals with (1) the Christian philosophy of history of which the common grace doctrine is a part, (2) the most comprehensive modern statement of this problem, (3) the salient features of the recent debate on the subject, and (4) some suggestions for further study.

The common grace[2] problem may quite properly be considered as being a part or aspect of the problem of the philosophy

1. The question of "point of contact" is multifaceted. For Van Til, "The point of contact for the gospel, then, must be sought within the natural man. Deep down in his mind every man knows that he is the creature of God and responsible to God." Cornelius Van Til, *The Defense of the Faith*, 4th ed., ed. K. Scott Oliphint (Phillipsburg, NJ: P&R Publishing Company, 2008), 116. Included in this point of contact is man's covenant relationship, in that all men are surrounded by an exhaustively personal environment, which is the presence of their God and Creator. Thus, being always in contact with the truth, both within and without, we can appeal to that truth in our defense of Christianity. For more on point of contact, see Van Til, *Defense of the Faith*, 90n2.

2. Though the question is a matter of debate we shall, for convenience, not enclose the phrase "common grace" in quotation marks. We use the phrase, and others like it, loosely.

of history. Dr. K. Schilder[3] speaks of Abraham Kuyper's[4] great three-volume work on "Common Grace" as an epic. And an epic it truly is. In setting forth his views on common grace Kuyper envelops the whole course of human culture in his field of vision. Common grace is said to be in large measure responsible for making history as a whole what it has been, is, and will be. On the other hand in rejecting the doctrine of common grace the Rev. Herman Hoeksema[5] in his various writings also takes the whole of history for his field. He argues that history can best be explained if we reject common grace. It may be well then if even at the outset we question ourselves about the Christian philosophy of history. Doing so at this early stage of our paper will help us in understanding both those who affirm and those who deny common grace.

3. Klaas Schilder (1890–1952) is perhaps best known as the father of the Gereformeerde Kerken (Vrijgemaakt), or "Liberated Churches" (known as the Gereformeerde Kerken onderhoudende artikel 31 van de Kerkenorde—"Reformed Churches supporting article 31 of the Church Order"). Schilder was educated in the Gereformeerde Gymnasium of Kampen from 1903 to 1909. In 1914, he graduated with honors from the theological school of the Gereformeerde Kerken in Kampen. From 1914 to 1933, he served six different congregations. After earning his Ph.D. from the University of Erlangen in Germany, his denomination called him to succeed A. G. Honig as professor of dogmatic theology. Schilder was arrested for opposition to the Nazis, after which, for other reasons, he was deposed from ministry in August of 1944. This led to the founding of the Liberated Churches that year. Controversy followed Schilder; his views of the covenant and of the church were controversial. Of specific concern here is that he debated Herman Hoeksema on the issue of common grace and covenant. Most popular among Schilder's works is the translation of his *Christus en cultuur*. See Klaas Schilder, *Christ and Culture*, trans. G. van Rongen and W. Helder (Winnipeg: Premier, 1977). For more on Schilder, see J. Geertsema, *Always Obedient: Essays on the Teachings of Dr. Klaas Schilder* (Phillipsburg, NJ: P&R Publishing, 1995).

4. Abraham Kuyper (1837–1920) was a theologian and politician. Prime minister of the Netherlands from 1900 to 1905, Kuyper sought to apply his Calvinistic theology in the area of politics. In theology, he is best known for his contributions in the areas of Christian worldview and theological encyclopedia and for his development of the Reformed doctrine of common grace. See Abraham Kuyper, *Encyclopedia of Sacred Theology* (New York: Scribner's, 1898); Kuyper, *Lectures on Calvinism* (Grand Rapids: Eerdmans, 1978); Kuyper, *De gemeene gratie* [Common grace], 2nd printing (Kampen: Kok, 1931–32); Kuyper, *Souvereiniteit in eigen kring* [Sovereignty in its own sphere] (Amsterdam: Kruyt, 1880). For an excellent analysis of Kuyper on worldview, see Peter S. Heslam, *Creating a Christian Worldview: Abraham Kuyper's Lectures on Calvinism* (Grand Rapids: Eerdmans, 1998).

5. It would not be overstating the case to affirm that it was, primarily, Herman Hoeksema (1886–1965) who began the debate on common grace in Reformed circles in the twentieth century. Hoeksema opposed the "Three Points of Common Grace" adopted by the Christian Reformed Church in 1924 (see the appendix in Van Til, *The Defense of the Faith*). His opposition to the notion of common grace led to his deposition from office in the Christian Reformed Church, after which he (and a few others who agreed with him) began the Protestant Reformed Churches of America. Hoeksema was a pastor and teacher in the Protestant Reformed denomination from 1924 to 1964.

In any philosophy of history men seek to systematize the "facts" of history. The many "facts" of history are to be brought into one pattern. Or, if we wish, we may say that the many "facts" of history are to be regarded *in the light of* one pattern. The philosophy of history is, accordingly, an aspect of the perplexing *One and Many* problem.[6]

Furthermore, in a philosophy of history the "facts" are regarded under the aspect of *change*. If there be other sciences that deal primarily with the "static," the philosophy of history deals primarily with the "dynamic" behavior of "Reality." It is natural, then, that in handling the problem of the philosophy of history the very existence of a single pattern of these *many*, and particularly of these *changing many*, should be called in question. That is to say, for one who *does not* base his thinking upon Christian presuppositions, it is natural to question the existence of an all-embracing pattern present in, and underneath, the changing "facts" of history. For one who *does* base his thinking upon Christian presuppositions it would, on the other hand, be unnatural or even self-contradictory to do so. For him the most basic fact of all facts is the existence of the triune God. About this God he has learned from Scripture. For the Christian, the study of the philosophy of history is an effort to see life whole and see it through, but always in the light of the pattern shown him in the Mount.[7] He cannot question, even when he cannot fully explain, the pattern of Scripture, in the light of which he regards the facts of history.

But to interpret facts—all facts and especially all facts in their changing aspect—in the light of an already fully given word of God is to be "unscientific" in the eyes of current science, philosophy

6. The "perplexing *One and Many* problem" is a philosophical problem that focuses attention on how we can relate individual facts (the many) to a more general, or universal, category (the one). This is not, we should note, a problem that plagues most people, but it has been a perennial problem in the history of philosophy. When philosophers deal with such things as the problem of meaning, they attempt to work through how a statement such as "I saw a dog" is meaningful. To be meaningful, there must be some notion of "dog" that is more than just an individual fact, so that anyone hearing the statement would employ a universal notion of "dogginess" in order to understand the statement about the individual dog that was seen. There has to be some relation between the many (individual dogs) and the one (dogginess).

7. Van Til is likely referring here to the pattern of the temple that Solomon built, which was given to his father David on Mount Moriah. Van Til used this as an analogy of how Christians should think about their cultural task. Like Solomon building the temple, they must think of it in terms that are laid down in God's Word.

and theology. Current methodology assumes the non-createdness of all the facts of the universe; it assumes the ultimacy of change. In this it follows the Greeks. With Cochrane[8] we may therefore speak of the classical-modern position and set it off against the Christian position.[9]

The believer and the non-believer differ at the outset of every self-conscious investigation. The "factness" of the first fact they meet is in question. The several schools of non-Christian thought have different principles of individuation.[10] Some find their principle in "reason" while others find it in the "space-time continuum." But all agree, by implication at least, that it is not to be found where the Christian finds it—in the counsel of God.[11]

It is sometimes suggested that though there is a basic difference between the Christian and the non-Christian explanation, there is no such difference in the mere description of facts. With this we cannot agree. Modern scientific description is not the innocent thing that we as Christians all too easily think it is. Sir Arthur Eddington's famed "ichthyologist" readily suggests this.[12] This "ichthyologist" explores the life of the ocean. In surveying his catch he makes two statements: (1) "No sea-creature is less than two inches long; (2) All sea-creatures have gills."[13] If an observer questions the first statement the "ichthyologist" replies that in his work as a scientist he is not concerned with an "objective kingdom of fishes." The

8. Charles Norris Cochrane, *Christianity and Classical Culture* (Oxford: Clarendon Press, 1940).

9. Charles N. Cochrane (1889–1945) was a Canadian. Educated at the University of Toronto and at Oxford, he spent his career teaching at the University of Toronto. The book to which Van Til refers traces the impact of Christianity on the Greco-Roman world.

10. A *principle of individuation* is that by which one thing can be distinguished from another. Going back at least to Aristotle, whose principle of individuation was tied to his theory of form and matter, it is one of the central aspects of the "one and many" problem that Van Til mentions above.

11. Van Til highlights "reason" and the "space-time continuum," apparently, due to Cochrane's discussion of those matters in the book referenced above.

By "the counsel of God," Van Til means God's triune agreement and decree to create and control all that is. What ultimately distinguishes one thing from another is God's determination in creation. As we will see, because the "counsel of God" is the counsel of the *triune* God, the problem of the one and the many has its source in the fact that God is both one (in essence) and three (in person).

12. Sir Arthur Eddington (1882–1944) was one of the most famous astrophysicists of the twentieth century. As Van Til notes in the next footnote, Eddington's ichthyologist analogy is found in his *Philosophy of Physical Science*, which published lectures originally given in 1938. The purpose of those lectures was to deal with scientific epistemology.

13. Arthur Eddington, *The Philosophy of Physical Science* (Cambridge: University Press, 1939), 16.

only fish that exist for him are those he has caught in his net. He makes bold to say "What my net can't catch isn't fish." That is to say, description is patternization. It is an act of definition. It is a statement of the *what* as well as of the *that*. It is a statement of connotation as well as of denotation. Description itself is explanation.[14]

Current scientific description is not merely explanation, but it is definitely anti-Christian explanation. Current scientific methodology wants to be anti-metaphysical.[15] It claims to make no pronouncements about the nature of reality as a whole. On the surface it seems to be very modest. In fact, however, current scientific methodology does make a pronouncement about the nature of Reality as a whole. When Eddington's "ichthyologist" says he is not interested in an "objective kingdom of fishes" he is not quite honest with himself. He is very much interested that that "objective kingdom of fishes" shall serve as the source of supply for his scientifically recognized fishes. Some of those "objective" fishes must permit of being graduated into fishes that have scientific standing. Some of them at least must be *catchable*. So the "facts," that is the "objective" facts, if they are to become facts that have scientific standing, must be *patternable*. But to be patternable for the modern scientist these "facts" must be absolutely formless. That is to say they must be utterly pliable. They must be like the water that is to be transformed into ice-cubes by the modern refrigerator.[16]

The scientist, even when he claims to be merely describing facts, assumes that at least some aspects of Reality are *non-structural* in nature. His assumption is broader than that. He really assumes that all Reality is non-structural in nature. To make a batch of ice-cubes Mother needs only a small quantity of water. But to hold

14. In the context of Eddington's argument, the net of the ichthyologist both defines and explains what "fish" are. If one were to ask about sea creatures that had gills and were less than two inches long, by the ichthyologist's definition, those could not be fish because his net could not catch them. So, as Van Til notes, explanation is reduced to definition, and connotation is reduced to denotation. The very definition of a thing is its meaning.

15. That is, current scientific methodology wants to explain the "facts" without reference to anything ultimate or to anything that would transcend the "facts" and give them their meaning.

16. Van Til's point here is that the fish that the ichthyologist defines and explains by his two criteria must have come from somewhere; they must have been somewhere prior to their description and explanation, when "caught" by the ichthyologist. Wherever they are, however, they can have no definition (hence, Van Til's notion of "formless") and can, therefore, be defined and explained according to any criteria the scientist chooses (hence, Van Til's notion of "pliable"). Like water transformed into ice cubes, they have neither form nor definition until such is imposed on them by outside factors.

the ice-cubes intact till it is time to serve refreshments, Mother must control the whole situation. She must be certain that Johnny does not meanwhile handle them for purposes of his own. So the scientist, if his description of even a small area, or of an aspect or a dimension, of Reality is to stand, must assume that Reality as a whole is non-structural in nature until it is structured by the scientist. The idea of brute, that is utterly uninterpreted, "fact" is the presupposition to the finding of any fact of scientific stand-ing.[17] A "fact" does not become a fact, according to the modern scientist's assumptions, till it has been made a fact by the ultimate definitory power of the mind of man. The modern scientist, pre-tending to be merely a describer of facts, is in reality a maker of facts. He makes facts as he describes. His description is itself the manufacturing of facts. He requires "material" to make facts, but the material he requires must be *raw* material. Anything else will break his machinery. The datum is not primarily *given*, but is primarily *taken*.[18]

It appears then that a universal judgment about the nature of all existence is presupposed even in the "description" of the modern scientist. It appears further that this universal judgment negates the heart of the Christian-theistic point of view.[19] Accord-ing to any consistently Christian position, God, and God only, has ultimate definitory power. God's description or plan of the fact

17. The notion of "brute fact" is one that has been misunderstood in Van Til's theology and apologetics. It is sometimes thought that Van Til's point was that, since there are no brute facts, all facts are what they are by virtue of our interpretation of them. This, how-ever, has more to do with postmodern relativism, and nothing to do with Van Til's view of fact. For Van Til, a brute fact is a mute fact. That is, it is a fact that does not "say" anything; it has no meaning unless and until a person, a scientist in this case, gives meaning to it. Thus, according to Van Til, there are no brute facts. But the reason there are no brute facts is not that every fact carries our interpretation with it. To think that way is to fall prey to relativism. For Van Til, there are no brute facts because every fact is a created fact. As created, therefore, every fact carries with it God's own interpretation. He speaks the facts into existence, and he speaks through that which he has created. But non-Christian science will not countenance any idea of the creation of facts by God.

18. The references to "*raw*" material and to a datum that is primarily "*taken*" are dif-ferent ways of describing the antimetaphysical posture of science. Since facts are thought to be "brute" facts, they can have no meaning until they are defined by science; they can have no structure until it is determined by the scientist. So facts can only be what they are when the scientist describes and delineates what they are. Prior to that description, they are simply "there" for the taking. This view has its roots in Immanuel Kant, who effectively eliminated the metaphysical as a source or ground of meaning.

19. This is a crucial point to grasp in Van Til's apologetic. Once science assumes the notion of "brute" facts, it has, as well, made a universal statement that facts are not what Christianity claims they are, namely, evidence and revelation of the true God.

makes the fact what it is. What the modern scientist ascribes to the mind of man Christianity ascribes to God. True, the Christian claims that God did not even need a formless stuff for the creation of facts. But this point does not nullify the contention that what the Christian ascribes to God the modern scientist, even when engaged in mere description, virtually ascribes to man. Two Creators, one real, the Other would-be, stand in mortal combat against one another; the self-contained triune God of Christianity and the *homo noumenon*, the autonomous man of Immanuel Kant, cannot both be ultimate.[20]

We conclude then that when both parties, the believer and the non-believer, are epistemologically self-conscious and as such engaged in the interpretative enterprise, they cannot be said to have any fact in common.[21] On the other hand, it must be asserted that they have every fact in common. Both deal with the same God and with the same universe created by God. Both are made in the image of God. In short, they have the metaphysical situation in common. Metaphysically, both parties have all things in common, while epistemologically they have nothing in common.[22]

Christians and non-Christians have opposing philosophies of fact. They also have opposing philosophies of law. They differ on the nature of diversity; they also differ on the nature of unity. Corresponding to the notion of brute force is the notion of abstract impersonal law, and

20. Kant's philosophy is difficult to summarize. As stated in footnote 18, Kant's philosophy is behind the antimetaphysical bias of secular science. The *homo noumenon* of Kant's philosophy is autonomous man because it is the *real* self, independent of all phenomenal limits.

21. The important notion of being "epistemologically self-conscious" will often be repeated in Van Til's discussion of common grace and apologetics. Note how Van Til qualifies the situation: "*when* both parties are epistemologically self-conscious, and *as such* engaged in the interpretive enterprise." Van Til is careful to make clear that the differences that obtain between the Christian and the non-Christian come to the fore to the extent that both parties are aware of, and explicit about, their epistemological and interpretive differences. If one is not epistemologically self-conscious, that does not mean that such differences do not obtain; it only means that they are not as clear.

22. It is necessary to highlight this statement and to keep it in mind, since so many who misunderstand Van Til either are unaware of it or ignore it altogether. *Metaphysically*, Christians have all things in common with non-Christians, in that all have the same triune God, live in the same created world, have all been created in the image of God, etc. *Epistemologically*, however, they have nothing in common, in that the non-Christian will interpret all things without reference to the true God and his creation. For the non-Christian, the counsel of God and his plan are automatically excluded at the outset of any and all interpretation of reality. As stated in the previous footnote, this epistemological motive is explicit to the extent that there is epistemological self-consciousness.

corresponding to the notion of God-interpreted fact is the notion of God-interpreted law. Among non-Christian philosophers there are various notions as to the foundation of the universals of human experience. Some would find this foundation "objectively," in the universe. Others would find it "subjectively," in man. But all agree, by implication at least, that it must not be found where the Christian finds it—in the counsel of God. The non-Christian scientist would feel hampered were he to hold to a Christian philosophy of fact. He would feel himself to be limited in the number, and in the kind of facts that he might consider. So also the non-Christian scientist would feel hampered were he to hold a Christian philosophy of law. To him this would introduce the notion of caprice into science. Law, he feels, must be something that has nothing to do with personality. When Socrates asked Euthyphro whether "the pious or holy is beloved by the gods because it is holy, or holy because it is beloved by the gods," he sought to make plain that all law must, in the nature of the case, be above all personality.[23] To find the essence of something we must, argues Socrates, go beyond what anybody thinks of a thing. To say that the gods love the holy is not to give us an insight into the essence of holiness. It is, as the Scholastics would say, merely to give an extrinsic definition of holiness. The *Good*, the *True* and the *Beautiful* as abstract principles, hovering above all gods and men—these are the universals of non-Christian thought.[24] Even so-called personalist philosophies[25]

23. Van Til is quoting from Plato's *Euthyphro*, in which Socrates is inquiring about the nature of the holy (or the good). If the "holy is beloved by the gods because it is holy," then holiness (or goodness) is ultimate; the *cause* of the gods loving it is in the holiness itself. If, on the other hand, something is "holy because it is beloved by the gods," then it is the gods who are ultimate, and what they determine to be holy is holy (or good).

24. Plato held that such ideas as the Good, the True, and the Beautiful, and not the gods, were ultimate. They are "abstract principles" because they are, by definition, impersonal. They have their origin in themselves, not in some person.

25. Van Til was interested in, and interacted with, personalist philosophy throughout his career. As he says in his lecture (see below), personalism was both a theology and a philosophy, and it has its roots in modern Methodist theology. Van Til's earliest published interaction with it was in a book review of Albert Knudson's *Doctrine of God*, in 1930 (*Christianity Today* 1, no. 8 [December 1930]: 10–13). The definition of it that Van Til seemed to work with was given by Knudson in his *Philosophy of Personalism* (New York: Abingdon, 1927), 87: "In the light of these facts we may define personalism as *that form of idealism which gives equal recognition to both the pluralistic and monistic aspects of experience and which finds in the conscious unity, identity, and free activity of personality the key to the nature of reality and the solution of the ultimate problems of philosophy.*" This quotation, and one of Van Til's interactions with personalism, can be found in "Boston Personalism," a lecture delivered to the faculty of the Boston University School of Theology on March 6, 1956 (unpublished). See also Van Til, *The Case for Calvinism* (Philadelphia: Presbyterian and Reformed, 1964), 62–64, 78–79.

like those of Bowne,[26] Knudsen [sic],[27] Brightman,[28] Flewelling[29] and others, are still impersonalist in the end.[30] Whether in science, in philosophy or in religion, the non-Christian always seeks for a daysman betwixt or above God and himself, as the final court of appeal.

Believer and non-believer have opposite philosophies of fact and opposite philosophies of law.[31] They also have, behind both of these, opposite views of man. Corresponding to the idea of brute fact and impersonal law is the idea of the autonomous man.[32] Corresponding to the idea of God-controlled fact and law is the idea of God-controlled man. The idea of creation out of nothing is not found either in Greek or in modern philosophy. The causal creation idea is obnoxious even to such critics of the classical-modern view

26. Borden Parker Bowne (1847–1910), a Methodist theologian and Boston personalist, received his B.A. (1871) and M.A. (1876) from New York University. He became a professor of philosophy at Boston University in 1876 and taught there for thirty years. He is most well known for his book *Metaphysics: A Study in First Principles* (New York: Harper & Brothers, 1882).

27. Albert C. Knudson (1873-1953) received an A.B. from the University of Minnesota, Minneapolis (1893), and an S.T.B. and Ph.D. from Boston University (1896; 1900), where he was presumably a student of Bowne. He did not teach at Boston University immediately after graduating, but later taught at their school of theology.

28. Edgar S. Brightman (1884–1953) earned his B.A. in 1906 and his M.A. in 1908, both from Brown University, and his Ph.D. from Boston University in 1912. He edited Knudson's Festschrift entitled *Personalism in Theology: A Symposium in Honor of Albert Cornelius Knudson* (Boston: Boston University Press, 1943).

29. Ralph Tyler Flewelling (1871–1960) studied at the University of Michigan, Alma College, and also at Garrett Biblical Institute (Evanston, IL) and Boston University (Ph.D., 1909). He became professor and chair of the department of philosophy at the University of Southern California, and in 1918 was appointed the chair of philosophy at the American Expeditionary Forces University in Beaune, France. He was ordained in the Methodist Episcopal Church in 1896. Flewelling was the founder and editor of the philosophical journal *The Personalist*, which he started in 1920; it was renamed *Pacific Philosophical Quarterly* in 1980.

30. To see why personalism is "still impersonalist in the end," see Van Til, "Boston Personalism," cited above. In sum, the focus on man's personality in personalism devolves into a focus on *abstract* human personality. Any focus on something abstract is, by definition, "impersonalist in the end." This harks back to Van Til's emphasis on "concrete thinking."

31. The believer affirms that facts and laws are created and controlled by God, but not so the unbeliever.

32. These three categories—brute fact, impersonal law, and autonomous man—are central to Van Til's entire apologetic, and they are, in various ways and with varying emphases, presupposed by any and all who reject Christianity. The extent to which one is aware of such presuppositions depends on the extent to which one is "epistemologically self-conscious." Brute facts are facts without meaning unless and until man gives them an interpretation; they are the antithesis of created facts, in and thorough which God speaks. The notion of impersonal law assumes that reality (or at least aspects of it) has a law-like structure, which no personal being maintains or controls. Autonomous man assumes that one is neither created nor governed by God, but is a law unto oneself. Understanding these three categories as the basic presuppositions of all non-Christians provides significant insight into much of what Van Til wants to argue.

as Cochrane, Reinhold Niebuhr[33] and the dialectical theologians.[34] Only the orthodox thinker holds to the creation idea. Accordingly only the orthodox thinker finds himself compelled to challenge the whole of classic-modern methodology.

Even so we are driven to make further limitations. Roman Catholics have taken no clear-cut position on the question of creation. They divide the field of factual research between autonomous Reason and Faith. "The natural" is said to be the territory of Reason and "the supernatural" is said to be the territory of Faith. In the territory of Reason believers and non-believers are said to have no difference. The question whether the mind of man is created or is not created, we are told in effect, need not be raised in this area. Rome is willing, in what it calls the field of Reason, to employ the ideas of brute fact, of abstract impersonal law and autonomous man, not merely for argument's sake, but without qualification.[35]

Arminians have, by and large, adopted a similar position. It is but natural that they should. Their theology allows for autonomy in man at the point of salvation.[36] Their philosophy, running in the same channel, ascribes autonomy to man in other fields.

It is therefore in Reformed thinking alone that we may expect to find anything like a consistently Christian philosophy of history. Romanism and Arminianism have virtually allowed that God's counsel need not always and everywhere be taken as our principle of individuation. This is to give license to would-be autonomous man, permitting him to interpret reality apart from God. Reformed think-

33. Reinhold Niebuhr (1892–1971) was a contemporary of Van Til and a highly influential neoorthodox theologian and pastor. The son of German immigrants, Niebuhr studied at Eden Theological Seminary and earned a bachelor of divinity from Yale Divinity School.

34. Among "dialectical theologians," Van Til certainly has in mind Karl Barth (1886–1968) and Emil Brunner (1889–1966). *Dialectical theology*, generally speaking, is another term for *neoorthodoxy* (also sometimes called the "theology of crisis"—see below), which seeks to affirm by way of negation and paradox. Paradox, as Van Til will discuss below, is really contradictory in dialectical theology. For example, in his commentary on Romans, Barth claims that God is to be understood as "the nonbeing of the world." For more on Barth and Brunner, see Cornelius Van Til, *The New Modernism: An Appraisal of the Theology of Barth and Brunner*, 2nd ed. (Philadelphia: Presbyterian and Reformed, 1947).

35. Van Til is referring here to the method employed by Thomas Aquinas and integral to Romanist dogma, which assumes a "natural" realm, in which there are no significant differences between a believer's and an unbeliever's use of reason, and a realm of "grace," in which those differences obtain. This "nature-grace" method of Romanism (and much evangelicalism) compromises biblical truth.

36. Because Arminian theology holds that, for man to choose freely, God must not be sovereign over that choice, Arminians allow for autonomy in a way that is similar to Romanists.

ing, in contrast with this, has taken the doctrine of total depravity seriously. It knows that he who is dead in trespasses and sins lives in the valley of the blind, while yet he insists that he alone dwells in the light. It knows that the natural man receives not the things of God, whether in the field of science or in the field of religion. The Reformed believer knows that he himself has been taken out of a world of misinterpretation and placed in the world of truth by the initiative of God. He has had his own interpretation challenged at every point and is ready now, in obedience to God, to challenge the thinking and acting of sinful man at every place. He marvels that God has borne with him in his God-ignoring and therefore God-insulting endeavors in the field of philosophy and science as well as in the field of religion. He therefore feels compelled to challenge the interpretation the non-Christian gives, not merely of religion but of all other things as well.

The significance of our discussion on fact, law and reason for the construction of a Christian philosophy of history may now be pointed out explicitly. The philosophy of history inquires into the meaning of history. To use a phrase of Kierkegaard, we ask how the Moment *is to have significance.* Our claim as believers is that the Moment cannot intelligently be shown to have any significance except upon the presupposition of the biblical doctrine of the ontological trinity.[37] In the ontological trinity there is complete harmony between an equally ultimate one and many. The persons of the trinity are mutually exhaustive of one another and of God's nature. It is the absolute equality in point of ultimacy that requires all the emphasis we can give it. Involved in this absolute equality is complete interdependence; God is our concrete universal.[38]

37. Søren Aabye Kierkegaard (1813–1855) is sometimes called the "father of existentialism." For him, "the Moment" (*ØjeblikketØjeblikket*) to which Van Til refers is the point (e.g., of decision) at which eternity and time intersect. In other words, "the Moment" was an attempt to give significance to the many aspects of reality (i.e., decisions) by way of the one (i.e., eternity).

By "ontological Trinity," Van Til means the triune God—Father, Son, and Holy Spirit—as he is *in himself*, and quite apart from his relationship to, and activity in, the world.

38. The term *concrete universal* comes from Hegelianism, which, in reaction to Kant's abstract universal, posited a universal that was embedded in reality, and which was in dialectic tension (between Being and Nonbeing). A concrete universal in Hegel's thought is that which is real and which includes everything in its scope. Van Til posits the true and triune God as our "concrete universal" (1) in order to speak to the philosophers in their own language, and, more importantly, (2) because God alone can transcend the reality and particulars of history, all the while being present in it to give it its true foundation and meaning.

We accept this God upon Scriptural authority. In the Bible alone do we hear of such a God. Such a God, to be known at all, cannot be known otherwise than by virtue of His own voluntary revelation. He must therefore be known for what He is, and known to the extent that He is known, by authority alone. We do not first set out without God to find our highest philosophical concept in terms of which we think we can interpret reality and then call this highest concept divine. This was, as Windelband tells us, the process of the Greeks.[39] This has been the process of all non-Christian thought. It is from this process of reasoning that we have been redeemed. On such a process of reasoning only a finite god can be discovered. It has been the nemesis of the history of the theistic proofs that this has been so frequently forgotten. Are we then left with a conflict between Faith and Reason? Have we no philosophical justification for the Christian position? Or are we to find a measure of satisfaction in the fact that others too, non-Christian scientists and philosophers as well as ourselves, have in the end to allow for some mystery in their system?

To all this we must humbly but confidently reply by saying that we have the best of philosophical justification for our position. It is not as though we are in a bad way and that we must seek for some comfort from others who are also in a bad way. We as Christians alone have a position that is philosophically defensible. The frank acceptance of our position on authority, which at first blush, because of our inveterate tendency to think along non-Christian lines, seems to involve the immediate and total rejection of all philosophy—this frank acceptance of authority is, philosophically, our very salvation. Psychologically, acceptance on authority precedes philosophical argument; but when, as epistemologically self-conscious grown-ups, we look into our own position, we discover that unless we may presuppose such a God as we have accepted on authority, the Moment will have no significance. The God that the philosophers of the ages have been looking for, a God in whom unity and diversity are equally ultimate, the "Unknown God," is known to us by grace. It has been the quest of the ages to find an interpretative concept such as has been given us by grace.

39. W. Windelband, *A History of Philosophy*, trans. James H. Tufts, 2nd ed. (New York: Macmillan, 1901), 34.

With this we might conclude our brief survey of the principles of a Christian philosophy of history. It is well, however, that we give further consideration to the modern notions of paradox and the limiting concept. Doing so will perhaps enable us to relate our own position more definitely to current speculation. Doing so may also prepare us for a better appreciation of the difficulties facing us when we deal with such questions as those with which we are concerned in the problem of common grace.

PARADOX

Our position is naturally charged with being self-contradictory. It might seem at first glance as though we were willing, with the dialectical theologians, to accept the really contradictory. Yet such is not the case. In fact we hold that our position is the only position that saves one from the necessity of ultimately accepting the really contradictory. We argue that unless we may hold to the presupposition of the self-contained ontological trinity, human rationality itself is a mirage. But to hold to this position requires us to say that while we shun as poison the idea of the really contradictory we embrace with passion the idea of the *apparently* contradictory. It is through the latter alone that we can reject the former. If it is the self-contained ontological trinity that we need for the rationality of our interpretation of life, it is this same ontological trinity that requires us to hold to the apparently contradictory.[40] This ontological trinity is, as the Larger Catechism of the Westminster Standards puts it, "incomprehensible." God dwells in light that no man can approach unto. This holds of His rationality as well as of His being, inasmuch as His being and His self-consciousness are coterminous. It follows that in everything with which we deal we are, in the last analysis, dealing with this infinite God, this God who hideth Himself, this mysterious God. In everything that we handle

40. When Van Til states that "we embrace with passion the idea of the *apparently* contradictory," he means that we must embrace with passion the Christian doctrine of the Trinity, and all that it entails. That doctrine is beyond our ability fully to comprehend, yet only by standing on the authority of God's revelation, and not our own reason, are we able to make sense of the world at all. His point, here, is to highlight that there are only two places on which one can stand with respect to knowledge—we either stand on God's authority in his revelation, or we stand on our own reason. The latter, Van Til makes clear, will end up destroying that same "reason" that we think is our foundation.

15

we deal finally with the incomprehensible God. Everything that we handle depends for what it is upon the counsel of the infinitely inexhaustible God. At every point we run into mystery. All our ingenuity will not aid us in seeking to avoid this mystery. All our ingenuity cannot exhaust the humanly inexhaustible rationality of God. To seek to present the Christian position as rationally explicable in the sense of being comprehensible to the mind of man is to defeat our own purposes. To do so we must adopt the standard of reasoning of our opponent, and when we have accepted the standard of reasoning of our opponent, we must rest content with the idea of a finite God.

To the non-Christian our position may be compared to the idea of adding water to a bucket that is already full of water. "Your idea of the self-sufficient ontological trinity," he will say, "is like a bucket full of water. To God nothing can be added. He cannot derive glory from His creatures. Yet your idea of history is like pouring water into the full bucket. Everything in it is said to add to the glory of God."

No Christian can answer this full-bucket difficulty in such a way as to satisfy the demands of a non-Christian epistemology. We can and must maintain that the Christian position is the only position that does not destroy reason itself. But this is not to say that the relation between human responsibility and the counsel of God is not *apparently* contradictory. That all things in history are determined by God must always seem, at first sight, to contradict the genuineness of my choice. That the elect are certainly saved for eternity must always *seem* to make the threat of eternal punishment unreal with respect to them. That the reprobate are certainly to be lost must always *seem* to make the presentation of eternal life unreal with respect to them.[41]

THE LIMITING CONCEPT

If we hold to a theology of the apparently paradoxical we must also hold, by consequence, to the Christian notion of a *limiting concept*. The non-Christian notion of the limiting concept has been

---

41. Van Til is elaborating on his point above that "at every point we run into mystery." Just exactly how a triune God who is altogether independent, eternal, and infinite can, really and sincerely, interact with his creation will always be mysterious to us; his ways are past finding out (see Rom. 11:33–36).

developed on the basis of the non-Christian conception of mystery. By contrast we may think of the Christian notion of the limiting concept as based upon the Christian conception of mystery. The non-Christian notion of the limiting concept is the product of would-be autonomous man who seeks to legislate for all reality, but bows before the irrational as that which he has not yet rationalized. The Christian notion of the limiting concept is the product of the creature who seeks to set forth in systematic form something of the revelation of the Creator.[42]

The Christian church has, consciously or unconsciously, employed the notion of the limiting concept in the formulation of its creeds. In these creeds the church does not pretend to have enveloped the fullness of the revelation of God. The church knows itself to be dealing with the inexhaustible God. The creeds must therefore be regarded as "approximations" to the fullness of truth as it is in God. This idea of the creeds as approximations to the fullness of the truth as it is in God must be set over against the modern notion of the creeds as approximation to abstract truth. The modern notion of approximation is based on the modern notion of the limiting concept. The modern notion of systematic logical interpretation as approximation is therefore based on ultimate skepticism with respect to the existence of any such thing as universally valid truth. The modern notion implies doubt as to whether any intellectual statement of any sort may be true at all. It is really no more than a hope, and that a false hope as we must believe, that there is in human interpretation an approximation to the truth. The Christian idea on the other hand rests upon the presupposition of the existence of God as the self-contained Being that Scripture presents to us. The Christian idea is therefore the recognition that the creature

42. For more on "limiting concept," see the foreword. The notion of a "limiting concept" is borrowed from philosophy, specifically from Immanuel Kant. In Kant's philosophy, there is much that can, presumably, be known by us in the phenomenal world. But there are other things that have to be posited, which cannot be known; Kant includes these as concepts of the "noumenal" realm. The noumenal things that are necessary (according to Kant), but nevertheless unknowable, are limiting concepts. The notion of *limiting* concepts presupposes Kant's agnosticism with respect to our knowledge (or lack of knowledge) of the noumenal realm. For Van Til, a limiting concept is that which is, at one and the same time, determined and defined by another limiting concept. Thus, the doctrine of election is a limiting concept with respect to our real and legitimate choices. It should be remembered that limiting concepts are not necessarily on a par with each other. God's election precedes our choices. Given creation, however, one (freedom) is best understood in the context of the other (election).

can only touch the hem of the garment of Him who dwells in light that no man can approach unto.[43]

If we have not altogether failed of our purpose, our discussion of the principles of a Christian philosophy of history will help us materially in understanding the literature that deals with common grace. In the first place it ought to enable those who affirm, and those who deny common grace to be conscious of the fact that only in Reformed circles could the question have arisen at all. Roman Catholics and Arminians could not be interested in the subject. Only those who are seriously concerned with interpreting the whole of history in terms of the counsel of God can be puzzled by the question of that which is "common" between believer and unbeliever. For both the Roman Catholic and the Arminian it is a foregone conclusion that there are large areas of life on which the believer and the unbeliever agree without any difference. Only he who is committed to the basic absolute of God's counsel can, and will, be puzzled by the meaning of the relative.[44]

The same thing must be said with respect to the Theology of Crisis. Of the dialectical theologians Barth claims to accept, and Brunner claims to reject, the doctrine of reprobation, but Barth no more than Brunner accepts this doctrine in the orthodox sense of the term. Hence their debate about creation-ordinances and common grace—Brunner affirming and Barth denying their relevancy to theology—has nothing except phraseology in common with the problem of common grace as discussed by orthodox theologians.[45] No one, we believe, can be seriously concerned with the question of common grace unless he seeks to be truly Reformed in his interpretation of life. Calvin, called the originator, and Kuyper, the great modern exponent, of the doctrine of common grace, were primarily concerned, in the whole thrust of their endeavor, to bring men

43. That is, when we confess that God is "infinite in being and perfection, a most pure spirit, invisible, without body, parts, or passions; immutable, immense, eternal, incomprehensible," as we do in the Westminster Confession of Faith, 2.1, we can know that what we confess is true because it is grounded in God's own revelation of himself, but we cannot plumb the depths of what these characteristics of God are in himself. For Kant, for example, what we can know about the phenomenal world is an "approximation," in that we can never know what that world really is; the "world-in-itself" is, by definition, hidden from us. Skepticism is the natural result of such approximations.

44. This is a tremendously significant point. A theology that confesses some kind of commonality between Christian and non-Christian will not see the need for a biblical doctrine of God's common grace; only in a Reformed context can such a doctrine find its home.

45. For more on this, see Van Til, *The New Modernism*.

face to face with the sovereign God. On the other hand, those who have recently denied common grace have done so, once more, in the interest of bringing men face to face with the sovereign God.[46]

In the second place, our discussion on the philosophy of history ought to make us realize that a question such as that of common grace admits of no easy and simple solution. We shall need to keep ourselves aware of the fact that we all need to employ the limiting concept, and that every statement of the truth is an approximation to the fullness of truth as it exists in God. Like the first point, this point, too, is a reason for common humility and mutual forbearance.

In the third place, our discussion ought to make us not only sympathetic in our understanding both of the work of those who have affirmed, and of those who have denied, common grace, but also critical of their efforts. We now have something of a criterion by which to judge whether men in their affirmation, or in their denial, of common grace have worked along lines that are really in accord with the Reformed Faith. The solution of the common grace problem, to the extent that it is to be found at all, must be found by looking more steadfastly into the face of God. To what extent have those that have engaged in the debate on common grace kept this point in mind? Have they sometimes allowed themselves to go astray along the by-paths of Parmenides, Heraclitus or Plato?[47] If we are even to *understand* the writings of Kuyper and others on the subject of common grace we must be both sympathetic and critical. How much the more then, if we are to *profit* by their work, should we both appreciate the good and avoid the mistakes they may have made?

46. Van Til is referring here to Herman Hoeksema and his followers.

47. Parmenides and Heraclitus were fifth-century B.C. pre-Socratic philosophers. Plato (429–347 B.C.) worked out his philosophy partly in reaction to, and dependence upon, the pre-Socratics. Van Til singles out these three philosophers because they represent three different notions of the problem of the one and the many, especially with respect to "Being" and "Knowledge." Heraclitus taught that all is in flux, so that whatever "is" and is "known" changes from moment to moment; all is "many." Parmenides, perhaps in reaction to Heraclitus, taught that Being is One, so that whatever was thought to be diverse was denied; all is "one." Plato sought to develop a middle position between these two. For Plato, Being can be either actual or potential. It is not necessary to choose either the static (Parmenides) or the flux (Heraclitus); his potentiality-actuality scheme seeks to include them both.

CHAPTER 2

ABRAHAM KUYPER'S DOCTRINE
OF COMMON GRACE

T urning now to an exposition of Kuyper's great work, we regret that we cannot begin with Calvin. (A reference, in passing, must be made, however, to the dissertation of Dr. Herman Kuyper,[1] *Calvin on Common Grace*, 1928).[2] We even pass by the pamphlet of Dr. Herman Bavinck on *Common Grace* with a remark or two.[3] Bavinck wrote his booklet (published in 1894) with the purpose of bolstering up the claim he made for the Protestant Faith in his earlier address on *The Catholicity of Christianity*

1. Herman Kuiper (1889–1963; Th.D., Free University of Amsterdam, 1928) was an ordained minister in the Christian Reformed Church in North America. "In 1953 he was appointed professor at Calvin Seminary to restore respect following a purge of almost the entire faculty" (Robert P. Swierenga, *Dutch Chicago: A History of the Hollanders in the Windy City* [Grand Rapids: Eerdmans, 2002], 343), and he became a professor of missions and dean at Calvin Seminary in 1956. It seems Van Til may have used an alternate spelling for his last name.

2. For a brief statement of the view of Charles Hodge, as well as for a more comprehensive statement of the exegetical foundation of the doctrine of common grace, see John Murray, "Common Grace," *Westminster Theological Journal* 5 (1942): 1–28.

3. Herman Bavinck (1854–1921), after a twenty-year stint as professor of dogmatic theology in the Reformed Seminary at Kampen, succeeded Abraham Kuyper in 1902 at the Free University of Amsterdam. Bavinck's work in systematic theology is the standard work of Reformed systematic theology from the Dutch tradition. His four-volume *Gereformeerde dogmatiek* has been translated into English as *Reformed Dogmatics* (Grand Rapids: Baker Academic: 2003–2008) (hereafter *RD*).

and the Church (published in 1888). It is Protestantism rather than Romanism, he avows in that earlier lecture, that expresses the truly catholic genius of the Christian religion. It is in accordance with this that he says in his pamphlet on *Common Grace,*

> Through this doctrine of *gratia communis* the Reformed [theologians] have on the one hand maintained the specific and absolute character of the Christian religion and on the other have been second to none in their appreciation of everything good and beautiful that God has given to sinful men. Thus they have simultaneously maintained the seriousness of sin and the rights of the natural. And thus they were protected against both Pelagianism and Pietism.[4]

A similar purpose has also controlled Kuyper in his work. It was the desire to press the catholic[5] claims of the truth of Christianity that led Kuyper as well as Bavinck to set forth this doctrine of common grace.

We shall first attempt to find the general characteristics of Kuyper's doctrine of common grace. Here a difficulty confronts us. There appears to have been a certain development in his views. In the first of his three volumes entitled *De Gemeene Gratie,* he tends to define common grace in more negative, while in the second he tends to define common grace in more positive, terms. In the first volume he speaks of the essence of common grace as being a certain restraint of God upon the process of the sinful development of history. In the second volume he speaks of the essence of common grace as being a certain positive accomplishment in history that the sinner is enabled to make by God's gifts to him. It looks as though Kuyper's conception of common grace grew gradually in his own mind to include a positive as well as a negative aspect. We shall look at each of these aspects in turn, in order then, as far as we can, to bring them together into one concept.

When Kuyper speaks of the restraint of the destructive process of sin as being the essence of the doctrine of common grace he makes plain that common grace, like special grace, presupposes

4. H. Bavinck, *De algemeene genade* (Kampen: G. Ph. Zalsman, 1894), 29.
5. Van Til uses the word *catholic* in the generic sense of "universal," not referring specifically to Roman Catholicism.

the doctrine of the sinner's total depravity. All men are born dead in trespasses and sins. "But," he adds,

> upon death follows a process of *disintegration* of the corpse. And it is the spiritual *disintegration* of the corpse that could be and was restrained, not *wholly* but in part. Not *wholly*, in order that the fearful results of sin might be apparent to all, but *in part*, in order that also in this manner the wealth of God's creation and of His recreating power in our sinful race might be glorified.[6]

He asserts a little later that the entire doctrine of common grace presupposes the fact of total depravity.[7]

Both types of grace, special and common, presuppose total depravity. The difference between the two must be indicated by the different effect they accomplish upon the totally depraved. Regeneration, a gift of special grace, Kuyper argues, removes the cancer of sin by taking out its roots. In the place of sin it gives the power of eternal life.

> But common grace does nothing of the sort. It keeps down but does not quench. It tames, but does not change the nature. It keeps back and holds in leash, but thus, as soon as the restraint is removed, the evil races forth anew of itself. It trims the wild shoots, but does not heal the root. It leaves the inner impulse of the *ego* of man to its wickedness, but prevents the full fruition of wickedness. It is a limiting, a restraining, a hindering power which brakes and brings to a standstill.[8]

Thus it is the restraint of the destructive force of sin that is said to be the essence of common grace.[9] Now as sin has affected the whole universe in the course of its historical development, we find, according to Kuyper, that common grace reaches out everywhere. Summing up his discussion on this point, he asserts:

6. A. Kuyper, *De gemeene gratie*, 3 vols. (Leiden: Donner, 1902), 1:243.
7. Ibid., 1:248.
8. Ibid., 1:251.
9. Ibid., 1:242.

Thus common grace began in *the soul* of man, by keeping the "small sparks" from dying out. It took its second point of support in the body of man by supporting its physical powers and thus pushing back the coming of death. In addition to this, common grace had to produce a third type of activity, namely, in the world of man.[10]

The essence of common grace is the restraint of the process of sin; its scope is man and his world. Its ultimate foundation, we must add, is the mercy of God. Says Kuyper: "Thus common grace is an omnipresent operation of divine mercy, which reveals itself everywhere where human hearts are found to beat and which spreads its blessing upon these human hearts."[11]

We cannot set forth in detail what Kuyper further says on the restraint of sin. At the moment we are looking for a broad perspective of the doctrine of common grace as a whole. It is well to hasten on, then, to Kuyper's statement of what we may call the positive aspect of common grace.

Kuyper distinguishes in his second volume between the *constant* and the *progressive* aspects of common grace. By the constant aspect of common grace he means largely what in the first volume he speaks of as the essence of common grace, namely, the restraint of the process of sin. God's purpose with common grace, he adds in the second volume, is not merely to make human life possible by the restraint of sin, but also to provide for its progress.[12] "There is," he says, "on the one hand the constant operation of common grace which began in Paradise after the Fall, and which has remained till this day precisely what it was in the beginning and this *constant* common grace itself consists of two parts."[13] These two parts are God's restraint of the power of destruction in nature and God's restraint "of the power of sin *in the heart* of man, to make possible the appearance of civil righteousness on the earth among sinners and heathen. . . . This is the common grace that leads to the *maintenance* and *control* of our human life."[14]

Continuing from this point Kuyper says:

10. Ibid., 1:261.
11. Ibid., 1:251.
12. Ibid., 1:600.
13. Ibid.
14. Ibid., 1:601.

Yet common grace could not stop at this first and constant operation. Mere maintenance and control affords no answer to the question as to what end the world is to be preserved and why it has passed throughout a history of ages. If things remain the same why should they remain at all? If life were merely repetition why should life be continued at all? . . . Accordingly there is added to this first constant operation of common grace . . . another, wholly different, operation . . . calculated to make human life and the life of the whole world pass through a process and develop itself more fully and richly.[15]

The course of history would, argues Kuyper, be wholly unintelligible if we forgot to bear in mind the progressive as well as the constant operation of common grace. Defining both aspects briefly again, he says:

The *constant* [operation] consists in this that God, with many differences of degree, restrains the curse of nature and the sin of the human heart. In contrast with this the progressive [operation] is that other working through which God, with steady progress, equips human life ever more thoroughly against suffering, and internally brings it to richer and fuller development.[16]

The "deep, incisive difference" between these two operations of common grace Kuyper signalizes by saying that in the constant operation God acts independently of man, while in the case of the progressive operation man himself acts as "instrument and co-laborer with God."[17] The history of civilization is here brought in as proof for his contention that man himself is the co-laborer with God. At a somewhat earlier point in the second volume Kuyper says: "Common grace is never something that is added to our nature, but is always something that proceeds from our nature as the result of the constraint of sin and corruption."[18] Here, though he speaks

15. Ibid.
16. Ibid., 1:602.
17. Ibid.
18. Ibid., 1:214.

without limitation, he is evidently thinking only of what he later calls the progressive operation of common grace.

We must now join the two aspects of common grace of which Kuyper speaks. In a general way we may affirm that, for Kuyper, common grace is primarily a restraining power of God, working either with or without man as an instrument, by which the original creation powers of the universe are given an opportunity for a certain development to the glory of God.

This very broad and unqualified definition of Kuyper's doctrine of common grace is perhaps the best we can do under the circumstances. Kuyper's exposition is not fully consistent and clear. Yet, in a well-rounded statement of his view Kuyper would wish us to include (a) the two operations spoken of and (b) the activity of man as the instrument of God at certain points.

Kuyper's statement of the doctrine of common grace has not gone unchallenged. In a number of pamphlets and books, as well as in a monthly magazine, *The Standard Bearer*, the Rev. Herman Hoeksema, the Rev. Henry Danhof and others have vigorously denied the existence of any form of common grace.

Hoeksema and Danhof argue that it is inconceivable that God should be in any sense, and at any point, graciously inclined to those who are not His elect. The wicked do, to be sure, receive gifts from God. But rain and sunshine are not, as such, evidences of God's favor.[19]

Moreover, the idea of common grace, Hoeksema and Danhof contend, virtually denies the doctrine of total depravity. Man is inherently a spiritual-moral being. If he is said to do any good, as Kuyper says he does, this good must be a spiritual good.[20] And if man does any spiritual good he is not totally depraved. When Hoeksema and Danhof[21] began to write against the idea of common grace they were ministers of the Christian Reformed Church. In 1924 the Synod of that Church virtually condemned their views. It did so by making a pronouncement on three points of doctrine.

19. H. Danhof and H. Hoeksema, *Van zonde en genade* (privately printed, 1923), 244.
20. Ibid., 131.
21. Henry Danhof (1879–1952), along with George Ophof and Hoeksema, is considered one of the founding fathers of the Protestant Reformed Churches, which were founded primarily as a protest against the doctrine of common grace espoused in the Christian Reformed Church, from which they came.

As these "three points" have ever since been at the center of the debate on common grace we include them at this juncture. As given in *The Banner*[22] they are:

"Synod, having considered that part of the *Advice of the Committee in General* which is found in point III under the head: Treatment of the Three Points, comes to the following conclusions:

"A. Concerning the first point, *touching the favorable attitude of God toward mankind in general, and not alone toward the elect,* Synod declares that it is certain, according to Scripture and the Confession, that there is, besides the saving grace of God, shown only to those chosen to eternal life, also a certain favor or grace of God which He shows to his creatures in general. This is evident from the quoted Scripture passages and from the Canons of Dort, II, 5, and III and IV, 8 and 9, where the general offer of the Gospel is discussed; while it is evident from the quoted declarations of Reformed writers of the period of florescence of Reformed theology that our Reformed fathers from of old have championed this view."

Note of the editor: The following Scripture passages are given as proof: Ps 145.9; Mt 5.44–45; Lk 6.35–36; Acts 14.16–17; 1 Tm 4.10; Rom 2.4; Ez 33.11; Ez 18.23. We need not print these texts since the readers can easily look them up. They can also find the passages of the Canons of Dort referred to in their copy of the Psalter Hymnal. However, inasmuch as they have no access to the declarations of the Reformed fathers, we should translate these; but since that will take considerable space we shall omit a sentence here and there, where this can be done without obscuring the thought.

Calvin: Book II, ch. II, 16: "Yet let us not forget that these are most excellent gifts of the Divine Spirit, which for the common benefit of mankind he dispenses to whomsoever he pleases. . . . Nor is there any reason for inquiring what intercourse with the Spirit is enjoyed by the impious who are entirely alienated from God. For when the Spirit of God is said to dwell only in the faithful, that is to be understood of the Spirit of sanctification, by whom we are consecrated as temples to God himself. Yet it is

22. Editorial by H. J. Kuiper, *The Banner* 74 (June 1, 1939): 508–9.

equally by the energy of the same Spirit that God replenishes, actuates, and quickens all creatures, and that according to the property of each species which he has given it by the law of creation . . ." Book III, ch. 14:2: "We see how he confers many blessings of the present life on those who practice virtue among men. Not that this external resemblance of virtue merits the least favor from him; but he is pleased to discover (reveal—K.) his great esteem of true righteousness by not permitting that which is external and hypocritical to remain without a temporal reward. Whence it follows, as we have just acknowledged, that these virtues, whatever they may be, or rather images of virtue, are the gift of God; since there is nothing in any respect laudable which does not proceed from him."

Van Mastricht, First Part, p. 439: "Now from this proceeds a threefold love of God toward the creatures: *a general,* Ps 104.31 and 145.9, whereby he has created, preserves, and rules all things, Ps 36.7 and 147.9; *a common,* directed to human beings in particular, not indeed to all and to *each,* but nevertheless to *all kinds,* without exception, the reprobate as well as the elect, of what sort or race they may be, to which he communicates his blessings; which are mentioned in Heb 6.4, 5; 1 Cor 3.1, 2."

Note: the third kind of divine love (toward believers) is not mentioned in this quotation since there is no disagreement regarding it.

* * *

"Concerning the second point, touching *the restraint of sin in the life of the individual and in society,* the Synod declares that according to Scripture and the Confession, there is such a restraint of sin. This is evident from the quoted Scripture passages and from the Belgic Confession, article 13 and 36, where it is taught that God through the general operations of His Spirit, without renewing the heart, restrains sin in its unhindered breaking forth, as a result of which human society has remained possible; while it is evident from the quoted declarations of Reformed writers of the period of florescence of Reformed theology that our Reformed fathers from of old have championed this view."

Note of the editor: The following Scripture passages are referred to: Gn 6.3; Ps 81.11, 12; Acts 7.42; Rom 1.24, 26, 28; 2 Thes 2.6, 7.

The same Reformed writers are quoted as under the first point:

Calvin, *Institutes*, Book II, ch. III, 3: "For in all ages there have been some persons who, from the mere dictates of nature, have devoted their whole lives to the pursuit of virtue. And though many errors might perhaps be discovered in their conduct, yet by their pursuit of virtue they afforded a proof that there was some degree of purity in their nature. . . . These examples, then, seem to teach us that we should not consider human nature to be totally corrupted; since, from its instinctive bias, some men have not only been eminent for noble actions, but have uniformly conducted themselves in a most virtuous manner through the whole course of their lives. But here we ought to remember that *amidst this corruption of nature there is some room for Divine grace, not to purify it but internally to restrain its operations* (we italicize—K.). For should the Lord permit the minds of all men to give up the reins to every lawless passion, there certainly would not be an individual in the world, whose actions would not evince all the crimes for which Paul condemns human nature in general, to be most truly applicable to him. . . . In his elect the Lord heals these maladies by a method which we shall hereafter describe. In others he restrains them, only to prevent their ebullitions so far as he sees to be necessary for the preservation of the universe."

Van Mastricht, II, p. 330: "God however moderates the severity of this spiritual death and bondage: (a) *internally* by means of some remnants of the image of God and of original righteousness . . . to which things is added an *internal restraining grace* . . . (b) *Externally*, through all kinds of means ("hulpmiddelen") of State, Church, Family, and Schools, by which the freedom and dissoluteness of sin is checked and restrained, and to which even an incentive to practice what is honorable is added."

* * *

"Concerning the third point, touching *the performance of so-called civic righteousness by the unregenerate,* the Synod declares that according to Scripture and the Confession the unregenerate, though incapable of any saving good (Canons of Dort, III, IV, 3), can perform such civic good. This is evident from the quoted Scripture passages and from the Canons of Dort, III, IV, 4, and the Belgic Confession, where it is taught that God, without renewing the heart, exercises such influence upon man that he is enabled to perform civic good; while it is evident from the quoted declarations of Reformed writers of the period of florescence of Reformed theology, that our Reformed fathers have from of old championed this view."

Note: The Scripture passages quoted are: 2 Kgs 10.29, 30; 2 Kgs 12.2 (compare 2 Chr 24.17–25); 2 Kgs 14.3 (compare 2 Chr 25.2 and vss. 14–16, 20, 27); Lk 6.33; Rom 2.14 (compare vs. 13. Also Rom 10.5 and Gal 3.12).

Note: Again we translate Synod's quotations from the writings of Reformed fathers:

Ursinus, Schatboek; on Lord's Day III: "Concerning an unconverted person it is said that he is so corrupt that he is totally incapable of any good. To understand this one must know what kind of good and what sort of incapability is spoken of here. There is a threefold good: (1) Natural (good), as eating, drinking, walking, standing, sitting; (2) Civic (good), as buying, selling, doing justice, some knowledge or skill, and more of such, which promote our temporal welfare. (3) There is also a spiritual and supernatural good, which is absolutely necessary for inheriting eternal life. It consists in this that one turns to God from the heart and believes in Christ. The last is meant here; in the other an unconverted man can even far excel a regenerated person although he has these (as a common gift) from God. See 2 Cor 3.5; Jas 1.17; Ex 31.2; Prv 16.1."

Van Mastricht I, p. 458: "Reformed (scholars) acknowledge indeed that the unregenerate person, apart from saving grace, is able . . . but they add to this that even these things are not done only through the exercise of the free will but through God's common grace working in the unregenerate all the moral good which is in them or which is produced by them. For example, all the natural art which was in Bezalel, Ex 31.2,

3, and all the moral good in those of whom it is said that they were enlightened by the Holy Spirit, tasted the good Word of God and the powers of the age to come, Heb 6.4, 5."

Van Mastricht, II, p. 330: " . . . There is a natural good, for example, eating, drinking, reasoning; there is a civic good as polite and friendly association with the neighbor, and offending no one; there is a moral or ecclesiastical good, as attending worship diligently, saying prayers, refraining from gross misdeeds, Lk 18.11, 12; and a spiritual good, for example, faith, hope, etc . . . in the state of sin the free will is indeed able to do a thing that is a natural, civic, or moral good, but not a spiritual good, which accompanies salvation."

We shall not pass in review the various criticisms made upon "the three points" by Hoeksema and his associates.[23] These criticisms, together with their relative validity or invalidity will appear in substance as we turn to a fuller discussion of the latest phase of the debate on common grace.

---

23. Cf. Herman Hoeksema:, *A Triple Breach in the Foundation of Reformed Truth* (Grand Rapids: Reformed Free Publishing Association, 1942); H. Hoeksema, *Calvin, Berkhof and H. J. Kuiper. A Comparison* (privately printed, 1928?), available online at www.prca.org; *The Standard Bearer.*

CHAPTER 3

COMMON GRACE IN DEBATE

I. RECENT DEVELOPMENTS

We must now turn to a brief survey of the controversy about common grace in its latest stage. Gradually the Reformed theologians of The Netherlands have interested themselves in the controversy so far largely carried on in America. And in recent years there has been a controversy in The Netherlands, as well as one between theologians of The Netherlands and theologians of America.

Broadly speaking there are in this latest struggle three parties. (a) There are those who would cling quite closely to the traditional, that is, the Kuyper-Bavinck point of view. Professor V. Hepp of the Free University of Amsterdam may be said to be the leading representative here.[1] (b) There are those who deny common grace.

---

1. Valentijn Hepp (1879–1950) graduated from the Free University of Amsterdam in 1903. He is perhaps best known as the successor to Herman Bavinck, taking the chair of systematic theology at the Free University in 1922, shortly after Bavinck's death. His inaugural address was entitled "Gereformeerde apologetiek" (Reformed apologetics). As the new dogmatician of the Free University, Hepp reacted to the American discussion on common grace with a series of articles in *De Reformatie* (of which he was the editor from 1920 to 1931) entitled "The Denial of Common Grace" (1922–1923). Hepp first came to America in the fall of 1924, when he gave forty-four sermons and fifty lectures, from coast to coast, including at Calvin College. His second visit was in 1930 to deliver the Stone Lectures at Princeton. Hepp was the third Free University professor to have this honor, after Kuyper (1898) and Bavinck (1908). Because Hepp was coming to America at just the time when Princeton was reorganized (culminating in the founding of Westminster Theological

Herman Hoeksema is now the recognized leader of this group. (c) There are those who would not deny common grace, nor yet affirm it in its traditional form, but reconstruct it. Dr. K. Schilder may be said to represent this group. It is naturally with the reconstructionists that we must chiefly concern ourselves now.

The reconstruction effort is closely related to a broad movement in theology and philosophy which attempts to build up the traditional Reformed position while yet to an extent rebuilding it. The Philosophy of Sphere Sovereignty[2] of Professors H. Dooyeweerd and D. H. Th. Vollenhoven represents a part of this movement.[3] It seeks to appreciate the concrete approach that Kuyper has given to the problems of theology and philosophy without clinging to certain abstractions that he retained.[4] We cannot further speak of this movement except to refer briefly to an article by the Rev. S. G. De Graaf on "The Grace of God and the Structure of God's Whole Creation."[5] In much the same way that Hoeksema argues, De Graaf argues that there can be no attitude of favor on the part of God toward the reprobate inasmuch as they are children of wrath.[6] Yet on the basis of such passages as Mt 5.45, he says, we must conclude that God loves His enemies.[7] Of the difference between grace or favor on the one hand and love on the other, he says:

Seminary), Hepp was under pressure to take a side on the issues in the Presbyterian Church. He decided that he could not do so. Because of that decision, his popularity and relationships with colleagues in America and the Netherlands began to decline. He was let go as editor of *De Reformatie* shortly after his return from the U.S. From 1937 to 1940, he was the editor of the periodical *Credo*.

2. "The Philosophy of Sphere Sovereignty" was initiated by Kuyper. His understanding was that there were various spheres of creation (such as the church and the state) that were each accountable to God and were also meant to function independently of each other. Thus, these institutions were "sovereign" in their own God-ordained spheres. Dooyeweerd and Vollenhoven attempted to interpret these ideas in the realm of philosophy.

3. Herman Dooyeweerd (1894–1977), together with his brother-in law, D. H. Th. Vollenhoven (1892–1978), were two pioneers of Christian philosophy in the twentieth century in the Netherlands. Though trained as a lawyer, Dooyeweerd's influence in philosophy surpassed Vollenhoven's, in part due to Dooyeweerd's three-volume work, *De wijsbegeerte der wetsidee* (The philosophy of the law-idea) in 1935–36. This work was later revised and translated into English as *A New Critique of Theoretical Thought*, ed. William S. Young, trans. David H. Freeman (Nutley, NJ: Presbyterian and Reformed, 1969). Seeing himself as an heir to Kuyper's thought, Dooyeweerd published over two hundred books and articles dealing with philosophy, culture, social theory, politics, and legal theory.

4. Cf. H. Dooyeweerd, "Kuyper's wetenschapsleer," *Philosophia Reformata* 4 (1939): 193–232; also C. Veenhof, *In Kuyper's lijn* (Goes: Oosterbaan & Le Cointre, [1939]).

5. S. G. De Graaf, "De genade Gods en de structuur der gansche schepping," *Philosophia Reformata* 1 (1936): 17–29.

6. Ibid., 18.

7. Ibid., 19.

The difference between grace or favor on the one hand and mercy and patience on the other is to be defined by saying that God in His patience gives his good gifts (*weldaden*), but withholds Himself from those to whom He gives these gifts, while in His grace He gives Himself, His own communion, as is the case with those to whom He grants His covenant.[8]

Of greater significance are the writings of Schilder. In his work on *Wat is de Hemel?* (*What is heaven?*) he seeks to offer a Christian philosophy of culture. The whole thrust of his thinking is an effort to proceed concretely. Accordingly he is critical of Kuyper's *Nebenzweck* (a secondary purpose or objective) of common grace, the provision for a history of civilization as such. He is also critical of what he thinks of as Kuyper's negative approach to the question of common grace. Culture is not to be based, he says, upon any foundation that we *still have* in common with the non-believer. Culture is rather to be based upon the original mandate given to man by God that he should subdue the earth. Thus we are brought back to the idea that man as office-bearer is called upon to glorify God in all he does. If therefore we speak of common grace at all, we should do so in connection with a "common curse."[9] There is restraint both of the full blessing and of the full curse. Keeping both in mind we are truly progressive rather than reactionary. We then think eschatologically and have an open mind for the idea of the catastrophic.[10] The popular notion of common grace as offering a neutral field of operation between Christians and non-Christians, Schilder rejects with vigor. It is not on the basis of one virtue in God; His patience, but on the basis of all His virtues that we must understand culture and history in general.[11]

The contribution made in this book is of great value. This contribution consists in stressing the need of concrete procedure in all our theological thinking. Schilder quite rightly attacks the idea of a territory that is common to believer and non-believer without

8. Ibid., 20.
9. K. Schilder, *Wat is de hemel?* (Kampen: J. H. Kok, 1935), 287.
10. Van Til will develop this point much more below. What he means is that common grace must be considered in the context of the establishment of the new heaven and new earth (the eschatological), as well as the context of the destruction of evil (the catastrophic). The *telos* of common grace, then, is the culmination of God's purpose for creation.
11. Schilder, *Wat is de hemel?* 289.

qualification. Yet he disclaims having dealt with the problem of common grace as a whole in this book.

Generally speaking it may be said that Hoeksema took some courage from the events we have so far related. He spoke with favor of the Philosophy of Sphere Sovereignty, but was displeased that its exponents did not, as he felt they should on their premises, deny common grace.[12, 13] He rejoiced to an extent in the work of Schilder and De Graaf.[14] Yet he doubted (in 1936) that Schilder really wanted to maintain the antithesis[15] and that De Graaf really denied common grace.[16]

More hopeful, from the point of view of Hoeksema, was an article in *De Reformatie* by Dr. S. Greydanus.[17] Greydanus argued about such gifts as those of rain and sunshine and asked the question whether, in view of the fact that the non-believer always misuses them and thereby adds to his punishment, they may be said to indicate a favor of God toward their recipients. He did not, in so many words, answer his question, but seemed to be very doubtful about the matter.[18]

We must hasten on, however, to relate something of a more specific nature. The "Three Points" of the 1924 Synod of the Christian Reformed Church came up for a fresh discussion. The Rev. Daniel Zwier[19] requested Schilder to state whether or not he was in agree-

12. H. H., "De twee-terreinen-leer," *The Standard Bearer* 12 (January 1, 1936): 176.

13. We need not discuss Klaas Schilder's detailed criticism of the formulation of the Three Points in "De scheuring in Amerika (II.)," *De Reformatie* 19 (May 19, 1939): 258–59, and "De scheuring in Amerika (XIII.)," *De Reformatie* 19 (August 18, 1939): 364–65.

14. S. G. De Graaf (1889–1955) was a prominent Amsterdam preacher of the gospel. His four-volume *Promise and Deliverance* (English translation of *Verbondsgeschiedenis*) has been highly influential in its presentation of redemptive history. For more on De Graaf, see "Translator's Introduction" in S. G. De Graaf, *Promise and Deliverance*, vol. 1: *From Creation to the Conquest of Canaan*, trans. H. Evan Runner (St. Catherines, Ontario: Paideia Press, 1979), 11.

15. H. H., "Een vergissing," *The Standard Bearer* 12 (May 15, 1936): 364.

16. H. H., "Loochening der gemeene gratie in Nederland," *The Standard Bearer* 12 (June 1, 1936); 393–94.

17. Seakle Greydanus (or Greijdanus; 1871–1948) was a Reformed theologian in the Netherlands who studied theology, specializing in dogmatics, at the Free University of Amsterdam. He was a minister in the Reformed churches of Rozenburg, Zuid-Beiherland, and Paesens-Moddergat. In 1917, he became professor of New Testament at Kampen Theological University. Greydanus was known for opposing Kuyper's ideas, joining Klaas Schilder in the Reformed Churches in the Netherlands (Liberated) in 1944. He was succeeded at Kampen by Herman Ridderbos.

18. H. H., "Dr. Greydanus stelt gewichtige vragen," *The Standard Bearer* 14 (February 1, 1938): 200.

19. Daniel Zwier (1879–1946) served the Synod of the Christian Reformed Church as its clerk for many years, including 1924, when the "Three Points" were produced. He was

ment with these three points. Zwier had been a member of the 1924 Synod and co-responsible for their adoption. In a series of articles in *De Wachter* (beginning April 4, 1939) he had expressed general agreement with Schilder's notion of the "Common Mandate." He professed a measure of sympathy with the general concrete approach to the problems of theology that Schilder was advocating. As a vigorous defender of the "Three Points" against Hoeksema, he, we can understand, was therefore much interested in Schilder's views on common grace.

The debate that followed discussed only the first point.[20] The Synod evidently said, or meant to say, that there is in God a certain attitude of favor toward the non-elect. Zwier so interprets the Synod's meaning. Schilder replied to Zwier that he was unable to accept the first of the "Three Points" as thus interpreted.[21]

In explanation of his position he criticizes the statement that God shows an attitude of favor "to His creatures in general." "Creatures in general" would include, he says, such things as lions and trees. But this is something quite distinct and different from "men in general." For in the case of men sin comes into the picture. And sin is not a creature. In actual men, therefore, we have to reckon with both factors, their creatureliness and their sinfulness. Accordingly it would be a mistake to conclude from the idea of God's favor toward creatures in general that there is a favor of God toward sinful, individual men. Again, "creatures in general" include fallen angels. And God certainly is not favorable to devils.

Synod failed therefore, argues Schilder, to distinguish between the mere creatureliness, and the office of man. We might say that, according to Schilder, Synod failed to bring into the picture the ethical as well as the metaphysical. Hoeksema, as well as he, says Schilder, will agree that God loves all creatureliness, even in the anti-Christ and in Satan.

With Zwier we believe that this criticism of Schilder's is not to the point.[22] For better or for worse, Synod meant to teach that God

also a minister in the Christian Reformed Church in Grand Rapids, Michigan.

20. See *De Reformatie*, May 12, 1939, and subsequent issues.

21. Klaas Schilder, "De scheuring in Amerika (XIV.): Intermezzo: antwoord aan ds. D. Zwier [I.]," *De Reformatie* 20 (October 20, 1939): 20–21.

22. Daniel Zwier, "Dogmatische onderwerpen: Syllogismen, die we onmogelijk kunnen aanvaarden," *De Wachter* 72 (November 21, 1939), 723–24; Zwier, "Dogmatische onderwerpen: Antwoord aan Dr. Schilder," *De Wachter* 73 (January 30, 1940): 67–68.

has a certain attitude of favor to all men as men. The use of the broad popular phrase "creatures in general" gives no justification for drawing such consequences as Schilder has drawn. Besides, the broad phrase itself expresses the fact that God loves all His creatures. And as for the idea that God loves all creatureliness as such, including the creatureliness of the devil, this is, we believe, intelligible only if we use it as a limiting concept. Schilder himself has warned us to think concretely. And thinking concretely implies the use of such universals as "creatureliness," as limiting concepts only.[23] Creatureliness as such can nowhere be found among men. It is a pure abstraction. Exegesis of Scripture may never, says Schilder, break the laws of thought which God has created in us.

The point of logic raised by Schilder is of a similar nature. Zwier replies that it is one thing to say that our Scripture exegesis must seek to be consistent, but quite another thing to say that our interpretation must accord with logic as that is generally taken. With this we must agree. If the second statement is not to be out of accord with the first, the logic referred to must be a genuinely Christian-theistic logic.

It may perhaps be said that much of the abstract reasoning of Hoeksema comes from his failure to distinguish between Christian and non-Christian logic. We do not mean, of course, that the rules of the syllogism are different for Christians and non-Christians. Hoeksema refers to the idea of insanity, saying that sin has not made us insane. We may agree if he means merely that the unbeliever can follow the technical processes of intellectual procedure as well as, or often better than, the believer. But when he says or assumes that God's revelation in Scripture may be expected to reveal nothing which will be apparently self-contradictory, we demur.[24]

He attempts to "harmonize" the revealed and the secret will of God, prayer and the counsel of God. His efforts on this score would not be accepted by unbelievers. He cannot solve the full-bucket

23. As a limiting concept, the notion of "creatureliness," since it is an abstraction, requires the "concrete" creature (e.g., the devil, a man, etc.) for its intelligibility and its proper application. For more on this, see the foreword.

24. Van Til is highlighting a crucial and central point in Reformed thinking—i.e., the foundational authority of Scripture. Scripture must guide our use and application of the way in which we understand and apply rules of thinking. If we deduce, for example, that since God has determined, from before the foundation of the world, those who will be eternally condemned, there can be no divine favor toward those people in history, we are using the logic of deduction to deny the clear teaching of Scripture.

difficulty, a difficulty which they think lies at the heart of the Christian religion. To them the whole idea of a God who is self-sufficient and all-glorious precludes the idea of anything taking place in history that should glorify Him. That, they argue, is to add water to a bucket that is already full. To say that no one resists the will of God, not even the murderer, is, for them, to say that we simply believe in fatalism. Have we then the right and the courage to say that Christianity does not contradict the laws of logic? We do, by pointing out that it is God, the self-sufficient God, in whom is no darkness at all, who has made us His creatures. Then it appears natural that there should be in all that pertains to our relation to God (and what does not?) an element of mystery.

As finite creatures we deal in all our contacts with an infinite and inexhaustible God. Schilder himself has, perhaps more than any other recent Reformed theologian, stressed the necessity of being open to the "catastrophic." The non-believer can allow for no such element. He seeks with Plato for a universal that is "rigidly universal" and as such essentially penetrable to the human mind.[25] The non-believer admits mystery, too. In fact for him mystery is ultimate, enveloping God as well as man.[26] His position therefore is rationalistic first and irrationalistic last. Unwilling to accept anything not essentially penetrable to the human mind, and thereby assuming the equality of the divine and human minds, he ends by facing a brute factual situation on the one hand and an empty universal on the other hand.[27] Thus the non-believer is illogical. He destroys the foundations of true logic. He may be ever so skillful in the manipulation of syllogisms, but he must still be said to be illogical.

On the other hand the Christian doctrine of God is the presupposition of the possibility of true logical procedure. The rules

25. "Rigidly universal truths" are those which are deducible with logical necessity from self-evident axiomatic principles.

26. As discussed above, for Kant, to use one example, the noumenal, which cannot be known, includes God, the transcendental ego, and things in themselves. These *cannot* be known, and thus are relegated to the noumenal. As Van Til's next sentence states, this means that non-Christian thinking includes an irresolvable dialectic of the rational (deducible principles—the phenomena) and the irrational (that which is not, and cannot be, known—the noumena).

27. The "brute factual" situation is the taking of phenomena in order to give them their initial interpretation; the would-be autonomous man takes facts and pretends to determine their meaning. Even so, some things are relegated to the noumena, and thus are "empty universals," in that they can have no content, factual or otherwise.

of formal logic must be followed in all our attempts at systematic exposition of God's revelation, whether general or special. But the syllogistic process must be followed in frank subordination to the notion of a self-sufficient God. We must here truly face the Absolute. We must think His thoughts after Him. We must think analogically, rather than univocally.[28] To reason as though we can remove all the "logical difficulties" which will naturally appear to be contained in the Christian system of truth is to say, in effect, that on the question of logic the believer and the non-believer occupy neutral territory and to assign to the unbeliever a competence he does not in reality possess.

It is well to observe in this connection that a natural concomitant of the failure to distinguish between a Christian and a non-Christian foundation for true logic is the denial of the genuine significance of the historical. Given the belief in a self-sufficient God, the idea of temporal creation and genuine historical development is absurd. So says the non-believer. And so says the Arminian, using the neutral application of the syllogism. Calvinism, we are told, makes history to be a puppet dance. The Arminian has not seen the necessity of challenging the idea of a neutral logic. He reasons abstractly, as all non-believing philosophy does. The Arminian therefore also rejects the Reformed conception of history. He thinks of it as he thinks of philosophical determinism.[29]

It is, we are compelled to believe, the essentially "neutral" logic, frequently employed by Hoeksema, that is back of his charge of "determinism" against those who maintain that the natural man

28. Van Til's notion of "analogy" and "analogical," as it applies to knowledge and to predication (which Van Til borrowed from Bavinck), is central to his theology and apologetic. Although the term itself is confusing, in that it tends to imply a host of assumptions in Thomism and elsewhere, it should not be confused or in any way identified with Thomas's understanding of analogy. For Thomas there is an analogy of being (*analogia entis*), but for Van Til the notion of analogy is meant to communicate the ontological and epistemological difference between God and man. To think analogically is to "think God's thoughts after him." Thus, such notions as "existence," "cause," and "necessity" must be understood in their proper context, with reference either to God or to the creature. One is original (God); the other is derivative (creation). This difference has been expressed historically in terms of an archetypal-ectypal relationship. For more on the latter, see Willem J. van Asselt, "The Fundamental Meaning of Theology: Archetypal and Ectypal Theology in Seventeenth-Century Reformed Thought," *Westminster Theological Journal* 64 (2002): 319–36.

29. In this paragraph, Van Til is explaining the difference between Calvinism's view of history, as meticulously planned and controlled by God (Eph. 1:11), and an Arminian view, which allows for the choices of man, rather than of God, to be determinative in history. Thus, some see Calvinism as destroying the significance of history.

does "good works" by common grace. The charge is identical in nature with the charge of determinism lodged against the Reformed doctrine of saving grace by the Arminian theologian. Secondly and more generally, it is, we believe, the use of an essentially neutral logic that leads Hoeksema to deny the possibility of (a) a certain attitude of favor on the part of God to the reprobate and (b) the ability of the reprobate to do good of a sort.[30]

Now Schilder has done much in his general works to teach Reformed Christians how to think concretely. We cannot grant, however, that in his general evaluation of the common grace controversy he has approached very closely to his high ideal. What he said about Scripture in relation to logic was not calculated to make men think concretely. And what he says about the Scripture material adduced by the Synod in support of the "Three Points" seems to us to indicate that he has frequently reasoned abstractly in the way that Hoeksema did.

We now turn to a brief consideration of his analysis of some of the Scripture pages involved.

(a) Ps 145:9.

The first passage is Ps 145:9, "The Lord is good to all; and his tender mercies are over all his works." Schilder argues, as before, that we have here the expression of God's pleasure in the fact of existence as such. God maintains the metaphysical situation and by so doing gives to "human existence the joyful feeling of existence and development" (Ps 145:9).

There is here no evidence of God's favorable attitude to any generality, says Schilder. In God's attitude His whole being in all its attributes is always involved. Hence God's justice must always be taken into consideration.[31]

With the last statement of Schilder we may well express agreement. We may add to it that in making up the balance all of the factors existing in man at any particular time in history must be taken into consideration. It is definitely a question of history before

30. In other words, on the basis of eternal election and reprobation (which all Calvinists hold), Hoeksema denies the possibility of God having a favorable attitude toward the non-elect. That conclusion may seem to be a necessary consequence of God's eternal decree, but it cannot be supported by Scripture, and thus is not a correct inference from election.

31. Klaas Schilder, "De scheuring in Amerika (XV.): Intermezzo: antwoord aan ds. D. Zwier [II.]," *De Reformatie* 20 (October 27, 1939): 28–29.

us. If we use no distinction of date at all we have the Arminian position, according to which God has the same attitude toward all men without qualification.[32] If we use only one distinction, that between creatureliness and office, as Schilder does, and say that God has an attitude of favor to his creation as such, we make the anti-Christ and the demons an object of favor. Schilder, although criticizing the Synod for holding to a position that would lead to the idea of favor toward Satan, is virtually in the same position himself when he would interpret Ps 145 as referring merely to the metaphysical situation as such.[33] Adding the further distinction of *date* enables us to approach somewhat more adequately, we believe, a full statement of the facts of the case.[34] When history is finished God no longer has any kind of favor toward the reprobate. They still exist and God has pleasure in their existence, but not in the fact of their bare existence. God has pleasure in their historically *defeated* existence. His justice has prevailed over their unrighteous *striving* in the course of time. Therefore God no longer in any sense *classifies* them in a generality with the elect. It was only at an earlier date, before the consummation of their wicked striving was made complete, that God even *in a sense* classified them with the elect.[35]

If we take this point back to the beginning of history we may find some further light shed on the subject. When God first spoke to Adam he did so as to the representative of all men. This does not mean that in God's mind the issue of each man represented was not already determined. It certainly was. Yet God undeniably dealt with the elect and the reprobate as being in some sense a generality.[36]

Adam was created perfect. When he fell all men *became* sinners; they became in Adam the objects of God's wrath (see Rom. 5:12–21). They *all* became sinners. They all became sinners *on the same day*

32. That is, there is no particular election unto salvation or reprobation; rather, God's acts depend on man's choice.

33. The "metaphysical situation as such" is, as Van Til says above, God's favor toward existence as such, without reference to any particular or any historical situation. This remains abstract, and thus is an unbiblical way of thinking. See the discussion of "concrete thinking" in the foreword.

34. In *Heidelbergsche Catechismus*, 4 vols. (Goes: Oosterbaan & Le Cointre, 1939–1940), 1:66, Schilder himself greatly stressed the importance of dates in history: "Het is overal *foederaal-historische* dateering!" ("The dating is thoroughly covenant-historical!").

35. What Van Til means by God's "classifying the reprobate with the elect" is that he shows favor and is good toward them all.

36. "In some sense a generality" refers to the fact that Adam was the covenant head of all, both elect and reprobate.

through the one act of a common representative. They all were confronted with the same conditional proposition. The elect and the reprobate are by one act of response to that single proposition led closer to their distinctive destinations. To be sure, this is true only in view of later events, the chief of which is the redemption in Christ of the elect. For all that, and because of that, there is a genuine sense in the word *common* when applied to believers and non-believers combined. It was by the same negative act to the same "offer" that *all* men lost the favor of God and became objects of the "common" wrath of God. While all men were perfect in Adam there was sameness with a difference. So when all men became sinners through Adam's sin there was again sameness with a difference.[37] It is of the essence of *historical development* that such should be the case.

The elect of God are always the objects of favor in the ultimate sense. In Adam, before the fall, they were perfect and, as perfect, God's favor rested on them. Thus their historical situation seemed to correspond to their eternal destiny. God's ultimate favor and His proximate favor seemed to correspond. Then the elect became sinners in Adam and as sinners the object of God's wrath. Yet God's ultimate attitude of favor did not change. Thus the elect, together with the reprobate, are objects of God's wrath. Yet there remains a difference. The elect are objects only of a "certain wrath" of God. Is not this a genuine wrath? If it were not, Christ would not have needed to die to "reconcile us to God."

When the elect are saved, the historical situation seems once more to accord with the ultimate attitude of God. Yet they are *closer* to God than they were before. There has been *progress.* The *process of particularization* has gone forward apace.[38] On the other hand they are still, to the extent that the "old man" in them remains active, the objects of God's displeasure.[39] The saints are told not to

37. The "sameness with a difference" with respect to Adam's perfection was that *all* were perfect in Adam, though the reprobate were perfect only due to Adam's headship. The "sameness with a difference" of all becoming sinners was that, while all became sinners, the elect were, nevertheless, objects of God's love.

38. The elect, when saved, are "*closer*" to God than before because of the reality of what takes place in history. The doctrine of election does not render the historical meaningless; real progress takes place in history. Part of that progress is the "process of particularization" (which Van Til elsewhere calls the "process of differentiation"), which means that the particular individuals who constitute "the elect" are those who are saved in history.

39. Van Til often used the "old man–new man" metaphor for unbelievers as well as believers. With respect to unbelievers, the "old man" is that aspect of man that retains the knowledge of God; it is the old man because it harks back to our being created in God's

grieve the Holy Spirit (Eph. 4:30). Thus there are genuine historical "downs and ups" upward by which the elect are brought to their particular destination.

In a similar fashion in case of the non-elect there are "ups and downs" downward leading them to their particular destination. And the process is in both cases genuine. This not in spite of, but because of, the fact that the destiny of both classes is fixed. History has, we believe as Christians, genuine significance because God's counsel is back of it and is being realized through it. Thus there is genuine progress, and therefore genuine variation, in the relations of the same men to the same God just because God's unvarying counsel is back of history. Why then should there not be genuine significance in the measure of generality through which God leads each class to its particular destiny? Every historical generality is a stepping-stone toward the final particularism that comes at the climax of history.[40]

(b) Mt 5:44, 45; Lk. 6:35, 36.

We pass on now to a brief notation on the other passages of Scripture cited by the Synod. We join the passages Mt 5:44, 5 and Lk. 6:35–36. Schilder sets aside what seems to be a common inter-pretation of these passages to the effect that we are to do good to the wicked in imitation of our Father in heaven who does good to them. Schilder says this common interpretation is illegitimate. From the presence of rain and sunshine as facts common to all we are not to conclude that there is a favorable attitude on the part of God toward His enemies. How then, says Schilder, can we expect to find God's attitude revealed in the facts of rain and sunshine?

To this we reply that Christ's words are positive as well as nega-tive. We are to show our attitude in our deeds, in imitation of God whose attitude we may therefore assume to be manifest in His deeds. When Schilder argues that we cannot legitimately reach a

---

image. The "new man" in the unbeliever is that which has fallen into sin. It is the new man because it harks back to Adam's fall, which presupposes the image of God. The "old man" in the believer is that "body of death" that remains in those who are born again (see Rom. 7:7–25).

40. In other words, the "generality" of the elect and the "generality" of the reprobate move in history toward the "particularism" of individuals, whose destinies comport with their respective generality. The generality of election, for example, has been particularized in the believer's historical salvation in Christ.

conclusion about God's attitude from the facts, we reply that we are specifically told that God's attitude is revealed in these facts. This is not to deny for a moment that, throughout it all, the rain and sunshine are means by which the wicked adds to his final punishment.

Again, when Christ is said to be χρηστός (this is typically translated as *kind*) to the "un-thankful and evil," (Lk. 6:35) Schilder would limit this to the elect, but unconverted, sinner. He speaks again of the mere continuation of the metaphysical situation as all that is implied for the unbeliever. He warns us again that the "facts" as such are no justifiable ground for a conclusion with respect to the attitude of God. We reply that there is here again a direct statement about the attitude of God, in the light of which the facts are interpreted.[41] All the facts of history manifest something of the attitude of God to men. If they did not, they would not be related to God and, therefore, be meaningless.

(c) Acts 14:16, 17.

The next passage is Acts 14:16, 17. It speaks of God not having left himself without a witness in times past, but giving gifts to men. Schilder points to the fact that Paul speaks of these gifts as being testimonies unto men of God's requirement upon them.[42] God is engaged in preparing judgment upon men, says Schilder; we are accordingly not justified in seeing a favorable attitude in the gifts of nature.

Again we cannot understand why the one cannot be true as well as the other. To be a witness of God, of the whole God, these gifts must show His mercy as well as His wrath. God's judgment is threatened because men reject God's mercies.

(d) 1 Tm 4.10. "God, who is the Saviour of all men, especially of them that believe" (1 Tm 4:10).

The word "Saviour" is by common consent taken to mean Preserver. Schilder again asserts that this refers merely to the

41. This is a clear example of Schilder reasoning "abstractly" and attempting to interpret Luke 6:35 accordingly. Van Til's point is that the verse speaks concretely of God's attitude of kindness, even toward those individuals who are under his wrath.

42. Klaas Schilder, "De scheuring in Amerika (XVI.): Intermezzo: antwoord aan ds. D. Zwier [III.]," *De Reformatie* 20 (November 3, 1939): 36–37.

continuation of the metaphysical situation. Zwier replies, we believe correctly, that God's preservation of the unrighteous is evidence of His favor toward them and that therefore there is some favor at least shown to the unrighteous in the fact of his preservation in this world. God is the preserver of all men, *especially* of the righteous. The "especially" cannot fairly be translated by "namely." "Especially" seems, therefore, to indicate some measure of favor, however small, to the unrighteous.[43]

There is another Scripture passage that has been much in dispute, but we shall refer to that in our last section, to which we now turn.

II. SOME SUGGESTIONS FOR THE FUTURE

We now make bold to submit a few remarks by way of suggesting the direction in which we may possibly hope for profitable discussion on the common grace question in the future. It is with hesitation and diffidence that we do so. And it is with the greatest of appreciation for the labors of such men as Kuyper, Bavinck, Hepp, Schilder, Hoeksema, Zwier, and others, that we say what we say.

A. The Danger of Abstract Thinking

It would seem to be obvious that if we are to avoid thinking abstractly on the common grace problem, we must seek to avoid thinking abstractly in the whole of our theological and philosophical effort. Perhaps the first question we should ask ourselves is whether the Kuyper-Bavinck form of theological statement in general, in which nearly all, if not all, who have been engaged in the recent common grace debate have been nurtured, does not, to some extent at least, suffer from the disease of abstraction. Perhaps the physicians have not altogether escaped the disease against which they have inoculated others. As a grateful patient it is my duty now to assert that in my humble judgment such is the case.

It will neither be possible nor necessary for our present purpose to discuss this matter at length. It must suffice to indicate what we have in mind by pointing to crucial instances. We shall deal with

---

43. For a helpful, concise analysis of this verse and its relationship to common grace, see Steven M. Baugh, "'Savior of All People': 1 Timothy 4:10 in Context," *Westminster Theological Journal* 54 (1992): 331–40.

the question of the knowledge of non-believers. More particularly we shall deal briefly with the question of natural theology. Rome's semi-Aristotelian epistemology influences, and accords with, its semi-Aristotelian ethics.[44] Rome's notion of the common area of Reason between believers and non-believers controls its conception of the common cardinal virtues. So also what Kuyper and Bavinck think of the reprobate's knowledge of God will influence what they think of the reprobate's deeds before God. We shall seek to intimate, be it all too briefly, that in the epistemology of Kuyper, Bavinck, and Hepp there are remnants of an abstract way of thinking that we shall need to guard against in our common grace discussion.

1. Kuyper. When we speak of Kuyper we may refer first to the booklet by C. Veenhof,[45] entitled *In Kuyper's Lijn.* Veenhof is concerned to show that the Philosophy of the Law Idea,[46] developed by Drs. D. H. Th. Vollenhoven and H. Dooyeweerd, professors at the Free University of Amsterdam, is working along the lines suggested by Kuyper, the founder of that university. In the course of his proof he speaks of the stress Kuyper laid on the fact that all the creation-ordinances are subject to the will of God.[47] These ordinances or laws admit of transgression by man, while yet they do not admit of abrogation.[48] "With great clarity Kuyper saw the law-organism which controls the world."[49] Veenhof further points out that Kuyper was opposed to the idea of neutrality. For him the attitude of the heart, the center of man's activity, was involved in all true scientific interpretation.[50] The whole idea of a science that is based on regeneration, as this is set forth in his *Encyclopedia,*[51]

44. That is, due to the influence of Aristotle on Aquinas, Rome holds to a measure of autonomous reason with respect to knowledge (epistemology) and morality (ethics).

45. Cornelis Veenhof (1902–1983), who received his doctorate in theology from Kampen, was, from 1946 to 1968, professor of pastoral theology at Kampen. He was indebted to Kuyper, as well as Bavinck, and he also learned much from the philosophy of Dooyeweerd and Vollenhoven. Attempting to follow "in Kuyper's line," Veenhof wrote not only the book Van Til mentions, but also *Souvereiniteit in eigen kring* (Sphere sovereignty), among others.

46. The philosophy of Dooyeweerd and Vollenhoven was called, in Dutch, *de wijsbegeerte der wetsidee,* which translates as "the philosophy of the law-idea."

47. Veenhof, *In Kuyper's lijn,* 29.

48. Ibid., 32.

49. Ibid.

50. Ibid., 32ff.

51. Some of volume 1 and all of volume 2 of Kuyper's three-volume *Encyclopaedie der heilige godgeleerdheid* (Amsterdam: J. A. Wormser, 1894) was translated into English

proves the correctness of Veenhof's contention on this point. It is well to emphasize again that it is from Kuyper, more than from any one else in modern times, that we have learned to think concretely. Both on the question of the universal and on that of the particular, Kuyper has taught us that we must build on our own presuppositions. Yet it must be said that Kuyper has not always been able to live up to this high ideal.

Kuyper has not always been able to live up to his own conception of the universal.[52] Dooyeweerd has shown this to be the case in his article on "Kuyper's Wetenschapsleer."[53] Dooyeweerd shows that Kuyper has all too uncritically employed the modern philosophical statement of the problem between the universal and the particular. We shall give some of the evidence to prove that Dooyeweerd was not mistaken.

Kuyper speaks of facts and laws or particulars and universals. The former correspond to our perception and the latter to our ratiocination.[54] Kuyper says that the whole of our ratiocinative process is exhausted by its concern for the universals.[55] Here Platonism is in evidence. The ratiocinative process, argues Kuyper, deals with concepts only. That is to say it deals with universals only. If we form a concept of a tree, a lion or a star, he says, we have no knowledge other than that which tells us how such a tree or lion or star is related to other objects or how the parts of such a tree, lion, or star are related to one another.[56] If this position were carried through consistently we should have the two worlds of Plato, the world of bare particulars and the world of bare universals standing in hopeless duality over against one another.[57] If this position were carried through, our "systems" of interpretation would be "approximations" in the Platonic, rather than in the Christian, sense of the word, our limiting concepts would be Kantian rather than Calvinistic, and our "as if" patterned

as *Principles of Sacred Theology* (Grand Rapids: Baker Book House, 1980) (hereafter *PST*).

52. Read, *Kuyper says that the objects of observation contain "moments" and "relations."*
53. Dooyeweerd, "Kuyper's wetenschapsleer" ("Kuyper's epistemology"), 193.
54. Kuyper, *Encyclopaedie der heilige godgeleerdheid*, 2:21, note (*PST*, 75, n. 1).
55. Ibid., 2:21 (*PST*, 75–76).
56. Ibid., 2:22 (*PST*, 76).
57. Plato's "theory of Forms" consisted of the real, which included our everyday experience, and the Ideal, which was the perfect Form of that which we experience. Thus, our "real" experience of a tree is an imperfect reflection of the "Ideal" (i.e., Form) of Tree-ness; it is a mere approximation.

after the *Critique of Pure Reason* rather than after the *Institutes*.[58] Kuyper, of course, does not carry through this sharp separation between ratiocination and perception. But he is able to escape the evil consequences suggested by no better means than that of inconsistency. Let us note the nature of this inconsistency.

Continuing his discussion of the relation of the intellectual process to the universals, he brings in two further notions. The universals themselves exist as a system. They are organically related to one another. Our ratiocinative process is adapted to penetrate this system of relations. And particularly our intellects are fitted to see through the higher relations. Here the gradational motif is injected in the process of describing the system of relations. This again is evidence of a non-Christian type of abstraction. A system cannot, if we start abstractly, exist otherwise than as a hierarchy.[59]

In the second place, Kuyper ushers in the notion of the active as well as the passive intellect. "Our thinking is wholly and exclusively adapted to these (highest) relations, and these relations are the objectification of our thought."[60] All this is still Platonic.[61] It is more than that: it is Kantian. Kuyper himself feels that we would, by going further along this path, soon fall into subjectivism. We are saved from subjectivism, argues Kuyper, by the fact that there is such a thing as a gradual transition from one relation to another. The results of these gradually changing universals we observe for the first time in that which for ages no human eye has discerned.[62] We remark here that subjectivism can in no wise be avoided in this manner. Plato himself tried to avoid it thus and failed. He sought to make the universals overlap one another. There was only one way open to him for the purpose, namely, the way of intermixture of the universals with what Adamson calls the "abstract essence of change."[63] But to intermingle

58. Some have called Kant's philosophy the "philosophy of the 'as if,'" since his positing of the noumenal means, in effect, that we operate "as if" those noumenal elements had a determining influence on us, even though we can have no knowledge of them.

59. That is, in an abstract system the best we can do is prioritize one over another; we have no real, concrete experience available to us that would otherwise distinguish the various elements.

60. Kuyper, *Encyclopaedie der heilige godgeleerdheid*, 2:23 (*PST*, 77).

61. Put generally, the passive intellect receives the Forms of things and the active intellect takes those Forms and "actualizes" them unto knowledge.

62. Kuyper, *Encyclopaedie der heilige godgeleerdheid*, 2:23 (*PST*, 77).

63. Van Til is probably referring here to Robert Adamson, *The Development of Greek Philosophy*, ed. W. R. Sorley and R. P. Hardie (Edinburgh: W. Blackwood and Sons, 1908).

universals with ultimate change is, in effect, to deny the universality of the universals.[64]

Kuyper, however, suddenly brings in the idea of an original Subject, who has thought the universals and has given them being. When we as human beings think ourselves into the relations of the universe we are simply thinking God's thoughts after Him.[65] The universals could not exist unless God had thought them. This is the Christian position. But how it is to be deduced from what up to this time has virtually been a Platonic procedure, is not apparent. Kuyper argues that we must stress the "identity of our thinking consciousness with the world of relations so far as to maintain that without an original Subject, who has thought them, and possessed the power to bring the product of His thought into dominance in the cosmos, they would not exist."[66]

Here the very existence of the relations is made to depend upon fiat creation by God.[67] But if fiat creation is to be their source, if the counsel of God is to be the source of the existence and validity of the relations, the Platonic procedure, to which Kuyper has clung in his discussion so far, must be dropped. Both Platonism in its final form and Christianity hold that the universals must have transition in them. But Platonism, not believing in temporal creation, ascribes this transition to the abstract idea of ultimate chance. On this basis the ideal of human knowledge must be that of identification of the subject's knowledge with objective universals. Yet it is a foregone conclusion that not even the first step toward the realization of that idea can be taken. The universals must be both abstractly unchangeable and abstractly changing.[68]

64. Universals, by definition, cannot change; they must be static abstractions or else they could not give us reliable knowledge of that which does change.

65. Kuyper, *Encyclopaedie der heilige godgeleerdheid*, 2:23 (*PST*, 77).

66. Ibid. (*PST*, 77).

67. That is, God "thought" of creation and all it contains, and then, by fiat (authoritative command), he created that which he thought.

68. Van Til is offering here a summary critique of Platonic, and much of Greek, philosophy. He is dealing with the basic question of epistemology (*wetenschapsleer*). What is it that would determine the relationship of the thinking subject to the object? If not God, then only pure "chance." Not only so, but in order to bring together the thinking subject, whose ratiocination is according to universals, and the object, which is always changing, the universal must both be unchanging (in order to provide true knowledge of the object) and changing (in order to apply to the changing object). There can be no true connection between subject and object in such a scheme.

Christianity, on the other hand, believing in temporal creation, ascribes the transition in the universals to the counsel of God. There is no abstract staticism and therefore no abstract change. On this basis the idea of human knowledge is to think God's thoughts after Him *analogically*. Hence man's intellectual effort cannot be said to be exclusively concerned with the relations; the relations do not exist otherwise than in correlativity with the "facts." Every intellectual effort deals with facts *in relations* and with relations *in facts*.[69] Thus the ideal of identification "of our thinking con-sciousness with the world of relations" must be entirely dropped. It is a remnant of the Platonic ideal. Kuyper cannot, except at the price of inconsistency, say that we are *in so far* to hold on to this ideal of identification as to warrant the Christian position with respect to God as the Creator of relations. If God is the Creator of the relations, we shall need to make a clean break with Plato. The abstract separation between facts and relations and the ideal of identification of the thinking consciousness with the world of relations, must both be dropped and dropped for good.

Kuyper has a weakness in the foundation of his epistemology. He did not start unequivocally from the presupposition of the ontological trinity. He has, to some extent, allowed himself to for-mulate his problems after the pattern of a modernized Platonism. In making this criticism we are aware of the fact that Kuyper himself sometimes joins perception and ratiocination closely. The strict analysis he has given, he holds, applies only if we deal with a "wholly elementary object."[70] But, we object, such a wholly elementary object does not exist. Hence the distinction between ratiocination and perception should have been made in the form of a limiting concept. But then the question would again arise as to whether this limiting concept were to be taken in the Christian or in the Platonic sense of the term. And there is evidence that indicates a lack of clarity in Kuyper's thought as to the distinction between the Christian and the non-Christian notion of the limiting concept. At times he argues as though the idealist's ideal of comprehensive knowledge is in itself a legitimate ideal for creatures to hold. If sin

---

69. This is an epistemological application of Van Til's previous point concerning the equal ultimacy of unity and diversity. There is a continual movement, in our thinking, between facts in relations (i.e., facts related to universals) and relations in facts (i.e., facts as diverse).

70. Kuyper, *Encyclopaedie der heilige godgeleerdheid*, 2:27 (*PST*, 81).

had not entered into the world, Kuyper says, the ideal of science reaching out toward the exhaustive interpretation of the whole of the cosmos, would be a legitimate idea.[71] In accordance with this he also speaks of *universality* and *necessity* as being of the very essence of the knowledge of cosmic law.[72]

But all this is, for the moment at least, to forget that for Adam in Paradise, no less than for us, God was the incomprehensible God. This incomprehensible God reveals something of Himself in cosmic history. He does so voluntarily and to the exact extent that it pleases Him. In searching out the ways of God's revelation, even perfect man should allow for what Schilder calls the catastrophic. He could not take for granted that the cosmos contains a set of thoughts, already fully expressed, of which man must simply seek to make a replica for himself. There is a qualitative, not merely a quantitative, difference between God and man.[73] Kuyper has not made a clear distinction between the Christian and the non-Christian ideal of knowledge. His universals sometimes resemble those of Plato a bit too closely.

Corresponding to this lack of clarity on the question of universals is a lack of clarity with respect to facts. The abstract separation between perception and ratiocination, to which we have called attention, already leads us to expect that such should be the case. Facts seem, according to Kuyper, to have a nature that does not fit them well for apprehension by intellectual categories. Kuyper has a sort of *Ding an sich* very similar to that of Kant.[74] Speaking of the knowledge process he says: "You behold the *morphe* [form] in your perception; you follow the *anaphoroi* of the relations[75] with your thought; but the *ousia* [essence] lies beyond your reach."[76] Individuality is said to be something that is inherently hostile to generalization, and as such obstructive of the progress of science.

71. Ibid., 2:38 (*PST*, 92).
72. Ibid., 2:36 (*PST*, 90).
73. That is, God is not simply "greater" or "bigger" than man (quantitatively different); he is of a wholly different nature (qualitatively different). He is spirit: infinite, eternal, immutable, etc.
74. A *Ding an sich*, in Kant, is a "thing in itself." For Kant, such things cannot be known, but are relegated to the noumenal realm, since there are no categories available for reason to grasp them.
75. *Anaphoroi* should actually be *anaphorai* (as it is in Kuyper's text), and means "relations." The clause should be translated "you follow the relations with your thinking."
76. Kuyper, *Encyclopaedie der heilige godgeleerdheid*, 2:39 (*PST*, 93).

Where individuality is most pronounced, there science meets with its greatest difficulty. At the climax of an argument on this point he says: "From a sharply drawn character it is scarcely possible to draw any conclusions."[77]

In this phenomenalism we have the counterpart to the semi-Platonic notion of complete comprehension.[78] If we hold to the ideal of absolute comprehension in knowledge we must conclude that the "facts," in so far as they do not lend themselves to this ideal, are unknowable.[79] For would-be-autonomous man it is quite consistent to hold to the ideal of complete comprehension, and at the same time to the notion of utterly irrational fact.

In contrast with this the Christian ought to abhor both the ideal of comprehensive knowledge and the idea of irrational fact. If the ideal of comprehensive knowledge were realized, it would be realized at the expense of the uniqueness of every fact of the cosmos and of the aseity of God.[80] If facts were irrational and not comprehensively known by God, they would not be known in any degree by man. Throwing overboard the non-Christian procedure entirely, the Christian should frankly begin his scientific work on the presupposition of the cotermineity of the universal and the particular in the Godhead.[81] With Warfield, paraphrasing Calvin, we would begin by saying: " . . . there is but one God; the Father, the Son, the Spirit is each this one God, the entire divine essence being in each; these three are three Persons, distinguished one from another by an incommunicable property."[82, 83]

On the basis of this conception of the ontological trinity we must hold that the facts and the universals of the created universe

77. Ibid., 2:40 (*PST*, 94).
78. That is, the counterpart to complete comprehension via the universal is the diversity of the facts, i.e., phenomenalism.
79. Remember the Eddington quote above—"What my net can't catch isn't fish." If facts do not or cannot "fit" my universal categories, then they are unknowable.
80. In other words, if we held to the ideal of comprehensive knowledge, we would know all things, even God, exhaustively and completely. He would thus not be independent, as he would be fully and completely known by us.
81. "The cotermineity of the universal and particular in the Godhead" refers to the triune God as one (unity) and three (diversity).
82. Benjamin B. Warfield, *The Works of Benjamin B. Warfield*, vol. 5: *Calvin and Calvinism* (New York: Oxford University Press, 1932), 232.
83. The "incommunicable property" refers to the Father as unbegotten, the Son as begotten, and the Spirit as proceeding. These properties cannot be communicated to another person in the Trinity, as they establish and distinguish the identity of each of the three persons. Even so, they are, each and together, the one God.

exist in correlativity to one another.[84] The ideal of science should be to describe this situation as far as it can. It should not seek in its intellectual effort to make contact with some abstract universal relations. Nor should it feel itself defeated to the extent that it cannot reduce individuality to abstract relations. Why should science consider itself foiled in its efforts when it finds that it cannot reduce the individuality of man to numerical relationships? Kuyper himself has taught us the idea of the sovereignty of spheres; but he has a sort of Kantian phenomenalism that keeps him from working out this idea consistently.

There is a vagueness inherent in Kuyper's treatment of common grace. He seems to be uncertain in his mind as to what is common to the believer and the non-believer. This vagueness, we are inclined to think, may be traced to the vagueness we have now spoken of.[85] Kuyper did not clearly see and hold to the correlativity of individual and universal that is involved in his own basic position. He has accordingly been handicapped when he sought to describe the scientific procedure. Wishing to do it according to Christian principles, he yet brings in elements of abstract non-Christian thought. Now that we have discussed briefly his failure to evolve a consistently Christian notion of universals and particulars, we call attention to his hesitation in the description of scientific procedure.

We have noted earlier that from a Christian point of view the most elementary description is done either on Christian or non-Christian presuppositions. Kuyper's own most basic views require us to hold to this. He has taught us the importance of stressing the difference in starting-point between those who do, and those who do not, work on the basis of regeneration.[86] With the drag of his semi-Kantian phenomenalism upon him, however, he is unwilling to draw a straight line of demarcation between the Christian and the non-Christian methodology of science. In saying this we are not thinking of his distinction between what is, and what is not,

84. Since in the triune God there is no priority of the one over the many, or vice versa, so also is there no priority of one or many in creation, since creation is a reflection of his character.

85. Note again the close relationship, in Van Til's mind, between epistemology and common grace. He has been analyzing problems in Kuyper's epistemology and then moves from that to the problems entailed in Kuyper's notion of common grace.

86. See Kuyper, *PST*, 150ff., or Kuyper, *Encyclopaedie der heilige godgeleerdheid*, 2:100ff.

strictly scientific. Says Kuyper: "To observe bacteria and microbes is in itself as little a matter of scientific interpretation as to observe horses and cows in a pasture."[87] We may readily allow the validity of this point. Nor are we thinking of another distinction Kuyper makes. He speaks with the German philosophers of natural and spiritual sciences, the former dealing, broadly speaking, with the *ponderabilia* (that is, the "facts" of the world that we can perceive and on which we can reflect[88]) and the latter, broadly speaking, with intangibles. We may readily allow a certain validity to this distinction, too. But it is with Kuyper's use of these distinctions that our difficulty begins. He seems to use these distinctions for the defense of his contention that there is an area of interpretation where the difference between those who build, and those who do not build, on the fact of regeneration, need not, and cannot, be made to count. His argument is somewhat as follows.

Kuyper shows how, because of the fact of regeneration, there must be a twofold development of science. Yet this twofold development could not, in the past, be clearly marked if for no other reason than that there is "a very broad territory where the difference between the two groups has no significance."[89] As a reason for this, Kuyper offers the fact that regeneration does not change our senses nor the appearance of the world about us. He therefore feels justified in concluding that the whole area of the more primitive observation, which limits itself to measuring, weighing, and counting is common to both. "The whole field of empirical research by means of our senses (aided or unaided) on observable objects falls beyond the principal difference that separates the two groups."[90] Kuyper does not want us to conclude from this, however, that the natural sciences as such are beyond dispute. He says the difference is excluded merely at the point where these sciences make their beginning. "Whether something weighs two or three milligrams, may be absolutely determined by any one able to weigh."[91] We are to accept gratefully the fact that at the beginning of scientific interpretation in the natural sciences, there

87. Kuyper, *Encyclopaedie der heilige godgeleerdheid*, 2:81 (*PST*, 134).
88. See Kuyper, *PST*, 93.
89. Kuyper, *Encyclopaedie der heilige godgeleerdheid*, 2:104 (*PST*, 157). To follow Kuyper's argument in the English translation, see *PST*, 157ff.
90. Kuyper, *Encyclopaedie der heilige godgeleerdheid*, 2:104 (*PST*, 157).
91. Ibid., 2:105 (*PST*, 157).

is a "*common* territory where the difference in starting-point and standpoint does not count."[92]

As a second area where the difference need not appear, Kuyper mentions the lower aspect of the spiritual sciences. Here too, says Kuyper, we deal with that which can be simply weighed and counted. Finally Kuyper speaks of a third territory that all have in common, namely, that of logic. "There is not a twofold but only one logic."[93] This allows, he says, for formal interaction between the two groups of interpreters.

On the ground of these three common territories Kuyper makes the following generalization: "As a result all scientific research that deals with the ὁρατά [things seen] only, or is carried on only by those subjective elements, which did not undergo a change, remains common to both. At the beginning of the road the tree of science is common to all."[94]

We call attention to two ambiguities in this argument. Kuyper has first led us to think of weighing and measuring as not being part of the scientific undertaking. Observation of microbes, even with the help of instruments, he says, is no more scientific in the strict sense of the term, than the observing of horses and cows. Yet Kuyper does include this weighing and measuring in the strictly scientific task when he says that it is this precisely which believers and non-believers have in common in their scientific endeavors. Which of these two positions are we to take as really representative of Kuyper's views? It would seem that we must take the second. If we do not take the second position, what is there left of the three territories that we are said to have in common?

If then, we take the second position, the position that weighing and measuring is a part of the scientific procedure, we are face to face with the second ambiguity. Kuyper argues for the commonness of the territories on the ground of their interpretative insignificance. It is because of the *externality* of weighing and measuring, and it is because of the *formality* of logic, that the three territories are said to be common to believer and non-believer. We are to hold, according to Kuyper's argument, that, where sin has not changed the metaphysical situation, the difference between believer and

92. Ibid., 2:106 (*PST*, 158).
93. Ibid., 2:107 (*PST*, 159).
94. Ibid., 2:116 (*PST*, 168).

unbeliever need not be brought to the fore. This is, in effect, to say that, to the extent that the objective situation has not changed, the subjective change need not be taken into account. To point out the ambiguity in the argument is, therefore, at the same time to point out its invalidity.

What do we mean when we say that the metaphysical situation has not changed because of sin? What do we mean when we say that even after the Fall man is a rational and moral creature still? We surely do not mean to deny total depravity. Accordingly there is no sinner who, unless regenerated, does not actually seek to interpret himself and the universe without God. The natural man uses his logical powers to describe the facts of creation as though these facts existed apart from God. He has rejected the common mandate. It is therefore in conjunction with the sinner's subjective alienation from God, as a limiting concept merely, that we can speak of anything as not having been destroyed by sin. In the interpretative endeavor the "objective situation" can never be abstracted from the "subjective situation." If we do abstract it, we fall back on the Scholastic position.[95] We may then say with Étienne Gilson,[96] the Roman Catholic, that Aristotle by the use of natural reason can think of *a* God, "one first being, the supreme principle and cause of nature, the source of all intelligibility, of all order, and of all beauty, who eternally leads a life of happiness, because, being thought itself, it is an eternal contemplation of its own thought" who yet must be the God "precisely because there is no other" God.[97]

No valid answer can be given the Scholastics by the device of reducing the area of commonness to ever smaller proportions. Any area of commonness, that is, any area of commonness without qualification however small, is a justification for larger areas of commonness, till at last there is but one common area. The only valid answer to the Roman Catholic is to say that in the whole of the area of interpretative endeavor the subjective difference makes

95. When Van Til mentions "the Scholastics" or "the Scholastic position," following Bavinck, he has in mind the Scholasticism of the Middle Ages. For him, Scholasticism was tied to an irrational nature-grace dialectic that allowed for neutrality with respect to reason.

96. Étienne Gilson (1884–1978) was an expert in medieval philosophical theology and is credited with reviving interest in the field in the twentieth century. His academic career spanned multiple decades.

97. Étienne Gilson, *Christianity and Philosophy*, trans. Ralph MacDonald (New York: Sheed & Ward, 1939), 35–36.

its influence felt. Weighing and measuring and formal reasoning are but aspects of one unified act of interpretation. It is either the would-be autonomous man, who weighs and measures what he thinks of as brute or bare facts by the help of what he thinks of as abstract impersonal principles, or it is the believer, knowing himself to be a creature of God, who weighs and measures what he thinks of as God-created facts by what he thinks of as God-created laws.[98] Looking at the matter thus allows for legitimate cooperation with non-Christian scientists; it allows for an "as if" cooperation.[99] Looking at the matter thus allows for a larger "common" territory than Kuyper allows for, but this larger territory is common with a qualification. Looking at the matter thus allows us to do full justice to "antithesis," which Kuyper has taught us to stress. It keeps us from falling into a sort of natural theology, patterned after Thomas Aquinas, that Kuyper has taught us to reject. If we are to hold to a doctrine of common grace that is true to Scripture, we shall need to build it up after we have cut ourselves clear of Scholasticism.

2. Bavinck. We turn now to the great work of Bavinck on Systematic theology, his *Gereformeerde Dogmatiek.* We observe at once that he is much concerned to point out that there is only one principle, according to which we are to set forth man's knowledge of God. He avows this in definite opposition to the scholastic position. There is a natural theology that is legitimate. It is such a theology as, standing upon the basis of faith and enlightened by Scripture, finds God in nature. But Rome's natural theology, he argues, is illegitimate. Its natural theology is attained by the natural reason without reference to Scripture. Against such a position Bavinck firmly asserts that theology must be built upon the Scriptures only. There must be only one principle in theology. "Even if there is a knowledge of God through nature, this does not mean that there are two principles in dogmatics. Dogmatics has only one princip-

98. This is one example of Van Til's insistence that the epistemological can never be severed from the ethical (or covenantal). The one who measures, weighs, and counts is either in Adam or in Christ. As such, he does such things in conformity to his covenant head. This does not preclude believer and unbeliever working together, as Van Til goes on to say. It does, however, allow for an apologetic challenge at any point—weighing, counting, or measuring—in a way that Kuyper's (and medieval Scholasticism's) view does not.

99. An "as if" cooperation means that believers can work with unbelievers "as if" the latter recognized their status before God as his image. This could only be applicable, however, up to a point.

ium externum, namely, the Scriptures, and only one principium internum, namely, the believing reason."[100, 101]

Bavinck has not always lived up to this conception. When he develops the principles which should control science,[102] he adopts a moderate realism.[103] He does this, to some extent at least, by accepting what he calls the good of empiricism and what he calls the good of rationalism, and dropping the evil of both. That is to say, the criticism he makes of rationalism might be made and has been made by non-Christian realists, and the criticism he makes of empiricism might be made and has been made by non-Christian rationalists.

Against the rationalist he argues that all men are naturally realists,[104] and that rationalism is bound to be stranded on the fact of plurality.[105] Against the empiricist he argues that all science must begin with unproved assumptions that have not been derived from experience,[106] and that science, in the nature of the case, is interested in the "general, the necessary and the eternal, the logical, the idea."[107] But, we object, the abstract principles of rationalism are not made concrete by bringing them into relation with the brute facts of empiricism, and the brute facts of empiricism are not made accessible by bringing them into relation with the abstract principles of rationalism.[108]

When Bavinck gives the distinguishing marks of the realism that he thinks theology needs for its foundation, he says no more than

100. H. Bavinck, *Gereformeerde dogmatiek*, 3rd ed. (Kampen: Kok, 1918), 1:74 (*RD*, 1:88).

101. *Principia* are the most fundamental foundations, or sources, beyond and behind which we cannot go. Typically in Reformed theology, we have two primary categories: the *principium essendi*, or foundation of being (or existence), which is God, and the *principium cognoscendi*, or foundation of knowledge, which is God's revelation. Bavinck is speaking of two aspects of the *principium cognoscendi*, which are the *principium externum*, or the objective or external foundation, which is Scripture, and the *principium internum*, or the subjective or internal foundation, which Bavinck says is regenerate reason.

102. Bavinck, *Gereformeerde dogmatiek*, 1:214ff. (*RD*, 1:207ff.).

103. Moderate realism takes various forms. In Bavinck's construal, it seeks to affirm the existence of universals, but those universals depend, to some extent, on our experience of the particulars in the world.

104. Bavinck, *Gereformeerde dogmatiek*, 1:217 (*RD*, 1:217).

105. Ibid., 1:218 (*RD*, 1:218).

106. Ibid., 1:222 (*RD*, 1:220–21).

107. Ibid. (*RD*, 1:221).

108. In other words, it is illegitimate to take two errant approaches and try to synthesize them into something true and accurate. Unless one excises the presuppositions of the various "isms," they remain errant, even when there is an attempt to employ only parts of them.

that against empiricism it maintains a certain independence of the intellect, and that against rationalism it maintains a dependence of the intellect upon sensation.[109] Accordingly, he does not make a thorough break with Scholasticism. His criticism of Scholasticism is at points little more than a matter of degree. "The fault of Scholasticism, both Protestant and Catholic, lay only in this, that it had done too quickly with observation, and that it thought almost exclusively of the confession as taken up into the books of Euclid, Aristotle, and the Church fathers."[110] The net result is that the moderate realism of Bavinck is not a specifically Christian position, obtained by the only legitimate principle of theology of which he has spoken.[111] Bavinck himself tells us that the only reason why we may hold our thought of reality about us to be correct in what it says is that back of our thought, and of the world about us, is the Logos.[112] But if this is true, no moderate realism based on a combination of rationalism and empiricism can afford a basis for theology. Bavinck has not kept this point in mind in the construction of the general principles of his epistemology.[113]

In consonance with his manner of derivation of a moderate realism is his manner of handling the question of the unknowability of God. The second volume of his *Dogmatics* begins with the sentence: "Mystery is the life of all dogmatics." The revelation of the infinite God to the finite creature, he points out, cannot be exhaustive of the being of God. God is incomprehensible. Here Bavinck should have distinguished more clearly the incomprehensibility of God from the non-Christian notion of mystery. The Christian and the non-Christian notions of mystery arc as the poles apart. The Christian notion rests on the presupposition of the existence of the self-contained ontological trinity of God, who dwells in light that no man can approach unto.[114] The non-Christian notion rests on

---

109. Bavinck, *Gereformeerde dogmatiek*, 1:228 (*RD*, 1:226).
110. Ibid., 1:229 (*RD*, 1:226).
111. Van Til notes above Bavinck's insistence that our *principia* in epistemology are Scripture (*externum*) and regenerate reason (*internum*). Moderate realism is derived from neither of these *principia*.
112. Bavinck, *Gereformeerde dogmatiek*, 1:235 (*RD*, 1:233).
113. For an extended discussion of Bavinck's realism and its attendant problems, see K. Scott Oliphint, "Bavinck's Realism, the Logos Principle, and *Sola Scriptura*," *Westminster Theological Journal* 72 (2010): 359–90.
114. In other words, for the Christian, mystery is not ultimate, since there is no mystery for God.

the assumption of the existence of would-be autonomous man who has not yet exhaustively interpreted the realms of ultimate chance. The Greeks held to the latter notion. The very notion of God, as Aristotle held to it, is obtained by abstraction till a final empty concept is reached. In Aristotle's case it is the emptiest of empty negations that is decorated with the name of God.[115]

Yet for all that, Bavinck sometimes speaks as though the concept of the incomprehensibility of God entertained by Christian theology and that entertained by pagan philosophy were virtually the same.[116] Greek philosophy, he says, has frequently taught the incomprehensibility of God.[117] This incomprehensibility, he says, was made the starting-point and foundation thought of Christian theology.[118] Scholastic theology at its best has made the same confession.[119] "The Reformation-theology has wrought no change in this."[120] When "this truth of the unknowability of God" was forgotten by theology, modern philosophy brought it to remembrance.[121]

It may be contended by some that in all this Bavinck is simply recounting history; that he is merely stating what has been and not what ought to be. But this can scarcely be maintained. Bavinck certainly considers himself a follower of the Reformation theology. Moreover, when he sets forth the doctrine of the incomprehensibility of God positively, he begins by saying: "To a remarkable degree this doctrine of the unknowability of God can be approved and accepted with gratitude."[122] Scripture and the church have, as it were, says Bavinck, accepted the premises of agnosticism and have been, even more deeply than Kant or Spencer, impressed with the limitations of man and the greatness of God.[123] Bavinck then points out that the church has refused to accept the conclusions of agnosticism. By revelation man can truly know something of God.

---

115. Aristotle's god cannot change, so cannot be material (because "matter" changes). Therefore, his god must be "thought"—and if so, it cannot think anything other than itself, or it would be dependent on that which it thinks. So Aristotle's god is "thought thinking itself." See Aristotle, "Metaphysics," 12.9, 1075b 34, in *The Basic Works of Aristotle*, ed. Richard McKeon (New York: Random House, 1968).

116. Bavinck, *Gereformeerde dogmatiek*, 2:10ff. (*RD*, 2:36ff.).

117. Ibid., 2:8 (*RD*, 2:34).

118. Ibid., 2:10 (*RD*, 2:36).

119. Ibid., 2:14 (*RD*, 2:40).

120. Ibid. (*RD*, 2:40).

121. Ibid., 2:16 (*RD*, 2:41).

122. Ibid., 2:23 (*RD*, 2:47).

123. Ibid., 2:24 (*RD*, 2:48).

Even in his constructive section then, Bavinck still speaks as though the only difference between the Christian and the non-Christian notions of the incomprehensibility of God were a matter of degree. This is the negative concomitant of the "moderate realism" obtained in part by Christian, and in part by non-Christian, principles of reasoning.

After what has been said, we are not surprised at Bavinck's manner of handling the "theistic proofs."[124] Having set them forth with fullness, he bewails the fact that they are spoken of as proofs. They should, he says, rather be thought of as testimonies. "Weak as proofs, they are strong as testimonies."[125] They are not to be taken as arguments that compel the unbeliever to believe in God. Taken individually they can be attacked (apparently he means that they can be refuted) at every point, and tend to obstruct the spontaneity of faith.

> Taken cumulatively they enable us to see Him as the divine being that must of necessity be thought by us, and must of necessity be thought of as existing, that is, the only, first, absolute cause of all creatures, that self-consciously and teleologically rules all things and that above all reveals Himself in conscience as the Holy one to whosoever believes.[126]

By means of them the believer can give himself an account of his own religious and ethical consciousness. They are as weapons to the believer by which he may defend himself against the unbeliever who "in any case has no better weapons than he."[127]

In his little book on *The Certainty of Faith*, Bavinck speaks in a similar vein. The "proofs," he says, enable the believer to defend himself against attack on the part of science "and show that there is as much and usually much more to say for the position of faith than for the position of unbelief."[128] These proofs may be unable

124. The "theistic proofs" are, typically, the proofs set forth by Aquinas (arguments from motion, causality, contingency, being, and design) and sometimes also by Anselm (the so-called ontological argument).

125. Bavinck, *Gereformeerde dogmatiek*, 2:73 (*RD*, 2:91).

126. Ibid. (*RD*, 2:91).

127. Ibid. (*RD*, 2:91).

128. H. Bavinck, *De zekerheid des geloofs* (Kampen: Kok, 1903), 64 (*The Certainty of Faith*, trans. Harry der Nederlanden [St. Catharines, Ontario: Paideia Press, 1980] [hereafter *CF*], 58).

to persuade men to faith, he adds, yet faith may accept their service, inasmuch as faith could not exist if the unhistorical character of the Christian revelation could be established.[129]

It appears anew from this treatment of the "proofs" that Bavinck has not altogether cut himself loose from non-Christian forms of reasoning. The proofs, as historically stated, are based upon the assumption that the non-Christian mode of reasoning is the only possible mode of reasoning. Would-be autonomous man sets for himself the ideal of universal comprehension in knowledge. Accordingly he speaks of a universal validity to which every rational being will readily agree. If he could establish this universal validity, every rational creature should be willing and able to accept his conclusions. Not being able by these "proofs" to establish universal validity for the existence of God, these proofs have somewhat less value, but are still probably, and to an extent, correct. Such is the usual procedure in handling these proofs.

Bavinck's position has failed to show that this procedure is basically mistaken. He virtually admits that the ideal of science is abstract universal validity, which every rational creature should be able and willing to accept. He finds the difference between scientific certainty and the certainty of faith in that the former demands universal acceptance while the latter does not. "Scientific certainty rests on grounds which are acceptable to all rational creatures, and whose validity can be shown to every creature gifted with rationality."[130] Religious certainty rests on revelation. "In this respect then, scientific certainty is in reality more general and stronger than that which is obtained by faith."[131] On the other hand, Bavinck admits that scientific certainty depends upon future inquiry which may disprove that which has been thus far believed. "The certainty of faith must therefore be of a different nature from scientific certainty. For scientific certainty, however solid and dependable, always retains this character, that it rests on the reasoning of men and that it can be overthrown by later and better research."[132] In science we are satisfied with human certainty but in religion we need divine certainty.[133] Speaking of the proofs and their value he

129. Ibid., 65 (*CF*, 59).
130. Ibid., 26 (*CF*, 23–24).
131. Ibid. (*CF*, 24).
132. Ibid. (*CF*, 24).
133. Ibid., 56 (*CF*, 51).

argues that they are limited in their application, inasmuch as only a few men are able to employ them. Then he adds: "In addition to this they may at any moment be invalidated entirely or in part by further investigation and deeper reflection."[134]

This position of Bavinck, it will be noted, is very similar to the old Princeton position,[135] and both are very similar to the Scholastic position. There are differences in degree between these three positions, but they agree in holding that all reasoning about Christian theism must be done on "common" ground.[136] It is difficult to distinguish the position of Bavinck from that of Gilson, whom we have already quoted as saying that natural reason can, with some probability, establish the existence of *a* God, whom we must then believe to be *the* God because there is no other. For all his effort to the contrary, Bavinck sometimes seems to offer us a natural theology of a kind similar to that offered by the church of Rome. The difficulty here is the same in nature as that which we have already noted in the case of Kuyper.

We cannot believe that the position of Bavinck on the theistic proofs is in line with the spirit of Calvin's *Institutes*. Calvin argues throughout his first book that men *ought* to believe in God, because there is, and has been from the beginning of time, an abundance of evidence of His existence and of His character. There is objective evidence in abundance and it is sufficiently clear. Men *ought*, if only they reasoned rightly, to come to the conclusion that God exists. That is to say, if the theistic proof is constructed as it ought to be constructed, it is objectively valid, whatever the attitude of those to whom it comes may be. To be constructed rightly, theistic proof ought to presuppose the ontological trinity and contend that, unless we may make this presupposition, all human predication is meaningless.[137] The words "cause," "purpose," and "being," used

---

134. Ibid., 66 (*CF*, 60).

135. The "old Princeton position" to which Van Til refers was the position that allowed for a neutrality of reasoning with respect to the theistic proofs. Van Til does not speak hypothetically here; as a student at Princeton, Van Til was taught this position by, among others, William Brenton Greene Jr.

136. The notion of "common ground" is first mentioned here, but will become a more significant aspect of discussions of common grace. For Van Til, the "common ground" at times appealed to by Bavinck, Old Princeton, and (medieval) Scholasticism is the supposed neutrality of reason.

137. This statement is an example of what Van Til called, early in his career, the "transcendental" approach. Here he states the "impossibility of the contrary," which is a part of that approach. For a concise description of the "transcendental method," see Cornelius

as universals in the phenomenal world, could not be so used with meaning unless we may presuppose the self-contained God.[138] If the matter is put this way one argument is as sound as the other. In fact, then, each argument involves the others. Nor is any one of the arguments then at any point vulnerable. And future research cannot change their validity.

If this be correct, we cannot say that the Christian may use these arguments as witnesses, though not as proofs. If they are constructed as all too often they have been constructed, they are neither proofs nor witnesses. Nor can we seek to defend our position with an argument which we really admit to be of doubtful validity. And it is out of accord with the idea of Paul, and of Paul's follower, Calvin, who stress the point that the created universe everywhere speaks of God (see Ps. 19:1–2; Rom. 1:18–20), to say that the Christian position is at least as defensible as other positions. We ought to find small comfort in the idea that others too, for example, non-Christian scientists, have to make assumptions. We ought rather to maintain that we are not in the position in which others are. We all make assumptions, but we alone do not make false assumptions. The fact that all make assumptions is in itself a mere psychological and formal matter. The question is as to who makes the right assumptions or presuppositions. On this point there ought to be no doubt.

We must, accordingly, frankly challenge the Roman Catholic notion that the natural man knows truly of God.[139] And we should

---

Van Til, *In Defense of the Faith*, vol. 2: *A Survey of Christian Epistemology* (Philadelphia: Presbyterian and Reformed, 1969), 10–11. For a more extended discussion of Van Til's method, see K. Scott Oliphint, "The Consistency of Van Til's Methodology," *Westminster Theological Journal* 52 (1990): 27–49. Unless the ontological Trinity is presupposed, no viable account can be given of any proposition. This is so, in part, because, as Van Til argued above, there can be no account given of the unity and diversity that is presupposed in any proposition.

138. Van Til uses these three "universals" because they are intrinsic to the theistic proofs. In Aquinas's five ways, for example, his second way is based on "causality," his fourth way is based on "being," and his fifth way is based on "purpose" (design). See, for example, Brian Leftow and Brian Davies, eds., *Aquinas: Summa Theologiae, Questions on God*, Cambridge Texts in the History of Philosophy (Cambridge: Cambridge University Press, 2006), 24–27. As Van Til has already argued, these "universals" cannot be fruitfully understood in relation to the "particulars" without presupposing the ontological Trinity, in whom the One and the Three are equally ultimate. Non-Christian philosophy has not been able to understand the relationship of these in any meaningful way.

139. What Van Til means here is that we ought to challenge the Roman Catholic notion that all people can, by virtue of the theistic proofs, know God truly. Van Til holds, with Paul (and Calvin) that all people do know God because he makes himself known, so that knowledge comes by way of God's natural revelation, not by way of some notion of neutral reason.

challenge the procedure by which the natural theology of Rome is obtained. We shall need to deny that true scientific certainty is something that can be demonstrated to every rational creature. True scientific certainty, no less than true religious certainty, must be based upon the presupposition of the ontological trinity. Both forms of certainty are psychological phenomena and as such are experiences of the human being.[140] But both forms of certainty need the same foundation if they are to be true. We shall need to challenge the possibility of either science or theology on any but a Christian foundation.

We need only to do what Bavinck has elsewhere told us to do in the matter of natural theology. He tells us that man cannot understand nature aright unless he places himself squarely upon Scripture. "For that reason it is a wrong method if the Christian in his handling of the *theologia naturalis* [natural theology] does, as it were, without Scripture and the illumination of the Holy Spirit . . ." The Christian must stand with both feet upon the bed-rock of special revelation in his study of nature. That is, we believe, the real position of Bavinck, but he has not been fully true to it.[141]

There is one further aspect of Bavinck's thought to which brief reference must be made.

When discussing what Bavinck says on the theistic proofs we dealt with what he calls the *cognitio Dei acquisita* (acquired knowledge of God). We would now add a word about what he says on the *cognitio Dei insita* (implanted knowledge of God). It is here that the question of the relation between the objective revelational and the subjective interpretational is most difficult. The two are found in such close proximity to one another that they are likely to be intermingled unless we make careful distinctions.

The question to be considered here is that of the κοιναὶ ἔννοιαι (ideas common to all) the *notiones impressae* (impressed notions), the *cognitationes insitae* (implanted knowledge). It is but natural that Roman Catholic theology, which holds that the natural reason can discover certain truths about God, should hold that there are ideas about God that are wholly common to the believer and the non-believer.

---

140. Because certainty is a subjective state, dependent on the individual subject, whether that individual subject is covenantally in Adam or in Christ will make all the difference as to whether or not certainty is obtainable.

141. Bavinck, *Gereformeerde dogmatiek*, 2:47. (*RD*, 2:74).

Gilson expresses this point of view when he argues that we can discover the same truths that Aristotle discovered, by the same reason unaided by special revelation.[142] Gilson further argues that Calvin, in holding to an "impression of divinity" or "common notion" or "innate idea" or "religious aptitude" in man, and in saying that "experience" attests the fact that God has placed in all men an innate seed of religion, virtually holds to the same position as that to which the Roman Catholic holds. He thinks the Calvinist faces an antinomy in connection with his view on this point:

> At first sight, it would seem that there could not be a better solution. But it is still true that this knowledge is confronted by the problem just as certainly as is the rational certitude which the Thomistic proofs of the existence of God claim to attain. Either it is a natural certitude, in which the right to criticize the Catholic position to suppress pure philosophy is lost; or it is a supernatural certitude, in which case it would become impossible to find a place for that natural knowledge of God, which is exactly what one was pretending to conserve.[143]

The question now is whether the innate knowledge of which Bavinck speaks is of such a nature as to be able to escape the dilemma before which Gilson places the Calvinistic position. We believe Gilson is fair enough in demanding that Reformed theology shall come to a self-conscious defense of its notion of natural theology in general. It cannot fairly limit itself to *diminishing the area* or *reducing somewhat the value* of the natural theology of Roman Catholic theology. As long as the natural theology of the Reformed theologian is still the same in kind as that of the Roman Catholic theologian, he will find it difficult to escape the dilemma with which Gilson confronts it.

Now both Kuyper and Bavinck, following Calvin, insist again and again that we shall break with the natural theology of Rome. They insist that a true natural theology is a frank interpretation of nature by means of the principle of interpretation that is taken from Scripture.[144] But we have noted that both Kuyper and Bavinck are, to an

---

142. It should be noted that Gilson's notion of following Aristotle is not original with him, but goes back to Aquinas.

143. Gilson, *Christianity and Philosophy*, 41.

144. This is a crucially important point with respect to Reformed theology. Van Til does not develop it because he assumes that his readers are familiar with it. For the Reformed,

extent, untrue to their own principles. Neither of them has been able to cut himself quite loose from a non-Christian methodology. Both allow, to a certain extent, the legitimacy of the idea of brute facts of Empiricism and the idea of abstract universals of Rationalism. This, as noted in the case of Bavinck, makes for allowing a certain truth value to the theistic arguments, even though they are constructed along rationalistic-irrationalistic lines.[145] Will we find something similar in his construction of the "common notions," the subjective counterpart to the theistic proofs?

To answer this question we do well to take careful note of a distinction of which we have spoken only in passing. It is the distinction between the psychological and the epistemological.[146] If there be such things as "common notions," psychologically speaking, it does not follow that there are such things as "common notions," epistemologically speaking.[147] Bavinck points to the fact that God's revelation is everywhere. That is to say, it is within man as well as in nature. "There is no atheistic world, there are no atheistic peoples, and there are no atheistic men."[148] When Bavinck says that there are no atheistic peoples and no atheistic men, we must be careful to understand this psychologically and not epistemologically. All that may be meant, so far, is that God's revelation is present in the activity of man's mind as well as elsewhere. "Because that which may be known of God is manifest in them; for God hath showed it unto them" (Rom. 1:19). The revelation of God about and within may take the form of

---

whatever natural theology is gained, can be understood properly only on the basis of God's revelation in Scripture. Thus, natural theology does not precede supernatural theology; rather, it depends on it.

145. The irresolvable rational-irrational dialectic is the foundation of all non-Christian thinking, according to Van Til. In this context, the rational refers to that which can be properly understood, and the irrational is the "noumenal" mystery that must be posited when the mind of man is unable to make sense of the facts.

146. This is another crucial distinction in Van Til. The "psychological" refers to the "psyche" or "soul" of man; it is the knowledge of God, or sense of deity, that all men have. Van Til sometimes uses the term interchangeably with "metaphysical" since it refers to the fact that all are, and remain, the image of God. (Included in the notion of "image" is the fact of true knowledge of God.) The "epistemological" is that which man thinks and infers. So, whereas the "psychological" has *God's* activity at its root (in that God reveals to us who he is, and thus we know him), the "epistemological" has in view what we ourselves *do* with that knowledge as we seek to think, analyze, understand, know, etc.

147. That is, all men know God, and thus have that knowledge "in common" (psychologically or metaphysically), but those who are in Adam take that knowledge (epistemologically) and suppress it in unrighteousness (Rom. 1:18).

148. Bavinck, *Gereformeerde dogmatiek*, 2:30 (*RD*, 2:56–57).

re-interpretation on the part of man. Paul speaks of the invisible things of God as being *clearly seen* (Rom. 1:20). Whether we take this to mean simply that they are clearly apparent, or whether we take this to mean that because clearly apparent they have been clearly observed, we are still in the field of the revelational.[149] We have not yet reached the point of ethical reaction.[150] When Adam was first created, he thought upon the works of God, and by thinking upon them interpreted them. This interpretation was still revelational. To be sure, this revelational interpretation was accompanied in his case with an attitude of belief. After the fall of man the same revelational interpretation continued. But after the fall this revelational interpretation was invariably accompanied by an attitude of hostility. Paul tells us that knowing God, having engaged in interpretative activity, psychologically speaking, the heathen yet glorified Him not as God (Rom. 1:21).

If then we are to avoid falling into a Roman Catholic type of natural theology, we shall need to make a sharp distinction between that which is merely psychological, and that which is epistemological in man's interpretative activity. For all the stress we need to place upon the invariable concomitancy of the merely psychological and the epistemological, we need to lay an equal stress upon the importance of the distinction. "Common notions" may be thought of as nothing more than revelation that comes to man through man. As an ethical subject man, after the fall, acts negatively with respect to this revelation. As made in the image of God no man can escape becoming the interpretative medium of God's general revelation both in his intellectual (Rom 1:20) and in his moral consciousness (Rom 2:14–15). No matter which button of the radio he presses, he always hears the voice of God. Even when he presses the button of his own psychological self-conscious activity, through which as a last resort the sinner might hope to hear another voice, he still hears the voice of God. "If I make my bed in hell, behold, thou art there" (Ps. 139:8). It is in this sense that we must, at least to begin with, understand the matter when we are told that there are no atheistic peoples and no atheistic men. Psychologically there are

149. Paul's point in Rom. 1:18–20 is that we know and understand clearly because God gets his revelation through to us, even in our depravity.

150. The "ethical reaction" is our suppression of the truth given by God and thus known by us (Rom. 1:18). This might better be dubbed a "covenantal" reaction.

no atheistic men; epistemologically every sinner is atheistic.[151] Has Bavinck kept this fact in mind?

Bavinck speaks of Cicero as saying that that on which all men agree, because of their common nature, cannot be wrong. Cicero no doubt meant that there is some basis of agreement between all men, epistemologically as well as psychologically. That is to say, for Cicero there was an area of common interpretation, however small, in which all men are epistemologically in agreement. It is on such notions as those of Cicero that Roman Catholic natural theology is built. Bavinck has not always kept this point in mind. When he speaks of Cicero, he fails to make the distinction between mere psychological commonness and epistemological agreement.

Moreover, he virtually contends that there is an epistemological as well as a mere psychological agreement when he adds that there is not so much difference of opinion among men about the existence as about the nature of God.[152] This distinction between the essence and the being of God fits in with Rome's natural theology. It does not fit in, we believe, with a Reformed conception of natural theology. To make a distinction between the bare *that* and the *what* is unintelligible in any field. We cannot intelligently speak of something and afterward determine what we have been speaking of. We may grow in clarity with respect to that of which we have been speaking, but we cannot speak of something that has no delineation whatsoever in our minds. Then, too, Paul tells us, in effect, that the voice of the *true* God, the only existent God, is everywhere present. He does not, to be sure, say that this God is present in the fullness of His revelation. Yet it is the *true* God, *the* God, not *a* God, that is everywhere to be heard, whatever button we may press. It is the *what* not merely the *that*, of God's existence that the heathen find impressed upon them. To this *what* they, willingly or not, give interpretative expression, thereby increasing the pressure of God's requirements upon their ethical powers of reaction.[153]

151. Given that, by God's revelation in and through creation, all men know God, there are no atheists. But given that all men, in Adam, suppress that knowledge and exchange it for a lie (Rom. 1:23, 25), all men, in Adam, are atheists. They will not honor and give thanks to the true God that they know.

152. Bavinck, *Gereformeerde dogmatiek*, 2:31 (*RD*, 2:57).

153. Recall what was said in the beginning about the denotation and the connotation.

We shall do well then to be careful with such notions as divinity *überhaupt* ("in general," i.e., generic theism). That is in itself an empty concept. To say that there are no atheists, strictly speaking, because no one denies divinity *überhaupt*, is to prepare the ground for an easy descent into the natural theology of Rome. We should rather say that there are no atheistic men because no man can deny the revelational activity of the true God within him. Atheists are those who kick against the pricks of the revelation of the true God within them. To be an atheist one need not deny divinity *überhaupt*.

Bavinck, however, seems to attribute too much value to belief in the existence of abstractions. In the same vein in which he reasons against the rationalists by the help of the empiricists he also argues against the innate ideas of the rationalists. A natural theology that is built upon the idea that man has within himself the information that he needs, he says, is utterly objectionable.[154] But this, he adds, is only one side of the story.

> Every science presupposes general principles which exist in their own right. All knowledge rests upon faith. All proof presupposes, in the last analysis, an ἀρχὴ ἀποδείξεως [a principle of demonstration]. There are logical, mathematical, philosophical, ethical and thus also religious and theological principles, which are, to be sure, very general and abstract, but which are accepted by all men in all ages and which have a character of naturalness and necessity. The laws of thought are the same for all; the doctrine of numbers is everywhere the same; the distinction between good and bad is known to all; there is no people without religion and knowledge of God. This is not to be explained otherwise than by the acceptance of *principia per se nota* [self-evident principles], κοιναὶ ἔννοιαι [ideas common to all], *veritates aeternae* [eternal verities], which are imprinted naturally on the human spirit. In the case of religion we must always, whether we will or no, come back to the idea of a *semen religionis* [seed of religion],[155] a

154. Bavinck, *Gereformeerde dogmatiek*, 2:47 (*RD*, 2:71).
155. For Calvin, the "seed of religion" (*semen religionis*) and the "sense of deity" (*sensus divinitatis*) were the same—the clear and true knowledge of the true God, given by the true God, to every human being, from the beginning of time into eternity. For more on Calvin's view, see K. Scott Oliphint, "A Primal and Simple Knowledge," in *A Theological Guide to*

sensus divinitatis [sense of divinity], an *instinctus divinus* [divine instinct], a *cognitio insita.*[156, 157]

Scripture tells us, says Bavinck, that man is made in the image of God, that in his νοῦς (mind) he has the capacity to see God in his works, and that the works of the law are written in his heart.[158] Rightly understood, says Bavinck, the idea of κοιναὶ ἔννοιαι means:

> That man has both the *potentia* [capacity] (*aptitudo, vis, facultas*) [aptitude or faculty] and the inclination (*habitus* [habit], *dispositio* [disposition]) so that in the course of normal development and in the midst of the environment in which God has given him life, he may of his own accord without compulsion, without scientific argumentation and proof, ἐμφύτως καὶ ἀδιδάκτως [inherently and intuitively], arrive at some solid, certain undoubted knowledge of God.[159]

In a case of normal development every man must come to such knowledge.

> As a man, opening his eyes, sees the sun and in its light sees the objects of the world about him, so man must, in accordance with his nature, when he hears that there is a God, that there is a difference between good and evil, etc., give his consent to these truths. He cannot avoid it. He accepts these truths involuntarily, without force or proof because they stand in their own right.[160]

In all this there has been a wavering between a Christian and a non-Christian concept of natural theology. On the one hand Bavinck comes back to the point that the true God has not left himself without a witness anywhere, and has spoken to man even

---

Calvin's Institutes: Essays and Analysis, ed. David Hall and Peter A. Lillback (Phillipsburg, NJ: P&R Publishing, 2008), 16–33.

156. The English translation has "innate knowledge"; I, with Bavinck, prefer the phrase *implanted knowledge*.

157. Bavinck, *Gereformeerde dogmatiek*, 2:47 (*RD*, 2:71).

158. Ibid.

159. Ibid., 2:48 (*RD*, 2:71).

160. Ibid., 2:49 (*RD*, 2:72).

through the depth of his self-conscious activity. The last sentence in the whole section is "It is God himself, who has not left Himself without a witness to every man." If the κοιναὶ ἔννοιαι were consistently explained along this line, we should come to the distinction between the psychological and the epistemological. We should then argue that *the* God, the only true God, has spoken to man from the beginning and everywhere. There are then no atheists in the sense that no one has been able to suppress this revelation of the true God within him and round about him.[161] On the other hand, Bavinck works with the distinction between the existence and the nature of God. In consonance with this distinction he then speaks about universal principles. He says that on the basis of the idea of κοιναὶ ἔννοιαι every man when he hears that there is *a* god, and when he hears that there is a difference between good and evil, must give his assent to *these truths.*

But how can Bavinck say that formal abstractions, such as the existence of *a* God and the idea of difference between good and evil as purely formal statement, are *truths?* They are in themselves the emptiest of forms and as such utterly meaningless. If they are to be spoken of as having content—and Bavinck speaks of them as such when he says they are truths—the question must be faced whence this content comes. If it comes from the revelation of God, if the revelation that there is *a* God comes from *the* God, if the idea of the *that* is to have its significance given it because it comes from the *what* of God's revelation, then we can not say that all men by nature will accept it, and as a consequence have a certain amount of true information about God. Man by his sinful nature hates the revelation of God. Therefore every concrete expression that any sinner makes about God will have in it the poisoning effect of this hatred of God. His epistemological reaction will invariably be negative, and negative along the whole line of his interpretative endeavor.[162] There are no general principles or truths about the true God—and that is the only God with whom any man actually deals—which he does not falsify. The very idea of the existence of

161. That is, even as Paul speaks of the suppression of the truth (Rom. 1:18), there is no possibility of *total* suppression, such that man does not know himself to be a creature of God and accountable to him. Paul explains what that suppression is in Rom. 1:23ff.

162. But keep in mind that for Van Til the epistemological presupposes the psychological, so that the negative reaction of the epistemological has its roots in the truth that is known by virtue of God's natural revelation.

COMMON GRACE AND THE GOSPEL

abstract truths is a falsification of the knowledge of the true God that every sinner involuntarily finds within himself.

Taken in its entirety, the section dealing with the *cognitio Dei insita* (implanted knowledge of God) has not escaped the ambiguity that we found in Bavinck's general treatment of the *principia*[163] in science, in his conception of mystery, and in his conception of the theistic proofs. It is the same ambiguity throughout that meets us. And it is the same ambiguity that we have found in Kuyper. These men have certainly led the way in modern times in the direction of working out a truly Protestant theology. But they have not quite had the courage to go consistently along the path they have marked out for us. There are elements of abstract reasoning in their procedure that lead to a natural theology which is not consistently set over against the natural theology of Rome at every point. When they deal with the objective aspect of the matter, that is with the revelational question, they cater, to some extent, to the idea of a probability position.[164] This probability position is the result of seeking for truth in the abstract way, combining impersonal principles with brute facts. When they deal with the subjective aspect of the matter, with the *common ideas*, they do not make a clear-cut, ringing distinction between that which is psychologically revelational and that which is epistemologically interpretative.

3. Hepp. Hepp has offered us a well-worked out discussion of Reformed epistemology. His book in which he does so is called *Het Testimonium Spiritus Sancti.* In the first volume he deals with what he calls the general testimony of the Spirit. It is to be followed by another, in which he is to deal with the special testimony of the Spirit.[165]

Hepp wants to build on what Bavinck and other Reformed theologians have done. In modern times Bavinck has come nearer than any one else to teaching a general testimony of the Spirit. But even he did not mention it by name. He only prepared the way for the idea.[166] When we come to the definitely constructive portion of

---

163. The *principia* are the basic, foundational principles.

164. That is, based on theistic proofs, a god *probably* exists. This is the best one can expect if such proofs are founded on a neutral notion of reason.

165. V. Hepp, *Het testimonium Spiritus Sancti* [The testimony of the Holy Spirit] (Kampen: J. H. Kok, 1914). The intended second volume was never published.

166. Ibid., 98.

Hepp's work, the argument he presents runs somewhat as follows. As the special testimony of the Spirit testifies within us to the truth of Scripture, so the general testimony of the Spirit testifies within us to truth in general.[167] The whole of the world about us is a manifestation of the truths of God. It is the Spirit's task to set forth the fullness of this revelation before the eyes of men. This may be called the *testimonium Spiritus Sancti externum* (the external testimony of the Holy Spirit). This external testimony reveals to man; but to this must be added the internal testimony to assure men of the truth of this revelation.

> Why? All revelation takes place by way of means. This is always true whether or not the revelation pertain to God or to created things. God never reveals Himself directly to us, but always through something that stands between Him and our ego. If not we should need to be able to look into the very essence of God, we should need to be fitted for a *visio Dei per essentiam* (vision of the essence of God).[168]

Revelation as such cannot give us certainty. If we had nothing but revelation, says Hepp, we should be compelled to believe in the objects on their own account. We should therefore rather say that the objects are but messengers of the Holy Spirit. Absolute certainty I, as a creature, can obtain only when the Holy Spirit, quite independently of the objects themselves, makes me believe that their revelation brings the truth to me. And that takes place when I receive the *testimonium generale internum* (general internal testimony).[169] This, says Hepp, is the essence of the testimony of the Spirit. It assures but does not reveal. It assures me of the truth of the revelation about me.

This general testimony, however, does not assure me of all truth. It assures me of central truths only.[170] These several truths do not relate to one another as members of a hierarchy. They are relatively independent of one another.[171] There are three groups of central truths, those pertaining to God, those pertaining to man, and those pertaining to the world.

167. Ibid., 140.
168. Ibid., 147.
169. Ibid., 148.
170. Ibid., 149.
171. Ibid., 151.

In connection with the truths pertaining to God, Hepp then discusses the value of the theistic proofs. His thought here is very similar to that of Bavinck. These proofs, he argues, put into set formulas that which comes to us from the cosmos as a whole. They press with power upon our consciousness, but cannot give us certainty.[172] General revelation, which is, as it were, concentrated in these proofs, would lead to a guess if it were not for the testimony of the Spirit.[173] Hepp is most insistent that we shall keep the two concepts, revelation and assurance, rigidly apart. Even in paradise Adam could not have lived by revelation as such. Without the general testimony there would have been uncertainty. Now doubt is sin, and in paradise there was no sin. We must therefore hold that even in paradise there was, in addition to general revelation, the general internal testimony of the Spirit to that revelation.

The second group of general truths centers about man. How is man to be certain of his self-existence? Only by the general internal testimony of the Spirit. How does man know that he can depend on his senses, on the axioms of his thought, and on the norms of his moral and aesthetic appreciation? Only by the general internal testimony of the Spirit.[174]

The third group of central truths deals with the world. This world presents itself as working according to *prima principia* (first principles). How do I know that this is true? Only by the general internal testimony of the Spirit.[175]

Thus the general internal testimony of the Spirit may be said to be the foundation of all science, religion, morality, and art.[176]

We come now to the most pivotal point of all.

From the marriage of the general testimony and revelation (here taken in its wide signification of God-revelation, man-revelation, and cosmos-revelation) *faith* is born. Wherever the internal testimony attests to the external testimony, man cannot withhold his assent. And faith always consists of giving assent by means of one's reason to some witness or other.[177]

172. Ibid., 153.
173. Ibid.
174. Ibid., 155.
175. Ibid., 156.
176. Ibid.
177. Ibid., 157.

Hepp calls this faith *fides generalis* (general faith). He says that modern philosophy has, quite generally, allowed for this *fides generalis*.[178] Yet, he adds, there is a difference, even a great difference, between the faith of modern philosophy and the general faith as we should hold to it.[179] For the modern philosopher, faith is, he says, after all, second to knowledge. For Christianity, on the other hand, faith offers far greater certainty than does science. "As for certainty knowledge cannot stand in the shadow of the *fides generalis*. For this rests on higher than subjective and objective grounds, on a direct operation of the Holy Spirit, on the testimony of God in the heart of every man."[180]

Now it is because of this *fides generalis*, resulting from the marriage of revelation and the general testimony, that men accept the general truths with respect to God, man, and the world. "Taken generally mankind does not deny the central truths. By far the greater majority of men recognize a higher power above themselves and do not doubt the reality within and beyond themselves."[181] Here we reach the climax of the whole matter. There are central truths to which the generality of mankind, because of the irresistible power of the Spirit's internal general testimony, must of necessity give their consent.

Our criticism of this position of Hepp will, quite naturally, be similar to that which we have made of Bavinck. As long as he is unwilling to argue along exclusively Christian lines, Hepp is unable to escape making concessions to a Roman type of natural theology. He makes many valuable negative criticisms against rationalism and empiricism. But he is not fully conscious, it seems, of the fact that even a negative criticism of non-Christian positions, must be undertaken from the presupposition of the Christian position. Hepp cannot effectively oppose the natural theology of Rome if he argues against it with the methods of a scholastic type of natural theology. He apparently has two methods of reasoning against false philosophies: one based on neutral premises, and, then, an additional one based on Christian premises.[182]

178. Ibid., 158ff.
179. Ibid., 161.
180. Ibid.
181. Ibid., 165.
182. Ibid., 133.

When Hepp deals with the "theistic proofs" he, like Bavinck, attributes a certain value to them even when they are constructed along non-Christian lines. Hepp says that Kant underestimated the value of these arguments. In his whole discussion of the proofs Hepp allows that an argument based upon would-be neutral ground, can have a certain validity. Of these proofs, constructed on a neutral and therefore non-Christian basis, Hepp says that they cry day and night that God exists.[183]

To this we reply that they cry day and night that God does not exist. For, as they have been constructed, they cry that a finite God exists. Nothing more could come from the procedure on which they have been constructed. They have been constructed on the assumption that we as human beings may make our start from the finite world, as from something that is ultimate. They take for granted that we already know from our study of the phenomenal world the meaning of such words as "cause" and "being" and "purpose," whether or not we have referred this phenomenal world to God.

To avoid a natural theology of the Roman sort, we shall need to come to something like a clear consciousness of the difference between a Christian and a non-Christian mode of argument with respect to the revelation of God in nature. God is, and has been from the beginning, revealed in nature and in man's own consciousness. We cannot say that the heavens *probably* declare the glory of God. We cannot allow that if rational argument is carried forth on true premises, it should come to any other conclusion than that the true God exists. Nor can we allow that the certainty with respect to God's existence would be any less if acquired by a ratiocinative process rather than by intuitions, as long as man was not a sinner. The testimony of the Spirit may well be conceived as originally controlling Adam's reasoning powers as well as his intuitive powers. On the other hand, when man has become a sinner, his intuitive powers are as sinful as his reasoning powers. There may be more area for error in a sorites (a form of logical argument) than in an intuition, but the corruption of sin has penetrated to every activity of man.

Thus the imperative necessity of introducing the distinction between the psychologically and the epistemologically interpreta-

183. Ibid., 153.

tive, becomes again apparent. God still speaks in man's consciousness. Man's own interpretative activity, whether of the more or of the less extended type, whether in ratiocination or in intuition, is no doubt the most penetrating means by which the Holy Spirit presses the claims of God upon man. The argument for the existence of God and for the truth of Christianity is objectively valid. We should not tone down the validity of this argument to the probability level. The argument may be poorly stated, and may never be adequately stated. But in itself the argument is absolutely sound.[184] Christianity is the only reasonable position to hold. It is not merely as reasonable as other positions, or a bit more reasonable than other positions; it alone is the natural and reasonable position for man to take. By stating the argument as clearly as we can, we may be the agents of the Spirit in pressing the claims of God upon men. If we drop to the level of the merely probable truthfulness of Christian theism, we, to that extent, lower the claims of God upon men. This is, we believe, the sense of Calvin's *Institutes* on the matter.

On the other hand, every man by his *sinful nature* seeks violently to suppress the voice of God that keeps on speaking within him through his *created nature*. One way sinful human nature has of suppressing the claims of God within itself, is by saying that the objective argument for the existence of God is of doubtful validity. Sinful human nature loves to speak of abstract principles of truth, goodness, and beauty. It loves to speak of a God because it hates *the* God.[185]

If we take both the original human nature and the sinful human nature, and realize that everywhere both are active, we have done once for all with the natural theology of Rome.[186] On the objective side we have done with it, inasmuch as we claim for the statement of the Christian position absolute validity. For science and philosophy,

184. What Van Til means to say is that there is nothing inherently wrong with the proofs themselves. It is certainly the case, for example (to use Aquinas's "second way"), that God is the first cause of all things. The problem, however, is that when the "objective" hits the subject, the terms and concepts in the otherwise valid proof are twisted by virtue of the suppression of the truth.
185. Any theism that is not Christian theism is idolatry. Generic theism is not "closer" to the truth than atheism; it is just another form of idolatry and thus of unbelief.
186. That is, the "original human nature" is man (male and female) in God's image, and thus man knowing God; the "sinful human nature" is man always and everywhere suppressing that which he knows. No room is left, therefore, for a neutral notion of natural theology.

as well as for theology, we frankly take our basic presuppositions from Scripture. Scripture tells us that God, the God who has more fully revealed Himself in Scripture than in nature, is yet speaking to us in the created universe about us. Scripture says that *from the beginning* He has spoken there (Rom. 1:20). It says that man has known this fact, and that by his efforts at perversion he has well-nigh succeeded in silencing the voice of revelation, but that deep down in his heart he is still aware of this revelation and will be held responsible for it. We must not lower these claims to the probability level. On the subjective side we have done with a Romanist type of natural theology, because we realize the sinful nature is everywhere active. There are no *capita communissima* (general principles), on which believers and non-believers can agree without a difference. There are no central truths on which all agree. The disagreement is fundamental and goes to the heart of the matter.

Thus we are no longer face to face with the dilemma with which Gilson confronts the Calvinist. As long as we seek refuge from Romanism by having less Romanism we shall not escape the sword of Gilson. To withdraw to the inner fortress of central truths, and make even these merely probable in the objective field, and to withdraw to the psychologically primitive (intu- itions, *beseffen*) in the subjective field, helps matters not at all. Gilson will find us still. Quite rightly he asserts that the atten- uations of language are of no help in this matter. If we speak of the sense of deity and of the seed of religion, and mean by that some degree of common epistemological response on the part of believer and non-believer, however small the area of agreement, and however primitive the nature of the response, Gilson has a right to confront us with his dilemma. The escape from the dilemma lies, we believe, as suggested, in doing what Kuyper and Bavinck and Hepp have all at one place or another told us to do, namely, offer an interpretation of life in its totality on the basis of the principle Scripture offers. That principle is the ontological trinity.

In answer to his challenge, we would tell Gilson that, unless he is willing with us to interpret nature and all things else in terms of the ontological trinity, he can get no meaning into human expe- rience. The interpretations of the natural reason, made by the aid of abstract principles and brute facts can, in the nature of the case, lead with rationalism (Parmenides) into a universal validity that is empty of content, or with empiricism (Heraclitus) to a particularism that has no universality, or to a phenomenalism[187] that is a compromise between these two positions and shares the weaknesses of both.

B. The Positive Line of Concrete Thinking

What has been said by way of criticism on the remnants of abstract thinking found in Kuyper, Bavinck, and Hepp has virtually suggested the direction of thought we would follow in approaching the question of common grace. The ontological trinity will be our interpretative concept everywhere. God is our concrete universal; in Him thought and being are coterminous, in Him the problem of knowledge is solved.[188]

If we begin thus with the ontological trinity as our concrete universal, we frankly differ from every school of philosophy and from every school of science not merely in our conclusions, but in our starting-point and in our method as well. For us the facts are what they are, and the universals are what they are, because of their common dependence upon the ontological trinity. Thus, as earlier discussed, the facts are correlative to the universals. Because of this correlativity there is genuine progress in history; because of it the Moment has significance.[189]

To make progress in our discussion we must, it seems, learn to take time more seriously than we have done. What does it mean to take time more seriously? It means, for one thing, to realize that we shall never have an exhaustive answer to the common grace problem. We have already made a good deal of the Christian concept of mystery. With all our admiration for Bavinck we yet found that he allowed himself to be influenced by the Greek ideal of the comprehension of God. This ideal works havoc with true Reformed

187. "Phenomenalism" in this context is a Kantian approach, described above.

188. The problem of knowledge, to which Van Til refers, is embedded, as he has said, in the problem of the relationship of the universal and the particular, the one and the many. It is "solved" in the triune God, not because we can completely comprehend that relationship, but because we know that since the One and the Three are coterminous and equally ultimate in God, reality will reflect that equal ultimacy. To see one way in which this can be articulated, see H. G. Stoker, "On the Contingent and Present-Day Western Man," in *The Idea of a Christian Philosophy: Essays in Honour of D. H. Th. Vollenhoven,* ed. K. A. Bril, H. Hart, J. Klapwijk (Toronto: Wedge Publishing Foundation, 1973).

189. See footnote 35.

theology. Perhaps we may here learn anew from the greatest of theologians, John Calvin.

Calvin lays great stress upon the incomprehensible will of God. This is particularly the case in his treatise on the predestination of God. In replying to Pighius[190] and Georgius[191] he falls back on this point again and again. In the first section of the book Calvin gives the doctrine of election "a slight touch." But even in this "slight touch" he refers to Rom 9:20. Of it he says: "The apostle in this appeal adopts an axiom, or universal acknowledgment, which not only ought to be held fast by all godly minds, but deeply engraven in the breast of common sense; that the inscrutable judgment of God is deeper than can be penetrated by man."[192] When we must answer such as argue along the lines of Pighius, says Calvin, we ask whether there be "no justice of God, but that which is conceived of by us." When men cannot see a reason for the works of God they are immediately "prepared to appoint a day for entering into judgment with Him."[193] "What do you really think of God's glorious Name? And will you vaunt that the apostle is devoid of all reason, because he does not drag God from His throne and set Him before you, to be questioned and examined."[194] Calvin steadfastly refuses to permit abstract universal ideas to rule God. We are to hold that the will of God, the will of the inscrutable God is "the highest rule of righteousness."[195] God's will is to be set "above all other causes."[196] Men who follow "their own natural sense and understanding" appeal to abstract justice, "because they presume to subject the tribunal of God to their own judgment."[197] We should rather rest content with the Word

190. Albert Pighius (1490–1542) was a Roman Catholic theologian, mathematician, and astronomer. His primary work against Luther and Calvin was *De libero hominis arbitrio et divina gratia* (The free will of man and divine grace) (1542).

191. Because Pighius had died by the time Calvin wrote his treatise on predestination, he makes clear that he is also addressing Georgius in the treatise. Giorgio Rioli (c. 1517–1551), surnamed Siculus, was a Roman Catholic monk who was executed as a heretic by the Inquisition. He spoke out against Calvin's teaching on predestination through his interpretation of 1 John 2:2.

192. John Calvin, *A Treatise on the Eternal Predestination of God*, in *Calvin's Calvinism*, trans. Henry Cole (Grand Rapids: Eerdmans, 1950), 32.

193. Ibid.

194. Ibid., 33.

195. Ibid.

196. Ibid., 34.

197. Ibid.

of God. May we keep our ears open to it and shut them to the voice of strangers.[198]

The problem Calvin is discussing is that of predestination. The objection raised against the doctrine of predestination is, of course, that it condemns secondary causes to insignificance. Pighius, says Calvin, "knows not how to make the least distinction between *remote* and *proximate* causes."[199] Pighius urges the full-bucket difficulty against Calvin's insistence that God's counsel is the ultimate cause of whatsoever comes to pass.[200] Calvin in turn insists that it is quite legitimate to urge man's sin as the proximate, and God's counsel as the ultimate, cause of man's final perdition.[201] Does he think he can offer an explanation of the relation between the ultimate and the proximate cause that will satisfy the demands of a logic, such as Pighius employs? Not for a moment. He calls on Pighius to forsake his logic with its phenomenal foundation. "Pighius, on the contrary, begins his building from the earth's plain surface, without any foundation at all."[202] Pighius would ask why God created such natures as he knew would sin. Pighius knows how to employ a well-turned syllogism. There is no escaping the force of his objection. If God is the ultimate cause back of whatsoever comes to pass, Pighius can, on his basis, rightly insist that God is the cause of sin. Calvin knew this. He attempts no answer by means of a non-Christian methodology. With Augustine he would throw man back into the consideration of what he is, and what is the capacity of his mind.[203] "Nay but, O man, who art thou that repliest against God" (Rom. 9:20). This is a reason for man and "all that is due him." That was Paul's answer and Augustine's answer. It is also Calvin's answer:

> Paul comparing, as he here does, man with God, shows that the counsel of God, in electing and reprobating men, is without doubt more profound and more deeply concealed than the human mind can penetrate. Wherefore, O man, consider (as the apostle adviseth thee) who and what thou art, and

198. Ibid., 36.
199. Ibid., 90.
200. Ibid., 85.
201. Ibid., 76.
202. Ibid., 74.
203. Ibid., 70.

concede more to God than the measure and compass of thine own nature.[204]

We are to remember, then, that on the question of the relation of God's counsel to what takes place in time "the wisdom of Christ is too high and too deep to come within the compass of man's understanding."[205] There is nothing "in the whole circle of spiritual doctrine which does not far surpass the capacity of man and confound its utmost reach."[206] When such a subject as predestination is discussed "numberless unholy and absurd thoughts rush into the mind."[207] How shall we meet these unholy thoughts and arguments in ourselves and in others? We shall not meet them by trying to defend such doctrines on the basis of a logic that assumes secondary causes to be ultimate causes. We shall not meet them on the basis of a logic that starts from brute facts, and handles them according to abstract universal principles. We shall meet them rather by offering the ontological trinity as our interpretative concept. This will at once lay us open to the charge of the full-bucket difficulty. We are not to be affrighted by the charge of holding the contradictory. "But I would repeat my being perfectly aware how much absurdity and irreconcilable contradiction these deep things seem to profane persons to carry with them."[208] We shall meet this charge of contradiction by asserting that we are the true defenders of the meaning of second causes. History has meaning just because God's counsel is back of it. Sin can be given as the reason for man's destruction just because men were "fitted for destruction" (Rom. 9:22), and faith can be given as a reason for man's final glory just because believers were "afore prepared unto glory" (Rom. 9:23). "Godly consciences"[209] need not be disturbed by the reasonings of rationalists, or irrationalists or rationalist-irrationalists. There is, in fact, a beautiful harmony between remote and proximate causes. The harmony exists—of that, faith is sure. Faith is reasonable—of that, faith is also sure. Faith alone is reasonable—of that, faith is once more sure. Faith

204. Ibid., 71.
205. Ibid., 82.
206. Ibid.
207. Ibid., 86.
208. Ibid., 88.
209. Ibid., 93.

abhors the really contradictory; to maintain the really contradictory is to deny God. Faith adores the apparently contradictory; to adore the apparently contradictory is to adore God as one's creator and final interpreter.

Says Calvin:

> If, then, nothing can prevent a man from acknowledging that the first origin of his ruin was from Adam, and if each man finds the *proximate* cause of his ruin in himself, what can prevent our faith from acknowledging afar off, with all sobriety, and adoring, with all humility, that *remote* secret counsel of God by which the Fall of man was thus preordained? And what should prevent the same faith from beholding, at the same time, the *proximate* cause within; that the whole human race is individually bound by the guilt and desert of eternal death, as derived from the person of Adam; and that all are in themselves, therefore, subject to death and to death eternal? Pighius, therefore, has not sundered, shaken or altered (as he thought he had done) that pre-eminent and most beautiful symmetry with which these *proximate* and *remote* causes divinely harmonise![210]

The "scholars of God," those who are "gifted, not with the spirit of this world, but with His own heavenly Spirit" may know the things freely given them by God;[211] but they know them because they have learned to know their places as creatures before the incomprehensible God.

There can be little doubt that if Calvin's conception of mystery were more closely adhered to in our discussion of common grace, we should lose less time and energy in misunderstanding one another. The charges of rationalism and irrationalism that have been hurled back and forth would subside to a considerable extent if we all learned to think less along rationalist-irrationalist and more along Calvin's lines. Any tendency toward either rationalism or irrationalism lowers the genuine significance of history.[212]

210. Ibid., 91.
211. Ibid., 96f.
212. Because the "genuine significance of history" has its roots in the plan and counsel of the triune God.

The imperative necessity of maintaining a clear-cut distinction between the Christian and the non-Christian conception of mystery in connection with any problem, and in particular with the common grace problem, may now become apparent. The common grace problem deals with this question: What do entities which will one day be wholly different from one another have in common before that final stage of separation is reached? We dare not expect to approach anything like a specific answer to this problem, so long as we allow our thinking to be controlled by abstractions. But abstractions will be with us as long as we do not distinguish clearly between the Christian and the non-Christian concept of mystery.

We have already observed that the invariable concomitant of confusing the two conceptions of mystery is the lowering of the claims for the objective validity of the Christian-theistic position. The theistic proofs are said to be objectively weak. They are said to be worth something but not a great deal.[213] Our position as Christians is merely said to be objectively *at least as good* as the position of our enemies. The result will naturally be that we relieve the pressure of God's claims upon created man. We say to him that, as far as the objective evidence is concerned, he is living up to the requirements of the case if he merely arrives at the existence of *a* God, at a divinity *überhaupt*. At least he need not feel that he is falling below the mark, if he is doubtful that the true God exists. Now apply this to man's moral attitude toward God. Both parties to the debate on common grace should be willing to agree that Adam and Eve had the requirements of God's law written on their hearts. We need not concern ourselves here with the distinction between the "works of the law" and the "law."[214] We are not speaking now of man's ethical reaction to God. We are speaking only of God's revelational relationship to man. And on that point all should be equally anxious to maintain that God originally spoke plainly to man, both in the "book of nature" and in the "book of conscience." Wherever man would turn he saw the living God and His requirements. Whether he reasoned about nature or whether he looked within, whether it was the starry heavens above or the

---

213. That is, if the theistic proofs are based on a neutral notion of what counts as "evidence," the best one can do is conclude that a god *probably* exists. But the proposition "God *probably* exists" is not only false, but another example of suppression of the truth.
214. In Rom. 2:15, Paul says that the "*work* of the law" is written on every heart.

moral law within,[215] both were equally insistent and plain that God, the true God, stood before him.

It should also be recognized that man was, from the outset, confronted with positive, as well as with natural, revelation. Dr. Vos[216] speaks of this as pre-redemptive special revelation.[217] God walked and talked with man.[218] Natural revelation must not be separated from this supernatural revelation. To separate the two is to deal with two abstractions instead of with one concrete situation. That is to say, natural revelation, whether objective or subjective, is in itself a limiting conception. It has never existed by itself so far as man is concerned. It cannot fairly be considered, therefore, as a fixed quantity, that can be dealt with in the same way at every stage of man's moral life. Man was originally placed before God as a covenant personality.

It is no doubt with this in mind that Calvin speaks of sinners as being *covenant-breakers.*[219] The phrase has come into common usage among Reformed theologians. Common as the usage of the phrase may be, however, the point we have made perhaps needs stressing. All too easily do we think of the covenant relation as quite distinct and independent of natural revelation. The two should be joined together. To speak of man's relation to God as being covenantal at every point is merely to say that man deals with the personal God everywhere. Every manipulation of any created fact is, as long as man is not a sinner, a covenant-affirming activity. Every manipulation of any fact, as soon as man is a sinner, is a covenant-breaking activity.[220]

215. Immanuel Kant, in his *Critique of Practical Reason*, claimed that the "starry heaven above and the moral law within" filled him with wonder.

216. Geerhardus Vos (1862–1949) was born in the Netherlands and came to the United States in 1881. He studied at Princeton Seminary and received his doctorate at Strassburg. Vos was the first to occupy the newly created chair of biblical theology at Princeton Seminary. His works include *Biblical Theology, The Pauline Eschatology,* and *Redemptive History and Biblical Interpretation.* The relationship of Van Til to his teacher at Princeton is indicated by Vos's request that Van Til preach at his funeral. The influence of Vos on Van Til was significant.

217. Geerhardus Vos, *Notes on Biblical Theology of the Old Testament* (Philadelphia: Westminster Theological Seminary, [1933]).

218. This is what Van Til means by "positive" revelation. Even in the garden, and quite apart from sin, it was necessary for God to speak in order for Adam and Eve to know what God required of them. Thus, special and natural revelation have always been together.

219. Calvin, *A Treatise on the Eternal Predestination of God,* 65.

220. In other words, because of God's revelation through creation, within and without man, man is always and everywhere accountable to God for his actions in God's world.

In this connection a word may be said about the question already touched upon as to whether any conclusions may be drawn about the attitude of God from observation of facts. In Schilder's discussion of the proof texts adduced by the Christian Reformed Church Synod of 1924, he speaks from time to time about "facts as such." From the "facts as such," he warns, we are not to conclude any such thing as an attitude of God toward the reprobate. "Beware, that you do not separate the facts from faith."[221] The point comes up again and again. As over against a Romanizing type of natural theology this warning of Schilder is no doubt in order. And we have observed that as Reformed theologians we have not yet outgrown Rome's natural theology entirely. We have already criticized the idea of brute fact. But there is another side to the story.

If there are no brute facts, if brute facts are mute facts,[222] it must be maintained that all facts are revelational of the true God. If facts may not be separated from faith, neither may faith be separated from facts. Every created fact must therefore be held to express, to some degree, the attitude of God to man. Not to maintain this is to fall back once again into a natural theology of a Roman Catholic sort. For it is to hold to the idea of brute fact after all. And with the idea of brute fact goes that of neutral reason. A fact not revelational of God is revelational only of itself.

Schilder tells us, further, that the attitude of God is revealed only to the extent that we know of the will of His eternal counsel. He speaks of this in connection with the story of the sons of Eli. In God's final purpose he has determined to slay the sons of Eli. Yet Eli is told to tell his sons that God desires not their death.

> The father Eli may, and must say to his sons: be converted, ye children of Eli, for Jehovah desires not your death; that is the revealed will, the command, which you are to obey. He hates

---

Because all men are the image of God, all men are covenant creatures; they are in a relationship to God, either as in Adam and under wrath or as in Christ and under grace. This point is central to Van Til's entire apologetic. For more on apologetics as covenantal, see K. Scott Oliphint, *Covenantal Apologetics: Principles and Practice in Defense of Our Faith* (Wheaton, IL: Crossway Books, 2013).

221. Klaas Schilder, "De scheuring in Amerika (XVII.): Intermezzo: antwoord aan ds. D. Zwier [IV.]," *De Reformatie* 20 (November 10, 1939): 44. See also *The Standard Bearer* 15 (1938–1939) and 16 (1939–1940).

222. That is, a brute fact, if there were such, would be a fact that doesn't say anything. But all facts declare the glory of God (see Ps. 19:1ff.).

sin. But in addition to this we are informed afterwards, that as far as the secret will of God is concerned, Jehovah did desire their death as just punishment; in part because of this they harden themselves against warning; inasmuch as wickedness is punishment as well as pollution. And in this hidden will it is that the *attitude* of God appears.[223]

Should Schilder wish to generalize the point he makes with respect to the sons of Eli, he would end up with the notion of brute fact. To set the problem before us as clearly as possible, we do well to think of it in connection with Adam in paradise. Would it be possible to maintain that only by the later revelation of God's final purpose could anything be known of His attitude toward man? Then Adam would at the beginning have known nothing of God's attitude toward him. No revelation of God's final purpose had yet been made. The whole future, as far as Adam's knowledge was concerned, was conditioned by his obedience or disobedience. But if this act of obedience or disobedience was to have any significance, it had to be obedience or disobedience with respect to God, whom he knew. His moral act could not be action in a void. He knew something of God and of God's attitude toward him without any unconditional revelation about God's final purpose.

We must go further than this. Man was originally created good. That is to say, there was, as a matter of fact, an ethical reaction on the part of man, and this ethical action was approved by God. It may be said that God created man with a good nature, but that the test was still to come as to whether he would voluntarily live in accord with this good nature. But surely Adam could not live for a second without acting morally. The "good nature" of Adam cannot be taken otherwise than as a limiting concept. The objective and the subjective aspects were correlative of one another. Further still, the decisive representative act was still to come. Granted that Adam's nature was an active nature, this active nature itself must be taken as a limiting concept in relation to the decisive ethical reaction that was to take place in connection with the probationary command. This goes to prove that the representative act of obedience or disobedience presupposed for its possibility the revelational

223. Klaas Schilder, "De scheuring in Amerika (XVIII.): Intermezzo: antwoord aan ds. D. Zwier [V.]," *De Reformatie* 20 (November 17, 1939): 52–53.

character of everything created. It goes to prove, further, that man's *good* ethical reaction must be taken as an aspect of that revelatory character of everything created. To be sure, this good reaction was not the consummated good that shall be attained in the case of those that will be in glory. Yet it was a good ethical reaction. It was good not so much in a *lower* sense as in an *earlier* sense.

The importance of stressing the idea of the *earlier* and the *later* needs to be insisted on. We know, of course, that in God's mind there are those that are reprobate and those that are elect. This fact being revealed to us, we know that some men will be finally rejected and some men will be finally accepted. And there is no dispute as to what is the ultimate cause with respect to this difference. Both parties to the debate are with Calvin, as over against Pighius, heartily agreed that God's counsel is the ultimately determinative factor. But the difference obtains with respect to the meaning of the historical. And here the problem is, more specifically, to what extent we should allow our notion of the earlier to be controlled by our notion of the later. We think that the notion of the earlier must be stressed more than has been done heretofore.

If we make the earlier our point of departure for the later, we begin with something that believers and unbelievers have in common. That is to say, they have something in common because they do not yet exist. Yet they do exist. They exist in Adam as their common representative. They have seen the testimony of God in common. They have given a common good ethical reaction to this testimony, the common mandate of God. They are all mandate-hearers and covenant-keepers. God's attitude to all is the same. God has a favorable attitude to all. He beheld all the works of His hands and, behold, they were good. God was pleased with them.

But this favorable attitude of God to this early common perfect nature must be taken as correlative to the representative moral act of Adam. We may and must hold that every fact was revelational. Every fact was the bearer of a requirement. But, even as such, it was expressive of a favorable attitude of God to man. *Without all this the ethical act of representation would have to take place in a void.* At the same time, this original situation was a historically unfinished situation. It required further ethical action as its correlative. The continuance of the situation required, on the part of man, the representative affirmation of God as God. And this correlativity implied that the situation would, in any case, be changed. Whether Adam was to obey or to disobey, the situation would be changed. And thus God's attitude would be changed.

We need at this point, as everywhere else, to be fearlessly anthropomorphic. Our basic interpretative concept, the doctrine of the ontological trinity, demands of us that we should be so. We have met the full-bucket difficulty by asserting that history has meaning, not in spite of, but because of, the counsel of God who controls whatsoever comes to pass. From the point of view of a non-Christian logic the Reformed Faith can be bowled over by means of a single syllogism. God has determined whatsoever comes to pass. Man's moral acts are things that come to pass. Therefore man's moral acts are determined and man is not responsible for them.[224] So Pighius argued against Calvin. Calvin replied, in effect, that just because God has determined everything, secondary causes have genuine meaning. Applying this to the case in hand, we would say that we are entitled and compelled to use anthropomorphism not apologetically but fearlessly.[225] We need not fear to say that God's attitude has changed with respect to mankind. We know well enough that God in himself is changeless. But we hold that we are able to affirm that our words have meaning for no other reason than that we use them analogically.

Accordingly we would not speak of God's love of creatureliness always and everywhere. Schilder uses this idea. He says that God greatly loves creatureliness everywhere, whether in the drunkard, the anti-Christ or the devil.[226] Creatureliness is then conceived of statically, as though it were something to be found anywhere and everywhere the same and always by itself. But creatureliness should be used as a limiting concept.[227] It is never found in moral beings, whether men or angels, except in connection with an ethical reaction, positive or negative. We cannot intelligently speak of God's

224. This is a good example of the fact that logic alone is insufficient, as are proofs, for understanding God and his ways in the world. What is crucial in logic and its proofs is the foundation upon which such things are posited. God's determination of every moral act does *not* undermine our responsibility for each act. As a matter of fact, God's determination *establishes* that responsibility.

225. "Anthropomorphism" (literally, "in the form of man") refers to ascribing human characteristics to God. For more, see the foreword.

226. See Zwier, "Syllogismen, die we onmogelijk kunnen aanvaarden," 723–24.

227. That is, "creatureliness," as a universal, and therefore abstract entity, must be thought of concretely, which means in the context of specific, individual creatures.

love of creatureliness in the devil. God's good pleasure pertains no doubt to the devil. But that is because the devil is frustrated in his opposition to God. God once upon a time loved the devil. But that was before the devil was the devil. We shall make no progress on the common grace problem with the help of abstractions.

We need not hesitate to affirm, then, that in the beginning God loved mankind in general. That was before mankind had sinned against God. A little later God hated mankind in general. That was after mankind had sinned against God. Is there any doubt that the elect, as well as the reprobate, were under the wrath of God? Calvin says that the whole human race is "individually bound by the guilt and desert of eternal death, as derived from the person of Adam."[228] So the elect and the reprobate are under a *common wrath*. If there is meaning in this—and who denies it?—there may and must, with equal right, be said to be an earlier attitude of common favor. Indeed, the reality of the "common wrath" depends upon the fact of the earlier "common grace."[229] But *after the common, in each case, comes the conditional.* History is a process of differentiation. Accordingly, the idea of that which is common between the elect and the reprobate is always a limiting concept. It is a commonness for *the time being.* There lies back of it a divine *as if.* One syllogism, based on non-Christian assumptions, would call this dishonesty. Pighius knew how to turn such syllogisms; but Calvin knew how to answer them. Invariably he answered them by turning to the words of Paul, "Who art thou, O man?" He answered them by rejecting the whole of the non-Christian methodology, based on the ideas of brute fact and abstract universal. Pighius cannot shake the symmetry with which the proximate and remote causes divinely harmonize, even though he can easily prove that no man can comprehend their connection. Man has sinned against the true God, whom he knew for what He is. When man first sinned he did not know God as fully as we know Him now, but he did know God for what

228. Calvin, *A Treatise on the Eternal Predestination of God*, 91.
229. Van Til is making the point that Calvin makes: because all were represented in Adam, it follows that when Adam fell, mankind fell. But presupposed in the wrath that accrued to mankind in Adam's fall was the favor of God toward all mankind in Adam. Van Til calls this pre-fall favor "common grace," but puts it in quotation marks in order to distinguish it from the common grace that comes after, and because of, the fall. The pre-fall "common grace" is actually God's attitude of favor toward all, in Adam, in that God's gracious offer of eternal life to Adam included all men. For a more complete explanation of this, see the foreword.

He is, as far as he knew Him at all. And it was *mankind,* not some individual elect or reprobate person, that sinned against God. Thus it was mankind in general which was under the favor of God, that came under the wrath of God.[230]

We have said that after the common in each case comes the conditional. What then is meant by the conditional? This question has caused much trouble. The synod of 1924 of the Christian Reformed Church, before referred to, gave the general offer of the gospel as evidence of common grace. Hoeksema, on the other hand, denies that there may be said to be any such thing as a well-meant offer of salvation to a generality of men, including elect and non-elect. He thinks he finds clear support in Calvin's treatment of the general offer in relation to predestination.

If any progress is to be made in the discussion of this most perplexing aspect of the perplexing problem of common grace we shall need, in our humble opinion, to stress, as we have tried to do throughout, the idea of the earlier and the later, that is to say, the historical correlativity of universal and particular. All too frequently our difficulty is needlessly enhanced in that those who affirm, and those who deny, employ in the defense of their positions such arguments as are constructed out of the ideas of brute fact and abstract law. A rather typical argument employed is that expressed in the following words of Hepp: "Is there not a sort of grace in the hearing of the gospel by the non-elect? They hear that God has no pleasure in their death, but rather that they be converted and live. As time-believers the Word may bring them joy." Here Hepp inserts a paraphrase of Heb 6:4, as proof that there may be a grace which is non-saving for the reprobate.[231] He then adds: "Let us not look at the lot of the non-elect in the congregation from the view-point of judgment only. Truly that judgment is a reality. But the enjoyments, which they sometimes have under the preaching of the gospel also have temporary reality, as a non-saving work brought about as they are by the Spirit."[232]

230. Again, Van Til is referring here to mankind as we are in Adam. In Adam, we were recipients of God's favor; when Adam sinned, we came under God's wrath.

231. Hepp offers much valuable material on the question of common grace in a series of articles in which he seeks to prove that common grace is taught in Scripture. Quoted here from the series is V. Hepp, "Het genadebegrip conform de Schrift (XV)," *Credo* 1 (July 1, 1938): 227.

232. Ibid.

Hepp here speaks as though it were already known who are and who are not elect. He speaks as though a preacher may approach a certain individual whom he knows to be reprobate, and tell him that God has no pleasure in his death. But this is to forget the difference between the earlier and the later. The general presentation comes to a generality. It comes to "sinners," differentiated, to be sure, as elect and reprobate in the mind of God, but yet, prior to their act of acceptance or rejection, regarded as a generality. To forget this is to move the calendar of God ahead.

Arguing as Hepp argues is virtually to accept the really contradictory. It at least approaches the idea that the same ultimate will of God wills, and yet wills not, the salvation of sinners. If it does not do this, as it is obviously not intended to do, it makes for a mechanical alignment of common and special grace. All agree that common grace is not a small quantity of special grace; yet if the matter of the conditional presentation be handled as Hepp handles it, there is great difficulty in escaping the quantitative idea. It may then, to be sure, be asserted that common grace is a *lower* kind of grace, a grace meant for this life only, but it is difficult to see how this lower grace is the result of the presentation of the gospel which deals with the highest grace, that is, saving grace.

The difficulties at this point are, we must believe, considerably reduced if we observe the ideas of the earlier and the later. Calvin does not hesitate to say of mankind that it was originally "placed in a way of salvation."[233] And while mankind in general was in a way of salvation, salvation was offered to all men. He recounts this as an historical fact. He argues with Pighius as to whether it was absolutely or conditionally offered, but he does not dispute the fact that it was offered to all men in Adam. "The truth of the matter is, that salvation is not offered to all men on any other ground than on the condition of their remaining in their original innocence."[234] From this fact that God did at the earliest point in history offer eternal life to all men, Calvin takes his departure. One who argues like Pighius is easily able to raise objections to this as being quite impossible. He will say: God, according to the doctrine of election, did not mean to save all men. Then what meaning has it to offer eternal life to all men? And how dare you say that God placed

233. Calvin, *A Treatise on the Eternal Predestination of God*, 92.
234. Ibid.

man in a way of salvation? But Calvin does not allow himself to be led astray by reasoning based on non-Christian assumptions. True reasoning, he says in effect, will rather maintain that the general offer has meaning and is possible because it has actually been made by God. And while it is true that this whole question of the universal offer of salvation is one of these things that can only "be fully understood or perceived by faith," we yet see such harmony between ultimate and proximate causes on the frankly revelational basis as cannot be seen otherwise.

It is with this background that Calvin then attacks the question of Christ's command to preach the gospel to all men alike. Pighius drew from the universality of this command the conclusion that God must mean all men to be saved. Against this Calvin argues that the promise is not unconditional. Speaking of the promise of Jer 31:33 to the effect that God will write His law in their hearts, he says: "Now a man must be utterly beside himself to assert that this promise is made to all men generally and indiscriminately."[235] It is evident that God by His counsel did not ordain all men to eternal life. Yet the fact of Christ's command remains. "It is quite manifest that all men, without difference or distinction, are *outwardly called* or invited to repentance and faith."[236] Pighius sees a contradiction here. And on non-Christian presuppositions there would be a contradiction here. But with the Christian distinction between ultimate and proximate causes we hold, though we cannot intellectually penetrate the question exhaustively, that, instead, there is genuine harmony here. There are, we can show Pighius, not two ultimate wills in God contradicting one another. Yet we need the idea of two wills, that of command and that of secret counsel. We harmonize the two, as far as we can harmonize that which involves the incomprehensible God, by the ideas of correlativity and conditionality as these ideas are themselves determined in their meaning by the concept of God.

The universality of the gospel presentation or invitation or promise or command—they all come to the same thing, and Calvin is not afraid to use them indiscriminately—comes to mankind in general. It comes to sinful mankind, to mankind that has once before, when "placed in a way of salvation," been offered salvation. It comes to

235. Ibid., 100.
236. Ibid., 95.

a generality that has once in common, in one moment, in one man, rejected the offer of eternal life through Adam. Mankind is now, to use words corresponding to the earlier stage, *placed in a way of death.*[237]

Meanwhile the fact of Christ's redemptive work, in promise or in fulfillment, has come into the picture.[238] Christ has not died for all men. He has died only for His people (see, for example, Matt. 1:21; John 10:11, 14–16; Eph. 5:25). But His people are not yet His people except in the mind of God. They are still members of the sinful mass of mankind. It is with them *where they are* that contact is to be made. The offer or presentation is not to those who believe any more than to those who disbelieve. The offer comes to those who have so far neither believed nor disbelieved. It comes before that differentiation has taken place. It comes thus generally, *so that differentiation may have meaning.* Christ is to be a savor of life unto life to some and a savor of death unto death to others. Those who eventually disbelieve will be the more inexcusable.[239]

The analogy of Calvin's argument here to his idea of original general revelation is apparent. As God's general revelation, natural and positive, plus the probationary command, originally *invited* all men to eternal life, as Calvin puts it, and men, of whom God had determined from all eternity that they should not inherit eternal life, yet were rendered inexcusable by the invitation when they rejected it, so now again, a second time, while it is still as certain as ever with God that they shall be lost eventually, and while historically they have by their sin placed themselves in the way of eternal death, they are rendered the more inexcusable by the gospel invitation, and have added to their condemnation by their second rejection of God.

Pighius objects that all this is to make of God a mocker. But Calvin introduces again his distinction between primary and secondary causes. Men "untaught of God" do not understand. They, he says in effect, use syllogisms "from the earth's plain surface, without any foundation at all." Believers, on the other hand, use syllogisms on the foundation of the ontological trinity. They know that all men

---

237. See the foreword for an explanation of Van Til's use of "earlier" and "later." Van Til is speaking covenantally in this paragraph. The earlier stage is the stage of mankind, in Adam, at the point of his disobedience. At that point, we were all under God's wrath.

238. Christ's work "comes into the picture" at Gen. 3:15.

239. Calvin, *A Treatise on the Eternal Predestination of God,* 95.

have placed themselves in the way of death. "For the nature of the whole human race was corrupted in the person of Adam."[240] How such as are chosen by God to eternal life, who are by God's secret counsel to be glorified, how, in short, the elect can yet, by historical representative disobedience, come under the wrath of God, they cannot understand.

Must we say that the wrath of God under which they rest, according to the revealed will of God, does not tell us of the real attitude of God to them? Must we say that the real attitude of God to them is revealed only in God's electing love? Must we say that the threat of eternal death to those that are the elect was meaningless because God willed, with His secret will, that they should finally be saved? The elect did actually disobey and they came actually under the wrath of God, while yet for all eternity they are under the favor of God.

Pighius here, if he desires, can use his charge of two ultimate wills in God. He may argue that, if the doctrine of foreordination is to be carried through consistently, history is naught but a puppet dance. We hold, as we are told in Scripture to hold, that the disobedience of the elect was a real disobedience and that on account of it they came under the wrath of God. For men "taught of God" it is possible to see the harmony here between the attitude of wrath, which, in this sense, the elect share with the reprobate, and the eternal attitude of God's favor to the elect only. They distinguish between primary and secondary causes. They hold to two wills in God.[241] They know there is no conflict between these wills. They know this not because they have been able to penetrate intellectually the relationship between the two. They know it by faith, and they know it intellectually so far as to see that, unless we may hold that harmony rests in God, all human experience is a farce. They do not hesitate to say to those of the mind of Pighius that only Christianity is rational, though not rationally penetrable by the mind of man.

This mode of reasoning Calvin applies to the case of the reprobate. Their case is not inherently more difficult than the case of

240. Ibid., 76.
241. Typically, the "two wills" of God are described as the decretive, by which God decrees and ordains whatsoever comes to pass, and the preceptive, which is God's revealed will, given to us in his revelation. These two are in complete harmony, although we are intellectually unable to harmonize them at every point.

the elect. How can we understand that they were first taken into a generality with the elect and said by God to be good?[242] Was not God's attitude to them displayed in that instance? Of course in God's mind there was a difference all the time. They were to him the children of wrath, even while they were pronounced good by Himself, in the earliest stage of their history. It was not some abstraction like creatureliness in them that was the object of God's favor. As concrete beings, eventually to be haters of God but not yet in history haters of God, rather, as yet in Adam good before God, the reprobate are the objects of God's favor.

But all this was conditional. God gave them, as it were, a sample of what would be theirs if they obeyed representatively in Adam. It was, as it were, a "lend-lease" proposition. How could God offer eternal life to the reprobate in Adam, if He did not finally mean to give it to them? Pighius would urge that to say that He did would be to make of God a mocker. Calvin would answer that God did it, and that it is the exact equivalent of God's threat of eternal death to the elect, which was involved in the same probationary command. That exactly is history. The Moment has significance, and can have significance, only against the background of the counsel of God. Threats and promises are real and genuinely revelatory of the attitude of God, just because of the counsel of God that is back of history. Thus "the calumny is washed off at once." We should not be surprised at the generality of the invitation to salvation. We should not argue that the general invitation reveals nothing of the attitude of God, on the ground that God's particular will is back of all.

> Wherefore, God is as much said to have pleasure in, and to will, this eternal life, as to have pleasure in the repentance; and He has pleasure in the latter, because He invites all men to it by His Word. Now all this is in perfect harmony with His secret and eternal counsel, by which He decreed to convert none but His own elect. None but God's elect, therefore, ever do turn from their wickedness. And yet, the adorable God is not, on these accounts, to be considered variable or capable of change, because, as a Law-giver, He enlightens all men

242. Van Til is here referring again to mankind covenantally in Adam.

with the external doctrine of *conditional* life. In this primary manner He calls, or invites, *all men* unto eternal life. But, in the latter case, He brings unto eternal life those whom He willed according to His eternal purpose, *regenerating* by His Spirit, as an eternal Father, *His own children* only.[243]

We are, therefore, to steer clear of Platonic abstractions. We are not to use the general offer of the gospel as an abstract idea. Schilder holds that, as a general truth, we may say to the anti-Christ or the devil that whosoever believes will be saved. But to make such a statement to the anti-Christ or to the devil as though it could involve them personally would be wholly meaningless. The anti-Christ and the devil are historically finished products. They are such as have finally disbelieved. The general gospel offer could make no point of contact with them. The conditional for them has passed. They have finally negated God and have been, or are being, frustrated by God; in their rejection of God they are epistemologically fully self-conscious. God loved the devil when the devil was an unfallen angel; God loved the anti-Christ and offered Him eternal life when he was in Adam; now that they have become the devil and the anti-Christ, God hates them exclusively. The general offer has meaning only with respect to those who are at an earlier stage of history. It has meaning with respect to the elect and the reprobate when they are, and to the extent that they are, members of an as yet undifferentiated generality.

In a non-Christian scheme of thought abstract universals and particulars stand over against one another in an unreconcilable fashion.[244] Such was the case in Plato's philosophy. Aristotle sought to remedy the situation by teaching that the universals are present in the particulars. But he failed to get genuine contact between them, inasmuch as for him the lowest universal (*infima species*[245]), was, after all, a supposed abstraction from particulars. Hence the particulars that were presupposed were bare particulars, having no manner of contact with universality. And if they should, *per impossible*, have contact with universality, they would

---

243. Calvin, *A Treatise on the Eternal Predestination of God*, 100.
244. Van Til made this point earlier, when noting that the problem of the one (e.g., universals) and the many (e.g., particulars) has never been solved in the history of philosophy.
245. In a movement from the more general to the least general, the *infima species* is the lowest limit of a species before accidental qualities are considered.

lose their individuality.[246] Pighius reasoned on the basis of such Platonic-Aristotelian assumptions. He therefore concluded that a general offer of salvation must destroy all differentiation and have universalism for its natural effect. If the general is to have any meaning, he argues, it must swallow up the particular. And if the particular is to have meaning, the meaning of the general must be denied.[247]

The whole thrust of Calvin's thought is opposed to this. For him the general and the particular are coterminous in God. That is implied in the doctrine of the ontological trinity.[248] And with this ontological trinity and the counsel of God as the background of history, it is possible to give genuine meaning to the general without doing despite to the particular. In fact the general is a means toward the realization of the particular. The very possibility of differentiation presupposes as its concomitant a correlative generality.

God as the lawgiver is working out His eternal plan. God has an attitude of favor toward the originally created good nature of man. The individual men are included in this generality. They are not contrasted with this generality as those that believe or disbelieve. It could not be said of this original promise that "the contents of this externally general message is particular and applies to the elect only."[249] Nor could we say that because this promise is conditional, "it is also particular and God in reality promises eternal life only to the elect."[250] Such, we are persuaded, is not Calvin's intention with his stress on the conditional character of the promise.

The burden of the whole matter lies in the fact that on any Platonic, or semi-Platonic, basis, the conditional can have no meaning. Only on a Christian, and more specifically only on a

246. There is a complicated argument behind Van Til's point here, but the summation is that, when that which is universal is *in the mind*, and that which is particular is *in the thing*, there has been no way given, in the history of philosophy, that would bring together what is in the mind and what is in the thing.

247. It should be noted that this is a unique, but ingenious, application of the problem of the universal and the particular. Being averse to abstraction, Van Til wants to maintain that any view that assumes that the universal can have no connection to the particular is fraught with unbiblical reasoning.

248. Since, in God, there is *both* one *and* three.

249. H. Hoeksema, *Calvin, Berkhof and H. J. Kuiper: A Comparison* (privately printed, 1928?), 32 (available online at www.prca.org).

250. Ibid.

consistently Christian, basis can the conditional have meaning. Certain as we are that this is true, certain as we are that Christianity is objectively valid and that it is the only rational position for man to hold, we are as certain that we cannot exhaustively explain the relation of the infinite to the finite. To do so would be to exhaust the being of God. In his article on Predestination, Warfield says that because Calvin believed in the freedom of God, he did not believe in the liberty of man to seek exhaustive knowledge of God.[251] Mystery, says Bavinck, is the heart of Dogmatics.[252] But it is Christian, not Platonic, mystery that constitutes this heart.

If, then, we think along the lines suggested by Calvin, we may think of the universal offer of salvation as an evidence of common grace. It is evidence of *earlier* rather than of *lower* grace. All common grace is earlier grace. Its commonness lies in its earliness. It pertains not merely to the lower dimensions of life. It pertains to all dimensions, and to these dimensions in the same way at all stages of history. It pertains to all the dimensions of life, but to all these dimensions ever decreasingly as the time of history goes on.

At the very first stage of history there is much common grace. There is a common good nature under the common favor of God. But this creation-grace requires response.[253] It cannot remain what it is. It is conditional.[254] Differentiation must set in and does set in. It comes first in the form of a common rejection of God. Yet common grace continues; it is on a "lower" level

251. Van Til is likely referring to the article in Benjamin B. Warfield, *The Works of Benjamin B. Warfield*, vol. 9: *Studies in Theology* (Bellingham, WA: Logos Research Systems, 2008), 177. Warfield references Calvin's debate with Pighius and Georgius.

252. Bavinck, *RD*, 2:29.

253. Van Til has in mind here the discussion he has mentioned of Calvin, against Pighius and Georgius, on eternal predestination. Calvin says in that treatise, "The truth of the matter is, that salvation was not offered to all men on any other ground than on the condition of their remaining in their original innocence." See Calvin, *A Treatise on the Eternal Predestination of God*, 92. By "their original innocence," Calvin is referring to the innocence of all men in Adam. Thus, there is "common grace" before the fall in that God graciously offers Adam, and thus all men, eternal life. It is not typical to speak of common grace before the fall, since common grace assumes the presence of sin. However, Van Til is attempting to show the significance and meaning of history—a philosophy of history—in light of God's eternal decree. So the "common grace" that is present at creation, and before the fall, is the common favor that God shows to all mankind, both elect and reprobate, in Adam.

254. Van Til likely emphasizes the conditionality here by virtue of Calvin's discussion in ibid., 96–100.

now; it is long-suffering that men may be led to repentance.[255] God still continues to present Himself for what He is, both in nature and in the work of redemption. The differentiation meanwhile proceeds. The elect are, generally speaking, differently conditioned from the non-elect. They are separated into a special people. In the New Testament period they have the influences of Christian surroundings brought to bear upon them. The non-elect are, generally speaking, conditioned in accordance with their desert; most of them never come within earshot of the external call of the gospel and have no Christian influence brought to bear upon them. Thus it becomes increasingly difficult to observe that which is common. We may be tempted to think of it as a merely formal something. We may, like the impatient disciples, anticipate the course of history and deal with men as though they were already that which by God's eternal decree they one day will be. Yet God bids us bide our time and hold to the common, as correlative to the process of differentiation (see Matt. 13:24–30).

Pighius would say that the universal offer of salvation must be taken as an unconditional promise that God will write His law on every heart, and we may be tempted to answer that the universal offer is formal and is, because conditional, after all only particular, but Scripture would have us use the notion of generality as a limiting concept still. Common grace will diminish still more in the further course of history. With every conditional act the remaining significance of the conditional is reduced. God allows men to follow the path of their self-chosen rejection of Him more rapidly than ever toward the final consummation. God increases His attitude of wrath upon the reprobate as time goes on, until at the end of time, at the great consummation of history, their condition has caught up with their state. On the other hand God increases His attitude of favor upon the elect, until at last, at the consummation of history, their condition has caught up with their state.[256] While in this world, though saved and perfect

255. The "'lower' level" is due to the ruin of the "common good nature" in Adam. Prior to Adam's sin, there was no long-suffering needed. Now, because of the fall, common grace presupposes God's patience with sin.

256. In other words, as history progresses, God is, more and more, calling his people to himself and passing over others, thus differentiating them according to his eternal decree.

in Christ, they are yet, because of their old nature, under the displeasure of God.

Again abstractions should be avoided. To say that God loves his people but hates their sin is to avoid the issue. Believers, in this life, are, and continue to be, both under the favor and under the disfavor of God. Sin is not an abstract something. The "new man" is responsible for the sin of the "old man." When Paul says it is no longer he but sin that dwelleth in him that performs certain actions, he does not seek to lift the "new man" from under the responsibility of the sin of the "old man." He merely means to prove that the "new man" is a genuine reality, whatever the appearance to the contrary (see Rom. 7:9–25). The idea of the old nature as a generality, as something the elect have in common with the non-elect, is still an important factor in the present situation. So, then, the ideas of common wrath and common grace must both be kept as constitutive factors in measuring the present historical situation by the Word of God.

What has been said may also help us to some extent in an intelligent discussion of the attitude of believers toward unbelievers. That attitude should, if our general approach be at all correct, be a conditional "as if" attitude. The attitude of Christ's followers is, as Christ has told us, to be in positive imitation of God's attitude. Hence we are to make practical use of the concept of "mankind in general." We are to use this notion as a limiting concept. We are not to forget for a moment that no such thing exists in any pure state. We are therefore to witness to men that in themselves they are enemies of God. We are to witness to them that this enmity appears even in such dimensions as that of counting and weighing.[257] This is done if, among other things, we build separate Christian day schools.[258]

And we are to oppose men more definitely to the extent that they become epistemologically more self-conscious. To say to the

As this differentiation increases, the conditional decreases in that more and more conditions obtain: the elect are effectually called, and the reprobate finally reject him.

257. This is contrary to Kuyper's approach. This does not mean that unbelievers cannot count and weigh properly; it means that even in their counting and weighing, they are in rebellion against God, as they assume such things exist and are possible "on their own," without need of God and his eternal plan and decree.

258. For more on Van Til's view of Christian education, see Cornelius Van Til, *Essays on Christian Education* (Phillipsburg, NJ: Presbyterian and Reformed, 1979).

anti-Christ that God loves sinners, and therefore may love him, is to cast pearls before swine. For all that, we still need the concept of "mankind in general." We are to think of non-believers as members of the mass of humankind in which the process of differentiation has not yet been completed. It is not to the righteous and to the unrighteous as fully differentiated that God gives His rain and sunshine. It is not to unbelievers as those that have with full self-consciousness expressed their unbelief that we are to give our gifts. We are to give our "rain and sunshine" as God gives them, on the basis of the limiting concept, to the as yet undifferentiated or at least not fully differentiated mass of mankind.

By thus substituting the ideas of earlier and later for lower and higher we may get something approaching a solution to the question of territories.[259] There is no single territory or dimension in which believers and non-believers have all things wholly in common. As noted above, even the description of facts in the lowest dimension presupposes a system of metaphysics and epistemology. So there can be no neutral territory of cooperation. Yet unbelievers are more self-conscious epistemologically in the dimension of religion than in the dimension of mathematics. The process of differentiation has not proceeded as far in the lower, as it has in the higher, dimensions. Does not this fact explain to some extent our attitude in practice? We seek, on the one hand, to make men epistemologically self-conscious all along the line. As Reformed Christians we do all we can, by building our own educational institutions and otherwise, to make men see that so-called neutral weighing and measuring is a terrible sin in the sight of God. To ignore God anywhere is to insult the God who has told us that, whether we eat or drink or do anything else, we are to do all to His glory. But when all the reprobate are epistemologically self-conscious, the crack of doom has come. The fully self-conscious reprobate will do all he can in every dimension to destroy the people of God. So while we seek with all our power to hasten the process of differentiation in every dimension we are yet thankful, on the other hand,

259. The "question of territories" refers to Kuyper's view that certain areas of thought and activity (i.e., "territories")—weighing, counting, measuring, logic—are religiously neutral.

for "the day of grace," the day of undeveloped differentiation. Such tolerance as we receive on the part of the world is due to this fact that we live in the earlier, rather than the later, stage of history. And such influence on the public situation as we can effect, whether in society or in state, presupposes this undifferentiated stage of development.

And this tolerance, on the one hand, and influence, on the other hand, extends, in varying degrees, to all dimensions. Because of the fact of undifferentiation we are tolerated in our religious life as we are tolerated in the field of weighing and measuring. And we have influence in the religious life as we have influence in the lower dimensions. Those who have no depth of earth yet, sometimes and in some cases, receive with joy the seed of the Word. They have a *temporal* faith (see Matt. 13:20–21). The problem of the inner ego and the more circumferential aspect of the human person, discussed by Kuyper with the help of the copper-wire illustration, need not much concern us.[260] It is not a question of psychology. Psychologically the whole individual is involved even to the depth of his being. When he receives the witness of the living God through nature about him, through his conscience within him, and by means of the preaching of the gospel, he is deeply engaged psychologically in an interpretative endeavor. But this deep psychological interpretative endeavor, by which he joins to himself all the multitudinous forms of the voice of God, is still, itself, merely the revelational voice of God. The question of his ethical response has not yet been broached.

The real question is one of epistemology and therewith of man's ethical attitude toward God. If men were fully self-conscious epistemologically they would violently suppress the psychologically interpretative voice within them. But to the extent that they are not self-conscious epistemologically, they may even taste of the heavenly gift, be made partakers of the Holy Ghost, and taste the good word of God and the powers of the world to come, and not rebel (see Heb. 6:4–6). They allow themselves to be affected by it to some extent. It is the nostalgia of the prodigal who has left the father's home but sometimes has misgivings. On his way to the far country he may halt, he may even turn back

260. See Kuyper, *PST*, 481ff.

for a distance, thinking that after all it was good and natural for a son to be in the father's home. Soon he will crucify unto himself the Son of God afresh, but for the moment the voice of God drowns out his own. He is at the moment not at all himself; he is *not yet* fully himself.

It is thus that we finally come to some fruitful insight into the problem of civil righteousness or the works of non-regenerate men.[261] It is not that in some lower dimension no differentiation, epistemological or psychological, needs to be made by believers. It is not that there is even a square foot of neutral territory. It is not that in the field of civics or justice, any more than in any other particular dimension, men, to the extent that they are epistemologically self-conscious, show any righteousness. The problem, as already suggested, faces us in every dimension.

There are non-believers who go to church, there are those who give to the cause of missions. Nor are they hypocrites, properly speaking. The hypocrite is a person who is epistemologically self-conscious to a large degree. He "joins the church" for the sake of reward. He may very well do the works of the law externally. Dillinger often walked well-dressed in fashionable society. May not a criminal give many and fine Christmas presents today to those whom he plans to murder tomorrow? He does the works of the law. Schilder makes much of the fact that the works of the law may be thus externally performed.

But the problem cannot be settled in this fashion. The very existence of the hypocrite requires us to go back of the hypocrite. To be able to act the hypocrite he must know the requirements of proper society thoroughly. How does he know the requirements of society? Because he has mingled in society and has had its requirements inscribed upon him as a demand. The very possibility of self-conscious hypocrisy presupposes an earlier undifferentiated state.[262] It is from that undifferentiated stage that we must make our beginning.

Schilder insists that we are not to interpret Paul's words in Rom 2:14 as though they meant that the heathen do the works of the law

261. This was the third point of the 1924 Synod statement on common grace, and is a point also taken up by Kuyper.

262. In other words, in order to transgress the norms of society, there must be presupposed a general knowledge of those norms.

by their own nature.[263] This is in itself true enough. Yet it is equally true that the question of general revelation is of basic importance for an understanding of Paul's words. The fact of general revelation may, and must, always be presupposed. Schilder himself allows for this possibility.[264] When seeking to explain the passage, he employs the idea of the remnants of the image of God and the idea of God's general providence. Yet he holds that the first reason for the performance of the works of the law, on the part of the reprobate, must be found in their sinful nature.[265] The sinner, says Schilder, does the works of the law hypocritically.

That is to say, Schilder would have us make a large degree of epistemological self-consciousness on the part of the non-believer the chief and primary point of departure. We shall get further in stating Paul's meaning if we make a low stage of epistemological self-consciousness our starting point. Paul is not saying that we deal with a group of people that are master simulators, having been in contact with the highest requirements of the law of God, and a group that is able to "dress as well as the best." On the contrary he is arguing that even those who have not had the special revelation of the oracles of God given to the Jews must yet be said to be sinners, that is, covenant-breakers.

All men need the justice of God, for all are sinners. Yet there is no sin unless there be transgression and there is no transgression unless there be knowledge of the law. Having not the externally promulgated law, the heathen yet have enough knowledge of the law or will of God to render them without excuse. Do some think that the wrath of God is revealed upon the heathen unjustly on the ground that they have no knowledge of the will of God? Let them realize, says Paul in effect, that the revelation of God is present with all men everywhere. Let them know that even from the beginning of history this knowledge has been about all men everywhere.

All men are responsible for the original positive revelation of God to mankind, as well as for the natural revelation that still surrounds them. Do some wonder whether that revelation of God has been persistent and insistent? Let them realize that that revelation is so close to all men as to be psychologically one with them. It is so close

---

263. Schilder, *Heidelbergsche Catechismus*, 1:87.
264. Ibid., 1:89.
265. Ibid., 1:90.

to them that, in spite of all their efforts to bury it, it speaks through their own moral consciousness. The law of God as a demand of God is written on their very hearts. The Westminster Confession does not hesitate to say that the law, not merely the works of the law but the law itself, was originally written on man's heart. And the reference given for that statement is Romans 2:14–15. To this is then added the fact that man originally had a true epistemological reaction to this revelation of God. Man was created in "knowledge, righteousness and true holiness." This original, true, epistemological reaction in paradise is in turn revelational and therefore further requisite for the sinner.

Sin has not been able to efface all this requisitional material from the consciousness of man. The very activity of his consciousness is a daily reminder to him of the will of God. Though he has tried over and over again to choke the voice of God he has not been able to do so. His evil nature would fain subdue the voice of the creation nature, but it cannot wholly do so. Involuntarily men think back, with the prodigal, to the father's home. And when the prodigal turns his face momentarily toward the father's house there comes to him the voice of approval. He may "with joy" receive the gospel though he have no depth of earth.

On the other hand, when he reasserts his true self, his self that is on the way to the swine-trough, there is still a voice pursuing him, this time the voice of disapproval. So he wavers as an unfinished product. He does the works of the law not as the devil or as the anti-Christ does them. They do them as arch-simulators of Christ and His people. The devil appears as an angel of light. Hypocrites imitate him. It is not thus that the average non-believer does them. If such were the case, the end of time would be here. If all non-believers did the works of the law primarily from their self-consciously developed evil nature they would, by force of their principle, seek to wipe all believers off the face of the earth. But "the man of sin," the "son of perdition, who opposeth and exalteth himself above all that is called God," is restrained (2 Thes 2:3–4). When no longer restrained he will attempt to make hypocrites of all unbelievers. He will work "with all deceivableness of unrighteousness in them that perish; because they receive not the love of the truth that they might be saved" (2 Thes 2:10). In punishment for their sin "God shall send them strong delusion, that they should believe a lie: that they all might be damned who believed not the truth, but had pleasure in unrighteousness" (2 Thes 2:11–12). Till such time as the "son of perdition" has not been given free power, and till such time as God has not in that connection sent a strong spirit of delusion, mankind in general is not fully self-conscious of its inherent opposition to God. The pressure of God's revelation upon men is so great that they are, from their own point of view, in a sort of stupor. With the prodigal they are on the way to the swine-trough, but with the prodigal they have misgivings in leaving the father's house. The heathen have such misgivings; those that hear the gospel may have such misgivings in a greater measure, as they taste the powers of the age to come.

In this manner the ideas of God's general providence, his general revelation, the remnants of the image of God in man, the general external call of the gospel, and man's evil nature may be brought into something of a harmonious unity. All things happen according to God's providence. That is basic. There is, according to this providence, to be a development in the direction of evil and a development in the direction of the good. These two developments grow in conjunction, in correlativity, with one another. Therefore all factors must be taken into consideration in all the problems with which we have to deal.

The general development of history, of which the two developments mentioned are subdivisions, comes about through God's presentation of Himself as He is, in varying degrees of self-revelation, to man, plus man's reaction to this presentation. God always presents Himself as He is. His attributes face man as man faces God. The revelation of God is always objectively valid. The greatest obscuration the sin of man can cast over the face of nature and his own consciousness, cannot destroy the validity of revelation. Vanity and corruption are, to be sure, seen in nature. But men ought, argues Calvin, to see even this as evidence of God's presence, of God's presence in judgment. Evil is found in man's heart. Again, even this is evidence of God's presence; man is pursued by the voice of accusing conscience. When the accusing conscience challenges the wisdom of his choice against God, the voice of God is heard again. The prodigal turns about for a moment, stands still, takes a few steps back, his conscience approving, his emotional life responding with joy; the remnants of the image of God appear even while he is on his general downward path.

In some cases the gospel call is heard. This tends to make some of those that hear it walk back a little farther still. But underneath it all the evil nature is operative. That nature accounts for the fact that all this turning and yearning is temporary and has not arisen from true faith in God. That nature accounts for the fact that the sinner will soon turn with more determination than ever toward the swine-trough. Even if he continues to do the works of the law, as well he may, he will do them more and more self-consciously for the sake of reward. Finally, he may become a worthy disciple of Satan who may appear as an angel of light to deceive, if it were possible, the very elect of God.

In this way, too, we may perhaps be on the way to seeing a bit more clearly the relation between common grace and total depravity.[266] If we stress the fact that common grace is earlier grace, it appears that it is something in connection with which total depravity shines forth in the fullness of its significance. Negatively, there is no possible toning down of the doctrine of total depravity; the attitude of favor spoken of is in no sense directed toward man's evil nature as such. It is directed toward the individual in so far as he is, epistemologically speaking, unconscious of the real significance of the path he is treading. And he is such an individual because he is a member of the mass of mankind which, in the providence of God, has not come to the climax of the process of differentiation.

Positively, common grace is the necessary correlative to the doctrine of total depravity. Total depravity has two aspects, one of principle and one of degree. The first representative act of man was an act that resulted historically in the total depravity of the race. This act was performed against a mandate of God that involved mankind as a whole; without that "common mandate" it could not have been done; without that common mandate the "negative instance" would have been an operation in a void. Thus mankind came under the common wrath of God.

266. The relationship of common grace to total depravity is a significant theological point, often misunderstood. The two doctrines are not two sides of one coin; rather, common grace presupposes total depravity. All men, in Adam, are totally depraved. In the context of that depravity comes God's common grace, applied and exhibited at various times and in various ways.

But the process of differentiation was not complete. This common wrath, too, was a stepping-stone to something further. The elect were to choose for God and the reprobate were each for himself to reaffirm their choice for Satan. The reprobate were to show historically the exceeding sinfulness of sin. Totally depraved in principle, they were to become more and more conformed in fact to the principle that controlled their hearts. They do this by way of rejecting the common call, the common grace of God. That is to say, they do it by way of rejecting God to whatever extent God reveals Himself to them. In the case of some this includes the gospel call, while in the case of most it does not. In every case, however, there is growth in wickedness on the part of those who have seen more of the common grace of God. So it appears that in every case of the historical process common grace is the correlative to total depravity.

Thus we have the "relative good" in the "absolutely evil" and the "relatively evil" in the "absolutely good." Neither the "absolutely evil" nor the "absolutely good" are epistemologically as self-conscious as they will be in the future. God's favor rests upon the reprobate and God's disfavor rests upon the elect to the extent that each lacks epistemological self-consciousness. In neither case is it God's ultimate or final attitude, but in both cases it is a real attitude. As there is an "old man" in the believer, so there is an "old man" in the unbeliever. As there are the remnants of sin in the believer, so there are the remnants of the image of God in the unbeliever. And as the "old man" in the believer does not, in the least, detract from his status as believer, so the "old man" in the unbeliever does not, in the least, detract from his status as unbeliever. Each man is on the move. He is, to use a phrase of Barth with a Reformed meaning, an *Entscheidungswesen* (a decision-making being).

Another parallel suggests itself. We are to regard the natural man as we regard nature. Or rather, we are to regard nature as we regard man. There is a parallelism between the two. They go through a similar history; they go together through the same history. They are aspects of the one course of events reaching toward the great climax at the end of the age. Both were originally created good. But it was a good that was on the move. Through the fall of man both came under the wrath of God. Nature as well as man is subject to vanity and corruption (Rom 8:19, 22).

But the vanity and corruption, which rest on man and nature by the curse of God, are also on the move. We must observe the "tendency" in both if we would describe either for what it is. Men ought, says Calvin, to be able to see the Creator's munificence in creation.[267] Men ought, in the second place, to see God's wrath upon nature. "For the wrath of God is revealed from heaven against all ungodliness and unrighteousness of men, who hold the truth in unrighteousness" (Rom 1:18). "The whole creation groaneth and travaileth in pain together until now" (Rom 8:22).

Thus there is a downward tendency in creation.[268] Men ought to conclude, argues Calvin, that history will end in judgment. When they do not see their own sins punished as they deserve to be punished, men ought to conclude that punishment is deferred, not that it is not coming. Thus there is a tendency toward a climax of wrath and a deferment of this climax in order that the climax may truly be a climax, the end of a process.

On the other hand, there is a tendency toward glory. The "earnest expectation of the creature waiteth for the manifestation of the sons of God" (Rom 8:19). In the "regeneration of all things" (see Matt. 19:28) the vanity and the corruption will be swallowed up in victory. He that would describe nature for what it actually is, must describe it as thus on the move. And so he that would describe man for what he actually is, must describe him as on the move.

Applying this to the unbeliever, who lives under earshot of the gospel call, we have the following. He must be looked at (a) as having been a member of an original generality that was good, (b) as having become a member of a second generality which is wholly corrupt in principle and is on the way to a grand climax of destruction, (c) as having become a member of that generality in the midst of which the supernatural redemptive process is operative, and as a member of a generality that lives under the long-suffering of God, which would lead it to repentance, (d) as a member of a generality that is, in some cases, crucifying to itself the Son of God

267. John Calvin, *Institutes of the Christian Religion*, ed. and trans. Henry Beveridge (Grand Rapids: Eerdmans, 1957), 1.5.1.

268. This should not be interpreted as some kind of premillennial disposition in Van Til, as the following paragraph makes clear. Rather, he speaks of a "downward tendency" with respect to the working out of evil in creation; its *telos* will be the final, consummating wrath of God.

afresh, (e) as a member of a generality in which that process of crucifixion is still incomplete.

All these generalities are presupposed in the meaning of each individual confrontation of the non-believer with the gospel; they are the correlative of the meaning of the conditional with which each one who hears the gospel is faced. All these generalities must be presupposed as still genuinely operative factors in any individual man. Not till all history is done may we drop any one of them. A fearless anthropomorphism based on the doctrine of the ontological trinity, rather than abstract reasoning on the basis of a metaphysical and epistemological correlativism, should control our concepts all along the line. A fearless anthropomorphism need not hesitate to say that the prodigal sometimes yearns for the father's house even when on the way to the swine-trough, and that the father *still* yearns for his son, the son that has broken "the law of his being."[269]

Summing up what has been said in this section, we would stress the fact that we tend so easily in our common grace discussion, as in all our theological effort, to fall back into scholastic ways of thinking. If we can learn more and more to outgrow scholasticism in our notions about natural theology and natural ethics, we shall be perhaps a bit more careful both in our affirmations and in our negations with respect to common grace. We shall learn to think less statically and more historically. We shall not fear to be boldly anthropomorphic because, to begin with, we have, in our doctrines of the ontological trinity and temporal creation, cut ourselves loose once and for all from correlativism between God and man.[270]

We shall dare to give genuine significance to historical conditional action just because we have, back of history, the counsel of God. Accordingly we need not fear to assert that there is a certain attitude of favor on the part of God toward a generality of mankind, and a certain good before God in the life of the historically

269. That is, a fearless anthropomorphism will affirm the reality that God yearns for the salvation of men.

270. In other words, our affirmation of the ontological Trinity entails that God alone is absolutely independent (*a se*), and our affirmation of temporal creation entails its total dependence on God. So there can be no ontological correlativity with respect to God and creation. God is who he is; creation is what it is, only because of who God is. When we think this way, we recognize that our fearless anthropomorphisms state, not God's ontological character as *a se*, but his covenantal character as "with us." For more on this, see the foreword.

111

undeveloped unbeliever. These assertions are not depreciatory of, but rather conditional to, a full assertion of the total depravity of the sinner. If we can say of one who is elect that he was at one point in his history totally depraved, we can, with equal justice, say of a reprobate that he was at one point in his history in some sense good.

Summing up our discussion as a whole we would stress the importance of looking at the common grace question as an aspect of our whole philosophy of history. And this requires for our day, it is our humble judgment, something of a reorientation on the question of Apologetics. Perhaps we may speak of a return to Calvin on this point. At least we hold it to be in line with his *Institutes* to stress, more than has recently been done, the objective validity of the Christian reading of nature and history.[271] Certainly no one would have hit upon the interpretation of nature and history that we as Christians have, if it had not been revealed by special grace. But this is primarily due to the fact that the natural man is blind. We dare not say that nature and history lend themselves quite as well to the non-Christian as to the Christian interpretation. That the non-Christian may present a plausible view of nature is quite true. That it is impossible to convince any non-Christian of the truth of the Christian position, as long as he reasons on non-Christian assumptions, is also true. All looks yellow to the jaundiced eye. But for all this we would still maintain, and this, we believe, is essentially Calvin's view, that he who reads nature aright reads it as the Christian reads it.

It is only when we thus press the objective validity of the Christian claim at every point, that we can easily afford to be "generous" with respect to the natural man and his accomplishments. It is when we ourselves are fully self-conscious that we can cooperate with those to whose building we own the title. God's rain and sunshine comes, we know, to His creatures made in His image. It comes upon a sinful human race that they might be saved. It comes to the believers as mercies from a Father's hand. It comes upon the non-believer that he might crucify to himself the Son of God afresh. The facts

271. The "reorientation on the question of Apologetics," of which Van Til speaks here, includes, at least, the recognition that the Christian position alone is true, and thus that the communication of Christian truth is the only communication that can be valid. Any truth that the non-Christian has and holds presupposes the truth of Christianity. It is not had or held in its own right.

of rain and sunshine, so far from being no evidence of anything in themselves, are evidences of all these things, simultaneously and progressively. Then why not cooperate with those with whom we are *in* this world but with whom we are not of this world? Our cooperation will be just *so far as* and *so far forth*. It will be a cooperation so far as the historical situation warrants.

We realize that the practical difficulties will always be great enough. We realize, too, that, theoretically, the question is exceedingly complicated. And we realize that we have a long way to go. But the direction in which we ought to work is, in our humble opinion, reasonably clear.

PART TWO

CHAPTER 4

PARTICULARISM AND COMMON GRACE[1]

I n the first lecture of this series Dr. Robert K. Rudolph[2] set forth for us the Reformed doctrine of God. He expounded the Westminster Shorter Catechism[3] definition of God as the One who is infinite, eternal and unchangeable in His being, wisdom, power, holiness, justice, goodness, and truth. This self-contained and self-sufficient Being by the sovereign act of His will created the world. And since their creation by God all things whatsoever in this world are being controlled by His providence. God controls "whatsoever comes to pass."[4]

This sovereign God gave man a task to perform. It was to till the ground, to bring out its powers, to act as prophet, priest, and king in the midst of the world that God had made. He was to engage in scientific, artistic, and philosophical enterprises of every

1. In September, 1951, the First Annual Institute of the Reformed Faith was held under the auspices of the Christ Bible Presbyterian Church of Philadelphia. The addresses given at that time were subsequently published in a booklet. The one dealing with *Particularism and Common Grace* was republished separately by L. J. Grotenhuis, Phillipsburg, NJ.
2. Robert Knight Rudolph (1906–1986) studied at the University of Pennsylvania, the Theological Seminary of the Reformed Episcopal Church (TSREC) and Westminster Theological Seminary. He studied under both J. Gresham Machen and Van Til at Westminster. For the bulk of his career (forty-nine years), he was a professor of systematic theology and ethics at TSREC.
3. Q & A 4.
4. Westminster Confession of Faith, 3.1.

conceivable sort. Such was man's cultural mandate. It was given to mankind as a whole. It was therefore a task that all men would have in common. Mankind was instructed with respect to this, its task, through its first representative, Adam. There was to be a reward for the faithful performance of it. He was to be given eternal life. And as his life when first given him was a life of perfection in a universe of perfection, so it may be thought that the eternal life that he would receive would be fullness of life with the rewards of his cultural labors all about him.

So far then we have (a) the sovereign God, (b) the universe created and controlled by God, (c) the representative of mankind confronted with the cultural mandate for all men, (d) with a reward of eternal life awaiting him on condition of love and obedience to God.

In the second lecture Professor John W. Sanderson[5] told us how Adam sinned for all mankind. He broke the covenant that God had made with him for them. "Wherefore, as by one man sin entered into the world, and death by sin; and so death passed upon all men for that all have sinned" (Rom 5:12). Thus all men come into the world as covenant-breakers. And they are as such under the *common* curse of God.

In the third lecture the Reverend Mr. George S. Christian[6] addressed us on the covenant of grace. He spoke of the immeasurable love of God, of God who so loved the world, the world of sinful, fallen mankind, that He sent His only Son into the world that whosoever should believe in Him might be saved. Again there was the note of commonness. First it was mankind as a unit that was given the common task of subduing the earth. Then mankind broke the covenant and God put all men under the curse, a common curse. After that it was Christ who came to save the *world*. And it is said that *whosoever* believeth on Him may be saved.

5. John W. Sanderson (1916–1998) was a graduate of Wheaton College, Faith Theological Seminary, and the University of Pennsylvania. He was ordained in the Bible Presbyterian Church in 1940. He served in pastoral ministry and as a professor at Westminster Theological Seminary (1957–1963), but the bulk of his career was spent in association with Covenant Theological Seminary.

6. George Spaulding Christian (1917–2008) was a teaching elder at Emmanuel Presbyterian Church (OPC) in Whippany, New Jersey. He was most well known for his essay *Let's Not Talk about a Split in the Bible Presbyterian Church* (privately printed, 1955).

PARTICULARISM

Yet it was the sovereignty of God and the particularism of the gospel that was stressed in all three lectures. The sovereign God has not seen fit to save all men. The gospel is not universally offered to all men everywhere. Millions have never heard of it. And though it is true that *whosoever* believeth on Christ shall be saved it is also true that of themselves men cannot believe. They love darkness rather than light (John 3:19). They are dead in trespasses and sins (Eph. 2:1). If they are to believe they must be made alive by the Spirit of God who takes the things of Christ and gives them to His people. It is they for whom and for whom alone Christ died. It is they and only they who were from all eternity ordained unto eternal life.

This gospel of particularism goes right back to the original plan of God. When God through Adam assigned to mankind its common task, He did so with the ultimate purpose in mind of saving a people for His own possession. God approached all mankind through one man, Adam, and by this means was effecting His purpose with respect to particular men in the future. In this intricate manner the particular and the universal are from the outset of history intertwined with one another. God approaches the mass of mankind through one man as their representative and He approaches each individual human being throughout history through the mass of mankind that has been thus approached through one man. When John Brown is born he may find himself in Africa or in Europe; he may look into the mirror and find himself to be black or white. He may be unable to play ball with other children because of infantile paralysis or he may be a better ball player than his fellows. All the factors of his inheritance and environment are mediated through, and are expressive of, the covenant relationship that God from the beginning established with mankind. All the facts of life about him speak of the mandate of God upon mankind, and therefore upon him. And all these facts also speak of the fact that mankind has, through Adam, broken the covenant with God. Thus self-consciousness for John Brown is identical with covenant-consciousness. John Brown knows he is a covenant breaker to the extent that he knows anything truly at all (see Rom. 1:18–20, 32; 2:14–15).

OBJECTIONS RAISED

It is to this scheme of things that men constantly raise their objections. Listen to what the objector has to say. "So then," he explains in triumph, "all that is done by John Brown is a farce, is it? He would have been saved or doomed no matter what he would have done. Adam had to fall or there would have been no people for your Christ to save. You want your Christ to save a *special* people. It was this *special* people that He had in mind from the beginning. He did not care for the rest of mankind. In fact your God must have hated the rest of mankind from all eternity. When you spoke of a common gift of life and a common mandate with the prospect of a common eternal life in glory, all that too was a farce and worse than a farce, was it not? God never meant to give the reprobate of whom you speak eternal life. He intended from the beginning to send them to hell for His own pleasure, regardless of what they might do.

"And as for the elect of whom you speak did not God plan to save them from all eternity? Then all their deeds are also a meaningless performance. These elect of yours would get to heaven no matter what they did. Christ would die to take away any sins they might perform. And the sins they would perform would not really be sins, for they would be done of necessity. Then why speak of these elect as being under a common curse with the reprobate? Or why speak of any curse upon any man since all men sin by necessity? And why has your Christ come into the world at all, since the elect will be saved of necessity and the reprobate will be condemned of necessity. The whole of man's moral standards are, on your basis, destroyed. Your God has no connection with anything that is moral according to the standards of civilized men."[7]

It is apparent from these words of the objector that he wants a "gospel" that is universal, that is favorable to all men. If he is to believe in a God it must be such a God as will do His best to save all men. He wants a God of love, a good God, One who is the cause of "good" and not of "evil." But then, it will be observed that the objector is bound also to follow Plato when he says: "Then God, if

---

7. This is a standard objection to the biblical doctrine of election. Van Til is using it to show the difference between thinking that is grounded in and bounded by Scripture and thinking that is grounded in unbelief.

he be good, is not the author of all things, but he is the cause of a few things only, and not of most things that occur to men; for few are the goods of human life, and many are the evils, and the good only is to be attributed to him: Of the evil, other causes are to be discovered."[8]

The "objector" then has a finite god.[9] It is this god that he substitutes for the sovereign God of Scripture. His god does not control whatsoever comes to pass, but is himself surrounded by Chance.[10] According to the Scriptures that, and that alone, is possible which is in accord with the plan of God; according to the objector *anything* is possible because possibility is beyond and above God. But to say that anything is possible, is to start with Chance. The objector has not been able to avoid assuming or presupposing something about the nature of all reality. He had to have something on which to stand in order to remove the scriptural doctrine of God, and that something on which he stands is the idea of Chance. And to interpret human experience in terms of Chance is wholly devoid of meaning.[11]

But all this has been neatly kept under cover. The objector himself is usually not fully aware of the fact that his own position involves the idea of Chance. In that case what he appeals to when he raises his objections to the gospel is "experience" and "logic." He says he experiences freedom. He asserts that this freedom enables him to initiate that which is wholly new in the world; and if this is so, it is illogical or contradictory to say that God controls "whatsoever comes to pass." The Christian, the objector asserts, holds that God is all glorious. God is full of glory in some such way as a bucket may be said to be full of water. At the same time, man, by his deed in history, by the exertions that proceed from his own choice, must seek to glorify God. That is as though he must add water to the bucket which he has himself said to be already full of water.

8. Plato, *The Republic*, in *The Dialogues of Plato*, trans. B. Jowett, 4 vols. (New York: Charles Scribner's Sons, 1885), 2:202.

9. This god is "finite" in the sense of being limited by that which is the cause of evil.

10. By "Chance" Van Til means indeterminacy. This god would be "surrounded by Chance" because he would be dependent on the cause of evil, over which he has no control, in order to respond or to act.

11. For example, suppose my human experience was to steal my neighbor's bicycle. What would that experience mean if governed by Chance? How could it be interpreted if it were completely indeterminate? It could only be something that "just happened," without meaning or value.

What is the Christian answer to such a charge as that?

Perhaps he feels the need of help. And does not the objection voiced above concern all Christians, and therefore the entire Christian church? Surely all Christians want to do justice to human freedom and responsibility; none therefore want to be determinists. It seems as though the objector is right when he says that if one is to do justice to experience and logic then one must preach a gospel which includes all men. Then the gospel cannot in any sense be particularistic. Then God must not merely offer salvation to all men everywhere, but He must have the intention of saving all men. If then all men are not saved this is, in the last analysis, due to their freedom to do that which is against the best intention and efforts of God. God's efforts are common without difference, and the differentiation among men comes in because of the ultimate choice of man. But would not this lead to indeterminism?

A CONFERENCE OF ALL CHRISTIAN THEOLOGIANS

Let us call a conference of all Christian theologians, Roman Catholic and Protestant, orthodox Protestant and modern Protestant, traditional Protestant and dialectical Protestant, and ask this conference what reply must be given to the objector. Among others present we note in particular those who speak for Thomas Aquinas, for Luther, for Calvin, for Arminius, for Schleiermacher,[12] for Ritschl,[13] and for Barth.

The First Session

What marvelous agreement there seems to be among these Christian theologians. They agree negatively against the objector that it will not do to subject God to the universe of Chance. "How terrible!" they shout. They agree positively that we must hold to God as man's Creator and Lord and that it is only through Christ that man can be saved. They also agree that human experience and human logic must be interpreted in terms of God and Christ

12. Friedrich D. E. Schleiermacher (1768–1834) is sometimes called the "father of modern theology," in part because he is the first well-known theologian to incorporate Kant's philosophy into his theology.

13. Albrecht Ritschl (1822–1889) was a liberal German Protestant theologian whose theology focused on the ethical dimension.

rather than that God and Christ must be interpreted in terms of human experience and logic.

What unison, what harmony!

But here we see that Socrates was right again. Men and gods agree so long as they talk of general principles. "But they join issue about particulars."[14] On the generalities mentioned even the objector might agree. Even he would be glad to say, as Plato said, that we must posit a *Good* that is above all the distinctions of good and evil that men make. But then it is to be understood, the objector would add, that this Good is "above all that men can say about it." It is above good and evil. It is indeterminate. It is a subjective ideal even when, as in the case of Plato, it is hypostatized and thus made "real."[15]

Kant would also agree that men must posit the idea of God as Creator and Ruler of the world, so long as it is made clear that it is impossible for the theoretical reason to say anything about Him.[16] Such a God, Kant would argue, must be an ideal of the practical reason, but cannot be known by means of the concepts of the theoretical or scientific reason. With such a God we can do justice to human experience and to logic too. For then the human mind is assumed to be a law unto itself, and therefore its "experience" of freedom is taken to be ultimate. And logic we then assume to be resting on this supposedly ultimate human experience. It therefore never pretends to make any assertions about anything that is beyond itself, Kant would say, and to talk of God as eternal is meaningless since man is temporal and has no experience of eternity. Any God that exists must be subject to the same limitations to which man is subject. If He is not, Kant would argue, then He is unknown and unknowable to man, and devoid of significance for man.

The Second Session

When thus challenged, as it were, by the objector to leave the formal introductory atmosphere of generalities and come to a

14. This comes up in Plato's *Euthyphro*, 8E, as Socrates dialogues with Euthyphro. See Plato, *Euthyphro; Apology; Crito; Phaedo; Phaedrus,* trans. Harold North Fowler, Loeb Classical Library (Cambridge, MA: Harvard University Press, 1966), 130–31.

15. Plato's "Good," because it cannot be associated with the world of experience, is the ultimate "ideal." As such, it is meant to be the ground of all other good and therefore "real," but there is no way to connect it with the particular "good things" of this world.

16. Because God is in the "noumenal," of which, according to Kant and his followers, there can be no knowledge.

discussion of particulars, the representative of Thomas Aquinas was given the floor first of all. As senior member of the fraternity he was entitled to this priority.

Surely, Aquinas argued, a synthesis must be possible between the objector and ourselves as representatives of the Christian church, for God has created man in His image. Do we not all agree on this? Therefore the reason of man, given by God Himself, must be honored as able to speak the truth in its own field. Let us listen then to Aristotle, the greatest representative of reason that has ever lived. He did not find it contradictory to believe in God. In fact he said that it is reasonable to believe in a first unmoved mover as the cause of the universe. And yet he started from experience as autonomous when engaged in his philosophical research. But Aristotle could not deal otherwise than with "essences." And theology deals with the personal God as One who *is*. So Moses must be added to Aristotle.[17] Theology must teach man that the Christian religion is only *above*, not *against*, human experience and logic.

The whole problem of the relation between the supernatural truths of faith and the natural truths of reason can be solved with Aristotle's idea of the *analogy* of being. Aristotle says there is one being, but God expresses the fullness of this being, and man expresses in a lower degree this same being. This idea of gradation or of potentiality developing into actuality solves all difficulties between God and man. It provides for the unity that reason requires (univocism) and it also provides for the diversity that the experience of freedom requires (equivocism).[18]

How marvelously authority and reason seem to have been brought together here. Here the authority of the living voice of Christ and the reason of Aristotle seem to be in perfect unison with one another.

The objector was much pleased with this representative of the Christian church. He knew, if the sentiment expressed in this first

17. Aquinas was clear about his method of doing philosophical theology. He began with a notion of reason that was thought to be universal and neutral. So he was content to borrow from Aristotle in much of his work and then to supplement that with "Moses" (i.e., revelation) when he thought it was needed.

18. There is much packed into this description. The basic point is that Thomas borrowed from Aristotle the notion that the universals are *in* the particulars (*contra* Plato), so that one can know a particular thing by the intellect abstracting the universal (form) from a thing ("a thing" is composed of form and matter). There is identity with respect to the universals, but no relation with respect to the particulars.

speech of our conference of Christian theologians would prevail, that then the gospel would be made common to men.

Why should the objector object to singing the praise *of being in general*?

To sing the praise of *being in general* would be to sing the praise of man as well as the praise of God. It would be to substitute the idea of man's participation in God and God's participation in man for the idea of creation of man by God. Thus man would not need to live by the instruction of God except as God gave him advice about the laws of the universe. Thus the idea of authority—that of good advice, not that of absolute authority— would be extolled. Thus all grace would be common because God would also need the grace or good fortune of the world of Chance about Him.[19] Here was the universalism the objector was looking for from the beginning. What was left of grace after the representative of Aquinas got through was nothing but the idea of the possibility of salvation, which possibility on Aquinas' scheme was not dependent exclusively on God after all, but also on Chance.

The Protestants agreed among themselves that it was somehow not right to join with the representative of Thomas Aquinas in his answer to the objector. With one accord they said that they must go to the Bible and not to the pope to get their instructions about the nature of the gospel and about answering the objector. Did not Protestantism recover the Bible, they asked. Are not all Protestants in agreement on this? Is not the Bible and what it teaches the end of all controversy?

THE CONFERENCE OF ALL PROTESTANT THEOLOGIANS

It is disappointing indeed that no general Christian answer could be found to give to the objector. But such was the sad situation. There was such a basic difference between the Protestants and Roman Catholics as to the source of Christian doctrine that they could not tell the objector clearly what, in the light of Christianity, was the basic error of the objector's position.

---

19. That is, whether or not man would accept God's offer of salvation was up to man, not God, and man's choice could in no way be sovereignly controlled by God—nor could it be free.

Roman Catholicism has sought to combine the word of God and the word of man in the form of tradition as the rule of faith, said the Protestant theologians. How then can it indicate clearly what is wrong in the position of the objector, who took the word of man alone as the rule of faith, they asked. So they met together in order to draw up an answer to the objector, and to show him that he needed the grace of God.

Again by the reason of seniority, the representative of Luther was first given the floor. He spoke in eloquent terms of the Scriptures as the word of God. "In terms of it alone, no matter what it teaches," he said, "we must interpret human experience. In it there is set forth, once for all, the system of truth by which men are to live."

In broad general lines he spoke of the contents of that system. He spoke of the triune God, sufficient to Himself from all eternity, causing the world to come into existence by an act of His will. He spoke of Adam and Eve in paradise and of how they were driven forth from the presence of God because they sinned against His express commandment. He spoke of men as sinners subject to the eternal wrath of God and headed for eternal doom because of their breaking of the law of God. He spoke of Christ who came into the world, who lived and died and rose from the dead. He said that those who believe in Christ should escape the wrath to come, and live forever in heaven in the presence of God and of their Savior.

At this point the representatives of Schleiermacher, Ritschl, and Barth simultaneously raised their hands asking for the floor. And when each of them in turn had spoken it appeared that there were two basically opposed conceptions of Scripture in the midst of this group of "Protestants."

They had agreed on the general statement that Scripture is the formal principle of Protestantism. But on the particulars as to how it is they disagreed. The three men mentioned stood over against the other three, the representatives of Luther, Calvin, and Arminius. The latter three said that the Bible is the direct revelation of God to man and as such contains a system of truth given once for all to men. The former three rebelled against this idea: they said that to hold such a position was worse than Romanism.[20]

20. Schleiermacher (the father of modern theology), Ritschl (the influential liberal theologian), and Barth (the neoorthodox theologian) denied the plenary, verbal inspiration and

The idea of the Bible as a direct revelation of God to man and as therefore containing a system of truth by which man must live, they contended, was to reduce the personal relation between God and man to the impersonal system of law. It is, they argued, to explain the world deterministically in terms of causes, rather than personalistically in terms of reasons. The idea of cause is a mechanical idea. To be sure, science needs such ideas as cause. But then science deals, in the nature of the case, with the relations of things within the world. It cannot say anything about the relation of the world as a whole to God.

If men wish to speak of the relation of the world as a whole, or of man, to God they must give up using the concepts of the theoretical reason. For if they use these concepts dualism always results. Men must then, as Plato did, attribute what they call "good" to a good God back of the world, and what they call "evil" to an evil God back of the world.[21] To avoid such dualism we must use the ideals of the practical reason and posit a God who is good, in whom the "good" and the "evil" of the theoretical reason are "somehow" united.

And, above all, to think of the Bible as containing a system of conceptually stated truth is to think of the atonement along legalistic lines. It is to think of God as giving men laws and of men as breaking these laws and being in consequence liable to eternal punishment. It is to think of the sufferings of Christ and His merits mechanically.[22] Men are then said to have the merits of Christ attributed to them in some such way as money may be transferred legally from one person to another.

True Protestantism, the representatives of Schleiermacher, Ritschl, and Barth argued, must start with faith in Scripture as the revelation of God. But the God of this Scripture must Himself be a faith-construct. He must be conceived independently of the systems of thought devised by man's philosophy, science, or even theology. He must be conceived as above the relative distinctions

inerrancy of Scripture. They thought such a view was an imposition of rationalism that made of the Bible a "paper pope."

21. Because "theoretical reason" must begin with experience, there is no way to posit a God who is only good; reasoning from experience requires a god who is good and a god who is evil.

22. To think of these things "mechanically," the modern theologians would aver, is to strip them of their "spiritual" meaning, since that which happens in the phenomenal world happens according to law, not according to freedom.

and differentiations of the human reason. He must therefore not be conceived as in any wise existing or as in any wise known otherwise than through Christ.

There must be no God in Himself, and no counsel of such a God according to which the course of the world is brought into existence and controlled.

There was therefore no original man, called Adam, who knew God and who broke the covenant that this God had made with him. Man, apart from his relationship to Christ, hovers on the verge of non-being. His reality consists in the fact that he is related to the Christ of whom the first Adam is but a sort of shadow.

Two things in particular these three men, the representatives of Schleiermacher, Ritschl, and Barth, wanted to stress as over against the position of Luther, Calvin, and Arminius. Both have to do with the centrality, and therefore the uniqueness, of the person and work of Christ. By enmeshing Jesus Christ in the realm of history as open to systematic interpretation by science, philosophy, or theology, the view of Luther, Calvin, and Arminius, they contended, virtually denied the very uniqueness of Christ that they were so anxious to maintain. The uniqueness and authority of Jesus Christ can be maintained, they argued, only if you introduce the notion of holy or primal history as over against secular or ordinary history.[23] In holy history God is God for man and man is man for God through Jesus Christ. In holy history God is truly free, free to turn into the opposite of Himself, free to become identical with man. In holy history man is truly free for God, free to partake of the very attributes of God. Thus there is nothing that keeps God from freely choosing man, for the man He then chooses is Jesus Christ. Jesus Christ is the electing God and also the elected man. The object of the grace of God is God Himself in man.

In the second place these three men claimed that in stressing the centrality of the person of Jesus Christ they had released the full and all-encompassing love of God for all mankind. If one holds to the idea of the Bible as the direct revelation of God, containing a system of doctrine, they said, then one cannot escape the hard

---

23. This is Kantian "dimensionalism," in which (for Barth, for example, whom Van Til mainly has in mind here) the events of history cannot, in and of themselves, be meaningful; events are meaningful only if we affirm a "dimension" that transcends the phenomena of events on a calendar. That "dimension," for Barth, was *Geschichte*, not *Historie*.

and fast dualism of some that are ultimately saved and of others that are ultimately lost. For on such a basis the love of God is not more ultimate than is the righteousness or justice of God. Therefore, on such a basis, there are those who are only the objects of the punishment of God and others who are only the objects of the love of God.

On the other hand, on the truly christological basis of Schleiermacher, Ritschl, and Barth, they contended, the reprobation of men is always reprobation in Christ. Men cannot reject Christ unless they are in Christ. They cannot sin unless they are aware of their sins as forgiven in Christ. This point of view, they argued, and this alone, can furnish the foundation for the truly Protestant doctrine of eternal security. For here is security that lies deeply imbedded in the eternal love of God. In that love all men have been saved from all eternity. They participate from all eternity in the saving work of Christ. Every idea of God as arbitrarily choosing some to eternal life and of casting others into everlasting doom is thus done away. All men, to be men, must have been men in Christ from eternity. They must have partaken in the act of revelation of God which is identical with Christ. The subject dispensing the grace of God is man himself in God and with God.[24]

In some such way as this the representatives of Schleiermacher, Ritschl, and Barth argued that they conceived of true Protestantism. They said that they had differences among themselves, and that they thought of these differences as important too. But they owned that their internal differences were as nothing in comparison with the great cleavage that separated them from Luther, Calvin, and Arminius.

For them Protestantism meant personal confrontation with God through Jesus Christ. And as long as one holds to the legalistic idea of the Bible as containing a system of truth one cannot meet God personally. Even the Romanist conception of the analogy of being, they contended, was not so impersonalistic as the orthodox Protestant doctrine of Scripture. If the representatives of Luther, Calvin, and Arminius really meant to be Protestants then why not join them in substituting the fully personal notion of the *analogy*

24. Van Til is here merging together some of the main tenets of modern theology, liberalism, and neoorthodoxy.

COMMON GRACE AND THE GOSPEL

of faith for the idea of a system of truth.[25] Then they would be free from every attack on the part of science and they would have a fully personal relationship to God.[26] They would then be able to answer the objector and yet hold to grace, even universal grace.

THE OBJECTOR AGAIN REJOICES

After the speeches of these representatives of Schleiermacher, Ritschl, and Barth, the objector was even more pleased than he had been when the representative of Thomas Aquinas had spoken. For he knew that this *analogy of faith* which these men were proposing as a substitute for the Romanist notion of the *analogy of being* was altogether in his favor. He knew that the philosophy of Kant, from which this purely "theological" idea of the *analogy of faith* had been taken, was even more hostile, if possible, to the Christian religion than was the philosophy of Aristotle on which the *analogy of being* was built. For it is of the essence of the *analogy of faith*, as proposed by these three men, the objector knew, that the ideas of God and man be thought of as correlative to one another. God is then nothing but what He is in relation to man through Christ, and man is nothing but what he is in relation to God through Christ. If the idea of correlativity between God and man was already involved in the *analogy of being*, it came to its full and final expression in the idea of the *analogy of faith*.[27]

According to the *analogy of faith*, thought the objector to himself, God apart from Christ is wholly indeterminate. How could He then have any control over man? How could He mean anything

25. Karl Barth argued that the true relationship between God and man is an "analogy of faith" in which we are confronted with the personal God. He was arguing, in part, against the Thomistic notion of the "analogy of being."

26. They would be "free from every attack on the part of science" because the "truths" to which they would hold would be beyond the phenomenal, scientific realm; they would be truths of the "noumenal," spiritual realm.

27. One example of this can be seen in Bruce McCormack, "Christ and the Decree: An Unsettled Question for the Reformed Churches Today," in *Reformed Theology in Contemporary Perspective*, ed. Lynn Quigley (Edinburgh: Rutherford House, 2006), 139: "Against the essentialism of the ancient Church, which made the self-identical element in God to consist in a mode of being which is untouched, unaffected, by all that God does, Barth said: there are no heights and depths in the being of God in which God is not already a God 'for us' in Jesus Christ. No wedge may be driven, therefore, between a being of God in and for himself and a being of God 'for us.'" But if God is *essentially* "for us," then, as Van Til says, there is a correlativity between God and man such that one cannot be what it is without the other. This view denies God's essential aseity, and thus is unorthodox at its root.

to man? Man could make God in his own image. And according to it man, apart from Christ, is wholly indeterminate. How could he sin against God except he be already forgiven in Christ? In this way man can project for himself a God who regards all men, however much they may violate His supposed commandments, as His children still. Man would, in short, project a God who would save all men if He could (save them and Himself, that is) from the unfortunate circumstances of a somehow hostile universe.

The objector laughed to himself as he thought of this conference of all Protestant theologians. He saw in this conference the means by which the gospel of the grace of a sovereign God might be most effectively destroyed from the world. If he could only get the representatives of Luther, of Calvin, and of Arminius to agree with the other three, then the church of Christ itself, the very agency that alone was preaching the gospel of particularism, would have sold itself out to the idea of common grace, grace common to all men everywhere, grace for God as well as grace for man, grace for all gods and for all men in a universe of Chance.

A CONFERENCE OF ALL ORTHODOX PROTESTANT THEOLOGIANS

The representatives of Luther, of Calvin, and of Arminius realized that they could not go along with the other three in answering the objector. They began gradually to sense the fact that the other three would preach only such a grace as is *common* grace, such a grace as the natural man himself is quite willing to accept, a grace that involves no repentance from sin. If God and man are made interdependent or commonly dependent upon a common universe then there can be no grace of God for man.

It was to point out this fact that the representative of Calvin spoke. He intimated simply that so long as one holds to the idea of interdependence between God and man in any form there could be no mention of grace. We have to come back to the system of Scripture according to which man is wholly dependent upon God because he is a creature of God, and to the idea that whatever comes to pass is controlled by God, he said.

The very idea of Scripture, he continued, would be meaningless unless it was the voice of such a God. How could we think of Scripture as the infallible and sovereign word of God if God Himself were no sovereign? How could the Scripture foretell the plan and purposes of God if He Himself were partly dependent upon forces outside Himself? It would be wholly devoid of meaning to say that God can predict what will happen if the universe is run by Chance.

"In particular," he said, "we shall have to stress that the will of man and all of its actions are genuinely significant within and only within the plan of God. And this shows," he said, "that our system of theology is a system based upon Scripture which is presupposed as being the word of God, and upon God who is presupposed as being the God of Scripture." For we cannot "prove," either deductively or inductively, or by the principle of coherence in the way that the objector would require, that man's will is genuinely significant within the plan of God. For if we did try thus to prove it, then this will of man would have to be woven into the being of God. And therewith we should be back to the *analogy of being* of Romanism or to the *analogy of faith* of the modern Protestantism of the three gentlemen who have just left us.

On the other hand, we cannot show by an appeal to experience that the will of man has genuine significance only in relation to the plan of God in the way that would satisfy the objector. For if we tried thus to satisfy the objector we would have to show that the plan of God is itself dependent upon the will of man and then there would be no plan of God in the biblical sense of the term. We need therefore to maintain that our system of truth which we set over against the idea of the *analogy of being* and over against the idea of *analogy of faith* is frankly based upon Scripture as the word of that God who controls whatsoever comes to pass.[28]

"Yet we can show negatively that unless the objector will drop his objections and stand with us upon the Scriptures of God and hold with us to the God of the Scriptures there is no meaning to his experience. Thus the law of contradiction may be used negatively as a means by which the two mutually exclusive views of life may be set apart from-one another. Thus it may be shown that if this law is to be used in the way that the objector would use it, then this very law would have no application to anything. On the assumption

28. This last sentence is a concise summary of the definitive and distinctive differences between the representative of Calvin and all other interlocutors, as Van Til will go on to show. We cannot construct our system of theology based only on induction, deduction, or experience; rather, it must be grounded, bounded, and founded only on the Word of God.

of the ultimacy of human experience, as involved in the position of the objector, the universe is a universe of Chance. And in the universe of Chance the law of contradiction has no fulcrum.[29] It is then like a revolving door resting upon chance moving nothing into nothing except for the fact that it then cannot move.

"When this has been shown to the objector, then it will appear objectively (whether he will accept it or not) that his own environment and his own heredity has all the while actually been controlled by the God of the Scriptures. Otherwise there wouldn't be any world. That is to say, it then appears that all the facts of this world, including the facts of man's own consciousness as well as the facts of his environment, must be seen in the covenantal perspective in which, as was pointed out, the Scriptures put them in order to exist at all.[30] All the facts therefore speak to all men everywhere of the fact that God once spoke to mankind in general about their common creation and confrontation by God. All the facts speak of the one event that took place at the beginning of history and therefore of the fact that God was favorably disposed toward mankind and that He offered them eternal life on condition of love and obedience to Him with their whole hearts."

It is thus, he argued, that the genuinely biblical idea of common grace to all mankind *has its foundation* at the beginning of history. It is thus also, he argued, that the genuine significance of the choice of the human individuals has its true foundation at the beginning of history. The two are interdependent. The choice of the individual man, Adam, was so overwhelmingly important that the eternal weal and woe of all men depended upon it. Such importance is nowhere else ascribed to the will of man. But such importance could be ascribed to the will of man only against the background of the fact that the sovereign God controlled whatsoever comes to pass. Without that background the will of man would have operated in a vacuum. It could have had no significance even for the individual himself, let alone for the whole of the human race.

29. That is, the law of contradiction, to be a law, requires that the universe be stable and, in some sense, predictable. But if Chance is the ultimate principle, there can be no law, because there is no stability or predictability.
30. The "covenantal perspective," as Van Til explains in what follows, includes, at least, the distinction between the ontological Trinity and creation, and the fact of Adam's covenantal representation of all mankind.

"And how, without the all-controlling counsel of God," he added, "could the consciousness of sin as it is found in every man, the consciousness of having broken the law of God, be seen for what it is? This consciousness can be seen for what it is, for what the Scriptures describe as being, only if seen in the light of the fact that God was originally favorable to mankind and that all mankind in Adam have turned against this favor of God given and offered to them.

"And how could the fact that the environment of man is anything short of what corresponds with the internal deserts of man, as utterly wicked, be explained except for the fact that God still extends favor even upon those who deserve nothing but to be cast into eternal separation from Him? How could even the punishments of God by which men are kept from breaking forth into utter violence be fully seen for what they are except as evidence of the favor of God?

"To be sure," he continued, "this general or common grace is not common in every sense. God's dealings with those who are to be in His presence and those who are to be finally driven forth from His presence is never wholly common, common without difference. From the beginning God's favor was common only for the purpose of setting before man his task and his responsibility. Commonness was from the outset correlative to difference in one common plan of God. How much more then shall common grace to sinners imply the fact that it is for the purpose of placing men before a significant choice?"

RAIN AND SUNSHINE

"When God therefore gives His gifts to men, the gifts of rain and sunshine in season, these gifts are the means by which God's challenge to man speaks forth. God's challenge means that men are asked to love God their Creator and to repent of sin and ask Him for His forgiveness. In long-suffering patience God calls men to Himself through these gifts. If they are not so conceived, then these gifts are not conceived according to their function in the plan of God. To say that the facts of rain and sunshine in themselves do not tell us anything of God's grace is to say in effect that the world and what is therein does not speak forth the revelation of God. But how can any fact in this world be a fact and be the kind of fact it is, except as revelational of the will of God to man? A fact in this world is what it is according to the function that it has to perform in the plan of God. Every fact is its function. And therefore every fact contains, in conjunction with all other facts, the covenantal claims of God upon man. *It is when seen as a part of this covenantal claim that the idea of common grace is seen for what it is.*[31]

When the sinner does not turn to God because of the challenge that comes to him through all the facts of the universe, his punishment is thereby greatly increased. The fact that the unbeliever who eventually turns out to have been a reprobate adds to his punishment because of his misuse of the gifts of rain and sunshine about him is not a proof against the idea that these facts are the gift of God's favor to him. On the contrary it were impossible that his punishment should be increased by his manipulation of the facts about him unless these facts were evidence of the undeserved favor of God in relation to him. From the beginning all the facts surrounding any man in the entire course of history were set in the framework of the covenant that God made with man. If they are in any wise separated from the framework then they become subject to the manipulation of the false logical and experiential requirements of the apostate man."

CHRIST FOR THE WORLD

"By thus placing all the facts of man's environment in covenantal perspective, the meaning of God's so loving the world that He gave His only begotten Son that whosoever should believe in Him should not perish but have everlasting life, will be seen for its breadth of sweep and for its sovereign particularity. Christ is sent to the world of sinful men. He is sent to save sinners. These sinners will ultimately show themselves to have been either elect or reprobate. They will show themselves with clarity to have been either elect or reprobate in the fact of their acceptance or rejection of Christ if confronted by Him.

"Sinners are challenged as a class to accept Christ. They are challenged through Him to undertake the cultural task that all mankind was originally given to do through Adam. Not all sinners

31. The "covenantal claim" is universal and personal, in that the triune God reveals himself through every fact. Thus, common grace "is seen for what it is," because it is seen in the light of God's clearly revealing himself, since creation, to all mankind.

are thus challenged. There is a delimitation as to the area where Christ comes to men. There are many to whom this second challenge and call does not come. This delimitation is due to the sovereign pleasure of God. All men were confronted with the cultural task and with the promise of eternal life with God at the beginning of history. When all men rejected God and broke the covenant then God did not owe any of them a second call. To be sure, He kept calling all men to repentance through all the facts about and within men. But He did not put the way of life positively before all men a second time. Many were left in the misery into which they had cast themselves through their first disobedience and fall in Adam. Yet Christ came to sinners as a class. He did not come to those who were already designated by Him as reprobate or as elect. To this class of sinners to whom He speaks through the preaching of the gospel, God says that He would have them turn unto Him and after repentance undertake the task of making all things subservient to the coming of the kingdom of God in Christ.

"The Apostle Paul tells us what God has in mind through the coming of Christ. Christ, he says, is the first born of every creature. By Him all things were created. By Him all things consist. It pleased the Father that in Him as the head of the body which is the church, all things in heaven and on earth should be reconciled to God (Col. 1:15–20).

"It is in this program of God, it is in connection with this work of Christ by which the world that was cursed of God should be reconciled unto Him for the greater glory of God, that common grace must have a part. All things in history must serve this glorious consummation. Even Satan and all his hosts must through his defeat by Christ serve the purpose of glorifying God. If men do not accept the Christ but reject Him, if perhaps they crucify the Son of God afresh, they have thereby shown sin to be exceeding sinful. Twice over, once in Adam and again in direct relation to Christ, they have refused to undertake under God, and for God, the performance of their cultural task. Twice over they have joined Satan in seeking to ruin the ultimate plan of God. Twice over they will be shown to have been defeated in their purpose. God will attain His purpose in spite of their rejection of Him both in relation to the first and in relation to the second Adam."

MAN'S RESPONSE TO THE GIFTS OF GOD

"However, God not only gives good gifts to men in general, He not only calls men with the good news of the gospel to a renewed acceptance of their original task, He also restrains the wrath of man. He keeps the negative, and therefore destructive, force of sin from breaking out in the fullness of its powers. All men everywhere are kept from working out self-consciously their own adopted principle as covenant-breakers and as the children of wrath. But none of them have reached maturity in sinning. If they had there would be no opportunity left for them to be frustrated in their evil efforts.

"For those who reject the Christ and those who have never heard of Christ, but who have sinned in Adam, are still laborers, even though unwillingly, in the cultural task of man. Being slaves to sin they are also partners in the defeat of Satan, unwilling slaves of God and His Christ. In spite of Satan's best efforts his followers are found to be contributors to the great edifice that is built by God through Him who is the first born of every creature. All the skills of those who are artificers in iron and brass, all the artistry of painters and sculptors and poets, are at the service of those who, under Christ, are anew undertaking the cultural task that God in the beginning gave to man."

THE RECIPIENTS OF SAVING GRACE

"In contrast with those who are slaves of sin and Satan, but who have to be unwilling workers in the performance of the cultural task of mankind, there are those who by the regenerating power of the Holy Spirit have been made alive from the dead. They are those who have by the power of God believed in Christ as their substitute. They are now through Him no longer subject to the wrath to come. They are now through Him the heirs of eternal life. To them the promise that God had made to mankind, the promise of eternal life in fullness of a glorified earth and heaven, shall be fulfilled.

With great enthusiasm they therefore undertake the cultural task of mankind. It is they who build the temple of the Lord in accord with the vision showed to them on the mount. The gifts of rain and sunshine they use in self-conscious subordination to their one great plan of accomplishing the cultural task that God has given to man. The master plan of their lives is therefore radically diverse from the master plan of those that are still covenant breakers. There is no common enterprise between covenant keepers and covenant breakers. That is to say there is no community project in which there is no difference of purpose.[32] The covenant keepers are in control of the situation. They are in control of the situation because they are servants of Christ. This is true even when their enemies may for the moment seem to be the lords of creation. It is the meek who shall inherit the earth. The earth and the fullness thereof belong to the Lord and to those to whom in His sovereign grace He gives it.

To them therefore belong all the common gifts of God to mankind. Yet that it may be the earth and the *fullness* thereof that is developed, the covenant keepers will make use of the works of the covenant breakers which these have been able and compelled to perform in spite of themselves. As Solomon used the cedars of Lebanon (1 Kings 5:8–10), the products of the rain and the sunshine that had come to the covenant breakers, and as he used the skill of these very covenant breakers for the building of the temple of God, so also those who through the Spirit of God have believed in Christ may and must use all the gifts of all men everywhere in order by means of them to perform the cultural task of mankind.

"How beautifully," the representative of Calvin said, "all things thus fit together according to the plan of God. Though the system that we thus construct is still, as noted before, only an analogical system, and it is therefore true only to the extent that it actually re-expresses the revelation of the word of God, yet we can see something of the symmetry of the truth of God. And we can see how radically different the system of Scripture is from the system of the objector. Both systems have in them an aspect of particularity and an aspect of universality. The system of the objector, and of the modern Protestant, has such universality as involves the identity of God and man. It has common grace which is common, but which is not grace. At the same time this system has such particularity as to destroy the very idea of unity or systematic coherence alto-

---

32. Notice Van Til's qualifying statement: "there is no common enterprise," in that "there is no community project [of believer and unbeliever] in which there is no difference of purpose."

gether. It has common grace which comes to such as have nothing in common because they live in total isolation.

"In contrast with such a system we as believers in the word of God and in the God of the word presuppose this word and this God.[33] We therefore presuppose the internal and eternal harmony between unity and diversity which lives within this internally self-complete God. It is on the basis of the presupposition of this God and of this word of God that there is both genuine individuality and genuine universality in the created world. Only on the basis of this presupposition can unity and individuality stand in relationship with one another without destroying one another. When we stress the commonness of the cultural task given to man, when we stress the commonness of the curse of God on man, the commonness of the non-saving grace of God to man, the commonness of the offer of the gospel to men, the commonness of all those who by birth are in the covenant of saving grace that God has made with believers and their seed, this commonness does not in the least tend to reduce the genuine significance of the particular. On the contrary, this commonness is required in order that the process of particularization may be accomplished.

"The commonness is one of the two indispensable factors of the covenant which God has made with mankind. The other factor is the genuineness of the choice of man. And through the two factors operating in dependence upon one another God accomplishes His one great purpose of glorifying Himself through the deeds of men. It is His all-encompassing plan in relationship to which and within which the course of history in its process of differentiation takes place. The choices of men therefore take place and have their significance in relation to the task that God has assigned to mankind as a whole. These choices are either an acceptance or a rejection of the responsibility of performing this task. But both the acceptance and the rejection take place in relation to the same task. And there would be no such thing as a common task in relationship to which the choices of men could have their genuine meaning unless there were one plan of God according to which

33. Van Til's method recognizes the two *principia*, or foundational principles, of Christianity—the foundation of existence (*principium essendi*) is God; the foundation of knowledge (*principium cognoscendi*) is the revelation of God.

all things come to pass. On the objector's basis there would be no true commonness in history.

"On the other hand there would be no truly significant choices of men, either by way of accepting or by way of rejecting the common task of mankind unless these choices are themselves subordinate to the one plan of God. There would be nothing in relationship to which human choice could take place if it were not for the common plan of God back of all things, and if it were not for the common task that God according to this one plan has set for men. Without this all things would be indeterminate. There would be and could be no culture, no civilization, no history.[34]

"Thus then we return to the particularism of the gospel, that was so greatly stressed in the other lectures. It is not to tone down this particularism but rather to support it and to show it in the breadth of its significance and in the depth of its foundation that we dealt with common grace.

"There is first the self-contained, eternally self-sufficient God. By His sovereign will this God created one world and through His providence He controls and leads this world to the end for which He has created it. At the beginning of the history of this world He created one human pair from whom all men were to spring. And through the first man, Adam, He dealt conditionally with the whole human race. Through Adam He confronted the entire human race with one cultural task. It was in relationship to this one task that Adam, representing all men, made his choice. His choice was therefore significant not in spite of, but because of, the fact that it took place in precisely such a situation and in such circumstances. What seemed to the objector to be determinism thus turns out to be the very condition for freedom and significant choice. If there was to be determinate experience for man it could not take place in a vacuum. It could take place only in relationship to the principle of unity back of all history, namely, the counsel of God, and in relation to the principle of unity within history, namely, the common cultural task set before man.[35]

34. Because culture, civilization, and history require the progress of *causality*, which indeterminism (Chance) cannot provide.

35. Van Til is stating here what is affirmed in the Westminster Confession of Faith, 3.1: "God from all eternity, did, by the most wise and holy counsel of His own will, freely, and unchangeably ordain whatsoever comes to pass; yet so, as thereby neither is God the author

"And so down through the ages each time the will of man is asked to function it functions in relation to the original cultural task that was given to mankind as a whole. For that cultural task continues to speak through every fact of man's environment. It speaks always to all men. It speaks more narrowly and more intensely to those to whom the gospel of saving grace is offered. It speaks still more narrowly and still more intensely to those who are born within the sphere of the covenant of saving grace. And as man's response to the original challenge was ultimately in the hands of the sovereign God and plan, so the acceptance or rejection of this task by men still rests upon the sovereign will of God. It is God that wills man to will and to do what is required of him.

"Thus the common task, the common curse, the common grace, the common call to the gospel, and a common participation in the promises of the covenant of grace are the background in relationship to which man's original disobedience, his continued rejection of God in the face of the facts within and about him, his rejection of Christ when called to Christ, and his breaking of the covenant have their significance. And thus a true biblical commonness is seen to be involved in a true particularism of the gospel of God."

The Lutheran and the Arminian Leave

At this point in the long address of the representative of Calvin those who stood for the views of Lutheranism and Arminianism raised their voices in protest. For a while it had seemed to them that things were not going so badly. But then when it appeared that only such a commonness was to be allowed as would fit within ultimate particularism of the gospel, they could keep silent no longer.[36]

Even though it was clearly shown to them that unless one held to such a concept of commonness as is correlative to, and therefore necessarily implied in, particularism, he will be carried on to commonness without difference and to difference without commonness: they were not satisfied. Said the representative of Luther: "Calvinism emphasizes the sovereignty of God in such a one-sided

---

of sin, nor is violence offered to the will of the creatures; nor is the liberty or contingency of second causes taken away, *but rather established*" (emphasis added).

36. Remember what Van Til said above (p. 119): "God approached all mankind through one man, Adam, and by this means was effecting His purpose with respect to particular men in the future."

141

manner that the countenance of grace is virtually obliterated."[37] Modern Calvinists teach with Calvin that "the purpose of the written Word is not to lead all men to faith and salvation, but to harden the hearts of the majority of the hearers."[38] "But over against the idea of the sovereignty of God, in which we too believe, we must place the counterbalancing notion of man's freedom. We must therefore say that God intends to save all men through Christ and that Christ died for the purpose of saving all men. Particularism, in whatever form it appears, is founded not on the Word of God, but on human speculation as to the will and work of God."[39] "But we know that though God in Christ intends to save all men, God's purpose is not accomplished in a part of mankind (Jn 3.18: 'He that believeth not is condemned already, because he hath not believed in the name of the only begotten Son of God')."[40]

The representative of Arminius agreed with this position. He spoke of it as a balanced position, a position in which justice was done to both God and man. Both the Lutheran and the Arminian were sure that when such a position was presented to the objector it might be expected that he would drop his objections and accept Christianity for himself. For the objector, they argued, was after all a reasonable person, and a "reasonable person" cannot refuse to admit that the Scriptures are the word of God, and that what they teach is true.[41]

Meanwhile, the objector was again rejoicing. He had been very sad when the representative of Calvin had spoken. He realized much better than the Lutheran and the Arminian did that grace is no more grace if God who must give the grace must Himself be dependent on man, and that the freedom of man is no longer freedom when it is cut loose from the plan of God as the only atmosphere in which it can function. The Lutheran and the Arminian did not want particularism. For it they substituted a common grace by which Christ died for all men with the intention of saving them all. But on this basis God's purpose may be and is foiled by men.

On this basis God Himself is involved in the realm of possibility: how then can He even make salvation possible for any one man,

---

37. Franz Pieper, *Christian Dogmatics*, 4 vols. (St. Louis: Concordia, 1950), 1:463.
38. Ibid., 1:275.
39. Ibid., 2:26.
40. Ibid., 2:27.
41. Cf. ibid., 1:310.

let alone making it possible for all men? If God is not the source of possibility then He cannot make salvation possible for men: and if He is the source of possibility then He is the source because He is in control of all actuality.[42]

The objector was glad when he saw that the Lutheran and the Arminian were once more following the road of the *analogy of being* of Romanism and of the *analogy of faith* idea of modern Protestantism. To be sure, he realized that they were doing it inadvertently. He realized that they meant to hold to the grace of God. He realized that they did not want to obliterate the difference between the being of God and the being of man as is done in part in the Romanist and completely in the modern positions. None the less he rejoiced when he saw that the Arminian and the Lutheran were willing to introduce such a notion of common grace as tended to turn into the same destruction of grace as is involved in the Romanist and especially in the modernist Protestant views. The Lutheran and Arminian types of universalism, according to which a finite God does the best He can to save men, by making it possible, so far as He can, that they should be saved has in it a tendency toward the identification of God and man. And having in it this tendency toward the identification of God and man it at the same time has in it a tendency that leads to the destruction of the significance of the will of man.

The objector realized all this. And so at last he was left alone with the representative of Calvin.

Only in the Reformed faith is there true commonness and true particularism. The particularism of Calvin's view cannot possibly be supplemented with the universalism of the Lutheran and Arminian view. Each system has its own particularism and its own universalism. The particularism of the Reformed faith requires a universalism that is based upon the Creator-creature distinction.

The particularism of the system of the objector requires a universalism in which there is no difference between God and man. The same must be said of the particularism of the modern Protestantism of Schleiermacher, Ritschl, and Barth. Romanist theology seeks to

42. That is, once one concedes that the free choice of man is in no way a part of God's plan (since if it were, it could not be free), then whether or not someone responds to what God has done is not up to God; it is, in the end, subject to Chance. It may or may not happen, but God has had no hand in its actuality.

143

occupy middle ground between Christianity and paganism. Then as to orthodox Protestant theology it is in the Lutheran and in the Arminian systems that there is some measure of non-Christian universalism or commonness, in the idea of Christ dying for all men and making salvation possible for all men. Here God is supposed to have the same attitude toward all men without difference. But the price the Lutheran and the Arminian pay for this identity of attitude is that of God's almighty and all-comprehensive control of all things. If the particularism of the Lutheran and the Arminian view is to be maintained, then God has to limit Himself when He creates man with a full will of his own. And so when God gave His commandments to men He was not asking them to react to a situation over which He had full control. He was really only able to give them good advice as to how best to get along in the universe. So man's will, in disobeying the law, was not really disobeying the law of God but making an exception to the orderly course of the universe. Therefore God could not make possible the salvation of man; He did not control the universe; He could do His best in the situation, but the situation was not fully under His control.[43]

Realizing all this the objector was finally compelled to face the choice between his own position and that of Scripture and the God of Scripture. Neither the Lutheran nor the Arminian was willing or able, according to his adopted principles, squarely to challenge the unbeliever and give him a reason why he should change his position.[44] The difference between the Christian and the non-Christian position could not be and was not clearly and fully made out except by Calvin. But at last it appeared that if there is to be true challenge of the natural man by the gospel of the sovereign God then the particularism of this gospel must be supported by a commonness of the call of God to all men everywhere. Common grace must support special or saving grace; saving or special grace cannot be adequately presented except in relationship to and in connection with common grace. Together they form the covenant framework in which the sovereign God deals with man.

---

43. This view, we should note, is the majority opinion of evangelicalism. In its more sophisticated form, it goes by the name of Molinism.

44. Once an element of neutrality (as in Romanism) or autonomy (as in the Lutheran/ Arminian view) is conceded, then it is impossible to challenge unbelief at its root, since both neutrality and autonomy are integral to unbelief. This is why the objector is not troubled by any of the positions represented, except the Reformed one.

CHAPTER 5

COMMON GRACE AND WITNESS-BEARING[1]

"Ye are my witnesses," said Jehovah God to Israel through the mouth of His prophet Isaiah. "This people have I formed for myself; they shall show forth my praise" (Is 43:21). In those words is summed up the whole task of the people of God in this world.

The New Testament through Peter tells us the same: "But ye are a chosen generation, a royal priesthood, an holy nation, a peculiar people; that ye should show forth the praises of him who hath called you out of darkness into his marvellous light" (1 Pt 2:9).

WE WITNESS TO THE UNBELIEVER

If God's people must bear witness of God, how did they come to be equipped for this task? The answer is that they have been "formed" by God for this purpose. They have not chosen this task. They have been chosen for it. They were not of themselves ready to obey when called to this task. Their hearts too were "deceitful above all things, and desperately wicked . . ." (Jer. 17:9). They were

---

1. Reprinted by permission from *Torch and Trumpet*, December, 1954–January, 1955.

of a piece with those who walk "in the vanity of their mind, having the understanding darkened, being alienated from the life of God through the ignorance that is in them, because of the blindness of their heart; who being past feeling have given themselves over to lasciviousness, to work all uncleanness with greediness" (Eph 4:17–19).

From this vain conversation received by tradition from their fathers, they have been redeemed "with the precious blood of Christ." And this Christ was Himself "foreordained before the foundation of the world" for this task of redeeming His people (1 Pt 1:20). So they are "chosen in him before the foundation of the world" (Eph. 1:4).

THE UNBELIEVER CHALLENGES OUR WITNESS

The Christ chosen to redeem them and they chosen to be redeemed by Christ! "What a neat little circle," someone will say. Your Christ came to save only you, your own little group of Calvinists, or at best your own group of Fundamentalists. Is that to the praise of the glory of His grace? Your Christ died for the elect only; is your witnessing for God limited to telling the world this fact? Why should the world be interested in such news as that? Have you no message of salvation for the world? Will you simply tell men that they are reprobate? Will you tell them that God intends to send them to perdition regardless of what they do? A "peculiar people" (1 Peter 2:9)! Indeed you are. You have a God who "appoints" men to eternal death or "elects" them to eternal life irrespective of their good or evil deeds. I dare you to preach on John 3:16. You are morally a Pharisee if you say that "whosoever will" may come. You have no love for men in your hearts. Or if you have, then you flatly contradict yourself. You say that whosoever will may come but you know that they cannot will to come. You ought to try preaching in a cemetery and see what results you have.

Seeking to satisfy this objector you assure him that God does not deal with men as with sticks and stones. According to our doctrine, you tell him: Man has lost, through Adam the first man, true knowledge, righteousness, and holiness which he originally had. He has lost what we call the image of God in the narrower sense.[2]

2. The image of God "in the narrower sense" includes, as Van Til just said, true knowledge, righteousness, and holiness (Col. 3:10; Eph. 4:24). Those were lost at the fall. But man

146

But he has not lost his rationality, his sense of moral responsibility and ability to will freely according to his nature.[3] Man's freedom and the contingency of second causes, you tell him, are not taken away by the idea of election.

But the objector is not satisfied. He asks: "Do you not hold that even Adam, though created with this true knowledge, righteousness, and holiness, *had* to sin? Was not the idea of his fall a part of the plan of God? Was not the Christ who should redeem your sinners chosen for that very purpose before the foundation of the world? And yet your Christ came only because of sin did He not? So in order that you might be redeemed in Him from sin unto good works, your God must have planned that you should be sinners. Is that not true?"

. . . Perhaps you will hesitate for a moment here. You know that sinners *are* dead and unable to come to life. You know that according to Scripture man is ethically bound to sin. He has no ethical free will by which, of himself, to accept the gospel offered him.[4] So you say that the case of Adam was different? Adam was free not to sin and free to sin?[5] Is it not because of his abusing this freedom that the slavery of sin has come upon all men? Yet you know that it was in accord with God's counsel that Adam should sin.

Try as you may, you soon discover that you cannot present your position without seeming to the man to whom you are speaking to be contradicting yourself. And try as you may to avoid it, you find that in answering the seemingly limited objection of your inquirer with respect to the matter of salvation in Christ, you must bring into the picture the whole idea of the plan of God controlling all things of history and the place of man as a moral and rational creature in this plan.

If you do not see this yourself, your questioner will soon force you to see it. He will push you back, from the question of Christ dying

---

continued as the image, in the broad sense, in that he continued as a covenant creature, knowing God and owing him all honor and thanks (Rom. 1:21–22).

3. In true Reformed fashion, Van Til makes clear that the will is what it is according to the nature of the one whose will it is. Even after the fall, man freely chooses what he wants. But he chooses according to his nature, which invariably wants sin.

4. Notice here that fallen man has "no *ethical* free will by which, of himself, to accept the gospel" (emphasis added). Though free to do what he wants to do, man will always want to do that which is contrary to God's will and character.

5. Before the fall, Adam's will was not enslaved to sin, so he was able freely to choose to obey God or to disobey him. In that way, the will of those who are redeemed are like Adam's pre-fall will, in that the redeemed can choose to obey or disobey.

for the elect only and yet being preached to all men, to the idea of this Christ as the Son of God, and the Logos, the Creator of the world, and the sustainer of it. He will say that if Christ is Himself God and if, with the Father and the Holy Spirit, He has from all eternity determined whatsoever comes to pass (thus determining that only some men shall be saved), then His weeping over Jerusalem (Matt. 23:37; Luke 13:34), and His bidding all that are weary and heavy laden to come to Him (Matt. 11:28), is but a farce and a sham. It is ethically reprehensible for Jesus to call man to Himself, if from all eternity He has determined that they shall reject Him. He may perform miracles before them in order to prove His divinity and in order to have them believe His message and yet He is also responsible for the words:

> But though he had done so many miracles before them, yet they believed not on him: That the saying of Esaias the prophet might be fulfilled, which he spake, Lord, who hath believed our report? and to whom hath the arm of the Lord been revealed? Therefore they could not believe, because that Esaias said again, He hath blinded their eyes, and hardened their heart; that they should not see with their eyes, nor understand with their heart, and be converted, and I should heal them. (Jn 12:37–40)

Christ performs miracles before their eyes so that they might believe, and yet He hath blinded their eyes and hardened their hearts so that they cannot believe. Is not that the plainest contradiction? the objector will say.

And then there is the point of the cosmic significance of Christ. Christ died to save only the elect, and yet Christ died "that in the dispensation of the fullness of times he might gather together in one all things in Christ, both which are in heaven and which are on earth" (Eph 1:10). "For it pleased the Father that in him should all fullness dwell; and, having made peace through the blood of his cross, by him to reconcile all things unto himself; by him, I say, whether they be things on earth, or things in heaven" (Col 1:19–20). So your Christ came to save the "world" yet not to save us. Do we not count for anything? Are we not part of the world? Or are you better than we?

Such then is the nature of the objection to the message of Christianity that, as Christians, holding to the Reformed faith, we are bound to meet. Your Christianity, the objector says, insults the intrinsic value and right of human personality. Your Christianity reduces man to the level of the machine. The God of Christianity is an arbitrary being, electing or rejecting men as He pleases apart from the actual merits of men. Even the Christ you offer, men say, contradicts Himself when He offers Himself to all sinners, since He as God intends to save only some of them.

HUMILITY IN OUR REPLY

Now what shall we say by way of response to this charge? In the first place we shall, of course, remember that all that we have received has been by grace. And if those who hold the Reformed faith do greater justice to the idea of God's grace in the salvation of sinners, then they ought to be the humblest of all men. They ought to enter most sympathetically into the mind and heart of him who makes this objection. Did they not themselves kick against the pricks and rebel against the overtures of God's grace?

And this attitude of humility holds over against those who with him name the name of Christ, as well as over against the unbeliever. With Bavinck let us say that all true Christians are at heart Augustinian[6] and with Warfield let us say that every Christian who calls out unto God in anguish of heart is really a Calvinist.[7]

NAY BUT—O MAN

But if we must follow the examples of Augustine and Calvin on the point of humility, shall we not also follow them when, in answer to the objector, they quoted Paul saying: "Nay but, O man, who art thou that repliest against God? Shall the thing formed say to him that formed it, Why hast thou made me thus" (Rom 9:20)? Submit yourself to God. Then you shall be saved and your works shall follow after you. If not, you will be lost and the profit of your labor will be given to the meek who shall inherit the earth.

6. Bavinck, *RD*, 2:377.
7. Benjamin B. Warfield, *Faith and Life* (Bellingham, WA: Logos Research Systems, 2008), 150.

That is the central point of our witness unto men. In the pride of their hearts, they worship and serve the creature, that is, themselves, more than the Creator (see Rom. 1:25). The natural man must be challenged in this, his assumed autonomy. He must be compelled to look into the face of God.

GENERAL REVELATION—ALL KNOW GOD

Men must be told that the revelation of God round about them and the revelation of God within their own constitution is clear and plain, rendering them without excuse.

> For the invisible things of him from the creation of the world are clearly seen, being understood by the things that are made, even his eternal power and Godhead; so that they are without excuse, because that, when they knew God, they glorified him not as God, neither were thankful; but became vain in their imaginations, and their foolish heart was darkened. (Rom 1:20–21)

All men know God. Every fact of the universe has God's stamp of ownership indelibly and with large letters engraved upon it.

All men know not merely that a God exists, but they know that God, the *true* God, the *only* God, exists. They cannot be conscious of themselves, says Calvin, except they be at the same time conscious of God as their creator.[8] This general revelation of God stays with man whatever his attitude toward God may be. When he sins against God, he must sin against this God whom he knows. Otherwise sin would be sin in a vacuum. Even in the hereafter, the lost and the evil angels still know God.

NONE KNOW GOD

Yet these same men to whom we must testify that they know God, must also be told that they *do not* know God (1 Thess. 4:5). They walk in the midst of this world which is an exhibition house of the glories and splendors of God, full as it is of the works of his

---

8. See John Calvin, *Institutes of the Christian Religion*, ed. John T. McNeill, trans. Ford Lewis Battles, Library of Christian Classics (London: SCM Press, 1960), 1.1–2.

hands, and they ask, mind you, *whether* God exists. They profess to be open-minded on the question. They say that they will follow the facts wherever these may lead them. But invariably they refuse to follow these facts. They constantly conclude that God does not exist. Even when they conclude that *a* god exists and that with great probability, they are virtually saying that God does not exist. For the true God is not surrounded by, but is the source of possibility. He could not possibly not exist. We cannot intelligently think away God's existence.

When working in the laboratory as scientists, men act as though they are not dealing with materials that belong to God. They are like a thief who, entering into your home and exploring all kinds of things within it, claims that the question of the ownership of the house is of no concern to him. They are like those who go hunting in a woods clearly marked "No Gunning," without a permit from the owner.

How absurd, says the objector. Do you mean to say that men really know that they are creatures of God, and that there is punishment awaiting them if they are not thankful and obedient to Him and yet pretend to be looking for Him if haply they may find Him? Do they know God and yet not know Him? How contradictory, how utterly absurd is this religion which you are asking me to believe. Your Bible is full of contradiction. It says that man is made in the image of God, with freedom to choose for or against God. Yet you say that man has no freedom; he simply *must do* what his God has determined shall be done. You say that by virtue of man's creation in the image of God, he knows God, and at the same time you say that these image bearers interpret all things amiss since they do not know God."

The answer is again: "Nay but, O man, who art thou that repliest against God?" If you do not accept this God, you are like a man swinging his arms in a vacuum.

GOD'S ATTITUDE

Once more: Not only do all facts reveal God but they, in revealing Him, manifest *His attitude toward men. God is love.* He loves Himself above all else. He loved Himself from all eternity when He had as yet made no creatures to love. But when He made creatures, He made them lovable like Himself. He loved them because in loving them, He loved Himself above all else. He made man perfect. And loving mankind, He offered them eternal life. It was seriously meant. It was no farce. All men disobeyed God. All came under His wrath and curse. God continued to love Himself; He therefore had to punish every insult to His holiness.

THE COMMON CURSE

To be sure, He had from all eternity chosen for Himself a people in Christ and He had from all eternity chosen Christ to redeem a people for Himself. Yet when those who are the elect of God, together with all men, were disobedient to God, they were under His wrath. So real was this wrath and so serious the threat of eternal punishment, that, if they were to be saved Christ had to be punished in their stead.

Those then whom God loved with an everlasting love, He at the same time regards as objects of wrath because of their sin.

How absurd, says the objector! How contradictory! Your witness for Christianity makes no sense to a self-respecting, intelligent person.

The objector has the same objection all the time. It is to the effect that we are insulting the dignity of human personality. We are running roughshod over his moral sensibilities and over the legitimate claims of his power of reason. Is he to be asked to believe that human personality is thus absolutely determined by the creation and the all-controlling providence of God?

LAW WRITTEN IN HEARTS (ROM 2:14–15)

To add insult to injury, the Bible tells us that all men as they know God, in that knowledge know the difference between good and evil. The requirement of God comes clearly home to the consciousness of man. In this sense the law of God is written in his heart. For every fact in revealing God requires man to use it to the glory of God. If the world is the Lord's and the fullness thereof (Ps. 24:1) then God wants man to own His sovereign sway over all things. He wants him not to act at any point as though he did not need to recognize God's ownership.

LAW NOT WRITTEN

At the same time the Bible says to these men that they do not have the law of God written in their hearts. According to the promise of God to Jeremiah (Jer 31:31) He will write His law upon the hearts of His people. Then they will be able to say: "O, how love I thy law" (Ps. 119:97). Man the sinner is told that he cannot know the truth and cannot love righteousness. Sinners are said to have their understanding darkened and to be enemies of God at the same time that they are told that they do know God and that they have the knowledge of right and wrong. And each time, the natural man is challenged to forsake his own judgment and submit to the judgment of God as He speaks in Scripture.[9]

COMMON GRACE

But what, you ask, does the question of *Common Grace* have to do with all this? Most of you will anticipate the reply. In the question of common grace there confronts us the same sort of situation that we have with respect to all other teaching of Scripture. Common grace presents us with a teaching that seems to contradict other teaching of Scripture.

Let us take the first and main point of the pronouncement made by the Synod of the Christian Reformed Church in 1924. In this first point mention is made of a favorable attitude of God to mankind as a whole, without distinction between elect and reprobate. As God was favorably disposed to the human race before the fall and offered the race as a whole eternal life,[10] so even after the fall God gives His good gifts to men everywhere, thereby calling them to repentance and to performance of their task. The Christian view of God in relation to man must always begin, as Berkhouwer has emphasized, from this idea that God at the beginning of history was favorably disposed to mankind.[11] And then in amazement we note that even after the fall, when mankind as a whole has become

9. This last sentence gets to the root of the objector's objections. Either one trusts one's own presumedly autonomous reason or one subjects that reason to the mind of God, as that mind is revealed in his Word.

10. By this point, it should be clear that Van Til is referring here to the existence of mankind *in Adam*, who was our covenant head and representative.

11. See G. C. Berkhouwer, *The Providence of God* (Grand Rapids: Eerdmans, 1952), 75ff.

153

the object of His wrath, God still continues to give good gifts unto men, and by these gifts He calls them to repentance. "Or despiseth thou the riches of his goodness and forbearance and long-suffering; not knowing that the goodness of God leadeth thee, (that is, is calculated to lead thee) to repentance" (Rom 2:4)?

Now how can this universal call to repentance be harmonized logically with the doctrine of election? God did not intend that all men should repent. Instead He intended from all eternity that some should not repent. How could they repent unless they heard the gospel of salvation through Christ? And to many millions of men this gospel was never offered. Many never heard of that only name by which they must be saved; and that is surely God's doing. The church is, no doubt, at fault if it is not zealous in its missionary enterprise. Ultimately, however, it was God's doing that millions of men lived in the darkness of heathendom and never heard the word of life.

But you say: "Paul does not assert that they were called to repentance in the sense that those who are confronted with the gospel are called to repentance unto eternal life." Even so the problem remains: How can God have an attitude of favor unto those men whom He so obviously has not included in the number that could possibly be saved through the gospel of the blood of Jesus Christ?

Well, the answer is that we cannot comprehend how it is possible, but the Scriptures reveal it to be true. And so we must learn to say to ourselves and to take seriously the words that, in following Paul, we say to the unbelievers: "Nay but, O man, who art thou that repliest against God?"

And what does this mean for us as Christians of the Reformed faith?

NOT WHAT IT MEANS TO BARTH

In the first place it means that we cannot join Karl Barth in reducing God as He is in Himself to a relation that He sustains to His people in the world.[12] Barth virtually seeks to meet the objector's charge that Christianity involves a basic contradiction by rejecting the idea of God as He is in Himself and of God's counsel as controlling all things in the world. He says that Calvin's doctrine of

---

12. See footnote 27 in the previous section.

God's counsel must be completely rejected. Only when it is rejected, is the grace of God permitted to flow freely upon mankind. And that means that God's love envelops all men. To be sure, for Barth there is reprobation but it is reprobation in Christ. The final word of God for all men, says Barth, is *Yes*. It matters not that men have not heard of the gospel of Jesus of Nazareth. For Jesus of Nazareth is not, as such, the Christ. All men are *as men*, of necessity in Christ. All grace is universal or common grace.[13]

From the historic Christian point of view this is simply to say that the concept of grace is so widened as no longer to be grace at all.

How truly Herman Bavinck anticipated, as it were, this most heretical of heresies of our day when he pointed out that in the last analysis one must make his choice between Pelagius and Augustine. The grace of God as Barth presents it is no longer distinguishable from the natural powers of man. All men to be men, says Barth, must have been saved and glorified from all eternity in Christ.

This is how Barth would meet the objection against the idea of the sovereign grace of God. There is no longer any sovereign God and therefore there is no longer any grace.

COMMON GRACE ACCORDING TO ROMANISM

In the second place there are the Roman Catholics. To be sure, they have not gone to the extremes of Barth or modern liberal Protestantism. They have not wholly reduced the being of God to a relationship to mankind. They have not, in modern Kantian style, made of God a projection into the void. Even so, they have no sovereign God. Their God does not control whatsoever comes to pass. For in their view man has ultimate freedom to set at naught the purposes of God. God, therefore, cannot reach the individual directly and determine his will and destiny. God can only reach *toward* the individual by means of *classes*.[14]

13. Van Til works through Barth's theology in a number of places. For a fuller explanation of this paragraph, see Cornelius Van Til, *Christianity and Barthianism* (Philadelphia: Presbyterian and Reformed, 1962); Van Til, *The Great Debate Today* (Nutley, NJ: Presbyterian and Reformed, 1971). For an excellent analysis of the differences in theology and focus between Van Til and Barth, see Edmund P. Clowney, "Preaching the Word of the Lord: Cornelius Van Til, V.D.M," *Westminster Theological Journal* 46 (1984): 233–53.

14. Van Til is likely here remembering Bavinck's discussion in *RD*, 2:545ff.

God cannot, on the Romanist view, unmistakably make His imprint of ownership upon man. The image of God in man does not reach down into the penetralium of the consciousness of the individual. If it did, the Romanist holds, man would lose his freedom. For freedom, in the Romanist sense of the term, means a bit of ultimacy or autonomy; a sharing in the freedom of God. The idea of man's participation in the being of God or his participation with God in a common being, precludes the idea of man's being truly made in the image of God.

It follows from this that Romanist theology speaks of Adam as being originally in need of grace. Man then needs grace because he is finite. Accordingly, after man fell into sin he needed the same grace, but still only the same grace. Thus, the concept of *nature and grace* takes the place of *sin and grace*. And the meaning of both sin and grace is thereby changed.[15]

Thus, once more the attempt is made to satisfy the objection against the sovereign grace of God and His electing sovereign power, by reducing the difference between special and common grace.

It is then not necessary to say: "Nay but, O man, who art thou that repliest against God?" For the idea of grace is largely made over to his taste. And though very vague on the subject Romanist theology therefore, like Barthianism and liberal Protestantism, holds that man's being lost is ultimately determined by man himself. Man is lost, Roman Catholic theologians often say, because he has not lived up to the light of nature that God has given him. And so the light that God gave unto the heathen for their conversion was really meant for their eternal salvation. And it is only because by their sins they live out of accord with that light, that God gives them over to eternal death. Thus it is again man, not God, who ultimately decides his eternal destiny. And thus the problem of "contradiction" is solved by removing one of the horns of the dilemma.

COMMON GRACE ACCORDING TO THE REMONSTRANTS[16]

Then thirdly come the Remonstrants or Arminians, who teach that "there are various kinds of election of God unto eternal life: the

15. For Bavinck's discussion of this, see ibid.
16. The Remonstrants were the followers of Jacob Arminius. They submitted five articles to the Synod of Dort (1618), which the Synod, in five points, ultimately rejected as outside

one general and indefinite, the other particular and definite; and that the latter in turn is either incomplete, revocable, non-decisive, and conditional, or complete, irrevocable, decisive, and absolute. Likewise: there is one election unto faith and another unto salvation, so that election can be unto justifying faith, without being a decisive election unto salvation."[17]

The central point of these words and similar ones from the *Five Articles Against the Remonstrants* is that the final determination of the destiny of individual men is still left in the hands of men instead of in the hands of God. Again God cannot reach the individual except through a general invitation. God may begin the process of salvation by offering general grace to all. But this must mean that God in a general way intends to save all. No answer is given to the question that if God intends to save all men, why did He not make salvation known to all through the spreading of the gospel news? There is reference to the idea that they have not used the *light of nature* aright and thus have made themselves unworthy of the better news of the gospel.

But again, on this basis, the answer to the objector against the sovereign grace of God is not voiced in the words: "Nay but, O man, who art thou that repliest against God?"

It is not till we assert that the ultimate destiny of all men everywhere, and therefore of each man individually is, in the last analysis, determined by God, that the problem of common grace comes clearly before us. For only when it is seen that according to Scripture God controls all of history and all the deeds of all men, evil deeds as well as good deeds, that the question is squarely before us as to how then God can have any attitude of favor to those whom He has from all eternity intended not to redeem.

REPROBATION MUST REST ON THE WILL OF GOD

We, therefore, cannot avoid taking note of a point of view sometimes advocated by those who are committed to the Reformed faith. I refer to the idea that reprobation rests ultimately upon

the bounds of Reformed theology.

17. Van Til is quoting here from the Canons of the Synod of Dort, First Head of Doctrine, Rejection of Errors, para. 2. For an English translation of this document, see the Christian Classics Ethereal Library at www.ccel.org.

the sin of man as the final cause. Reprobation is then said to be an act of punishment of God upon sin as committed by man. In this respect reprobation is said to differ from election. Election is said to proceed from God's eternal plan directly. But reprobation is not thus directly an act of the eternal plan of God. Reprobation is thus said not to be equally ultimate with election.

But surely, it is apparent that such a point of view leads us off the highway of the Reformed faith and tones down our witness to the world. The world needs the sovereign God of Scripture. Hence we must say that reprobation is not ultimately an act of justice with respect to the sin of man. It is rather an act of the sovereign will of God. The fully Biblical, and therefore fully Reformed, position is not reached till God in His sovereign decree is made the ultimate cause of *all* that comes to pass in this world through the deeds of men, whether these deeds lead to their final destruction or by God's grace to their final glory. Hence, too, we dare not say that Adam could, in the last analysis, have chosen to be obedient just as well as disobedient. The fall of man is the proximate cause of reprobation (*propinqua repro-bationis causa*). But, says Bavinck, and again: "For that reason the fall of Adam, sin in general and all evil, is not only seen in advance but also in a sense willed and directed by God. There must therefore be, though hidden from us, a reason why God willed the fall: There is an *altius Dei consilium* [higher plan of God] which precedes the fall."[18] Once more: There is but one and that an all-comprehensive plan of God.

Quite properly Bavinck refers in this connection to the reply that Calvin gave to Pighius when the latter objected to the counsel of God as the final source of the determination of the destinies of all men. In dealing with the 9th chapter of Romans and, therefore, with the difference between Esau and Jacob, Calvin says:

Now if this "*afore prepared* unto glory" is peculiar and special to the elect, it evidently follows that the rest, the non-elect, were equally "*fitted* to destruction" because, being left to their own nature, they were thereby devoted already to certain destruc-

18. Bavinck, *RD*, 2:364.

tion. That they were "fitted to destruction" by *their own wickedness* is an idea so silly that it needs no notice. It is indeed true that the wicked procure to themselves the Wrath of God, and that they daily hasten on the falling of its own weight upon their heads. But it must be confessed by all, that the apostle is here treating of the difference made between the elect and the reprobate, which proceeds from the alone secret will and counsel of God.[19]

Then Calvin goes on to treat of the passage from Isaiah already quoted, in which he speaks of the blinding of man's eyes. He points out how utterly destructive of the idea of the sovereign grace of God it would be if anything that is done by men is made the ultimate or final cause of their destiny. All men were corrupted in their nature by the fall of Adam. If this their corruption were the *ultimate* cause of their reprobation then God Himself would be confounded when seeking to save men. For all would then be bound to be reprobate.

If the wickedness of man be still urged as *the cause* of the difference between the elect and the non-elect, this wickedness might indeed be made to appear more powerful than the grace of God which He shows toward His elect, if that solemn truth did not stand in the way of such an argument: "I will have mercy on whom I will have mercy."[20]

Of the words of John (John 12:37ff), who also quotes the passage from Isaiah, Calvin says:

Now, most certainly, John does not here give us to understand that the Jews were prevented from believing by their sinfulness. For though this be quite true in one sense, yet *the cause* of their not believing must be traced to a far higher source. The secret and eternal counsel of God must be viewed as the original cause of their blindness and unbelief.[21]

19. John Calvin, *A Treatise on the Eternal Predestination of God*, in *Calvin's Calvinism*, trans. Henry Cole (Grand Rapids: Eerdmans, 1950), 76.
20. Ibid., 81.
21. Ibid.

PROXIMATE AND ULTIMATE CAUSE

In answer to all objections made by those who seek the ultimate issues of life and death in man, Calvin distinguishes between *proximate* and *ultimate* causes. Man is the *proximate* and *responsible* cause of his eternal punishment. Men must be told that they will be eternally lost if they persist in their rebellion against God. They must be called to repentance. Even so, back of their belief or unbelief is the sovereign will of God. It is of that God that we must witness. If men object and disbelieve we yet reply: "Shall not the Judge of the whole earth do right?" (Gen. 18:25).

Quite in accord with Calvin, Bavinck asserts that the difference between the Reformed and other approaches to the doctrine of grace is that they—following Augustine—did not stop with secondary causes but dared to climb up to God as the first and ultimate cause and therein found rest for their thought.[22]

But in finding rest for their thought did they think that they could logically penetrate the mystery of the relation of this ultimate will of God to the will of man as the secondary cause either of obedience or of disobedience? Not at all. With Calvin they would say: "Here let human reasonings of every kind that possibly can present themselves to our minds cease forever."[23]

Shall we not say this to ourselves, and mean it, with respect to the problem of common grace? How can God have an attitude of favor unto those who are according to His own ultimate will to be separated from Him forever? The first and basic answer is that Scripture teaches it. But then we can see that in order to be disobedient and, therefore, to be punished for their own sin, they must be confronted with God in all that they do. Historical causes have genuine meaning just because of God's ultimate plan. God reaches down into the self-consciousness of each individual. If the heathen are adding to their sins and to their punishment, and if for additional sin they are, as Paul tells us, given over unto still further sin by God (see Rom. 1:24, 26, 28), we can see that they

---

22. Bavinck, *Gereformeerde dogmatiek*, 3rd ed. (Kampen: Kok, 1918), 2:393. The passage to which Van Til alludes is this: "The sole difference is this: Reformed Christians, with Scripture in their hands and Augustine as their leader, did not stop at the consideration of secondary causes but ventured to push on to faith in the primary cause, that is, the will of God, in which alone they experienced rest for their mind and life." *RD*, 2:379.

23. Calvin, *A Treatise on the Eternal Predestination of God*, 67.

must have the fact of God, as long-suffering and as calling them to repentance, before them (see Rom. 2:1–4). And we can also see that, therefore, the restraint of God by which men are kept back from greater sin and from greater punishment is something that is an unmerited favor unto them.[24]

We have not come into full sight of this problem till with Calvin and Bavinck we trace all things back to the sovereign will of God. Only then does the problem appear of how such a God, who ultimately has fixed the destinies of men, yet promises or threatens what appears to be opposed to this destiny. And the problem is as acute in the case of the elect as it is in the case of the reprobate. How are good deeds of men called *their* good deeds if they are gifts of God?

Moreover, when I add with Bavinck that though sin and its eternal punishment for some men is a part of the plan of God and, therefore, in a sense willed by God, yet they are not willed in the same sense and in the same manner as are the grace and salvation of the elect—I have not thereby met the objection of him who charges the Christian religion with contradiction.[25] We shall need simply to hold both to the genuine meaning of historical causes and to the all inclusiveness of God's will as the ultimate cause.

On the other hand, I cannot meet the objector by trying to show him that God is quite consistent with Himself since He, by His will, has determined to elect some and not elect others. If I say that God's work in the direction of reprobation and in the direction of election differs not at all, then I am merely saying to the objector, in effect, that I would solve his problem by denying the meaning of secondary causes altogether. I must then wipe out the

24. The fact that God gives men over to more and deeper sin implies that he restrains sinners from what they would otherwise desire to do and to be.

25. Bavinck, *Gereformeerde dogmatiek*, 2:405. The passage to which Van Til alludes is this: "The fall, sin, and eternal punishment are included in the divine decree and in a sense willed by God, but then always only in a certain sense and not in the same manner as grace and blessedness. God takes delight in the latter, but sin and punishment are not occasions of pleasure or joy to God. When he makes sin subservient to his honor, he does it by his omnipotence, but this is contrary to the nature of sin. And when he punishes the wicked, he does not delight in their suffering as such; rather, in this punishment he celebrates the triumph of his perfections (Deut. 28:63; Ps. 2:4; Prov. 1:26; Lam. 3:33). And though on the one hand, with a view to the comprehensive and immutable character of God's counsel, there is no objection to speaking of a "double predestination," on the other hand we must bear in mind that in the one case predestination is of a different nature than in the other." *RD*, 2:389.

distinction between the revealed and the secret will of God. And I must say therefore that God's eternal election of men implies that He had no attitude of disfavor unto them even for their sins. Thus I would wipe out the necessity for their atonement in history through the redemptive work of Christ. Says Calvin: "Let no one deceive himself by vain self-flattery. Those who come to Christ were before sons of God in His divine heart, while they were, in themselves, His enemies."[26]

Let us, rather than try to meet the objector's desires for supposed consistency in logic, not deny the fact of God's revelation of His general favor to mankind or the fact of God's wrath resting upon the elect. To meet the objector and satisfy him we should have to deny the meaning of all history and of all secondary causes. We should need to wipe out the difference between God and man. To the objector it is contradictory to say that God controls whatsoever comes to pass and also to say that human choices have significance.[27]

ALL TEACHING OF SCRIPTURE IS APPARENTLY CONTRADICTORY

Rather let us say with Calvin: "And most certainly there is nothing in the whole circle of spiritual doctrine which does not far surpass the capacity of man and confound its utmost reach."[28] If we are really to witness to men for God, then it must be the God of Scripture, the sovereign God of whom we testify. This God demands that we submit our whole man, with all its powers, to Him. This God, therefore, wants us to tell men that they have really met Him; that they are really confronted with Him; that they really know Him; that their deeds of obedience or disobedience have genuine meaning in His sight; that if they believe they will be saved and that if they do not believe they will be lost. They must be shown that they are kicking against the pricks always and everywhere, since they do not submit their thoughts captive to the obedience of God or of Christ. And we do not thus witness if we ourselves reduce history to something that is meaningless.

26. Calvin, *A Treatise on the Eternal Predestination of God*, 84.
27. Notice that Van Til is here again pressing the point that one can either base one's objections on supposed autonomous principles of reason, and thus require God to make sense of his actions, or one can submit to the clear teaching of Scripture.
28. Calvin, *A Treatise on the Eternal Predestination of God*, 82.

NATURAL THEOLOGY AND COMMON GRACE

But there is another side to the story. If we are to witness to the God of Scripture we cannot afford to deny common grace. For, as noted, common grace is an element of the general responsibility of man, a part of the picture in which God, the God of unmerited favor, meets man everywhere. But neither can we afford to construct a theory in which it is implicitly allowed that the natural man, in terms of his adopted principles, can truly interpret any aspect of history. For the natural man seeks to interpret all the facts of this world immanentistically.[29] He seeks for meaning in the facts of this world without regarding these facts as carrying in them the revelation and therewith the claims of God. He seeks to determine what can and cannot be, what is or is not possible, by the reach of human logic resting on man himself as its foundation.

Now surely, you say, no Reformed person would have any commerce with any such view as that. Well, I do not think that any Reformed person purposely adopts such a view. But we know how the Roman Catholic conception of natural theology did creep into the thinking of Reformed theologians in the past. And the essence of this natural theology is that it attributes to the natural man the power of interpreting some aspect of the world without basic error. Even though men do not recognize God as the Creator and controller of the facts of this world, they are assumed to be able to give as true an interpretation of the laws of nature as it is possible for finite man to give. It is admitted that man as a religious being needs additional information besides what he learns by means of his own research. But this fact itself indicates that on this basis the knowledge of God about salvation has no bearing upon the realm of nature. The realm of nature is said to be correctly interpreted by the natural man.[30]

On this basis it is quite possible for Christians to join with non-Christians in the scientific enterprise without witnessing to them of God. The Christians and non-Christians have, on this basis,

29. To interpret facts "immanentistically" means that they are understood or interpreted only with regard to themselves and to that which is "immanent," not in light of that which transcends the facts and thus gives meaning to them—namely, God and his Word.

30. This is a good description of what is sometimes called the "nature-grace dialectic." It is dialectical in that one is not able to connect with the other. In such cases, there is no way to reconcile one to the other.

a certain area of interpretation in common. They have *common ideas* in the sense that they agree on certain meanings without any difference. It is not merely that they are together confronted with the natural revelation of God. It is not merely that men are, all of them together, made in the image of God. It is not merely that they have in them the ineradicable sense of deity so that God speaks to them by means of their own constitution. It is not merely that, as Kuyper stressed, all men have to think according to the rules of logic according to which alone the human mind can function. It is not merely that all men can weigh and make many scientific discoveries.

WITNESS-BEARING IN THE LABORATORY

All these things are true and important to maintain. But it is when in addition to these it is said that there are *common notions*, common *reactions*, about God and man and the world to all this speech of God, on which there is no basic difference between Christians and non-Christians, that natural theology is confused with natural revelation. And it is allowed that those who assume that the facts of this world are come from chance and those who presuppose that the facts of this world are created and controlled by God, have essentially the same interpretation of these facts. Thus the Christian and the non-Christian scientist could work together in the laboratory for days, for weeks and years and the Christian would have no other witness to give to his friend than to invite him to the prayer meeting or the Sunday service.

The Christian would on such a basis only reap the reward of his little faith were his friend to refuse to be interested in his religion. This friend, more consistently than the Christian, gives witness to his own faith. He will insist that he cannot believe in such a God as the Christians want him to bow unto since this God has created and determined all things. This God, he will say, does not allow men to experiment freely in the laboratory. The non-Christian may give witness to his faith in such words as these: "Your God hampers me in the making of my hypotheses. If I believe in Him I may make only such hypotheses as are in accord with the doctrines of creation and providence. I could not then think of evolution as a legitimate hypothesis with respect to the origin of man. Does not your God say in your Bible that man has not come from animal ancestry but is directly created in the image of God? Moreover your God, besides taking away from me the idea that any hypothesis may be taken as on a par with any other at the outset of an investigation, insists that I shall accept the contradictory position that supernatural things may happen and influence the order of the natural. That," he says, "makes the realm of natural law itself something that can be arbitrarily interfered with at will."

Thus the Christian working in the laboratory is confronted with the necessity of leaving the laboratory, giving it over entirely to the unbeliever or witnessing to the fact that only if Christianity is true is science possible and meaningful.

Are we then to fail to witness for our God in the field of science? Is it only because the unbeliever has never been confronted with the full implication of Christianity for the field of science that he tolerates us in his presence still? And are we to have a theory of common grace that prohibits us from setting forth the witness of God before all men everywhere? Is not the Christ to be set forth in His cosmic significance by us after all? Is it not true that there could be no science if the world and all that is therein is controlled by chance? Is it not true that the non-Christian does his work by the common grace of God? A theory of common grace based on a natural theology is destructive of all grace, common or special.[31]

Surely the witness to the God of the Scriptures must be presented everywhere. It must be, to be sure, presented with wisdom and with tact. But it must be presented. It is not presented, however, if we grant that God the Holy Spirit in a general testimony to all men approves of interpretations of this world or of aspects of this world which ignore Him and set Him at naught.

The non-Christian scientist must be told that he is dealing with facts that belong to God. He must be told this, not merely in the interest of religion in the narrower sense of the term. He must be

31. A theory of common grace based on natural theology would destroy *common* grace because it presupposes total depravity; it presupposes that no one can please God in any endeavor. The only good that is accomplished, therefore, by the nonbeliever is accomplished because of what God, not the nonbeliever, has done. A theory of common grace based on natural theology would also destroy *special* grace because any notion of man's reason and will that is thought to be neutral allows for the initiation of salvation by man himself, not by God. "Grace," in this context, is not the unmerited favor of God, but his reaction to man's good and proper, supposedly free, choice.

told this in the interest of science too, and of culture in general. He must be told that there would be no facts distinguishable from one another unless God had made them and made them thus. He must be told that no hypothesis would have any relevance or bearing on these same facts, except for the providence of God. He must be told that his own mind, with its principles of order, depends upon his being made in the image of God. And then he must be told that if it were not for God's common grace he would go the full length of the principle of evil within him. He would finish iniquity and produce only war. His very acts of courtesy and kindness, his deeds of generosity, all his moral good is not to be explained, therefore, in terms of himself and the goodness of his nature but from God's enabling him to do these things in spite of his sinful nature. "Will you not then repent in order to serve and worship the Creator more than the creature?" (see Rom. 1:25).

INFRA- AND SUPRALAPSARIANISM[32]

Our conclusion then on the problem of common grace may, I hope, be along the lines marked out by Bavinck on the issue of infra- and supralapsarianism. Bavinck sought to avoid extremes in either direction. And how avoid extremes? How attain a balanced view? By not allowing our logic to dominate over the teachings of Scripture.

Supralapsarianism, when held without full regard for all scriptural data, led to a stressing of the final destiny of men through election and reprobation to such an extent as to render the means by which that end is attained of little value. It led to a virtual denial of second or historical causes.[33]

Infralapsarianism, when held without full regard for all scriptural data, so stressed the significance of the historical fact of sin as the cause of the lost condition of men, as to endanger the basic importance of the fact that back of all the historical choices of men is the

32. The "lapsarian" debate gained prominence among the Reformed in the sixteenth century. The debate has to do with the logical order of the particulars of God's decree. Supralapsarians hold that the order is God's election, creation, then the fall. Infralapsarians hold that the order is creation, the fall, then God's election. Bavinck holds both to be out of place and insufficient, though the infralapsarian position has been the majority view among the Reformed. See Bavinck, *RD*, 2:365–92.

33. This would be the case because, logically speaking, God elected a people without reference to creation or the fall. The means through which his election comes are incidental.

one all-controlling plan of the sovereign God. It led, sometimes, to a virtual denial of God's plan as the first or last ultimate cause as controlling all finite causes.[34]

We shall not thus, argues Bavinck, permit our reason to legislate with respect to scriptural data. Ours is a sovereign God. His glory is the end of all things. But we cannot say that this glory, in the case of the reprobate, is manifested only and exclusively in the righteousness of their punishment. There is while they are in this world, proceeding from them that which cannot be explained exclusively in terms of their reprobation. So also we cannot say that God's glory, in the case of the elect, is accomplished exclusively in God's grace to them in Christ. There is much of sin in them that displeases God. That which proceeds from their "old man" is not from, but against the grace of God. So in the case of the reprobate; their doings are better than their principle of evil, if not governed by God's common grace, would lead one to expect.

Supra- or infralapsarianism, taken as some advocates of these views have taken them, were faulty in their imposing of the reach of human logic upon the data of revelation.

Is it not thus with us who love the Reformed faith today? Do we not need to come to an "agonizing re-appraisal" with respect to the whole matter?[35] Our witness must come clearly before the world. We all love to honor God for the work of the Reformers. That work found its climax in the idea of the sovereign grace of God freely proclaimed unto men.

Shall we, the sons of that Reformation, bedim its challenge to men by going off on tangents in order to satisfy the illegitimate objections of sinful men?

A BALANCED VIEW OF COMMON GRACE

There lies before us the highway of the Christian faith. May we ever drive upon it, without veering either to the left or to the right.

34. This would be the case in that, logically speaking, creation and fall take place without reference to God's electing and predestinating purposes. Thus, there are aspects of history—notably creation and the fall—that take place without reference to God's decree.

35. The "agonizing re-appraisal" quote is likely one from John Foster Dulles, who was Secretary of State from 1953 to 1959. With respect to foreign policy, he said: "If E.D.C. [the European Defense Community] should fail, the United States might be compelled to make an agonizing reappraisal of its basic policy."

If the wheels of an automobile are out of line the car will gradually tend to run off the pavement. You cannot drive an automobile effectively with one wheel on the pavement and the other on the soft shoulder next to the road. Let us, in all kindness, warn one another not to go off the highway either to the left or to the right.

Going off to the right by denying common grace or going off to the left by affirming a theory of common grace patterned after the natural theology of Rome is to fail, to this extent, to challenge the wisdom of the world.

In neither case is the call of God to man made truly universal. In denying common grace we say, in effect, that God does not really call some men to repentance at all. In affirming a natural theology type of common grace, we fail to show that God calls all men everywhere and in all dimensions of life.

In neither case do we show man the full glory of the gospel and of the Christ, the Savior of the world.

Ye are my witnesses!

CHAPTER 6

A LETTER ON COMMON GRACE[1, 2, 3]

Dear Friend:

Recently you wrote me asking about my views on common grace. You remarked that somebody had made a statement in your hearing to the effect that if he were to take my position on common grace he did not see how he could make any use of the results of the scientific work of those who are not Christians. This gentleman apparently got the impression that on my view the non-believer must be thought of as being unable to discover any truth at all of any sort in any field.

A criticism of a similar nature is to the effect that I do not think that unbelievers can do anything that is good in any sense.

1. This chapter deals with the work of Dr. William Masselink, Th.D., Ph.D., entitled *Common Grace and Christian Education* (privately printed, 1951). Because this chapter was prepared before the publication of Dr. Masselink's more recent book, *General Revelation and Common Grace* (Grand Rapids: Eerdmans, 1953), it has been impossible to take note of this later work.

2. The original publication date of this "letter" was 1952.

3. William Masselink (1897–1973) graduated from Grundy College and Seminary with a diploma in 1918 and from Princeton Theological Seminary with a Th.M. in 1919. He attended Chicago Divinity School in 1920 and earned a Ph.D. from Southern Baptist Theological Seminary in 1921 and a Th.D. from the Free University of Amsterdam in 1937. He was ordained in the Christian Reformed Church in 1922. He held several pastorates in Indiana, Michigan, and Illinois in the Christian Reformed Church, after which he taught at Reformed Bible College from 1952 to 1963. Significant for the discussion that follows is the fact that Masselink wrote his dissertation at the Free University of Amsterdam, and defended it in 1938, under Valentijn Hepp.

It is said, in short, that I have *too negative* a view of the "natural man." I am said to teach *absolute* instead of *total* depravity. That is to say, I am said to teach that man is as bad as he can be, thus not allowing for the fact that he can, because of the operation of God's common grace upon him, do much that is morally though not spiritually good.

In all this I am said to draw "too near to Herman Hoeksema." Have not I criticized Abraham Kuyper, and that not on a point of detail but on his very epistemology? In short I am said to hold to an "absolutist position," a position that involves "intellectual Anabaptism,"[4] a position that is out of accord with the Reformed confessions, which speak of the "natural light" that remains in men after the Fall and of the "remnants" of the knowledge of God and of morality that they still possess.

My position is reported to be part of a *reconstruction theology*, a theology of rebellion against the views of Abraham Kuyper and Herman Bavinck of Holland, and of the view of the "Old Princeton theology" of such men as B. B. Warfield and J. Gresham Machen. To be sure, I am said not to belong to the drastic reconstructionists, like Klaas Schilder and Herman Hoeksema, but to the more moderate ones like Professors D. H. Th. Vollenhoven and H. Dooyeweerd.

Much of this sort of criticism of my position has found expression in the book *Common Grace and Christian Education*, published in 1952 by Dr. William Masselink, a professor of the Reformed Bible Institute in Grand Rapids, Michigan.[5] Dr. Masselink seeks to show that "the old traditional view of Common Grace is the only tenable position."[6] And since I am, in his eyes, undermining this traditional view, he seeks to prove that my views are untenable.

Dr. Masselink is very frank in his admiration of the theology of his teacher at the Free University of Amsterdam, the late Dr. Valentijn Hepp. His assumption is that Hepp's views are identical with the traditional position and are, to all intents and purposes, identical

4. "Intellectual Anabaptism" is meant to be a pejorative metaphor signaling a radical separation with regard to the intellect. This is S. J. Ridderbos's way to communicate, not only how radically Van Til separates the knowledge of believers and unbelievers, but also that Van Til's view, as an "anabaptist" view, is not Reformed. See also Cornelius Van Til, *The Defense of the Faith*, ed. K. Scott Oliphint (Phillipsburg, NJ: P&R Publishing, 2008), 1–27, esp. 12–13.
5. The publication date was actually 1951.
6. Masselink, *Common Grace and Christian Education*, 3.

with those of Kuyper and Bavinck. He therefore adheres strictly to the criticisms that Hepp has made of Schilder, of Vollenhoven, of Dooyeweerd, and of others. He agrees in the main with the criticism made of my position by Dr. S. J. Ridderbos in his booklet *Rondom het Gemene Gratie Probleem* (1949) (*Concerning the common grace problem*). He quotes Ridderbos with approval to this effect. "If one continues to reason in this line the possibility is cut off to acknowledge the 'glimmerings' of the 'natural knowledge of God.' "[7]

It is not my intention in this letter to deal with the general criticism of my position outlined above in full. My main purpose is to seek to remove some misunderstandings that have developed with respect to my views. These misunderstandings may be my own fault, no doubt, in considerable measure. My terminology may sometimes be ambiguous. But I cannot believe that such misconstruction of my view as is now being advertised is fairly found in anything that I have written or said.

I shall deal first with Dr. Masselink's analysis of my view of facts, the objects of human knowledge; then I shall deal with the human mind, with the subject of human knowledge, and in particular with the "natural man."

1. Facts Or The Object Of Knowledge

In describing my view of fact, Dr. Masselink says: "To the question, 'What is a fact?' the non-Christian answers, 'Only that which has been defined, interpreted, and patterned by man.' Therefore all 'facts' are anti-metaphysical. Anything which man cannot define is not a 'fact.' There may be 'brute facts,' that is, not real 'fact,' but an interpreted 'fact.' This, according to the non-Christian, is the presupposition to the finding of any 'fact.' Therefore the non-Christian himself determines what is a 'fact.' He makes a 'fact' by his interpretation of it."

"According to the Christian, on the one hand, God only can define a 'fact.' God's description or His plan of the 'fact' makes a 'fact' a 'fact.' What modern science ascribes to man, namely, power to make facts, the Christian ascribes to God. Therefore, as far as the epistemology is concerned, Christians and non-Christians have no

7. Ibid., 98.

'facts' in common."[8] Then, after two paragraphs on what I have said on the place of law and of man, Dr. Masselink adds: "Now you ask, What is the view of Van Til? I think we find the answer on page 70 of 'Common Grace,' where he expresses his agreement with Schilder."[9] And on what am I said to agree with Schilder? It is on the point that from "facts as such" we are not to conclude to any such thing as an attitude of God toward the reprobate. "Therefore, according to Schilder and Van Til, facts cannot be separated from faith. In other words, a "fact" is impossible with a non-Christian."[10]

On this description of my position I may remark as follows: (1) It leaves out two qualifications that are essential for a fair treatment of my view. First, I said that the non-Christian *virtually* ascribes to man what the Christian ascribes to God on the matter of "making facts." Man needs *material*; he does not pretend to *produce* material. The exact point in comparison is that of *definitory power*. On this point, I argued, the non-Christian ascribes to man what the Christian ascribes to God. Dr. Masselink's presentation is calculated to leave the impression that, according to my view, the natural man claims to create out of nothing as God is said to do in the Genesis narrative. This is not at all what I said.

In the second place, I said that,

> When both parties, the believer and the non-believer, are epistemologically self-conscious and as such engaged in the interpretative enterprise, they cannot be said to have any fact in common. On the other hand, it must be asserted that they have every fact in common. Both deal with the same God and with the same universe created by God. Both are made in the image of God. In short, they have the metaphysical situation in common. Metaphysically, both parties have all things in common, while epistemologically they have nothing in common.[11]

My statement that epistemologically Christians and non-Christians "have nothing in common" is meant to hold only to the extent that men are *self-consciously engaged in the interpretative enterprise*.

8. Ibid., 66.
9. Ibid.
10. Ibid.
11. Cornelius Van Til, *Common Grace* (Philadelphia: Presbyterian and Reformed, 1947), 5.

172

Why did Dr. Masselink, in presenting my views, omit this obviously all-important qualification? It is this qualification which, later in my argument, allows for commonness "up to a point" between believer and non-believer.

It is equally evident that my statement just referred to has for its correlative the other statement to the effect that "metaphysically speaking, both parties have all things in common." This point too is of basic importance. Suppose someone had seen fit to make me out to be a "relativist." He might then have said: "According to Van Til, believers and non-believers 'have every fact in common. Both deal with the same God and with the same universe created by God. Both are made in the image of God. In short, they have the metaphysical situation in common.' "[12] He would merely have omitted such words as "epistemologically they have nothing in common." Yet his description of my full position would not, in point of adequacy, be far behind that of Dr. Masselink.

(2) Dr. Masselink asserts that I agree with Dr. Schilder in saying that we must not conclude from "facts as such" to any such thing as an attitude of God toward believers. The exact reverse is actually the case. The whole thrust of the section from which the quotation is taken is to the effect that I *disagree* with Schilder on this point. I make one minor concession to him. It is to the effect that over against a Romanizing type of natural theology such a warning is in order. Dr. Masselink presents this minor concession as being identical with agreement on the main issue. But the following words indicate quite the opposite; immediately after making this concession the following paragraph appears:

> If there are no brute facts, it must be maintained that all facts are revelational of the true God. If facts may not be separated from faith, neither may faith be separated from facts. Every created fact must therefore be held to express, to some degree, the attitude of God to man. Not to maintain this is to fall back once again into a natural theology of a Roman Catholic sort. For it is to hold to the idea of brute fact after all. And with the idea of brute fact goes that of neutral reason. A fact not revelational of God is revelational only of itself.[13]

12. Ibid.
13. Ibid., 70.

It is precisely because I believe that such facts as "rain and sunshine" *do* manifest an attitude of God, and that a *favorable* attitude to men as His own creatures, that I have defended the first of the "three points" formulated by the Synod of the Christian Reformed Church in 1924 against Schilder's criticism of it.[14]

Dr. Masselink asserts that according to my view a "fact" . . . "is impossible with a non-Christian."[15] This sentence is the conclusion of the quotation given above. He finds corroboration for this assertion in another agreement of mine with Schilder. And this time it is a real agreement.

Schilder rejects the idea that there is a neutral territory of interpretation between believers and unbelievers. I agreed by saying: "Schilder quite rightly attacks the idea of a territory that is common to believer and non-believer without qualification."[16] It is commonness "without qualification," that is, the idea of *neutral* territory of interpretation between believers and non-believers that I reject.

Is it this idea of neutral territory that Dr. Masselink would defend? Is it his understanding that that is the traditional and only defensible view? And must one who believes in commonness but in commonness *with* qualification be spoken of as one who has made the break between God and man complete? Such seems to be the view of Dr. Masselink as the following quotation, in addition to the others already given, seems to indicate:

> It is therefore clear that both Van Til and Schilder reject "with vigor" every idea of "common territory" or, "common ground" between the believer and the non-believer. This, we believe, means that both Schilder and Van Til accept not only an absolute ethical antithesis between God and "natural man," but an absolute logical and absolute aesthetic antithesis as well. The break between God and "natural man" is then complete.[17]

14. It must be said here that, for whatever reason, the criticisms of Van Til thus far mentioned from Masselink are inexcusable. Masselink either did not read carefully or purposely misrepresented Van Til, attributing to him the opposite of what he actually said. His criticisms in this regard should be afforded no credibility whatsoever.

15. Masselink, *Common Grace and Christian Education*, 66.

16. Van Til, *Common Grace*, 25.

17. Masselink, *Common Grace and Christian Education*, 67.

Our discussion so far has been on the basis of the first part of Dr. Masselink's book. The second part of his chapter deals with my "disagreement with the Old Reformed Theologians in their epistemology."[18] The list of headings and descriptions under this general topic is as follows:

I. Van Til's Criticism of Kuyper
   1. Van Til states that Kuyper is not Calvinistic but Platonic and Kantian in his conception of the universals.
   2. Van Til accuses Kuyper of being like Plato and Kant in his conceptions of facts.
   3. Van Til says that Kuyper is like Catholics, Aristotle and Scholastics in his views as to what believers and non-believers have in common.

II. Van Til's Disagreement with Bavinck and the "Old Princeton Theology"
   1. He says Bavinck must be charged with "Moderate Realism and Scholasticism."
   2. Van Til says that Bavinck identifies the Christian and pagan conception of the unknowability of God.
   3. Van Til says that Bavinck uses "non-Christian form of reasoning" in his theistic arguments.
   4. Van Til accuses Bavinck of wavering between a Christian and non-Christian concept of natural theology.
   5. Van Til summarizes his disagreement with Kuyper, Bavinck and the "Old Princeton Theology" as follows [Here follows a long quotation from pages 50 and 52 of *Common Grace*].

III. Van Til's disagreement with Hepp follows the same line of thought.[19]

Under each heading there is a quotation of material taken from *Common Grace*. These can easily be checked by any interested reader. The section ends as follows:

18. Ibid., 68.
19. Ibid., 67.

From all this we come to the conclusion that there is a *basic disagreement between Van Til on the one side, and Kuyper, Bavinck, Hepp and the "Old Princeton Theology" on the other side,* in regard to their views on Common Grace,—especially concerning that which Van Til correctly considers to be fundamental to our whole conception of Common Grace, namely Epistemology.[20]

At various points in his work Dr. Masselink comes back to this matter of my disagreement with all the great Reformed theologians of the recent past. He sums it all up as follows:

When Van Til characterizes the views of the Old Reformed Theologians on epistemology as being "Kantian," "Platonic," "Non-Christian," etc., we maintain that the difference between the views of these Theologians and the heathen philosophers, to amplify beyond Romanism, is so drastic that it does not admit of a comparison. We will only mention a few self-evident facts:

1. The worldly heathen philosophers do not admit of Christ. Theirs is a Christless philosophy, even though there may be remnants of truth in what they have to say. The Reformed Theologians, of course, base all their views of epistemology on the Covenant of Common Grace, which is based upon Christ's atonement.

2. The heathen philosophers admit of no Ontological Trinity. The Reformed theologians take this as their starting point.

3. The heathen philosophers have no Bible as basis for their thinking. The Reformed Theologians proceed from the Scripture.

To say, as Van Til does, that the views of these Reformed Theologians relative to epistemology are "Kantian," "Platonic," "Non-Christian," etc., because they acknowledge some elements of truth in the philosophies of the world, and say that some of these truths because of God's Common Grace may even be traced to them, is, to say the least, surprising to us.[21]

20. Ibid., 2.
21. Ibid., 81.

Dr. Masselink has thus far tried to prove that my basic alignment on the matter of what unbelievers may know about "facts," and even on epistemology in general, is with the "drastic reconstructionist," Schilder, and away from the great Reformed theologians, such as Kuyper, Bavinck, Hepp, Warfield, and Machen. The evidence for the first part of this claim is the one point that with Schilder I do not hold to the idea of a neutral territory of knowledge between believer and unbeliever. On this point I may say that if the idea of a neutral territory does fairly represent the "traditional view," then I can only disagree with it.

The second point is calculated to make the reader think that my disagreement with these great theologians goes to the root of their theology. Dr. Masselink finds it necessary to point out as against me that these theologians, in distinction from such men as Plato, Aristotle, and Kant, were Christians and that they believed the Bible. Well, has there been in anything I have ever said or written as much as an insinuation that the root of their thinking was not from the Bible?

It is well to emphasize again that it is from Kuyper, more than from anyone else in modern times, that we have learned to think concretely. Both on the question of the universal and on that of particular, Kuyper has taught us that we must build on our own presuppositions. Yet it must be said that Kuyper has not always been able to live up to this high ideal.[22]

In similar words I began my section on Bavinck by praising him for having shown, better than any one before him, the necessity of building up one's theology from one basic principle, namely, Scripture; adding that "Bavinck has not always lived up to this conception."[23] As for "Old Princeton Theology" in the booklet on Common Grace, I have scarcely referred to it. Elsewhere I have expressed disagreement with its *apologetics*. In this I was following Kuyper. But never have I expressed a basic difference with its theology or its basic epistemology. Dr. Masselink might better have followed Dr. S. J. Ridderbos on this point as he has done on others. Dealing with the same point with which Dr. Masselink deals,

22. Van Til, *Common Grace*, 35.
23. Ibid., 45.

Ridderbos says that I have criticized "subdivisions" of the theology of Kuyper and Bavinck.[24] This was in accord with the facts.

The impression is given that there is full agreement between the "Old Princeton Theology" on the one hand and the Amsterdam theologians on the other hand, on the question of common grace and of general epistemology. But in a former publication Dr. Masselink himself has made a good deal of the differences between the views of Warfield and those of Kuyper. In particular does he point up the "departures" of Machen from what he considers the full Reformed position as maintained by Hepp. Some of the criticisms he makes of Machen's views have a bearing on the problem now under discussion. Some of them do not. We shall give some indication as to the general nature of the criticism made by Dr. Masselink.

1. He says that Machen agrees with Warfield, A. A. Hodge, and Patton as against Kuyper and Hepp on the place to be assigned to apologetics. In assigning to apologetics the introductory place to all the theological sciences, Warfield "was a follower of Schleiermacher" and Machen a follower of Warfield.[25]

Kuyper assigned to apologetics the subordinate task of defending dogma. According to Warfield, Kuyper did this because he makes "too absolute the contrast between the 'two kinds of science'—that which is the product of the thought of sinful man in his state of nature, and that which is the product of man under the influence of the regenerating grace of God."[26]

2. Machen follows Warfield as against Hepp on the question of method in apologetics. "Our criticism against Prof. Machen's apologetics becomes more pronounced when the question is raised about *The Method of Apologetics According to his Conception*."[27]

The question arises, does Machen make sufficient allowance for the "super-rational" element in his Apologetics. We believe

24. Simon Jan Ridderbos, *Rondom het gemene-gratie-probleem* (Kampen: J. H. Kok, 1949).

25. William Masselink, *Professor J. Gresham Machen: His Life and Defence of the Bible* (privately printed, 1938?), 140.

26. Quoted in *ibid.*, 140–41, from Warfield's introduction to Francis R. Beattie's *Apologetics or the Rational Vindication of Christianity* (Richmond: Presbyterian Committee of Publication, 1903).

27. Masselink, *Professor J. Gresham Machen*, 145.

not. . . . The apologetics of the past, as well as the Roman Apologetics of today, make the mistake of trying to justify the religion before the bar of natural intellect. Such attempts are vain. How can there be any affinity between the unregenerate reason and the depths of the Christian religion which makes the understanding possible. The Apologetics which is based upon rational proofs, has always ignored the word of Paul and the psychic, the unspiritual man, does not understand the things of God. We believe that these conclusions to which Prof. Hepp has come, are sound and cannot be refuted.[28]

Here then Dr. Masselink signalizes a deep difference between the Old Princeton theology which, he says, Machen closely follows, and the Amsterdam theology. Princeton charges Amsterdam with stressing too much the difference between unregenerate and the regenerate men with respect to their ability to know the truth about the facts that surround them. If the unity of science is to be maintained there must be no such sharp distinction between knowledge of the unregenerate and the knowledge of the regenerate man. On the other hand, Amsterdam charges Princeton with failing to do justice to the fact that there is not *any affinity* between the unregenerate reason and the depths of Christianity which makes understanding possible. Dr. Masselink agrees with Amsterdam as against Princeton in saying that there is not *any* affinity for the truth of Christianity in the unbeliever. Just how does this position differ from what I said on the "absolute ethical antithesis?"[29]

3. Machen, says Masselink, had too high an estimate of the "Theistic proofs." "We do not share Prof. Machen's views regarding *The Relationship Between Natural Theology and Faith.*"[30] Machen would establish faith in God by these proofs. After some quotations from Machen, Dr. Masselink concludes, "From these and many other similar quotations from Machen we conclude that Machen bases the

28. Ibid., 147.
29. For more on Van Til's analysis of Amsterdam and Old Princeton, see Van Til, *Defense of the Faith*, 345–82. The "absolute ethical antithesis" of which Van Til speaks is better dubbed an absolute *covenantal* antithesis in which every person is either in Adam or in Christ. Those who are in Adam suppress the truth in unrighteousness; their "ethical" reaction to God's revelation is one of disobedience and thus is dishonoring to God (Rom. 1:18–23). Those who are, by grace through faith, in Christ accept the truth as it is found in him.
30. Masselink, *Professor J. Gresham Machen*, 147.

Christian Faith upon Theistic proofs of God which can be derived from Natural Theology."[31] But in his doctoral dissertation on the Testimony of the Holy Spirit, Hepp has taught us that general revelation cannot give us certainty of knowledge. "This is because all revelation takes place through means. We cannot know the essence of things except through things themselves. If this revelation, therefore, would have to give us certainty in regard to these matters, it would have to do it through the things themselves. These would then in turn become the basis of our certainty. This we have already observed cannot be, as then the certainty is in the creation itself and not in the Creator. The absolute certainty I receive only then, when the Holy Spirit gives me assurance that these things are so apart from the external revelation."[32] "The 'theistic proofs,' therefore, cannot be the basis of Faith, as Machen says."[33]

From what has been said so far it appears that there was, according to Dr. Masselink himself, a considerable difference between the position of Kuyper and that of Warfield on the question of facts and their knowledge by unbelievers. In his dissertation Dr. Masselink contends that Amsterdam and Old Princeton stand over against one another on the question how the unity of science may be preserved. Kuyper wants to maintain the unity of science by basing it upon frankly Christian foundations; the non-Christian, having not *any affinity* for Christianity, cannot maintain the unity of science. Warfield wants to maintain the unity of science on the basis of a rationality which all men, non-believers as well as believers, have in common. All men can interpret the facts of their environment correctly up to a point. The theistic proofs, as historically formulated, are for Warfield and for Machen sound as a foundation for belief in Christianity. Dr. Masselink chooses against the Warfield-Machen position and for the Kuyper-Bavinck position.

In his later work Dr. Masselink speaks as though the Kuyper and Warfield points of view were in agreement with one another on the question of science and as though I have departed from a position that Old Princeton and Amsterdam had in common. He criticizes me for not following both Kuyper and Warfield at the same time.

31. Ibid.
32. Ibid., 150.
33. Ibid., 153.

A few years ago he did essentially the same thing for which he now charges me with being a reconstructionist.

* * *

I may now add a few words about my view of the nature of facts and of the unbeliever's knowledge of them.

1. I hold that all the facts of the universe are exhaustively revelational of God.
   a. This is true of the facts of man's environment in nature and history.
   b. This is also true of man's own constitution as a rational and moral being.
2. In consequence of these two points I hold that all men unavoidably know God and themselves as creatures of God (Rom 1).

A brief explication of each point may be in order. Dr. Masselink contends that according to my view the natural man has no knowledge of either God or morality. The reverse is true. I have greatly stressed the fact that all men know God. Following Dr. Machen I hold that Christianity is capable of scholarly defense.[34] And this is so, I believe, because the facts of the universe clearly and unmistakably show forth the existence of God and of His truth.

Speaking of my view of man's natural knowledge of God, Dr. Masselink says: "The denial of 'natural knowledge of God' and sense of morality is, to our mind, in conflict with Synod's declaration."[35] The reference is to the declarations of the Synod of the Christian Reformed Church relative to the matter of Common Grace (1924). But I do not

---

34. There is a good bit of discussion on the relationship of Machen's apologetic to Van Til's. Much of the discussion (e.g., "Was Machen a presuppositionalist?") is anachronistic. Muether's analysis is accurate: "The longstanding debate over apparent differences between Machen and Van Til tends to obscure the more basic similarity between the two. What Van Til learned from his teacher and what Machen admired in his student was an unrelenting insistence on the coherence of both Christian theology *and* apologetics. Christianity is a *system* of truth, and Westminster promised to present that system with a methodological consistency that Princeton, now tainted with Auburn Affirmationists, could not." John R. Muether, *Cornelius Van Til: Reformed Apologist and Churchman* (Phillipsburg, NJ: P&R Publishing, 2008), 68.

35. Masselink, *Common Grace and Christian Education*, 96.

deny the "natural knowledge of God" or the "sense of morality." To be sure I do deny that this natural knowledge of God and of morality is the result of common grace. I think it is the *presupposition* of common grace. It is the presupposition also of saving grace.[36]

First then, if there is to be a natural knowledge of God all the facts must clearly speak of God. Calvin maintains that they do and I have closely followed him. The following quotations and references are from the syllabus to which Dr. Masselink makes reference: *An Introduction to Systematic Theology.*

After quoting from Calvin's exposition on Romans chapter 1:20 these words appear: "What Scripture therefore emphasizes is that even apart from special revelation, men *ought* to see that God is the Creator of the world."[37] Again, men ought to see the munificence of God.[38] Even the result of sin in no wise reduces the perspicuity of God's revelation.

> We would think of a man in the midst of heathendom and remember the elements in the revelation at his disposal in order to see then what logical conclusions he ought to draw if he reasoned correctly.
>
> In the first place, he ought to think of God as the creator of this world. In the second place, he ought to believe in the providence of God. In the third place, he ought to think of the presence of a certain non-saving grace of God.[39]

Then the revelation through the facts of nature is brought into close relation with the original supernatural revelation that God gave to the human race through Adam.[40] At the beginning of history man was in direct contact with the living God through supernatural revelation and "man remains responsible for these facts."[41]

---

36. This is an important theological point. The fact that all men know the true God is entailed in all men being the image of God. It is, therefore, the presupposition of common (and saving) grace, not the product of it.

37. Cornelius Van Til, *An Introduction to Systematic Theology: Prolegomena and the Doctrines of Revelation, Scripture, and God,* 2nd ed., ed. William Edgar (Phillipsburg, NJ: P&R Publishing, 2007) (hereafter *IST*), 140.

38. Ibid.

39. Ibid., 145.

40. Ibid., 146.

41. Ibid., 147.

The facts of man's constitution no less than the facts of his environment reveal God to man. Calvin says: "For, in the first place, no man can survey himself without forthwith turning his thoughts toward God in whom he lives and moves because it is perfectly obvious, that the endowments which we possess cannot possibly be from ourselves, nay, that our very being is nothing else than subsistence in God alone."[42, 43]

Sin has not effaced this natural knowledge of God. A sense of deity is "indelibly engraven on the human heart."[44] Try as men will they cannot suppress this knowledge of God; "for the worm of conscience, keener than burning steel, is gnawing within them."[45, 46] So also the seed of religion is divinely sown in all. Men should have recognized God; the revelation from without and from within is a daily challenge to them to turn to God.[47] God's power and divinity

are still displayed in man as well as about him, in the fact of the self-conscious activity of his person, in his own negative moral reaction to the revelation about and within him, in his sense of dissatisfaction with all non-theistic interpretations, and in a measure of involuntary recognition of the truth of the theistic interpretation as the true interpretation of the origin of the world.[48]

It is therefore utterly impossible for any man not to know God and morality.

The natural man has knowledge, true knowledge of God, in the sense that God through nature and man's own consciousness impresses his presence on man's attention. So definitely and inescapably has he done this, that try as he may, man cannot escape knowing God. It is this point that Paul stresses

---

42. Ibid., 156.
43. Van Til is referring here to John Calvin, *Institutes of the Christian Religion*, ed. and trans. Henry Beveridge (Grand Rapids: Eerdmans, 1957), 1.1.
44. Ibid., 1.3.3.
45. Van Til, *IST*, 158.
46. Calvin, *Institutes of the Christian Religion*, 1.3.3.
47. Van Til, *IST*, 158–59.
48. Ibid., 169.

in the first two chapters of Romans. Man has the sense of deity indelibly engraven upon him. He knows God and he knows himself and the world as God's creation. This is objective revelation to him. Even to the extent that this revelation is within man, i.e., in his own constitution, and as such may be called "subjective," it is none the less objective to him as an ethically responsive creature, and he is bound to react as an ethical person to this objective revelation.[49]

Or again:

The actual situation is therefore always a mixture of truth with error. Being "without God in the world" the natural man yet knows God, and, in spite of himself, to some extent recognizes God. By virtue of their creation in God's image, by virtue of the ineradicable sense of deity within them, and by virtue of God's restraining grace, those who hate God, yet in a restricted sense know God, and do good.[50]

If this be kept in mind, it will be seen that if, as Reformed theology has contended, both the doctrines of the absolute ethical antithesis of the natural man to God and of his relatively true knowledge and relatively good deeds must be maintained, we are not led into any inconsistency or self-contradiction.[51]

In an essay on "Nature and Scripture" published in *The Infallible Word*[52] the same sort of stress is found on the clarity of God's revelation to man in his environment and within himself. This is done over against the Roman Catholic concept of *analogia entis* (analogy of being).[53] "God is light and in him is no darkness at all (1 John 1:5). As such he cannot deny himself (2 Tim. 2:13). This God naturally has an all-inclusive plan for the created universe. He has planned all the relationships between all the aspects of created being. All

49. Ibid., 65.
50. Ibid.
51. Ibid., 66.
52. Cornelius Van Til, "Nature and Scripture," in *The Infallible Word*, ed. N. B. Stonehouse and Paul Woolley (Philadelphia: Presbyterian and Reformed, 1946).
53. See chapter 3, footnote 29.

184

created reality therefore displays this plan. It is, in consequence, inherently rational."[54]

Or again,

> By the idea of revelation, then, we are to mean not merely what comes to man through the facts surrounding him in his environment, but also that which comes to him by means of his own constitution as a covenant personality. The revelation that comes to man by way of his own rational and moral nature is no less objective to him than that which comes to him through the voice of trees and animals. Man's own psychological activity is no less revelational than the laws of physics about him. All created reality is inherently revelational of the nature and will of God. Even man's ethical reaction to God's revelation is still revelational. And as revelational of God, it is authoritative. The meaning of the Confessions' doctrine of the authority of Scripture does not become clear to us till we see it against the background of the original and basically authoritative character of God's revelation in nature. Scripture speaks authoritatively to such as must naturally live by authority. God speaks with authority wherever and whenever he speaks.

At this point a word may be said about the revelation of God through conscience and its relation to Scripture. Conscience is man's consciousness speaking on matters of directly moral import. Every act of man's consciousness is moral in the most comprehensive sense of that term. Yet there is a difference between questions of right and wrong in a restricted sense and general questions of interpretation. Now if man's whole consciousness was originally created perfect, and as such authoritatively expressive of the will of God, that same consciousness is still revelational and authoritative after the entrance of sin to the extent that its voice is still the voice of God. The sinner's efforts, so far as they are done self-consciously from his point of view, seek to destroy or bury the voice of God that comes to him through nature, which includes his own consciousness. But this effort cannot be wholly successful at any point

54. Van Til, "Nature and Scripture," 269.

in history. The most depraved of men cannot wholly escape the voice of God. Their greatest wickedness is meaningless except upon the assumption that they have sinned against the authority of God. Thoughts and deeds of utmost perversity are themselves revelational, revelational, that is, in their very abnormality.[55] The natural man accuses or else excuses himself only because his own utterly depraved consciousness continues to point back to the original natural state of affairs. The prodigal son can never forget the father's voice. It is the albatross forever about his neck.[56]

In the pamphlet *The Intellectual Challenge of the Gospel* the same procedure is followed as in the foregoing. The revelation of God to man in the created universe is said to be clear. Men therefore cannot help but know God. Man's own consciousness is part of the revelation of God to himself as an ethical reactor.

Paul makes bold to claim that all men know deep down in their hearts that they are creatures of God and have sinned against God their Creator and their judge.[57]

Paul knows that those who cling to the "wisdom" of the world do so against their better judgment and with an evil conscience. Every fact of "theism" and every fact of "Christianity" points with an accusing finger at the sinner, saying: "You are a covenant-breaker; repent and be saved!"[58]

It is only against the background of this stress on the perspicuity of the natural revelation of God about and within man, and these as related to the original supernatural revelation vouchsafed to Adam in paradise, that the meaning of the statement that the natural man and the regenerated man have nothing in common epistemologically must be taken. *It is constantly put in that context.* The point is that when and to the extent that the natural man is

55. In other words, for something to be deemed "evil" or "abnormal," a standard of "good" or "normal" must be presupposed. The fact of abnormality depends on that which is the "norm" or "standard," which is God himself. So also for that which is evil and good.
56. Van Til, "Nature and Scripture," 265–67.
57. Van Til, *The Intellectual Challenge of the Gospel* (London: Tyndale Press, 1950), 5.
58. Ibid.

engaged in interpreting life in terms of his *adopted principles then*, and *only* then, he has nothing in common with the believer.[59] But man can never completely suppress the truth.[60] On necessity he therefore knows that it is wrong to break the law of God. This point will receive further discussion under our second head dealing with,

II. MAN AS THE SUBJECT OF KNOWLEDGE

It is well to hear what Dr. Masselink has to say on my view of the natural man as the subject of knowledge. Something of this has already appeared in the preceding section; we now turn to the matter explicitly.

Says Dr. Masselink:

Our great difficulty with Van Til's philosophy of Common Grace is his premise or starting point, namely, the absolute ethical antithesis between God and man. This premise controls his whole system of thinking. All of the objections which follow are immediately related to this primary premise, which Van Til himself declares is his starting point.

Van Til says: "We must begin by emphasizing the *absolute ethical antithesis* in which the 'natural' man stands to God" (*Introduction to Systematic Theology*, p. 25).[61] All Reformed Theology, of course, asserts that there is an ethical antithesis between God and fallen man. The question is whether it is *absolute*. According to Webster's dictionary the term *absolute* means without qualification, limitation or restriction. The question is whether the term *absolute* is not too sweeping and far-reaching here.[62]

Dr. Masselink assumes that by the idea of the "absolute ethical antithesis" I must mean that man is as bad as he can be. "*The absolute*

---

59. These qualifications, highlighted and emphasized by Van Til, are crucial to a proper understanding of his argument. Notice that it is "to the extent" that the natural man interprets life in terms of his sinful principle; then and only then does he have nothing in common with the believer.

60. Thus, those who are in Adam can never live and act consistently according to their own sinful principle. To do so would be to attempt to annihilate oneself. (Neither, by the way, can those who are in Christ live and act consistently according to their own regenerate principle.)

61. Van Til, *IST*, 64–65.

62. Masselink, *Common Grace and Christian Education*, 73.

ethical antithesis of God is the devil. If we place man ethically, in the same category with the devil, then what becomes of the image of God in man?"[63]

> Reformed theology distinguishes between *total* and *absolute* depravity. By *total* depravity we mean that human depravity extends to every function of the soul, intellect, will and emotions. . . . By *absolute* depravity we mean that man is as bad as he can be. With absolute depravity there can no longer be any curbing of sin through Common Grace. . . . The Devil and the Lost in Hell are absolutely depraved, because there is no Common Grace in Hell. The absolute ethical antithesis between God and 'natural man,' as Van Til says, must imply absolute depravity. By affirming the *absolute ethical antithesis* we fail to see how there can be any room left for Common Grace.[64]

On this analysis of my view the following remarks are in order:

1. If Dr. Masselink had consulted my usage of the expression "absolute ethical antithesis" instead of going to the dictionary he would have found: (a) that I usually imply the expression *total* depravity. Apparently Dr. Masselink has been unable to find the expression *absolute depravity* in my booklet on *Common Grace*. The expression *total depravity* is there constantly used. (b) For me the idea of total or absolute depravity means that the sinner is *dead* in trespasses and sins (Eph 2:1). In *principle* man is therefore blind. If he is to see the truth about God and himself he must be born again. He must be born again *unto* knowledge.[65] But in spite of the fact that man is spiritually dead, dead in principle, absolutely dead, not half or partly dead in principle, he may know and do much that is relatively good.

Here we should again bring in the fact of the non-saving grace of God. In the case of Satan, the folly of his interpretation

63. Ibid., 74.
64. Ibid., 75.
65. Cf. Charles Hodge, *Systematic Theology*, 3 vols. (London: James Clarke, 1960), 3:17.

appears very clear. In the case of the sinner, however, we have a mixed situation. Through God's non-saving grace, the wrath of God on the sinner has been mitigated in this life. This appears along the whole line of man's interests. It appears along the line of man's physical life. Man is given an abundance of food and drink. It is shown in the fact that man's body, though weakened, is even so, particularly in some instances, a usable tool for the soul of man. It is shown in the fact that man's mind is not fully and exclusively bent upon evil. Though basically man is at enmity against God so that he is prone to hate God and his neighbor, this enmity against God does not come to full expression in this life. He is not a finished product.[66]

(c) The burden of the entire discussion in *Common Grace* is to the effect that it is fully consistent with the fact of total depravity to maintain that there is a genuine commonness between believer and unbeliever. There are those who have denied common grace. They have argued that God *cannot* have any attitude of favor at *any stage* in history to such as are the "vessels of wrath." But to reason thus is to make logic rule over Scripture. Against both Hoeksema and Schilder I have contended that we must think more concretely and analogically than they did, allowing ourselves to be led only by scriptural exegesis.

All the truths of the Christian religion have of necessity the appearance of being contradictory.[67] But since we build our thinking on the ontological trinity and therefore on the revelation of this triune God as given in Scripture, we think analogically. We do not fear to accept that which has the appearance of being contradictory. We know that what appears to be so to us is not really so.

So also in the case of the question of common grace. We are not to say that God cannot have any attitude of favor to a generality of mankind, including both reprobate and elect, because our logic seems to require us to do so. In the case of common grace, as in the case of every other biblical doctrine, we should

66. Van Til, *IST*, 168.
67. Van Til is paraphrasing the statement from Bavinck that mystery is the lifeblood of theology.

seek to take all the factors of Scripture teaching and bind them together into systematic relations with one another as far as we can. But we do not expect to have a logically deducible relationship between one doctrine and another. We expect to have only an *analogical* system.

For this reason then we must not hesitate to say that God has a *common* attitude of favor to all mankind as a generality. We must not fear to assert that though the ultimate end of God for the elect is their salvation, they yet are under God's displeasure when they do not fully live up to His requirement for men. Similarly we must not fear to assert in the case of the reprobate that though they are ultimately vessels of wrath they yet can be in history, in a sense, the objects of the favor of God.

The case is similar with respect to the knowledge of unbelievers and their ability to do that which is relatively good. The fact that they are *in principle* opposed to God and would destroy the very foundation of knowledge and ethics, yet, in spite of this, because of God's common grace they can discover much truth and do much good.

We say that this is one factor of the whole situation. We do not say that it is the only factor. God loves the works of his hands, and the progress that they make to their final fulfillment. So we may and should rejoice with God in the unfolding of the history of the race, even in the unfolding of the wickedness of man in order that the righteousness of God may be most fully displayed. But if God tells us that, in spite of the wickedness of men, and in spite of the fact that they misuse his gifts for their own greater condemnation, he is long suffering with them, we need not conclude that there is no sense in which God has a favor to the unbeliever. There is a sense in which God has a disfavor to the believer because, in spite of the new life within him, he sins in the sight of God. So God may have favor to the unbeliever because of the "relative good" that God himself gives him in spite of the principle of sin within him. If we were to think of God and his relation to the world in a univocal or abstract fashion, we might agree with those who maintain that there is no qualitative difference between the favor of God toward the saved and toward the unsaved. Arminians and Barthians virtually do this.[68] Or, we might agree with those who maintain that there is no sense in which God can show favor to the reprobate. On the other hand, if we reason concretely about God and his relation to the world, we simply listen to what God has told us in his Word on the matter. It may even then be exceedingly difficult to construct a theory of "common grace" which will do justice to what Scripture says. We make Scripture the standard of our thinking, and not our thinking the standard of Scripture. All of man's activity, whether intellectual or moral, is analogical; and for this reason it is quite possible for the unsaved sinner to do what is "good" in a sense, and for the believer to do what is "evil" in a sense.

With respect to the question, then, as to whether Scripture actually teaches an attitude of favor, up to a point, on the part of God toward the non-believer, we can only intimate that we believe it does. Even when we take full cognizance of the fact that the unbeliever abuses every gift of God and uses it for the greater manifestation of his wickedness, there seems to be evidence in Scripture that God, for this life, has a certain attitude of favor to unbelievers. We may point to such passages as the following: In Ps 145.9, we are told, "The Lord is good to all; and his tender mercies are over all his works." In seeking the meaning of such a passage, we must be careful. In the first place, it is to be remembered that God is constantly setting his own people in the center of the outflow of his goodness to the children of men. So, in Exodus 34.6, 7, we read: "And the Lord God passed before him, and proclaimed, The Lord, The Lord God, merciful and gracious, long suffering and abundant in goodness and truth, keeping mercy for thousands, forgiving iniquity and transgression and sin, and that will by no means clear the guilty; visiting the iniquity of the fathers upon the children, and upon the children's children, unto the third and fourth generation." In this passage we are, as it were, warned to think concretely on the question before us. God's

68. Arminian theology does this when it holds that God's love for every individual person is indiscriminate, and is discriminated only at the point of one's free decision; Barthian theology does this when it holds that all people, to *be* people, must be in Christ. Thus, the former theology is univocal, seeing an identity in God's love for every person, and the latter theology is abstract.

mercy and grace is primarily extended to those whose sins are forgiven. If in any sense it is given to those whose sins are not forgiven, it must always be remembered that God does not overlook iniquity. We may therefore expect that in Ps 145 the Psalmist teaches nothing that is out of accord with what has been taught in Exodus 34. Thus, the primary meaning of Ps 145 is again that God's great favor is toward his people. Even when God gives great gifts to non-believers, they are, in a more basic sense, gifts to believers. Gifts of God to unbelievers help to make the life of believers possible, and in a measure, pleasant. But this does not detract from the fact that the unbeliever himself is, in a measure, the recipient of God's favor. There is a certain joy in the gift of life and its natural blessings for the unbeliever. And we may well think that Ps 145 has this in mind. Such joy as there is in the life of the unbeliever cannot be found in him after this life is over. Even in the hereafter, the lost will belong to the works of God's hands. And God no doubt has joy that through the works of evil men and angels, he is establishing his glory. Yet that is not what the Psalmist seems to mean. There seems to be certain satisfaction on the part of God even in the temporary joy of the unbeliever as a creature of himself, a joy which will in the end turn to bitterness, but which, nonetheless, is joy while it lasts.

Another passage to which we briefly refer is Matthew 5.44, 45. "But I say unto you, bless them that curse you, do good to them that hate you, and pray for them that despitefully use you, and persecute you; that ye may be the children of your father which is in heaven: for he maketh his sun to rise on the evil and on the good." In this passage, the disciples of Jesus are told to deny themselves the selfish joy of expressing enmity against those that hate them. They are not to express their attitude of hostility. But this is not all they are to do. They are to replace the attitude of hatred with an attitude of love. He does not know but that this one who now hates him may one day become a believer. This is one factor in the total situation. Yet this is not to be made the only factor. It is not even the expressed reason for loving his enemy. The one guide for the believer's action with respect to the enemy is God's attitude toward that enemy. And the believer is told definitely to love his enemy in imitation of God's attitude toward that enemy. God's attitude toward that enemy must therefore in some sense be one of love. It is no doubt the love of an enemy, and, therefore, in God's case, never the same sort of love as the love toward his children. And to the extent that we know men to be enemies of the Lord, we too cannot love them in the same sense in which we are told to love fellow-believers. God no doubt lets the wheat and the tares grow together till the day of judgment, but even so, though God's ultimate purpose with unbelievers is their destruction and the promotion of his glory through their destruction, he loves them, in a sense, while they are still kept by himself, through his own free gifts, from fully expressing the wicked principle that is in them.[69]

(d) It is not in accordance with fact to say that the absolute ethical antithesis, even when taken as being such *in principle only,* is for me the starting point when dealing with the relation of the believer and the non-believer. As the preceding quotations imply, my starting point is always the fact that God originally made man in His image and that He placed him in an exhaustively revelational context.[70]

To be sure, we cannot agree with the Roman Catholic position. According to this position there is an area of knowledge, an area of interpretation, which believers and unbelievers have in common without difference. Similarly, the Arminian position calls for such a common or neutral territory of interpretation.[71] Over against this we must take into consideration the fact that the natural man is

---

69. Van Til, *IST,* 381–83.

70. That is to say, Van Til's starting point is the *covenant*—man as God's *image,* thus meant to reflect God's character in God's presence, and, given his omnipresence, the *revelational* context in which all men always and everywhere live.

71. Cf. Bishop Butler's *Analogy.* Bishop Joseph Butler (1692–1752) was the most influential Protestant apologist of the eighteenth century. The book to which Van Til refers, *The Analogy of Religion Natural and Revealed to the Constitution and Course of Nature* (1736), was a defense of Christianity against the prevalent deism of the day. Butler uses a double negative argument to attempt to argue from the natural religion of the deists to the probability of revealed religion as well (i.e., given x in natural religion, it is not so irrational to believe y in revealed religion). The basic thrust of Butler's argument is that this (observed) life and the (unobserved) afterlife, taken together, exhibit features that resemble known features of this life taken alone. For example, we can infer that this life is a training-ground for the next life from the way in which the early years of this life are a training-ground for the later ones. Parenthetically, the reader should note that the term *analogy* is not used in the same way by Butler, Aquinas, or Van Til, which is one reason why confusion remains with respect to the term itself in apologetics.

ethically depraved, ". . . wholly defiled in all the parts and faculties of soul and body."

We need to recognize this complexity, and to see the problem it involves. It will not do to ignore the difference between Christians and non-Christians and speak of *reason* in general. Such a thing does not exist in practice. As dangerous as it is to speak of method in general without distinguishing clearly between the Christian theistic and the non-theistic method, so dangerous is it to speak of reason in general or of a "common consciousness" in general. We must therefore begin with:

(a) The *Adamic consciousness*, or, the reason of man as it existed before the fall of man. This reason was derivative. Its knowledge was, in the nature of the case, true, though not exhaustive. This reason was in covenant with God, instead of at enmity against God. It recognized the fact that its function was that of the interpretation of God's revelation. In paradise Adam had a true conception of the relation of the particulars to the universals of knowledge with respect to the created universe. He named the animals "according to their nature," that is, in accordance with the place God had given them in His universe. Then, too, Adam could converse truly about the meaning of the universe in general and about their own life in particular with Eve. Thus the subject-object and the subject-subject relationship was normal. In paradise man's knowledge was self-consciously analogical; man wanted to know the facts of the universe in order to fulfill his task as a covenant-keeper.

(b) Then, secondly, we must think of the sinful consciousness, i.e., of the human reason as it became after the entrance of sin. Looked at from the point of view of its unredeemed character, we may speak of it as the *unregenerate consciousness*. This is the "natural man," "dead in trespasses and sin." The natural man wants to be something that he cannot be. He wants to be "as God," himself the judge of good and evil, himself the standard of truth. He sets himself as the ideal of *comprehensive* knowledge. When he sees that he will never reach this ideal he concludes that all reality is surrounded by darkness. As a child would say, "If I cannot do this, no one else can," so the "natural man" today says in effect that, since he cannot grasp knowledge comprehensively, God cannot either. The non-regenerate man takes for granted that the meaning of the space-time world is imminent in itself, and that man is the ultimate interpreter of this world, instead of its humble re-interpreter. The natural man wants to be creatively constructive instead of reconstructive.[72]

It is only after we have dealt with what men have in common that we turn to that which separates them as sinners saved and sinners not saved. The fallen consciousness wants in principle to be *creatively constructive*. The regenerated consciousness wants, in principle, to be *receptively reconstructive*. So we might expect that two such mutually exclusive principles of interpretation could have *nothing* in common. But we cannot take such an absolutist position.

> We are well aware of the fact that non-Christians have a great deal of knowledge about this world which is true as far as it goes. . . . That is, there is a sense in which we can and must allow for the value of knowledge of non-Christians.[73]

We do not make this point as a concession but rather as a fact taught directly by Scripture itself and as such observed in daily experience.

The question how those who are totally depraved *in principle* can yet do the natural good and have true knowledge "has always been a difficult point." But no more or less difficult than all other Christian teaching. Pighius argues against Calvin that commonness must always be *commonness* without qualification. He contends that therefore the attitude of God to all men must be the same without difference. Hoeksema argues that since God has determined some men to be elect and others to be reprobate there must be *nothing but difference between them*. But the truly Reformed position does not go off on a tangent toward Arminianism, nor does it go off on a tangent with Hoeksema. Both types of thinking are univocal instead of analogical, abstract instead of concrete.

72. Van Til, *IST*, 62–63.
73. Ibid., 63.

We therefore do not expect to be able to settle this difficult point, *or any other difficult point,* to the full satisfaction of either Hoeksema or the Arminians. We would do with this problem as we must do with all other theological problems. We would take all factors into consideration simultaneously and thus "hem in the question." That is all that the fathers did when at Chalcedon they established the relation of the two natures of Christ to one another. They were not able to satisfy and neither did they desire to satisfy the "logical" demands of either the Eutychians who wanted a confusion of natures lest there be no identity between them, nor of the Nestorians[74] who wanted two persons lest there be no difference between God and man.

Now, "In order to hem in our question we are persuaded that we must begin by emphasizing the *absolute ethical antithesis* in which the 'natural man' stands to God."[75]

From the point of view that man, as dead in trespasses and sins, seeks to interpret life in terms of himself instead of in terms of God, he is wholly mistaken. "From this ultimate point of view[76] the 'natural man' knows nothing truly. He has chains about his neck and sees shadows only."[77, 78]

Dr. Masselink quoted this passage as though it controlled the whole discussion of the relation of the knowledge of believers and unbelievers. Nothing could be further from what is actually said. *The very idea of man's ethical depravity as absolute in principle presupposes that men are inherently and originally in possession of the truth about God and themselves.*

74. Eutychianism was a Christological heresy in the fourth and fifth centuries that taught that Christ had only one nature. Nestorianism was a fifth-century Christological heresy that taught that the two natures of Christ were actually two persons. The Chalcedonian Creed (451 A.D.) denounced such views. It affirmed that Christ is to be "acknowledged in two natures, inconfusedly (ἀσυγχύτως), unchangeably (ἀρέπτως), indivisibly (ἀδιαιρέτως), and inseparably (ἀχωρίστως)."

75. Van Til, *IST*, 64.

76. Notice again the important and crucial qualification: "from this ultimate point of view."

77. Van Til, *IST*, 64.

78. Van Til's reference to the natural man who "sees shadows only" is significant. He is referring to the "Allegory of the Cave" that was set forth by Plato, in his *Republic* (book 7). Plato (through Socrates) describes people who are confined to a cave and who see shadows only. Eventually, they begin to interpret the shadows as the true reality. The philosopher, on the other hand, is the one who escapes the shadows of the cave and thus ascribes true forms to reality. Similarly, the natural man sees shadows only and thinks that such shadows are the substance of true reality. He is never able to get to the basic truth of the matter.

We must therefore distinguish between natural man's knowledge of God by virtue of the revelational character of all created reality, himself included, and the natural man's being without God in the world and blind because of sin. "The natural man has knowledge, true knowledge of God, in the sense that God through nature and man's own consciousness impresses his presence on man's attention."[79] But man seeks to suppress this revelation of God about and within him. "Having made alliance with Satan, man makes a grand monistic assumption.[80] Not merely in his conclusion but as well in his method and starting point he takes for granted his own ultimacy."[81] He needs therefore, as Warfield put it, new light and new power of sight.[82] The natural man has cemented colored glasses to his face. And all things are yellow to the jaundiced eye. So then "to the extent that he works according to this monistic assumption he misinterprets all things, flowers, no less than God."[83] However, lest someone should draw absolutistic conclusions, conclusions dictated by a supposed logic rather than by Scripture from what has been said, we hasten to add:

Fortunately the natural man is never fully consistent while in this life.[84] As the Christian sins against his will, so the natural man "sins against" his own essentially Satanic principle. As the Christian has the incubus of his "old man" weighing him down and therefore keeping him from realizing the "life of Christ" within him, so the natural man has the incubus of the sense of Deity weighing him down and keeping him from realizing the life of Satan within him.

79. Van Til, *IST*, 65.
80. A "monistic assumption" is to assume that reality is, at bottom, *one*. In philosophy, it takes the form, for example, of an "All is . . ." assumption. Less technical, but no less disastrous, is the assumption that there is no distinction between God (as the "I Am") and man (as his image). Thus, everything is thought to be on the same plane of existence. This is clearly seen, for example, in the notion of evolution; man's status is equivalent to that of animals, trees, etc. So man takes for granted his own ultimacy because he alone defines reality and gives it its meaning.
81. Van Til, *IST*, 65.
82. Benjamin B. Warfield, "Inspiration of Scripture," in *The Works of Benjamin B. Warfield*, vol. 5: *Calvin and Calvinism* (Bellingham, WA: Logos Research Systems, Inc., 2008), 70.
83. Van Til, *IST*, 65.
84. Notice that the natural man is never fully consistent with his unbelief, because he is God's image and because God restrains his sinful principle. But this in no way negates the principle and its foundational importance.

The actual situation is therefore always a mixture of truth with error.[85] Being "without God in the world" the natural man yet knows God, and, in spite of himself, to some extent recognizes God. By virtue of their creation in God's image, by virtue of the ineradicable sense of deity within them and by virtue of God's restraining general grace, those who hated God, yet in a restricted sense, know God and do good.[86]

It appears then that the section in which I did use the expression "absolute ethical antithesis" is mainly directed against those who would interpret the idea of the antithesis to mean that man is as bad as he can be. The whole burden of the argument is that to hold to the idea of absolute or total ethical depravity does not *need to*, and *must not* lead to, the idea that man is now satanic. Since the antithesis is ethical and not metaphysical, God's restraining grace keeps man from being as bad as he can be.

* * *

From the preceding discussion it will also be clear what reply I would make to another charge made by Dr. Masselink. He says: "The absolute ethical antithesis is in conflict with our conception of the Divine image in 'natural man.' " And again, he adds: "If we assert that there is an *absolute ethical antithesis* between God and fallen man, then how can we speak of fallen man as bearing the image of God, unless with Hoeksema we restrict this to the strictly formal sense, meaning thereby that man is merely 'capable of bearing God's image.' "[87]

But I have argued at length, particularly against Barth, that the image of God in man consists of actual knowledge content. Man does not start on the course of history merely with a capacity for knowing God. On the contrary, he begins his course with *actual*

85. This deserves to be highlighted. Again, the principle is all-important in that it allows us to see the covenantal condition of unbelief, but the *actual* situation—meaning the *practical* situation—is that there is a mixture of truth and error. The unbeliever sees the flower and knows it is a flower, and can even define its various parts, but he will never say that it is what it is, as a flower and in its parts, because of the plan and purpose of God. Thus, his knowledge (and description) of the flower is a "shadow" of the reality itself.

86. Van Til, *IST*, 65.

87. Masselink, *Common Grace and Christian Education*, 74.

knowledge of God. Moreover, he cannot even eradicate this knowledge of God. It is this fact that makes sin to be sin "against better knowledge." In this I think I am in line with Reformed theology in general and with Calvin in particular.

At this point there no doubt emerges a difference between Dr. Masselink and me on the question of the function of common grace. I do not think it is the function of common grace to maintain the metaphysical *status quo*. Roman Catholic theology thinks of the creature as beginning as it were from the borders of non-being. There is, according to Roman theology, in man, as in created reality generally, an inherent tendency to sink back into non-existence. Hence the need of supernatural aid from the outset of man's being.[88] There is in Roman theology a confusion between the metaphysical and the ethical aspects of man's being.

If there is any one thing on which Bavinck has laid great stress throughout the four volumes of his *Gereformerde Dogmatiek*, it is that true Protestantism is a matter of restoring man, the creature of God, to his true *ethical* relationship with God.[89] The destructive tendency of sin is not to be seen in a gradual diminution of man's rationality and morality. Man is not less a creature, a rational moral creature of God when he turns his back to God and hates his maker than he was before.[90]

Therefore when God gives to man His grace, His saving grace, this does not reinstate his rationality and morality. It reinstates his *true* knowledge, righteousness, and holiness (Col. 3.10; Eph. 4.24). It restores man *ethically*, not metaphysically. So too, if we take common grace to be that which has to do with the restraint of sin, then it is an *ethical* not a *metaphysical function* that it performs. It does not maintain, as Dr. Masselink seems to contend, the creatural characteristics of man. It does not sustain the image of God in "the

88. Van Til's reasoning here, though complex, includes at least the following: Because, on a Romanist scheme, man was not perfect and complete at creation, there was need of a *donum superadditum* (an added gift) in order for him to will the good. Evil, according to Romanism (following the early Augustine) is nothing; it is a privation, a lack. To the extent that man wills evil, he is closer to nothing, to nonbeing, and has rejected that which is supernatural, i.e., the *donum superadditum*. So, man is near to nonbeing at the beginning of creation.

89. "*Ethical*" here could best be read as "*covenantal*," including as it does the image of God and man's essential and responsible relationship to God.

90. As it was in the beginning, is now, and ever shall be, man is either in Adam, or, by grace, in Christ.

wider sense," consisting of man's rationality and morality. It keeps the man who will be rational anyway, by virtue of his creation in the image of God, from expressing his hostility to God in the field of knowledge to such an extent as to make it impossible for himself to destroy knowledge.[91] And in restraining him in his ethical hostility to God, God releases his creatural powers so that he can make positive contributions to the field of knowledge and art.[92] Similarly, in restraining him from expressing his ethical hostility to God there is a release within him of his moral powers so that they can perform that which is "morally" though not spiritually good. The rationality and morality of man had not diminished through sin. Man cannot be *amoral.* But by sin man fell ethically; he became hostile to God. And common grace is the means by which God keeps man from expressing the *principle* of hostility to its full extent, thus enabling man to do the "relatively good."

True, we have to speak of sin as, in principle, destructive of the work of God. We have to speak "as if" sin might prevent God's plan for the universe from being realized. And this would seem to indicate that the world, metaphysically speaking, would have been destroyed by sin. And it might seem to indicate that common grace keeps the metaphysical situation intact. At the same time we know that sin and Satan were bound to be defeated. God planned this

91. It is, therefore, to refer again to our example above, because man is the image of God, and because his sin is restrained by God, that he can affirm that a flower is a flower. Based on his own principle, man would deny reality itself, because reality reveals God, and his constant rebellion requires that he suppress that revelation.

92. Calvin's view in this regard is worth quoting here: "Meanwhile, we ought not to forget those most excellent benefits of the divine Spirit, which he distributes to whomsoever he wills, for the common good of mankind. The understanding and knowledge of Bezalel and Oholiab, needed to construct the Tabernacle, had to be instilled in them by the Spirit of God [Ex. 31:2–11; 35:30–35]. It is no wonder, then, that the knowledge of all that is most excellent in human life is said to be communicated to us through the Spirit of God. Nor is there any reason to ask, What have the impious, who are utterly estranged from God, to do with his Spirit? We ought to understand the statement that the Spirit of God dwells only in believers [Rom. 8:9] as referring to the Spirit of sanctification through whom we are consecrated as temples to God [1 Cor. 3:16]. Nonetheless he fills, moves, and quickens all things by the power of the same Spirit, and does so according to the character that he bestowed upon each kind by the law of creation. But if the Lord has willed that we be helped in physics, dialectic, mathematics, and other like disciplines, by the work and ministry of the ungodly, let us use this assistance to suffer just punishment for our sloths. But lest anyone think a man truly blessed when he is credited with possessing great power to comprehend truth under the elements of this world [cf. Col. 2:8], we should at once add that all this capacity to understand, with the understanding that follows upon it, is an unstable and transitory thing in God's sight, when a solid foundation of truth does not underlie it." Calvin, *Institutes of the Christian Religion,* 2.2.16.

defeat before the foundation of the world. These two notions are limiting or supplementative concepts. They modify one another. We cannot make linear deductions from one of these principles taken by itself. Therefore we cannot say that the world was on the way to being destroyed by sin except for the fact that common grace came in and saved it from destruction. We must rather reason from the fact of God's all-comprehensive plan and make relative distinctions within it. Then we conclude that common grace, by restraining sin, influences the condition of the universe as planned by God.

According to Dr. Masselink the created powers of the universe themselves tended to disappear into nothingness and have to be kept in existence through common grace. On this, then, there is disagreement between Dr. Masselink and me; I would think of common grace as an ethical attitude on the part of God to mankind and an ethical response which is otherwise than this response would be if sin were allowed to go unchecked.

Conscience

Dr. Masselink also criticizes me for thinking of conscience as revelational of God.

> Van Til speaks of consciences as a means of general revelation. We cannot at all agree with this. There is a vast difference between God's general revelation and human conscience. God's general revelation is objective, whereas conscience is subjective; God's general revelation is divine, whereas conscience is human; God's general revelation is infallible, whereas conscience is fallible. Conscience is man's answer to God's general revelation. The Holy Spirit witnesses within man's heart that God is holy and an avenger of evil, and conscience is man's response to this internal witness. If there is an *absolute ethical antithesis* between God and man all functions of human conscience become impossible.[93]

This criticism is the same in intent as that made with respect to Machen in Dr. Masselink's dissertation. "In the fifth place we

93. Masselink, *Common Grace and Christian Education*, 75.

do not like the way in which Prof. Machen speaks of *conscience as a means of revelation*."[94] In criticizing Machen's view Dr. Masselink deals with Rom 2.14, 15, and concludes by saying: "Also here God's general revelation namely, the work of the law, and conscience are distinguished."[95] He quotes Hepp as follows with approval: "To be sure the Holy Spirit is active in all of this, yet only in a mediate way. So there is a difference in principle between conscience and the General testimony which is directly a testimony of the Holy Spirit."[96]

The main charge against Machen and me is therefore that we have confused the divine and the human; but neither Machen nor I has done such a thing. Leaving out Machen's views, I may point out that, as has appeared even in the quotations given, I take conscience to be an *aspect* of the created consciousness of man. And everything created is revelational of God. In this broad sense even the sinful reaction of man to the revelation of God in the narrow sense is still revelational of God's general purpose.[97] It is only by thus thinking of all created reality as revelational that the ethical actions of man can be properly focused. Without thus making all created reality revelational of God the ethical reaction of man *would take place in a vacuum.*

To be sure, the revelation of God in the consciousness of man is psychologically subjective. It is the human subject which, in its very constitution and function, speaks of God. Calvin wonders at the marvelous working of the human mind and heart as revelational evidence of the work of God. And Dr. Masselink admits that "also 'conscience' was often conceived as a means of revelation by the old Reformed theologians, but that 'conscience' was conceived of in a very *broad* way."[98] Well, it is in a broad way that I am taking it.

Nor was it only the "old Reformed theologians" who spoke of conscience as revelational in this broad way. Bavinck himself does so not once but repeatedly. Speaking of the comprehensiveness of God's general revelation, he says: "He reveals himself also in the heart and conscience of every man, Job 34.8; 33.4; Prv 20.27; Jn 1.3–5, 9, 10; Rom 2.14.15; 8.16. This revelation

94. Masselink, *Professor J. Gresham Machen*, 155.
95. Ibid., 158.
96. Ibid., 157.
97. That is to say, for example, that sin shows us something of God's holiness, in that his character is opposed to it, and it shows us the wrath of God (see Rom. 1:18–32).
98. Masselink, *Professor J. Gresham Machen*, 156.

of God is general, in itself observable and intelligible to every man."[99] Discussing the principles of religion, Bavinck speaks as follows: "Thus there is not only an external, objective, but also an internal, subjective revelation."[100] Elsewhere he signifies the testimony of the Holy Spirit by which man accepts the truth of Scripture as revelational. "Objective revelation is therefore not sufficient; it must in a sense be continued and completed in subjective revelation."[101] Other passages of similar import could be cited.

The main point is that if man could look anywhere and not be confronted with the revelation of God then he could not sin in the biblical sense of the term. Sin is the breaking of the law of God. God confronts man everywhere. He cannot in the nature of the case confront man anywhere if he does not confront him everywhere.[102] God is one; the law is one. If man could press one button on the radio of his experience and not hear the voice of God then he would always press that button and not the others. But man cannot even press the button of his own self-consciousness without hearing the requirement of God.

The Theistic Proofs

The question of the theistic proofs also involves the idea of the all-comprehensiveness and the perspicuity of general revelation in man's consciousness as well as in the facts about him. Dr. Masselink rejects Machen's view of conscience as revelatory of God. That is the question of revelation in and through the human subject. So he also rejects Machen's acceptance of the "theistic proofs" as foundational to the truth of Christianity. That is the question of revelation in and through the facts of the universe in general. Following Hepp's line of reasoning Dr. Masselink says that in the former case we would be making our certainty to rest upon the human subject, and in the latter case we would be making our certainty to rest upon the created object. In both cases we would be depending upon a creature. And certainty rests in God alone.

99. Herman Bavinck, *Gereformeerde Dogmatiek*, 3rd ed. (Kampen: Kok, 1918), 1:321 (*RD*, 1:310). The Job reference should not be 34:8, but 32:8.
100. Ibid., 1:290 (*RD*, 1:279).
101. Ibid., 1:534 (*RD*, 1:506).
102. Note how important God's covenantal *presence* is for a proper understanding of revelation, of man, and of sin against God.

With Hepp we must speak of the general internal testimony of the Holy Spirit as witnessing to general revelation. Then by this general testimony of the Spirit we have certainty.

Even the general external testimony of the Spirit, says Dr. Masselink, cannot by itself give certainty to man.

> It is a revelation which comes to us as a witness. A revelation is a disclosure of the thoughts of God. The whole creation is full of God's thoughts and they come to us in the General External Testimony of the Spirit. This general External Testimony of the Spirit can reveal God's thoughts to us, but cannot give us certainty with regard to them. Why not? you ask. This is because all revelation takes place through means. We cannot know the essence of things except through the things themselves. If this revelation, therefore, would have to give us certainty in regard to these matters, it would have to do it through the things themselves. These would then in turn become the basis of our certainty. This we have already observed cannot be, as then the certainty is in the creation itself and not in the Creator. The absolute certainty I receive only then, when the Holy Spirit gives me this assurance that these things are so apart from the external revelation.[103]

The point of importance here is again the question of revelation, especially of general revelation. This revelation discloses the thoughts of God. These thoughts come through the general external testimony of the Holy Spirit. But though the general external testimony reveals God to us this testimony cannot give us certainty. The reason is that this revelation or testimony takes place through means, and the means are created facts, objective or subjective. So, since they are not God Himself, they cannot give us certainty with respect to God. Hence the need of a direct internal witness added to the external witness of the Spirit.

On this construction of Hepp's the following remarks are apposite:

1. It is not found in Kuyper and Bavinck or in the "Old Princeton theology." Hepp himself says that Bavinck came near to his

103. Masselink, *Professor J. Gresham Machen*, 150.

idea of a general testimony of the Spirit, but that he did not quite attain unto it.

2. It is out of analogy with the relation of Scripture and the special internal testimony of the Holy Spirit witnessing to the truth of Scripture; this in spite of the fact that Hepp seeks to carry through the analogy. Calvin's doctrine of the internal testimony of the Spirit does not presuppose the lack of certainty in the revelation given in Scripture. On the contrary, for Calvin all revelation is objectively true and certainly true. But the sinner does not want to believe that which is in itself certain and clear as day. So the Holy Spirit in regenerating and converting man enables him to accept that which as unregenerate and unconverted he could not accept. It brings him back, in principle, to the normal state of affairs. The testimony of the Spirit within man is to the objective and certain[104] truth of that which comes to man through external revelation.

3. Even the "immediate testimony" of the Holy Spirit has, at last, to terminate upon man. It has to be mediated to man through man's own consciousness. Otherwise it has no content. The human mind must think upon and reconstruct for itself the objective revelation given to it whether through Scripture or through "nature." But to think upon it is a psychological activity. It is an activity of the human mind. It is to the thinking subject that the internal testimony of the Spirit comes. It terminates upon this subject. It is unavoidably mediated to the ethically responsible subject through this very subject itself. Without mediation through both object and subject there is no revelation and no reception of revelation. Subjectivity in the objectionable sense of the term does not come into the picture of Christian thinking by the insistence that both the created object and the created subject are nothing but what they could not help but be, namely, revelational, exclusively revelational of God. Subjectivity of the objectionable sort comes into the Christian's thinking only if he tones down this objective certainty. For if he does and then tries

---

104. The notion of certainty, as in this case, is very often used without clear definition or explanation. The concept itself is not used uniformly across the literature, and its meaning is tied to the context in which it is used. Generally speaking, *epistemic* certainty accrues to a proposition if there is no proposition that is more warranted than it. *Metaphysical* certainty, on the other hand, often has reference to the impossibility of the contrary, i.e., "recognizing what must be true in order for our world to be the kind of world it is." Robert Audi, *The Cambridge Dictionary of Philosophy* (Cambridge: Cambridge University Press, 1995), 113. Van Til has the latter kind of certainty in mind here.

to make up for it by the idea of an internal testimony of the Spirit, then the directness of this testimony unavoidably partakes of the nature of identification of the creature with God. It leads to the position that only God can know God to be God with certainty.[105]

* * *

Dr. Masselink's criticism of my evaluation of the theistic proofs is quite different from his criticism of Machen's acceptance of these proofs. But the unity of these two criticisms lies in the fact that both Machen and I are out of agreement with Hepp's evaluation of them. And this evaluation of them by Hepp rests upon his doctrine of the external and internal general testimony of the Holy Spirit. Dr. Masselink's criticism of my view will be given first, then the views of Hepp stated; and after that an analysis made of the idea of the general testimony of the Spirit.

1. Dr. Masselink asserts that I deny any truth value to the theistic proofs.[106] "According to Van Til, Bavinck's 'Theistic Proofs' have no value whatsoever. This too is a logical consequence of his major premise of the *absolute ethical antithesis* between God and natural man."[107]

This is again simply contrary to fact.

The argument for the existence of God and for the truth of Christianity is objectively valid. We should not tone down the validity of this argument to the probability level. The argument may be poorly stated, and may never be adequately stated. But in itself the argument is absolutely sound. Christianity is the only reasonable position to hold. It is not merely as reasonable as other positions, or a bit more reasonable than

105. Van Til is here critiquing the position of Masselink and Hepp. Masselink, following Hepp, is arguing that, since certainty can only come from and be produced by God, there can be no certainty *by means of* our conscience (subjective) or the external world (objective). Van Til's point is that certainty can come through both the subjective and the objective, given that God speaks in and through both means (see Rom. 1:18–2:15). If God speaks through both, and if both means produce knowledge, then certainty should be the result. If, on the other hand, certainty can only be obtained immediately, then there must be an identification of the creature's certainty with God (because the certainty is unmediated and thus direct), and therefore an identification of the creature with God.

106. Masselink, *Common Grace and Christian Education*, 83.

107. Ibid., 85.

other positions; it alone is the natural and reasonable position for man to take. By stating the argument as clearly as we can, we may be the agents of the Spirit in pressing the claims of God upon men. If we drop to the level of the merely probable truthfulness of Christian theism, we, to that extent, lower the claims of God upon men. This is, we believe, the sense of Calvin's *Institutes* on the matter.[108]

To say that the argument for Christianity and for the existence of God is absolutely valid I am merely applying the idea that God's revelation without and within man is perspicuous.[109] If then man rightly interprets this revelation he has an absolutely valid argument for the truth. But the sinner, so far as he works from his adopted principle which rests in himself as autonomous, does not interpret the facts of the universe rightly. How could he? He assumes himself to be ultimate. He therefore assumes also that the facts of the universe are not created but exist in themselves. He also assumes that man's reasoning powers are ultimate and that they must therefore be determinative of what is possible and what is impossible in the realm of being.

Now *in principle*, the natural man interprets human experience upon these false assumptions. *In principle* he interprets all things in terms of man as the final reference point. And so he comes to the conclusion that god is some abstract principle beyond the cosmos, is some unifying principle within the cosmos, or is identical with the cosmos.

But the facts of the universe about him testify against such a distortion of them. Men ought to know, and know they ought to know and see God as their Creator and benefactor. They ought to see God as manifesting His wrath upon men when they behold the evils of nature. Similarly, they *ought* to see God as the Creator and benefactor when they behold themselves as image bearers of

108. Van Til, *Common Grace*, 62.
109. The problem with the theistic proofs, generally speaking, is *not what* they say, but *to whom* they say it. As we noted earlier (see chapter 3, footnote 184), it is certainly true that God is the first cause. But, to the extent that the unbeliever is true to his own sinful principle, he will either reject such a notion or understand causality univocally, such that it applies to both God and man in an identical way. Not only so, but if the proofs are thought to appeal to that which is neutral, then the method itself will be faulty (since there is no neutrality with respect to the notion of cause, etc.).

Him. They ought to see God as their judge when their conscience witnesses in approval or in disapproval of their deeds (Rom. 2:15).

> In order to receive knowledge we must also have God's general revelation and God's general internal revelation.[110]

So the interpretative effort, *so far as it is self-conscious*, is a means by which the natural man seeks to suppress the truth about God and the World that he has both about and within himself. But he cannot ever completely suppress the knowledge of God and of morality within himself. Dr. Masselink at one point expresses himself in a similar vein:

> Can this disposition to receive knowledge ever be lost by sin? The answer is *no*, as it belongs to the image of God. The disposition through which we receive knowledge, however, is now corrupt. In the state of integrity before the Fall, the three means by which knowledge was received—disposition, natural revelation, and historical revelation—were all pure but now there is corruption. In Hell these three means continue too. The consciousness of the "I" is unchanged by sin, but the nature of "I" is changed.[111]

> This general revelation is basis for *Common Grace*, and not vice versa—Common Grace is basis for general revelation,—since general revelation is before the fall, and therefore existed before Common Grace. The image of God cannot be removed for two reasons: First, because it belongs to the essence of man, and, second, because man receives internal and external revelation.[112]

Therefore *prior* to *Common Grace*, as its presupposition, we presuppose that man is of necessity confronted with the truth about himself as the creature of God. This objective truth about man himself, this ineradicable truth, this inescapable confrontation by God, man, *so far as he thinks from his sinful principle*, seeks to suppress. But he

110. Masselink, *Common Grace and Christian Education*, 129.
111. Ibid., 130.
112. Ibid.

cannot suppress it. It comes to him with the pressure of God, the inescapable One. God's revelation is everywhere, and everywhere perspicuous. Hence the theistic proofs are absolutely valid. They are but the restatement of the revelation of God, which, as Dr. Masselink says, is infallible. God the Holy Spirit presses the revelation of God, external and internal, upon man. I have not denied the general testimony of the Spirit any more than I have denied the validity of the theistic proofs. God the Holy Spirit presses upon men the revelation of God as being infallible, not as inherently unable to give certainty.[113]

Even so, it is imperative that a distinction be made between what is the objective revelation of God, both external and internal, and what is our interpretation of that revelation. In preaching, the Reformed minister of the gospel seeks to bring the system of truth as given him in Scripture. But he does not claim that any sermon of his infallibly mediates the revelation of God to man. His sermons are true so far as they reflect the revelation of God. So too with the formulation of the theistic proofs, these are true so far as they reflect the revelation of God. They are true when they reflect scriptural procedure. And scriptural procedure involves making the ontological trinity the foundation of all predication.

But these arguments have often been stated otherwise. In the first place men have often formulated them and have built them upon the assumption of man as autonomous. This is, for instance, the case with Aristotle, with Descartes, with the British empiricists, with the rationalists, etc.[114]

When the theistic proofs are thus constructed they do not convey the revelation of God; they then become the means of suppressing that revelation in terms of the monistic assumption of the natural man.[115] How could "the theistic proofs" then be sound, for if they

113. Note that the theistic proofs, according to Van Til, are "absolutely valid" and "are but the restatement of the revelation of God." Because these proofs are themselves restatements of God's revelation, they are infallible. As with God's special revelation, his general revelation comes to us without error, and when it comes to us, it always accomplishes the purpose(s) for which God sent it (see Isa. 55:9–11).

114. Van Til's point here is that the history of philosophy—from Aristotle to the present—with respect to theistic proofs, has not taken into account the truth of Scripture, and so has not wanted to demonstrate the reality of the triune God; it has, rather, been content to try to show that a god (probably) exists.

115. See footnote 80 above.

"prove" that the God of Aristotle exists, then they disprove that the God of Christianity exists.[116]

Now it is the difference between theistic proofs when rightly and when wrongly constructed that I have been anxious to stress. It is this that I think has not been adequately stressed even in Bavinck. And this in spite of the fact that he has given us, perhaps better than other Reformed theologians, the means by which to distinguish between the right and the wrong way of reasoning about God. He has rejected the scholastic idea of natural theology. It was this scholastic natural theology that took into the Christian camp the false way of reasoning about God. It took over to a large extent the method of Aristotle. Bavinck himself has signalized the proofs as formulated wrongly as being invalid. Kuyper did the same thing. He assigned a subordinate place to apologetics just because he assumed that it sought to prove to "reason" that of which "reason" cannot be the judge.

In this criticism of the validity of the theistic proofs Kuyper too had a different position from that of "Old Princeton apologetics."[117] When I arrived at Princeton Seminary as a student, Professor William Benton Greene was the professor of apologetics. The method of apologetics that he taught was to a large extent based on Bishop Butler's *Analogy*. It was based on the idea, as expressed by Butler, that there is an area or territory of interpretation on which Christians and non-Christians agree. To ask men to believe Christianity we must ask them only to apply the same principle of interpretation to Christianity and its phenomena that they have already applied to the realm of nature. Then they would have to admit that Christianity is very probably true as they had already admitted that God very probably exists.

116. Elsewhere, Van Til says: "In not challenging this basic presupposition with respect to himself as the final reference point in predication the natural man may accept the 'theistic proofs' as fully valid. He may construct such proofs. He has constructed such proofs. But the god whose existence he proves to himself in this way is always a god who is something other than the self-contained ontological trinity of Scripture. The Roman Catholic apologete does not want to prove the existence of this sort of God. He wants to prove the existence of such a God as will leave intact the autonomy of man to at least some extent. Rome's theology does not want a God whose counsel controls whatsoever comes to pass." Van Til, *Defense of the Faith*, 101.

117. For more on Kuyper's and Warfield's views of apologetics, see Van Til, *Defense of the Faith*, 345ff.

In this method it is assumed that the reason of the natural man quite properly takes itself to be the judge of what is possible or impossible. Says Charles Hodge,

> Christians concede to reason the *judicium contradictionis* [judgment of contradiction], that is, the prerogative of deciding whether a thing is possible or impossible. If it is seen to be impossible, no authority and no amount or kind of evidence can impose the obligation to receive it as true.[118]

Now I have criticized this Old Princeton *apologetics* in the way that Kuyper and Bavinck and Hepp have criticized positions similar to it. Dr. Samuel Volbeda[119] says that this method of apologetics does not do justice to the Pauline statement that the natural man cannot receive the things of the Spirit since they are spiritually discerned.

> *Methodologically* the Warfieldian scheme of Apologetics does not fit in with Reformed Hamartology and Soteriology. With you I believe that Apologetics should be so defined as not to carry with it implications contradictory of 1 Cor 2.14.[120]

The Princeton method, so far as it worked by this method of appeal to the reason of man as such as the judge of the possible and the impossible, was flatly opposed to Old Princeton theology, according to which only that is possible which God in His sovereign will determines shall come to pass.[121] Princeton apologetics did not live up to its own teaching in theology to the effect that the natural man must be born again unto knowledge. Princeton apologetics started with the non-believer from an abstract idea of possibility, based upon its calculations of what

118. Charles Hodge, *Systematic Theology*, 1:51.

119. Samuel Volbeda (1881–1953) was born in the Netherlands and came to the United States in 1886. After graduating from Calvin Theological Seminary in 1904, he pastored two congregations. He then studied at the Free University at Amsterdam and received his D.D. in 1914. He was professor of church history at Calvin Theological Seminary from 1914 to 1926, professor of practical theology from 1926 to 1952, and president of the seminary from 1944 to 1952.

120. From a letter to Gerrit G. Hospers, quoted in the latter's pamphlet *Apologetics* (New York, 1922), 28.

121. This statement reiterates Van Til's emphasis that one's apologetic *must* be consistent with one's theology, in that it flows from that theology.

might probably happen, and then concluded that Christianity is very probably true.

But David Hume has long since shown the invalidity of such an argument.[122] Abstract possibility presupposes the idea of Chance. And in Chance there are no probabilities, no tendencies one way or the other. And a Christianity that is probably true is not the Christianity of the Scripture.

So far as choice had to be made between the two positions, I took my position with Kuyper rather than with Hodge and Warfield. But there were two considerations that compelled me finally to seek a combination of some of the elements of each position. Negatively Kuyper was surely right in stressing that the natural man does not, on his principles, have any knowledge of the truth. But Hodge and Warfield taught the same thing in their theology. It was only in their apologetics that they did not lay full emphasis upon this teaching. Positively Hodge and Warfield were quite right in stressing the fact that Christianity meets every legitimate demand of reason.[123]

Surely Christianity is not irrational. To be sure, it must be accepted on faith, but surely it must not be taken on blind faith. Christianity is capable of rational defense. And what the Princeton theologians were really after when they said that Christianity is in accord with reason, is that it is in accord with the reason that recognizes its creatureliness and its sinfulness. It is only that the difference between the Christian and the non-Christian concepts of possibility and probability has not been adequately brought out by them.

> The reason why these differences do not appear on the surface is that, as a matter of fact, all men are human beings who were created in the image of God. Even the non-regenerate therefore have in their sense of deity, though repressed by them, some remnant of the knowledge of God, and consequently of the true source and meaning of possibility and probability.

---

122. David Hume (1711–1776) was the most radical of the empiricists, arguing, among other things, that there could be no empirical basis for the notion of cause and effect. For a discussion of the relationship of Hume to theology and apologetics, see Van Til, *Defense of the Faith*, 160–66, esp. 164.

123. It is important to see that Van Til's approach includes aspects *both* of Kuyper *and* of Warfield and Hodge.

It is to this remnant of a truly theistic interpretation of experience that Hodge really appeals when he speaks of the laws of belief that God has implanted in human nature. It is, of course, not only quite legitimate, but absolutely imperative to appeal to the "common consciousness" in this sense. But in order really to appeal to this "common consciousness" that is repressed by the sinner we must refuse to speak of a "common consciousness" that is not suppressed by the sinner.

The non-regenerate man seeks by all means to "keep under" this remnant of a true theistic interpretation that lingers in his mind. His real interpretative principle, now that he is a covenant-breaker, is that of himself as ultimate and of impersonal laws as ultimate. It is he himself as ultimate, by means of laws of logic that operate independently of God, who determines what is possible and probable. To the extent, then, that he proceeds self-consciously from his own principle of interpretation, he holds the very existence of God, and, of the creation of the universe, to be not merely improbable, but impossible. In doing so he sins, to be sure, against his better knowledge. He sins against that which is hidden deep down in his own consciousness. And it is well that we should appeal to this fact. But in order to appeal to this fact we must use all caution not to obscure this fact. And obscure it we do if we speak of the "common consciousness" of man without distinguishing clearly between what is hidden deep down in the mind of natural man as the revelation and knowledge of God within him, and what, in rejecting God, he has virtually adopted as being his final interpretative principle.[124]

Again in the case of Kuyper and Bavinck, is it not to the common consciousness of mankind as involved in Calvin's idea of the sense of deity, as involved in the very idea of the image of God that they can and do allow as a legitimate point to which we may appeal with the gospel? In spite of their rejection of apologetics as that discipline which must establish the foundation of the truth of Christianity, and in spite of their insistence that the natural man has no affinity for

124. Van Til, *IST*, 82–83.

the truth of Christianity, they yet themselves appeal to that which lives in the consciousness of every man but which every man as a sinner seeks to suppress. Further, through criticizing the sort of method that was used at Old Princeton, Kuyper and Bavinck often used that very same method themselves. They, too, often appealed to a common consciousness of man as containing a body of truth on which there is not much disagreement between Christians and non-Christians.

Of course it was with great diffidence and hesitation that I sought a solution for the apologetic problem and for the problem of common grace by the means of thus sorting out, rejecting the weaknesses in both positions, and building upon the solid foundation in both, derived from Calvin and ultimately from St. Paul. But it was impossible to ignore the differences between the two positions. It was also impossible to agree with the Old Princeton position to the effect that appeal must be made to reason without differentiating between a reason conceived of as autonomous and reason conceived of as created.[125]

Finally, it was impossible to agree with what seemed to be a lowering of the claim for Christianity by Kuyper and Bavinck when they concluded from the fact that sinful man cannot of himself accept the truth to the idea that there is no objectively valid reason to be given for the truth.

Here then is, so far as I am now able to see, the direction in which we ought as Reformed Christians to travel.

1. The foundation of the thinking of both the Amsterdam and the Old Princeton men was that which both derived via Calvin from Paul, namely, the fact that God has unavoidably and clearly revealed Himself in general and in special revelation. The whole triune God is involved in this revelation. The whole triune God testifies to man in this revelation. This is the general testimony of the Father, the Son, and the Holy Spirit. It is nothing more than the Reformed philosophy of history. God controls and therefore manifests His plan in "whatsoever comes to pass." It is His will of decree that comes to expression in a measure, in nature and in

---

125. It should be remembered here that, while Van Til refers (primarily) to Warfield as the representative of the Princeton apologetic, he himself was a student at Princeton and learned Warfield's approach from William Brenton Greene Jr. His analysis of "Old Princeton," then, comes primarily from his own experience of studying there.

history. In this decree lies the basis, the unity, and the guarantee of the success of "science."

2. Both the men of Amsterdam and the men of Old Princeton agree that God has promulgated to mankind in Adam His will of command. He set before mankind the task of subduing the earth. Here lies the command for all men to engage in the scientific enterprise. Here also lies the expression of the generally benevolent attitude of God to mankind. This is not grace, for grace presupposes sin. But it presupposes God's favorable attitude toward man. All men are responsible for proper reaction to this assignment of task.

In His will of command God deals with man as a created person; He deals with him conditionally. God wants self-conscious covenant reaction to His will of command and promise. But the entire covenantal transaction takes place according to the counsel of God.

3. Amsterdam and Old Princeton agree that the relation between the will of decree and will of command cannot be exhaustively understood by man.[126] Therefore every point of doctrine is a "difficult problem." As men we must think analogically. God is the original and man is derivative. We must not determine what can or cannot be by argument that starts from the will of decree apart from its relation to the will of command. In particular we must not say that God cannot display any attitude of favor to the generality of mankind because we know that He intends that ultimately some are "vessels of wrath." On the other hand we must not argue from the revealed will of God with respect to man's responsibility to the denial of man's ultimate determination by the will of decree. We need therefore at this point, which is all-inclusive, to be "fearlessly anthropomorphic."[127]

> Applying this to the case in hand, we would say that we are entitled and compelled to use anthropomorphism not apologetically but fearlessly.[128]

126. That is, we cannot plumb the depths of how God's eternal decree, by which he creates and controls whatsoever comes to pass, fits with his commands, for example, to believe and obey. We know from Scripture that they *do* fit together, but just *how* they fit together is beyond our intellectual capacity to understand.

127. For an attempt at, and example of, "fearless anthropomorphism" with respect to the relationship of God's eternal decree to his commands, see K. Scott Oliphint, *God with Us: Divine Condescension and the Attributes of God* (Wheaton, IL: Crossway Books, 2012).

128. Van Til, *Common Grace*, 73.

And to think analogically, to be fearlessly anthropomorphic, is to think concretely, for it is to take all the factors of revelation into consideration simultaneously. It is to admit that no theological problem can be fully solved exhaustively. The Council of Chalcedon excluded logical deductions based on anything short of a combination of all the factors of revelation with respect to the God-man.[129] So in the problem of common grace we must not argue for differences without qualification or for identities without qualification. The former is done by Hoeksema; the latter is done if we insist that there must be a neutral territory between believers and unbelievers.

4. Amsterdam and Old Princeton agree on the doctrine of sin. Both teach total depravity. Total depravity for both means that sin has affected man in all his functions. But it does not merely mean that. It also indicates how *deeply* sin has affected all his functions. Man is "wholly defiled," not partly defiled in all his functions. He hates God and his neighbor. He therefore seeks to suppress the truth within him. He worships and serves the creature more than the Creator. He *cannot but* sin.

5. Amsterdam and Old Princeton agree on the doctrine of election. Both teach that God from all eternity planned to redeem a people unto Himself. Disregarding the differences between infra- and supra-lapsarianism, all Reformed theologians, in accord with the Reformed confessions, teach that God is redeeming a people unto Himself. Those who are God's people are *totally* saved. They are saved in their every function. They are *absolutely* saved in principle. Paul calls them righteous and holy *without qualification*. John says they *cannot* sin.

6. Amsterdam and Old Princeton agree on the genuine significance of human responsibility. Their position has been called absolutist and determinist. It has been charged that with their doctrines of election and reprobation the "free offer of the gospel" would be meaningless. But Scripture teaches both the ultimate determination of the destiny of men by God and the fact that men die because of their sin. So both Amsterdam and Old Princeton, following Calvin, argued that the conditional is meaningful not in spite of, but because of, the plan of God in relation to which human responsibility takes place.

---

129. This is a foundational point to keep in mind. The Council of Chalcedon could have begun with the supposition that theology was meant to be conformable to rational principles.

Hence both preached with conviction the universal or general offer of salvation to men as a class. They were not deterred by those who would impose "logic" upon Scripture either by way of rejecting election in favor of the sincerity of the general offer of the gospel, or by way of rejecting the sincerity of the offer of the gospel in favor of election. They thought concretely and scripturally rather than abstractively and deductively from one aspect of revelation.

7. Both Amsterdam and Old Princeton therefore taught common grace as well as the common offer of the gospel to the generality of mankind. From the beginning God had in mind His ultimate plan with respect to the final differentiations between men. Both infra- and supralapsarians agree on this. But this did not reduce the favorable attitude toward mankind at the beginning of history.[130] Why then should God's general favor not continue upon man even after the fall? *Only if sin were taken to be the act of a being that is itself ultimate would that be the case.*[131] From eternity God rejected men because of the sin that they would do as historical beings. So He elected others because of the work that Christ would do for them and the Spirit would do within them in history. It is as true and as important thus to assert the significance of the historical whether as contemplated by God or as realized in fact as it is to say that history is what God intends by His plan that it shall be.

Thus the general favorable attitude toward mankind at the beginning of history becomes the sincere offer of the gospel and common grace to those who have sinned. All men were, because of sin, in *the way of death* (Calvin).[132] To man as a class God comes with the sincere offer of *the way of life* (Rom 2). That is the general witness of the triune God to men.

Therefore God's good gifts to men, rain and sunshine in season, are genuinely expressive of God's favor unto them. At the same time they are a general testimony by which the Spirit of God labors with men to call them to repentance, and therefore to the fulfillment of the task originally assigned to mankind in Adam.

Therefore also through common grace the natural man is enabled to do "good works."

130. That is, God's favorable attitude toward mankind via Adam as our federal head.
131. Van Til makes this point in order to emphasize that Adam's act of sin was not the ultimate determiner of everything that has followed from it; God's decree alone determines whatsoever comes to pass.
132. See, for example, Calvin's commentary on Jeremiah 21:8.

Total depravity has two aspects, one of principle and one of degree. The first representative act of man was an act that resulted historically in the total depravity of the race. This act was performed against a mandate of God that involved mankind as a whole; without that "common mandate" it could not have been done; without that common mandate the "negative instance" would have been an operation in a void. Thus mankind came under the common wrath of God. But the process of differentiation was not complete. This common wrath, too, was a steppingstone to something further.[133] The elect were to choose for God and the reprobate were each for himself to reaffirm their choice for Satan. The reprobate were to show historically the exceeding sinfulness of sin. Totally depraved in principle, they were to become more and more conformed in fact to the principle that controlled their hearts.[134]

It will now be apparent why I have found it impossible to agree with Hepp in his evaluation of *the* theistic proofs. There are two ways of constructing a proof for the existence of God. These two ways are mutually exclusive. The one is in accord with the basic construction of Reformed theology; the other is destructive of it. The one begins with the presupposition of the existence of the triune God of the Scriptures. The other begins with the presupposition of man as ultimate.

The true theistic proofs undertake to show that the ideas of existence (ontological proof), of cause (cosmological proof), and purpose (teleological proof) are meaningless unless they presuppose the existence of God.[135]

This involves interpreting human reason itself in terms of God. It involves saying that unless human reason regards itself as being what Scripture says it is, created in the image of God, that then it has no internal coherence. To this must be added that it involves the fact of sin as darkening the understanding and hardening the

133. The "common wrath" of which Van Til speaks here is the wrath of God toward Adam, as representative of the human race. The "something further" is the historical working out of that common wrath on those who "become more and more conformed in fact to the principle" of that depravity.

134. Van Til, *Common Grace*, 91.

135. The ontological proof was initially put forth by Anselm (1033–1109). The cosmological and teleological proofs are two of Thomas Aquinas's "five ways."

will. Yet no one but a Christian will admit these two truths about himself. By nature all men seek to suppress the facts of their sinfulness and creaturehood. They cannot succeed in fully suppressing this truth. As you cannot mop the figure off the surface of an indelible linoleum so man cannot erase his creatureliness and sinfulness, try as he may.

One of the most subtle and apparently effective ways by which the natural man seeks to cover his guilt is by "proving the existence of God" to himself. By that means he makes an idol for himself. Worshiping his idol, his god, he seeks to make himself believe that he has done all that may be expected of him.

That the gods produced by the "theistic proofs" are frequently nothing but idols is plain to any one familiar with the history of philosophy. Aristotle proved the existence of a god; there must, he reasoned, be an unmoved Mover back of all movement. Thomas Aquinas used essentially the same method that Aristotle did in proving the existence of God. Yet the god of Aristotle did not create the world, does not control it, is not even a person. Aquinas wanted to prove to those whose standard of judgment is reason rather than revelation that it is proper to believe in God. But the only god that he can rightfully hold to on this basis is such a god as no Christian should call God.

In modern times Descartes used the ontological argument.[136] But he started from the idea that he knew his own nature as man without first or at the same time knowing that God exists. This assumption is the exact opposite of that from which Calvin starts. Calvin argues that not a word can truthfully be said about man himself unless it be presupposed that he is a creature of God. Accordingly Descartes, as well as Aristotle, had at best a finite god. And a finite god is, from the Christian point of view, an idol.

136. René Descartes (1596–1650) was perhaps the seminal philosopher of the modern era. In his *Meditations on First Philosophy*, Descartes attempted to extend certain knowledge of mathematical truths to other domains of knowledge. His method was to accept universal doubt in order to ascertain at least one indubitable truth. The indubitable truth that he claimed to find was his own existence. His famous dictum, "*Cogito, ergo sum*" (I think, therefore I am), became the hallmark of modernist thought. Van Til regularly juxtaposes Descartes and Calvin. Whereas Descartes thought he had gained universal truth by way of his own indubitable existence, Calvin begins his *Institutes* by inextricably linking any self-knowledge with knowledge of God. Thus, Descartes's view exhibits autonomy, while Calvin's view entails our dependence upon God. This is a running theme in Van Til's thought. Descartes borrowed from Anselm in using the ontological argument.

It is therefore quite impossible to speak intelligently of *the* theistic proofs without distinguishing between the method by which a Christian believer and the method by which a non-Christian uses them.

It is therefore the essence of Protestantism, and in particular of the Reformed theology to reject the "natural theology" of Rome. Kuyper and Bavinck have done so in no uncertain terms. And so has Hepp. And the whole genius of "Old Princeton" was against it.

A truly Reformed apologetic cannot be worked out unless one follows closely in Calvin's wake. Men *ought* to see God's being as the being who is self-sufficient and self-contained. Men *ought* to see themselves as creatures, as beneficiaries of their Creator's bounties. They ought to see themselves as under the law of God. And men *cannot but* see themselves as such. Yet such is the folly of sin, that men hold down the truth in unrighteousness. They do this by assuming that they participate in the being of God, or that God's being is of a piece with theirs. So their systems of philosophy, based as they are on this monistic assumption, are means by which men seek to suppress the truth about themselves. The result is folly and ruin to themselves.

Either presuppose God and live, or presuppose yourself as ultimate and die. That is the alternative with which the Christian must challenge his fellow man.

If the Christian thus challenges his fellow man then he may be an instrument of the Spirit of God. The proofs of God then become witnesses of God; and witnesses of God are God witnessing to men. The theistic proofs therefore reduce to one proof, the proof which argues that unless *this* God, the God of the Bible, the ultimate being, the Creator, the controller of the universe, be presupposed as the foundation of human experience, this experience operates in a void. This one proof is absolutely convincing.[137] To be sure, in so far as it is an interpretation of biblical and general revelation it cannot be assumed to be infallible. Only revelation *to* man (which includes revelation *through* man as a psychological being) is infallible. When man, even redeemed man, reinterprets this revelation, it cannot be said to be infallible in detail. Reformed theology does not attribute infallibility to its confessions. Yet the main points of doctrine of these confessions are, by Reformed men, assumed to

137. It would be "absolutely convincing," that is, if man's mind were not enslaved to sin (Rom. 8:7).

be, for all practical purposes, a faithful reproduction of the truths of revelation.

It will now be apparent why I cannot agree with Hepp's estimate of the proofs. Hepp does not distinguish between such proofs as are constructed upon true and such as are constructed upon false presuppositions. He simply speaks of *the* theistic proofs. He assumes that the non-believer can and does correctly interpret the revelation of God. After warning us against overestimating the value of the proofs Hepp says:

> The so-called proofs for the existence of God are not at all without value. They teach us that nature within us and round about us witnesses of God. They convey in set formulas, the speech which comes to us from the cosmos as a whole (cosmological proof), from the world of ideas (ontological proof), from the moral world (moral proof), from history (historical proof), from the purposiveness nature of things (teleological proof) and testify to us constantly that God reigns and that He is the Creator of the ends of the earth who does not faint or grow weary. They press powerfully upon our consciousness. But—they cannot give us the last ground of certainty.[138]

Against the type of argument developed by the Old Princeton apologetics Hepp therefore objects because it claims *certainty* for the proofs. But certainty, says Hepp, cannot be derived from revelation, since revelation comes through media, whether subjective or objective. Certainty, he contends, comes from the testimony of the Spirit only.

In this objection of Hepp's against too great a reliance on the theistic proofs he leaves untouched what constitutes, we believe, the one great fault in them. Hepp ignores the basic difference between a theistic proof that presupposes God and one that presupposes man as ultimate. And this is not an oversight. Hepp's whole doctrine of the *general* testimony of the Spirit is constructed with the purpose of showing that there are certain *central truths* on which all men agree. Non-Christians as well as Christians can,

138. V. Hepp, *Het testimonium Spiritus Sancti* [The testimony of the Holy Spirit] (Kampen: J. H. Kok, 1914), 152.

he argues, correctly interpret God's general revelation. They can together put this revelation in set formulas, as they do in the case of the theistic proofs. Thus they can and do, together believe in *certain central truths.*

Here then the Christian and the non-Christian together interpret God's general revelation and together come to the same conclusion, namely, that God exists. But they are not certain of this truth, for revelation cannot give certainty. So the Holy Spirit testifies within them, so as to bring certainty within them with respect to the conclusion of their process of reasoning.

All this is in effect to have lapsed into the natural theology of Romanism. The doctrine of the general testimony of the Holy Spirit as developed by Hepp is in itself no cure for natural theology. Hepp assumes that the natural man can and does, even on his own interpretative principle, correctly interpret the revelation of God on central questions. There is then an area of fact, of revelation which non-Christians and Christians together interpret correctly. There is then a *neutral territory,* a "territory between," where men can positively build together on the house of science.

In this area the Holy Spirit does not testify to the non-believer through the believer to the effect that he must turn from idols to the service of the living God. On the contrary, in this area the Spirit testifies to both believer and unbeliever that they are right in believing God. The Spirit, as it were, testifies to Calvin that he is right in thinking of God as his Creator and Judge, and also testifies to Spinoza that he is right in believing in the existence of God as identical with all reality. Or, if this be not so, then the Spirit must testify to the contentless *form* of God, it must testify to the fact *that* God exists without any indication as to *what* is the nature of that God.

Now either idea, the idea that the Spirit should testify to the existence of a finite god, or to the existence of a mere *form,* devoid of content, is directly contrary to Scripture. Nature within man and through the facts about man testifies that God as Creator, as controller of all things, and as judge, exists. It is to this that the Spirit testifies. And testifying to the existence of *this* God it testifies *against* the existence of such gods as men have made for themselves, often by means of the "theistic proofs."

It is in this conception of *the* theistic proofs and of the general testimony of the Spirit witnessing to what they express, to this idea of central truths on which Christians and non-Christians are in agreement, that I have rejected. I have rejected it for the same reason for which I have rejected the method of the Old Princeton apologetics. And I have rejected both in view of my close adherence to the Old Princeton and the Amsterdam theology. It is, in short, because I hold the appeal to reason as autonomous to be both illegitimate and destructive from the point of view of Reformed faith that I am bound to reject Hepp's position as well as that of Old Princeton apologetics. But happily I can do so in view of the theology that I have learned from Old Princeton and Amsterdam.

In this connection I may explain to you a remark I made recently on the occasion when Dr. Masselink and I debated the question of common grace. I argued that on the basis of such an apologetics as Old Princeton furnished us we were still on an essentially Romanist rather than on a Reformed basis. For it is of the essence of Romanism to argue with the non-believer on the ground of a supposedly neutral reason. No Reformed person could espouse such a position and then honestly claim that his position was uniquely Calvinistic and as such calculated to save science.

In this context I contended that a doctrine of common grace that is constructed so as to appeal once more to a neutral territory between believers and non-believers is, precisely like Old Princeton apologetics, in line with a Romanist type of natural theology. Why should we then pretend to have anything unique? And why then should we pretend to have a sound basis for science? Nothing short of the Calvinistic doctrine of the all-controlling providence of God, and the indelibly revelational character of every fact of the created universe, can furnish a true foundation for science. And how can we pretend to be able to make good use of the results of the scientific efforts of non-Christian scientists, if, standing on an essentially Roman basis, we cannot even make good use of our own efforts?

Why live in a dream world, deceiving ourselves and making false pretense before the world? The non-Christian view of science:

(a) presupposes the autonomy of man;
(b) presupposes the non-created character, i.e., the chance-controlled character, of facts; and,
(c) presupposes that laws rest not in God but somewhere in the universe.

Now if we develop a doctrine of common grace in line with the teachings of Hepp with respect to the general testimony of the Spirit, we are incorporating into our scientific edifice the very forces of destruction against which that testimony is bound to go forth. Then "we might as well blow up the science building with an atom bomb." I have apologized for that statement. But to the meaning intended then I subscribe today. We should as Reformed Christians be able to present a well-articulated philosophy of knowledge in general and of science in particular in order to justify our independent educational institutions.

CHAPTER 7

A REPLY TO CRITICISM[1]

I n his syllabus *Common Grace and Christian Education*, Dr. William Masselink charged me with beginning my whole system of thought with the idea of the *Absolute Ethical Antithesis*. I made reply to this charge in *A Letter on Common Grace*. There I made it clear that I begin rather with the creation of man as made in the image of God. Following Calvin, I then speak of all men as unavoidably knowing God (Rom 1:19). All men, even after the fall, know, deep down in their hearts, that they are creatures of God; that they should therefore obey, but that they have actually broken, the law of God.

After the fall, therefore, all men seek to suppress this truth, fixed in their being, about themselves. They are opposed to God. This is the biblical teaching on human depravity. If we are to present the truth of the Christian religion to men we must take them where they are. They are: (a) creatures made in God's image, surrounded by a world that reveals in its every fact God's power and divinity. Their antithesis to God can never be metaphysical. They can never be anything but image bearers of God. They can never escape facing God in the universe about them and in their own constitution. Their

---

1. As Van Til notes at the beginning of this book, this chapter first appeared as an appendix to *An Introduction to Systematic Theology*. It can be found at the end of earlier publications of that syllabus, and after chapter 2 in the edition edited by William Edgar.

antithesis to God is therefore an *ethical* one.[2] (b) Because of God's common grace, this ethical antithesis to God on the part of the sinner is *restrained*, and thereby the creative forces of man receive the opportunity of constructive effort. In this world the sinner does many "good" things. He is honest. He helps to alleviate the sufferings of his fellow men. He "keeps" the moral law. Therefore the "antithesis," besides being ethical rather than metaphysical, is limited in a second way. It is one of *principle*, not one of full expression. If the natural man fully expressed himself as he is in terms of the principle of ethical hostility to God that dwells within his soul, he would then be a veritable devil. Obviously he is often nothing of the sort. He is not at all as "bad as he may be."

All of this is found in my various writings. It was pointed out especially in *A Letter on Common Grace*. Yet Dr. Masselink keeps repeating the idea that I start my whole system of thought from the idea of the Absolute Ethical Antithesis, and insists that I mean by this that man "at present is as bad as he can be."[3] Masselink says that according to Reformed theology the antithesis is "principial," not absolute. "I do not believe that Reformed Theology ever speaks of an 'absolute ethical antithesis.' By 'Principial Antithesis' is meant that natural man *in principle* is dead in sin and completely depraved."[4] "Natural man, however, is absolutely depraved in principle."[5]

Masselink therefore also uses the term *absolute* with respect to the total depravity of man. And I have repeatedly used the qualification that the depravity is absolute only *in principle*. The only difference at this point seems to be that I add one more qualification than does Masselink. I am careful to note that the antithesis is *ethical*, and not metaphysical. I do not discover this distinction in Masselink. Perhaps this failure accounts for the fact that at other points he reasons as though the antithesis is not absolute in principle, even when this antithesis is conceived of ethically. I refer to the fact that

2. A metaphysical antithesis would mean that man is no longer the image of God. "*Ethical*" here might be better termed "*covenantal*." Man, though created in the image of God, is covenantally in Adam, and therefore, since the fall, has been opposed to God and a slave to sin.

3. William Masselink, "The New 'Common Grace' Issue," *Torch and Trumpet* 3, no. 6 (February-March 1954): 15; cf. also Wm. Masselink, "New Views regarding Common Grace," *The Calvin Forum* 19 (April 1954): 172–77.

4. Masselink, "New Views regarding Common Grace," 174.

5. Masselink, "The New 'Common Grace' Issue," 15.

he follows Dr. Valentijn Hepp in his idea that there are general ideas of God, of man, and the universe on which Christians and non-Christians have no *principal difference*.[6]

In passing it may be noted that the usage of the phrase "absolute antithesis" is not so unheard of as Masselink surmises. So, for instance, Dr. Herman Kuyper uses it, and ties it in closely with the absoluteness of Christianity. He says:

> In this connection it is in place to note that Calvin's conception of common grace can help us in upholding the absoluteness of Christianity. Especially in recent years many who profess Christianity are unwilling to subscribe to the orthodox conception of Christianity as the only true religion. Instead of maintaining that there is an absolute antithesis between Christianity and all non-Christian religions, they prefer to look upon Christianity as the highest development of the seed of religion which is implanted in the heart of every man.[7]

A second point of criticism made on my views by Masselink and others pertains to the laws of logic. Says Masselink:

> In his recent publication, "A Letter on Common Grace," Van Til says of reason in general that "such a thing does not exist in practice." The issue between us and Van Til does not at all concern a degree of difference in knowledge between the Christian and the non-Christian, but rather whether we with Kuyper can say that the *laws of logic in natural man* have not been completely destroyed by sin.[8]

The reader will at once observe that it is wholly counter to the approach taken in this book to say that the laws of logic have been destroyed in the sinner. The whole point of the distinction between the antithesis as being ethical rather than metaphysical is that as a creature made in God's image, man's constitution as a rational

---

6. Cf. Cornelius Van Til, *A Letter on Common Grace* (Phillipsburg, NJ: L. J. Grotenhuis, n.d.).

7. Herman Kuiper, *Calvin on Common Grace* (Goes: Oosterbaan & Le Cointre, 1928), 231.

8. Masselink, "New Views regarding Common Grace," 174.

and moral being has *not* been destroyed. The separation from God on the part of the sinner is ethical. How could it be metaphysical? Even the lost in the hereafter have not lost the power of rational and moral determination. They must have this image in order to be aware of their lost condition.

And this has a bearing on Masselink's point that in my view the sinner's consciousness would be entirely "devoid of ethical content." "If this 'God-consciousness and moral consciousness' were entirely devoid of ethical content our Confession would be untrue when it speaks of 'civil righteousness.' "[9] But the distinction between a metaphysical and an ethical antithesis is made for the specific purpose of avoiding the idea that there could ever be a stage in which man can be entirely devoid of moral consciousness. It is because on the Romanist position this distinction cannot be made that the effect of sin is thought of in terms of the scale of being. Under the Aristotelian idea of the analogy of being, man, when "*in puris naturalibus,*"[10] is well nigh devoid of ethical consciousness. It takes the *donum superadditum*, a metaphysical notion, in order to give him such a moral consciousness, even in paradise. Then after the entrance of sin, when this *donum superadditum* is removed, man sinks down close to the bottom of being and almost loses his ability to discern good and evil.[11]

It will be difficult for Masselink to keep from falling into this line of thinking. He seems to operate with the idea of the scale of being in the sentence following the one quoted. "In hell the antithesis between God and natural man is absolute. There is no common grace nor civil righteousness in perdition." Now it is true that there is no common grace in the estate of the lost. But are the lost "devoid of ethical content?" Does not their conscience smite them forever for having offended the holiness of God? Masselink makes the very idea of "ethical content" to depend upon the presence of common grace. He thereby shows that on his view common grace, in restraining the principle of sin, keeps men from falling into a state where they are no longer able to have moral awareness. This is in line with the Romanist idea of sin as having

9. Masselink, "The New 'Common Grace' Issue," 15.
10. That is, man in a pure state of nature (i.e., before the fall).
11. See footnote 88 in the previous chapter.

a deleterious metaphysical effect on man; it is out of line with Reformed thinking.[12]

The whole question of the influence of sin, whether it is ethical or metaphysical, is centrally expressed in the idea that except for the entrance of common grace, the whole world, including man, would have fallen to pieces. Herman Kuyper quite rightly rejects this notion when he says:

> We also refuse to subscribe to Calvin's teaching in II, 2, 17 to the effect that the fall of man would have resulted in the destruction of our whole nature, including our reasoning power, if God had not spared us. Calvin here seems to forget that the revolt in the world of angels did not have for its result that the devils have lost all reasoning ability, and he also leaves out of consideration the fact that the lost souls who will one day inhabit the place of torment will remain men and will retain a certain measure of intellectual power.[13]

In *A Letter on Common Grace*, I expressed the idea that we need to use the ideas of "metaphysical" and "ethical" in connection with the fall of man as limiting or supplementative notions. We have to speak *as if* sin would have destroyed the work of God. That was certainly its ethical intent. But we know that this is not an ultimate metaphysical possibility, for it was already, from all eternity, a part of the plan of God that sin should be defeated through the work of the Christ.

Genuine advance in Reformed thinking has come about in the last generation by means of the use of Christian supplementative, or limiting concepts. This use has enabled G. C. Berkouwer and others to avoid some of the scholasticism that must otherwise obtain. Scholasticism appears when, on the ground of the idea of election, we deduce that God cannot in any sense whatever have any attitude of favor to mankind as a group.[14] It also obtains when, because

12. The reason hell will be a place where "the worm never dies" (Mark 9:48), and where there will be weeping and gnashing of teeth (Matt. 8:12; 13:42, 50), is that there the conscience will be ever and always accusing the lost of their perpetual rebellion against God in this life.

13. Kuiper, *Calvin on Common Grace*, 226.

14. Van Til may be thinking here of G. C. Berkouwer, *Man: The Image of God* (Grand Rapids: Eerdmans, 1962), 154ff.

we hold to the idea of responsibility, we hold also that there can therefore be no election. It obtains too when we say there can be no equal ultimacy of the idea of election and reprobation in God, or when we say that Adam's choice for obedience was equally ultimate with his choice for disobedience. In short, without thinking of our theological concepts as being supplementative of one another, we fall into logicism. We reduce the significance of the stream of history to the static categories of logic.

The gift of logical reason was originally given by God to man in order that he might order the revelation of God in nature for himself. It was not given him that he might by means of it legislate as to what is possible and what is actual. When man makes a "system" for himself of the content of revelation given him in Scripture, this system is subject to, not independent of, Scripture. Thus the idea of system employed by the Christian is quite different from the idea of system as employed in modern philosophy.[15]

It is therefore pointless for Christians to tell non-Christians that Christianity is "in accord with the law of contradiction" unless they explain what they mean by this. For the non-Christian will take this statement to mean something entirely different from what the Christian ought to mean by it. The non-Christian does not believe in creation. Therefore, for him the law of contradiction is, like all other laws, something that does not find its ultimate source in the creative activity of God.[16] Accordingly, the non-Christian will seek to do by means of the law of contradiction what the Christian has done *for* him by God. For the Christian, God legislates as to what is possible and what is impossible for man. For the non-Christian, man determines this for himself. Either positively or negatively the non-Christian will determine the field of possibility and therewith the stream of history by means of the law of contradiction.

This means that for the non-Christian the concepts that he employs while using the law of contradiction are taken to be

15. Because the Christian must submit his thinking to the truth of Scripture, any systematizing of God's revelation will have, at root, the notion of mystery. It could not be otherwise, since God's judgments are unsearchable and his ways are inscrutable (Rom. 11:33).

16. Notice that the law of contradiction has its source, not in "God's logic" (whatever that might mean), but in God's "creative activity." Logic is a product of creation, and a created reflection of God's character. For more on logic, see Vern S. Poythress, *Logic: A God-Centered Approach to the Foundation of Western Thought* (Wheaton, IL: Crossway, 2013).

exhaustive of the "essence of the thing" they seek to express. By taking each concept as wholly expressing the essence of a thing, non-Christian thought seeks to express the whole of reality, even of temporal reality, in terms of concepts that are static. Even when it is admitted, as it generally is in modern thought, that reality is exhaustively temporal and therefore not at all, or not fully, expressible in terms of concepts, still it is maintained or assumed that what is expressed by means of concepts is all that man can know. Men may then speak of revelation as another means of knowing reality. They may even say that this other reality is more basic than the reality that is known through conceptual manipulation. They will then posit a dualism between the idea of faith by which this wholly other reality is "known" and reason by which the world of phenomena is known. In any case the genuine significance of the facts of history is destroyed.

This is most clearly illustrated in the case of dialectical theology, In order to maintain the uniqueness of the facts of history this theology thinks it necessary to speak of *primal* history (*Geschichte*) in distinction from *ordinary* history (*Historie*). Ordinary history cannot, say Barth and Brunner, manifest anything unique. Ordinary history is history as the secular mind thinks of it. That is to say, history must be interpreted by means of concepts, and these concepts, in their view, kill all individuality. Concepts, we are told, can deal only with abstract essences. The individual is by means of these concepts reduced to an instance of a class. In fact, the individual is wholly lost in the concepts that describe it.[17]

It is only in Reformed theology that the means are available to oppose this modern approach. That is not because Reformed theology has access to some means of manipulation of reality not open to other men. It is rather because only in Reformed theology is full justice done to the idea of God as man's creator. If God is really man's creator then man's thinking must be thought of as being analogical. Therefore his concepts cannot rightly be employed as

17. Van Til is saying here that Barth and Brunner were wed to a Kantian idea of reality (i.e., phenomenal-noumenal), such that the phenomena of this world operate according to the laws of this world, the concepts by which we organize the data of the world are abstract categories of the mind, and for there to be anything that is meaningful, there has to be something that transcends the mundane and routine phenomena of *Historie*. That something, for Barth, was *Geschichte*, which was thought to be a category that alone was able to provide spiritual meaning to history.

the instruments of a deductive system. These concepts must be employed as means by which to display the richness of God's revelation. When the apparently contradictory appears, as it always must when man seeks to know the relation of God to himself, there will be no denial of concepts such as election or human responsibility in the name of the law of contradiction.

Applied to the general problem of common grace, the idea of limiting or supplementative concepts means that we shall not deny common grace nor, on the other hand, hold to a common grace that creates a neutral territory between believers and unbelievers.

THE IMAGE OF GOD IN MAN

The necessity for the use of the idea of the limiting or supplementative concept may be illustrated further by observing what happens if it is not used with respect to the idea of man as the image-bearer of God.

It is customary in Reformed circles to distinguish between the image of God in the wider and the image of God in the narrower sense. But difficulty develops if we do not clearly stress that this distinction is not to be carried through deductively. This difficulty may be indicated by a brief summary of the work on *The Image of God* (*Het Beeld Gods*) by Abraham Kuyper, Jr. The image of God in the *wider* sense, Kuyper says, must be found in the essence of man.[18] And this essence of man remains unchanged in fallen man.[19] "Man has been permitted to keep much, and is, in spite of his deep fall, capable of much, because he has kept the image of God in its essence and because Common Grace came to his assistance."[20] "This image of God cannot be lost since, if man could lose it, he would at the moment of losing it, cease to be a human being. The image of God in the wider sense (*sensu latiore*) has reference to the human in man, to that whereby man, in

18. Abraham Kuyper, Jr., *Het beeld Gods* (Amsterdam: De Standaard, 1929), 62.
19. Ibid., 69: "De natuurlijke mensch, die als zondaar leeft, heeft zeer zeker de rede, het verstand de kennis, het intellect, hoe men het noemen wil. Kennis behoort tot het wezen van den mensch, de mensch is immers, ook de gevallen mensch, een redelijk-zedelijk wezen." ("The natural man, who lives as a sinner, certainly has reason, understanding, knowledge, intellect, whatever one might call it. Knowledge belongs to the essence of man; man is, after all, even fallen man, a rational-moral being.")
20. Ibid., 75.

distinction from all other creatures, is man and not an angel or an animal or a plant."[21]

Summarizing his own discussion of the image in the wider sense as being the unchangeable essence of man, Kuyper says that it must be sought in the first place in the "I through which man is a person, and then further in the two capacities which this marvelous 'I' controls, the capacity to know and the capacity to will . . ."[22]

The image of God in the *narrower* sense is said to consist of true knowledge, righteousness and holiness. As usual, Eph 4.23–24 and Col 3.10 are quoted in support of this. Kuyper also speaks of immortality as part of the image of God.[23] But we need not, for our purpose, follow his analysis in detail. Our interest turns to the fact that this image in the narrower sense is said to be lost. "Thus the image of God in the narrower sense consisted of *true* knowledge, righteousness and holiness. This image was lost, and in its place there came blindness, guilt, and sinfulness."[24] This image is *lost*, it disappears.

What, we are tempted to ask, is the effect of the disappearance of this image in the narrower sense upon the image in the wider sense? The latter, it will be remembered, *cannot*, according to Kuyper, Jr., be lost. It is therefore called "the image as such" (*als zoodanig*).[25] And the knowledge of this image *as such* is called knowledge *as such*.[26] Yet through sin the reason which belongs to the unchangeable essence of man is said to be darkened.[27] His immortality that he possessed in paradise is lost.[28] There is no longer any righteousness in his will.[29] Can we then continue to say that the essence of man, his person, his reason and will, have in no wise been affected by the true righteousness, true knowledge, and true holiness? Or if we continue to say that the essence of man remains unchanged while his nature changes, does anything then remain to be said about this essence at all? Has it not become an entirely featureless entity?

21. Ibid., 123.
22. Ibid., 68.
23. Ibid., 92.
24. Ibid., 126.
25. Ibid., 130.
26. Ibid., 69.
27. Ibid., 70.
28. Ibid., 92.
29. Ibid., 126.

Similar problems confront us with respect to the image of God in the narrower sense. Is it so loosely, so "accidentally" related to the essence of man that it can be lost without affecting that essence at all? Is the essence of man, the human personality, the image as such, with knowledge as such, completely devoid of ethical content? If so, is the ethical content to be a gift of pre-redemptive common grace after the fashion of the Romanist *donum superadditum?* Then special grace after the fall would be *greater grace*, but grace of the *same sort* that man was given before the fall. Thus the initial antithetical distinction between a changeless essence and a changing nature turns into its opposite. Since the essence cannot in every sense be maintained to be unaffected by the loss of the perfect nature, sin has a damaging effect on the essence of man after all. Common grace is then required to save the metaphysical situation intact.

> God the Lord intervened with Common Grace, a grace given to man as man, through which sin was restrained, the curse was checked, and natural life on earth, however drastically changed, was maintained. A human race could develop itself, and history could begin its course. Without the entrance of Common Grace this would have been altogether impossible.[30]

On the other hand the remnants of the image of God that remain in the sinner are said to be remnants of the image in the narrower sense. "The image of God does not consist only in true knowledge and service of God, and in righteousness and holiness, of which remnants are preserved in the religious feeling and in the moral life of the natural man, but also in the kingly control over the earth by man."[31] It is in line with this that the author says: "Without the entrance of Common Grace man would have lost the image of God, and would have come to the full expression of bitter hostility to God and to a life explosive with sin and unrighteousness. The life of his soul would have become like that of a devil, with respect to whom we cannot speak of common grace at all."[32]

Thus common grace is interchangeably said to be that which preserves some remnants of the image of God in the wider sense,

30. Ibid., 180.
31. Ibid., 200.
32. Ibid., 181.

234

and some of the remnants of the image of God in the narrower sense. In the former case common grace is required to save the metaphysical situation intact. Thus we are virtually back with the Romanist concept of the *donum superadditum*. In the latter case common grace seems to be a means of toning down the doctrine of total depravity. The "remnants" of the image of God in the natural man then appear to be little specks of true knowledge, true righteousness, and true holiness. The difference between the believer and the unbeliever then becomes one of degree.

It appears then that if we do use such concepts as "essence" and "nature" without stipulating that they are limitative and supplementative of one another, we not only get into confusion and contradiction, but we are inadvertently led into positions which we were trying to avoid.

All this is not surprising. In a non-Christian methodology such as Romanism took over from Aristotle, man is the final point of reference in predication. On this basis man is not regarded as the creature of God. His intellect is therefore not thought of as being dependent upon God. To be sure, the word analogy is used to describe the relation of human to divine thought. But on the Aristotelian basis this idea of analogy is based upon the idea of participation rather than upon the idea of creation. Man is thought of as participating in the being of divinity by means of his intellect. By means of his concepts he is supposed to discover the essence of reality as something that is wholly changeless.[33] Change in the created universe is then taken to be the same as Chance. Individual facts of the created world are taken to be characterized by Chance. Or if they have any reality at all it must be because they somehow participate in the eternity of the divine being. The result is that when man seeks to order the facts of the temporal world he must find their reality in a world of essences that are non-temporal. To thus explain the facts of history is, therefore, on this basis, to explain away the individuality that was to be explained. In using this Aristotelian scheme and applying it to the idea of the image of God in man, Romanist theology was driven to the idea of the scale of being. Near to non-being is man *in puris naturalibus*. He is there practically without ethical content. The ethical content must

33. That is, according to Aristotle (and Aquinas), man knows by way of universals, which do not change, and not by way of particulars.

be placed upon him artificially by means of the idea of potential participation in divinity.

Surely it is of the greatest importance for Reformed theology to use the concept of the image of God in man in truly analogical fashion, that is, with the definite intent to think as creatures who are called upon to give order to the revelation of God. Using human concepts analogically means to be deeply conscious, moment by moment, that each concept employed must constantly be subject to the whole of the revelation of God. And this implies the setting of such concepts as the essence of man and the nature of man in a definite relationship of correlativity to one another. The idea of the essence of man simply cannot be taken as standing for something wholly unchangeable. And the idea of nature cannot stand for something that can wholly change. So we find that in actual practice modifications are constantly being used. The essence is said to be affected by the change the nature undergoes. And the nature is itself in need of a "nature" within itself that is not wholly subject to change. When, therefore, the two notions are taken as being self-consciously in supplementation of one another, better justice is done to the content of the revelation that one intends to express. Then the man who is created perfect, who falls into sin, who is the recipient of common and in some cases special grace, is seen in his historical development.

Then too, the doctrine of common grace can do better justice to the historical development of man. The scholastic view is in the nature of the case bound to do injustice to the significance of history. One of two things always takes place. Either an absolute and artificial separation is made between the essence and the nature of man, or, if the separation is overcome, it is overcome by reducing the distinction to one of degree. The metaphysical and the ethical are either wholly separated or they are reduced to differences of degree.

Looking to the past, this appears in the following manner. The idea of grace, whether special or common, is said to be wholly inapplicable to pre-redemptive man because it is exclusively applicable to man who has become a sinner. This might seem to be in the interest of stressing the significance of the historical, that is, the significance of the fact of the fall of man. In reality this would lead to the destruction of the historical by reducing it to the non-rational or irrational.

It is the sort of thing that one finds when it is asserted that Adam's choice in paradise for good was equally ultimate with his choice for evil. This is the essentially Arminian idea that God does not control whatsoever comes to pass but that man's deeds are ultimate.

On the other hand, when, on this scholastic basis, a continuation is sought between God's attitude toward man before and after the fall, this is sought along metaphysical rather than along ethical lines. That man is not wholly a demon (an ethical notion) is reduced to, or at least commingled with, the idea that man has the power of distinguishing good and evil, which Satan and the lost hereafter also have. Then common grace becomes interchangeably that which maintains the remnants of the image of God in the wider or the image of God in the narrower sense of the term. In order to avoid the idea that man should be wholly devoid of ethical content it is thought necessary that he have remnants of the "true knowledge" and true morality such as Adam had.

With singular sagacity Calvin avoided this scholastic approach when he spoke of the revelation of God as penetrating into the penetralia of man's psychological being. The sense of deity is the principle of continuity which he presupposes as that in relation to which the ethical reaction of man takes place.[34] And this means that man is always reacting ethically to this revelation of God. He first lives under the *general favor* of God and reacts favorably.[35] Then he reacts unfavorably and comes under the curse of God. So far as his ethical attitude is concerned this is *in principle* entirely hostile to God.

Then grace comes upon the scene, both saving and non-saving grace. It does not preserve some remnants either of the image of God in the wider or in the narrower sense, if these should be taken in scholastic form. How can common grace keep sin from being principal hostility to God? There are no degrees in the principle of depravity. In this narrower sense the image of God has been lost. On the other hand, common grace does not preserve remnants of the image in the wider sense, if this image is thought of as that which is unchangeable. How can remnants be saved of that which was never subject to change?

34. In other words, since all men, at all times and places, know the true God, their relationship to God has its roots in that revelational knowledge that he gives and in their response to it, either in suppression of it or in faith and trust.

35. As was the case, initially, in Adam as our covenant head.

237

Nor is it adequate to say, "By Common Grace He curbs sin, by Special Grace He purges from sin."[36] (After criticizing me for not doing justice to the "positive operations" of common grace, Masselink continues to define common grace in purely negative terms.) Special grace restrains sin as well as does common grace. In fact, if it were not for the restraining activity of saving grace in the world there would be no restraining activity of common grace.[37]

On the other hand, not only saving grace acts positively; common grace does too. It enables man to do many positive things which he would otherwise not be able to do. And the principle of continuity presupposed in all this is the idea of the image of God as itself revelational of God. The Holy Spirit testifies to man through his own constitution as well as through the facts of the universe around him, that he is God's offspring and should act as such (see Acts 17:28).

The sinner seeks to suppress this revelation within himself and around him. He cannot do so fully. He continues to be an image bearer of God; even the lost hereafter will be image bearers of God. They will continue to receive the revelation of God within their own constitution; they cannot be devoid of ethical reaction. So the remnants of which the confession speaks cannot refer to the fact of man's religiosity or to the fact that he knows the difference between good and evil. His knowing this difference is the presupposition of his sinning against God, and therefore also of his being in any wise the recipient of God's grace, either saving or non-saving. Common grace is therefore a favor to sinners by which they are kept from working out to the full the principle of sin within them and thereby are enabled to show some measure of involuntary respect and appreciation for the law of God that speaks to them even through their own constitution as well as through the facts of the world outside.[38]

36. William Masselink, *Common Grace and Christian Education* (privately printed, 1951), 39.

37. In other words, common grace is meant to serve the purpose of God in his application of special grace.

38. Remember again how Paul explains this in Romans 1:24–25. The fact that "God gave them up" presupposes that their sinfulness had previously been restrained by God, such that "their conscience also bears witness, and their conflicting thoughts accuse or even excuse them" (Rom. 2:15).

CHAPTER 8

"REFORMED DOGMATICS"
OF HERMAN HOEKSEMA

A Calvin College student sat, spellbound, listening to the young preacher who had just come to the Eastern Avenue Christian Reformed Church in Grand Rapids, Michigan. The preacher had the physique of a blacksmith and the mien of a Napoleon. But his name was Herman Hoeksema.

With flaming eyes and resonant voice the preacher said: "All flesh is grass, and all the goodliness thereof as the flower of the grass" (Isa. 40:6).

Hoeksema was, throughout his life, a great preacher. The many doctrinal treatises that later flowed from his pen were all written while he continued to be the pastor of a large congregation. His work on *Reformed Dogmatics* is the last and most comprehensive of these works.

Two earlier works may be mentioned here.

1. In 1936 Hoeksema published a book under the title *The Protestant Reformed Churches in America*. These churches sprang into existence, argues Hoeksema, as a Reformation movement. After 1924, when the Synod of the Christian Reformed Church adopted the "doctrine of Common Grace" as a practical addition to its confessional standards, there was no longer any room for an unqualified preaching of the sovereign grace of God in that church. By

the adoption of the "doctrine of Common Grace" the door was set ajar for Arminianism to enter into the church.

To be sure, it was Abraham Kuyper's view of Common Grace and not that of Arminius that the Christian Reformed churches were raising to virtual confessional status. But Kuyper's view led easily to "the Arminian conception of common grace and to the Pelagian conception of the natural man . . ."[1]

In fact, says Hoeksema, the teaching of the doctrine of common grace as adopted by the Christian Reformed Church actually "lapses into the Arminian conception" of grace in that, according to it, "the saving grace of God is intended for all men individually."[2]

Hoeksema distinguishes between *common* and *general* grace.

> By common grace is meant the grace of God, not saving, common both to the elect and the reprobate. . . . By general grace the theory is denoted that holds that the saving grace of God is *general*, i.e., intended for all men individually. The latter theory is a denial of sovereign election and reprobation and of particular atonement and teaches that Christ died for all, but that the application of His atoning death depends upon the choice of the will of the sinner.[3]

Is the Christian Reformed Church now ready to betray the Synod of Dordt? Are they going to allow the preaching and teaching of the sovereign grace of God to be sullied by toning down the biblical and confessional teaching with respect to the total depravity of the natural man? In God's name, this must not and shall not be.

2. In 1943 Hoeksema began the publication of an exposition of the Heidelberg Catechism.[4] In this work Hoeksema not only seeks to defend but also to develop the teachings of the Heidelberg Catechism. If in his Reformation efforts Abraham Kuyper had found it convenient to write an exposition of the Heidelberg Catechism,

---

1. Herman Hoeksema, *The Protestant Reformed Churches in America* (Grand Rapids: First Protestant Reformed Church, 1936), 305–6.

2. Ibid., 312.

3. Ibid., 322.

4. The Heidelberg Catechism (1563) was one of the earliest of the Reformed creeds and was written by Zacharias Ursinus (1534–1583). It is one of the three creeds to which Reformed churches in the Dutch tradition subscribe, the other two being the Belgic Confession (1561) and the Canons of Dort (1619).

Hoeksema did the same. In the nature of the case the "doctrine of common grace" comes in for renewed criticism.

This doctrine is now seen to be destructive of the whole Reformed "system" of theology as the Heidelberg Catechism sets it forth. It is also shown that if "common grace" is to appear in all its pernicious nature then the covenant of God with man must be conceived of in a strictly supralapsarian sense. "History may be, and no doubt is, *infra* in its order of events. But God's eternal purpose and good pleasure dare not be conceived otherwise than according to the supralapsarian order: what is the ultimate in history or in the realization of God's pleasure is first in his eternal counsel."[5]

Only on a supralapsarian view can one see that God's covenant with man is unilateral. It is absurd "to speak of the covenant as an agreement, a mutual alliance, between the infinite God and the speck of dust that is man . . ."[6] How "can man ever be a party, a contracting party in relation to the living God . . . ?" How can the relation of the creature to his Creator "ever be or become an agreement or pact according to which man may merit something higher than he has already attained, even eternal life. Shall I make an alliance with the worm that crawls at my feet?"[7]

How, then, can man, as a "speck of dust," be said to be truly responsible for his deeds? To be sure, the confessions speak of a "natural light" that remains in man even after his fall into sin. True, says Hoeksema, the confessions do speak of natural light. It is true that in "a certain sense man remained a prophet" after his fall into sin.

His light was not changed into darkness in the sense that he ceased to be an intellectional and volitional, a rational and moral being. Even though also from a natural viewpoint the light of his knowledge does not shine any more in its original brilliancy, he does retain some remnants of natural light, by which he has some knowledge of God and of the difference between good and evil, remnants of light that are sufficient to leave him without excuse. Even though he does no longer

5. Herman Hoeksema, *The Heidelberg Catechism (An Exposition): The Triple Knowledge*, 10 vols. (Grand Rapids: Eerdmans, 1951), 6:148.
6. Ibid., 6:142.
7. Ibid., 6:138–39.

clearly discern the Word of God in creation, by the light of the remnants of his natural knowledge, he knows that God is, and that He must be thanked and glorified, and that man is called to declare the praises of the Most High. For, on the other hand, creation remained a medium of revelation of the glorious power and wisdom of God. The invisible things of God are clearly seen, being understood through the things that are made. The light shines in the darkness, even though the darkness comprehendeth it not. God does not leave Himself without witness, even in the conscience of the natural man. Because of this continued speech of God concerning Himself in the works of His hands, and this work of the law written in man's heart, and the remnants of natural light, man is still a prophet, even though through sin he became a false prophet.[8]

Even so, we must not "ascribe the remnants of natural light to the operation of a certain common grace of God, even as did the old Remonstrants."[9]

The theory "that through a certain operation of common grace man's natural light represents a remnant of his original wisdom and knowledge, is not only a theoretical error, but from a practical viewpoint a damnable heresy and pernicious fallacy."[10]

3. Hoeksema's work for the reformation of the church expressed itself finally in his work on *Reformed Dogmatics*. His son, Professor Homer C. Hoeksema, speaks of this work as "the major work of his many-sided and busy ministry of almost fifty years." For more than thirty years Hoeksema "occupied the Chair of Dogmatics in the Theological Reformed Churches." The present work, his son informs us, "is the clearest, the most systematic, and the most complete statement of his theology."[11] Hoeksema did not live to see the publication of his *magnum opus*, for "the Lord took him to his heavenly reward on September 2, 1965."[12]

When Karl Barth began to write his *Dogmatik* in 1927 and his *Kirchliche Dogmatik* (*Church Dogmatics*) in 1932, something of the

8. Ibid., 3:51–52.
9. Ibid.
10. Ibid., 3:53.
11. Homer C. Hoeksema, "Editor's Preface," in *Reformed Dogmatics*, by Herman Hoeksema (Grand Rapids: Reformed Free Publishing Association, 1966), v.
12. Ibid.

existential pathos of his *Romerbrief (Commentary on Romans)* of 1919 was no longer in evidence. The case is similar with Hoeksema. In the first book mentioned above Hoeksema says of Professor Louis Berkhof[13] that his soundness of doctrine on such questions as "revelation, inspiration, the canonicity of Scripture—books and the miracles"—is "largely due to an inconsistent drawing of sound conclusions from unsound principles."[14] Did not Berkhof, in his defense of the doctrine of the common and general grace virtually open the door to Arminianism and Pelagianism?

In the *Dogmatics* Hoeksema writes more calmly. Not as though the severity of his condemnation of the "doctrine of common grace" has abated. Says Hoeksema: "The truth of the total depravity of man" is still being corrupted in Reformed circles by means of the doctrine of common grace. With obvious allusion to the teachings of Kuyper's work on *Gemeene Gratie (Common Grace)* Hoeksema says:

It was found that there was much in the life of the sinner that could not well be harmonized with the confession that man is truly totally depraved, incapable of doing any good, and inclined to all evil. There is much in man, so it was judged, that is truly noble. Consider his serious attempts to improve the world. Consider also his manifestation of power and ability. Consider the work of art and science that is being developed in the world. How much of noble attempt to help one another in misery one beholds in the world. When thus one looked about in the world, the truth of Scripture and of the confessions that the natural man is totally depraved seemed out of harmony with reality. One did not infrequently express the judgment that the children of the world could be an example for the children of God. Thus the sinful judgment of the sinful mind of man was preferred above the judgment of Scripture, which declares that there is no one that doeth any good, no, not one. And when this conclusion was reached, an explanation was sought and invented for this apparent contradiction

13. Louis Berkhof (1873–1957) was a professor at Calvin Seminary from 1906 to 1944, and would have taught Van Til systematic theology. He studied at Princeton from 1902 to 1904 under Warfield and Vos. His most influential work is his *Systematic Theology*, which is dependent on Dutch Reformed theology, especially Herman Bavinck.

14. Hoeksema, *The Protestant Reformed Churches in America*, 24–25.

243

between the judgment of Scripture and the confessions and that which was discerned in the world and which was characterized as the good of the natural man. It was then and on that basis and with this motivation that the theory of common grace was invented. According to this theory, there is a grace, an operation of the Holy Spirit, whereby sin was restrained in man's heart and mind, as well as in the community, and in the power of which the natural man could accomplish all these good things. Of himself man could certainly do no good; he was totally depraved. But all men received a certain grace; and through this grace man is not regenerated: his heart remains always evil. But the evil operation of his heart was restrained. Yea, what is more, he is somewhat changed to the good, so that in temporal, natural and civil things he could do good before God. And thus hocus-pocus was played with the confessions.[15]

In the *Dogmatics*, then, Hoeksema continues to carry on the task of church reformation he had, from the beginning of his career, set for himself.

In each of the six loci of dogmatics he discusses, Hoeksema seeks to hold forth, with more biblical faithfulness than his predecessors have done, the sovereign grace of God to His people.

This does not mean that Hoeksema differs very radically at every point from such Reformed dogmaticians as Herman Bavinck and Louis Berkhof. It means rather that he seeks to go *beyond* them in stressing the primacy of the grace of God to sinful men.

There is, says Hoeksema, no such thing as natural theology. God is "always greater than his revelation." While he is known "He is still the Incomprehensible."[16] On the other hand, through the fall man "lost the image of God, and all his light was changed to darkness." "There is, therefore, only one recipient of the revelation of God, the new man in Christ Jesus."[17]

It is even at this early stage that Hoeksema's difficulties reveal themselves. When he says that there is "only one recipient of the revelation of God" he means that only through the redemption in Christ and through the regeneration of the Holy Spirit can

15. Hoeksema, *Reformed Dogmatics*, 272–73.
16. Ibid., 41.
17. Ibid., 42.

one receive and accept the revelation of God for what it is. This is perfectly true. When some Reformed theologians of the past accepted the validity of the so-called "proofs" for the existence of God, this was inconsistent with their basic commitment. The proofs presuppose the idea of the autonomy of man. So far we must agree with Hoeksema.

However, there is another side to the story. It is true that no argument is sufficient to prove the existence of God to one that refuses to bow before the revelation of the living God Himself and that contradicts His word.[18] However, this only proves that the natural man cannot, of himself, see the revelation of God for what it is. It does not prove that this revelation is not present to him. Nor does it prove that this revelation is not clear. A blind man cannot see the light of the sun but the sun is there for all that. In fact, the blind man is blind only in relation to the light of the sun.

Hoeksema could have helped us forward indeed if he had made this simple but telling point. As it is, Hoeksema leaves us where Bavinck left us, with respect to the "proofs" for the existence of God. Following Bavinck, Hoeksema says: "While all these so-called 'proofs,' therefore, have their significance and value for him that believes, as so many witnesses of the invisible God, as strictly logical proofs, that must convince unbelieving reason, they must be said to lack all power."[19]

Now the "proofs" presuppose the idea that the natural man can and does interpret himself and the universe rightly at least up to a point. As he handles these "proofs" the natural man is trying to penetrate by his logical power what the ultimate nature of Reality is, even while, at the same time, he insists that Reality is unknowable. In spite of himself Hoeksema virtually allows a measure of validity to the "proofs." They are for him "so many witnesses of the invisible God."[20]

But the "proofs" do not "witness" at all. If they had any validity then they would have *absolute* validity. If they prove anything they prove that all Reality is and can be only that which man, by his logical power, says that it can and must be. If they have any validity then even Parmenides and Spinoza would get more than they

18. Ibid., 47.
19. Ibid.
20. Ibid.

desired to get. They then would get their own complete absorption into a timeless Unity.[21]

If then the "proofs" are, in any sense, to be retained as witnesses, they must do so because they have no logical validity at all. The "invisible God" to which these "proofs" point as witnesses then becomes the wholly other, the wholly unknowable God of medieval nominalism and of modern neo-orthodoxy.[22]

The "proofs," then, cannot be taken "as evidences of revelation" of the God of Scripture.[23] On the contrary, they presuppose that the God of the Bible does *not* exist and is therefore *not* revealed in the world. To all intents and purposes the "proofs" constitute an attack on the clarity of God's revelation in the created universe. A child in a home need not and cannot seek to *prove* the existence of his father. If he knows himself at all in any proper sense, this child knows himself as a child of his father. The prodigal son of the parable was what he was because he was constantly trying to make himself believe that he was not the son of his father.

Calvin starts off his discussion of theology in his *Institutes* by saying that man's consciousness of himself and his consciousness of God are involved in one another. In saying this he is only reflecting what Paul so clearly says in his first chapter of the epistle to the Romans when he speaks of man as unavoidably knowing God.

Hoeksema rightly lays great stress on the total depravity of man. But man's total depravity spells his ethical disobedience to his Creator. Man cannot become and remain apostate except in relation to the revelation of God's character and will that is everywhere and always present in him.

Hoeksema does not approve of the distinction often made by Reformed theologians between the image of God in the wider and in the narrower sense. He prefers to distinguish between the image

21. In this paragraph, Van Til is not denying what he has affirmed earlier, namely, that the proofs are objectively valid. What he is doing is taking Hoeksema's affirmation of the proofs as "witnesses" to its logical conclusion. If the proofs are witnesses to the natural man, in the way that the natural man has construed them, then they testify that the natural man can, on his own, determine the nature of ultimate reality. The mind of man can, therefore, postulate an ultimate, unchanging principle (i.e., a god) which must itself become *the* universal principle.

22. This universal, unchanging principle, which is the logical implication of the proofs (as defined and determined by the natural man), must transcend all particulars (because it must be a universal and thus unchanging). It is, therefore, "wholly other"; it is beyond the particular things of this world.

23. Hoeksema, *Reformed Dogmatics*, 43.

"in a formal and in a material sense." "By the former is meant the fact that man's nature is adapted to bear the image of God." It "requires a rational, moral nature to bear that image of God."[24]

In terms of the formal image man is "a personal being with a rational moral nature, capable of standing in a conscious, personal relation to God, capable of knowledge of God, of righteousness, and of holiness."[25]

It is this formal image by which man does not stand but is capable of standing in an ethical relation to God that was not lost through the fall. "Through sin man did not change essentially. He is still the same personal, rational, moral, psychological, material earthly being. And from a natural point of view, he still stands in the same relation to the world about him."[26] Thus since "the influence of sin is of a spiritual and ethical nature," the formal essence of man was not changed by it. After his fall man "still remains man." In this fact lies the capability of his restoration to a true ethical relation to God. Thus though the "Christian is fundamentally and principally renewed through the work of regeneration . . . also this change is not an essential change, but a spiritual and ethical conversion. Also the regenerated man remains man. His nature remains a spiritual, ethical, moral, psychological, material, earthly nature."[27]

Who, then, is "man as man, by virtue of his creation?"[28] His essence lies in his *capability* of ethical relationship to God, whether in *malum* or in *bonam partem* (whether in an *evil* or a *good manner*). But even though the essence of man remained unchanged through the fall "from a natural point of view he lost much of his original power and of his natural gifts. He only retained a few and small remnants of them."[29] Then when "God through Jesus Christ by His Holy Spirit realizes His covenant with man, it becomes his solemn responsibility to love the Lord his God with all his heart . . ."[30]

It is thus that by his substitution of the distinction between the formal and material for the distinction between the wider and the narrower aspects of the image of God and man that Hoeksema

24. Ibid., 208.
25. Ibid., 209.
26. Ibid., 543.
27. Ibid., 542; cf. 462.
28. Ibid., 540.
29. Hoeksema, *Reformed Dogmatics*, 543.
30. Ibid., 445.

seeks to maintain the biblical teaching with respect to the total depravity of fallen man. The latter distinction is "dangerous," says Hoeksema, "because it prepares room for the further philosophy that there are remnants of the image of God left in fallen man, and that therefore the natural man cannot be wholly depraved."[31] The distinction between the image in the wider and in the narrower sense "lends itself very easily to support the view of those who insist that there is a certain common grace by virtue of which natural man is not so depraved as without that grace he would have been. And if this is not a denial of the doctrine of total depravity, words certainly have lost their meaning."[32]

We must now ask whether in what Hoeksema says on the question of the "remnants," on the question of "proofs," and on the question of the "image" Hoeksema has really helped us forward in our struggle to maintain the biblical teaching of total depravity and the primacy of the sovereign grace of God.

Basic to all three of these questions is the idea that the only "recipient of the revelation of God" is "the new man in Christ Jesus."[33]

This idea is basically unscriptural. In the clearest possible language Paul asserts that man "knowing God" rebels against God. Hoeksema quite rightly insists that man is inherently a covenant being. This is his *humanum* (that is, his *humanity*, or what makes him human). In all his reactions to every aspect of his environment the "natural man" is confronted with God's revelation. This means that always and everywhere every man is face to face with the requirement of God's holy will. Unless this were the case man would have to identify himself in a vacuum and then operate in a vacuum. In particular, man could not be totally depraved if he were not totally enveloped by the revelation of God.

Hoeksema rightly says that by the fall man's activity has turned into reverse. This constitutes his apostasy. But apostasy does not take place in a vacuum.

When, therefore, in their confessions the Reformed churches speak of *reliquiae* (remnants) and *vestigial* (vestiges) they mean to say that the light of the revelation of God always remains as the presupposition of man's ethical depravity.

31. Ibid., 207.
32. Ibid.
33. Ibid., 42.

To be sure, the idea of "remnants" is a dangerous one. It has sometimes been interpreted in such a way as to impinge upon the idea of total depravity. And when the notion of "common grace" is taken to imply a "neutral territory" of interpretation between believers and unbelievers, then it is destructive of the doctrine of total depravity. Taken properly, however, the idea of common grace, like the idea of the remnants, presupposes as it expresses the universal presence of the revelation of God. Taken as such the idea of common grace as well as that of the remnants supports the idea of total depravity. Both stress the fact of the inescapable presence of the face of God to every man. Hoeksema overreaches himself when, in seeking to stress the idea of total depravity, he takes away the foundation on which alone it stands.[34]

Hoeksema also overreaches himself when he says that "it is absurd to speak of the proofs of the existence of God."[35] Says Hoeksema, "No one is able to demonstrate with mathematical certainty that God exists, nor can reason reach out for Him by means of a syllogism. For whatever can be so demonstrated and proven must needs belong to the world of our own understanding and experience and therefore is not God."[36]

In saying this Hoeksema is giving altogether too much credit to the natural man. The proofs are built on the assumption that the natural man can properly identify facts and employ logic with respect to these facts without presupposing God's revelational requirements in them.

Hoeksema would have advanced the cause of Reformed theology if he had argued the "absurdity" of the proofs on the ground that they presuppose a man who must identify himself in a vacuum in order then to identify facts in a vacuum, in order then to bring these facts into logical relation to one another. The idea of the "remnants" and the idea of common grace, properly understood, would have helped him to help the Reformed community as it is

34. This could be one of the most important points in the debate on common grace, since it shows Hoeksema's lack of understanding of the image (and thus the knowledge) of God. To deny common grace is to deny that God's natural revelation gets through to the unbeliever, and that he is unable completely to eradicate it. Thus, "remnants" of that revelation will come through at times.

35. Hoeksema, *Reformed Dogmatics*, 43.

36. Ibid.

now threatened with extinction by the neo-orthodoxy of such men as Emil Brunner and Karl Barth.[37]

Emil Brunner also introduced the distinction between the formal and the material aspect of man as the image-bearer of God into his theology. For him this distinction is required by his dialectical view of the relation of God to man. Brunner's dialectical theology denies the historicity of man's creation and fall. It denies the direct revelation of God to man in history at any point, even in Jesus Christ. Accordingly, the loss of man's image through the fall of the first Adam and the restoration of the believer's image through the second Adam is not historical at all in any but a Pickwickian sense of the word.[38]

Yet, in his zeal to guard the teaching of man's total depravity against the common grace idea of those who with him stand for historic Christianity in general and for Reformed theology in particular, Hoeksema does nothing to distinguish his view of the formal-material distinction from that of his contemporary, Emil Brunner.

Nor does the distinction of the formal and material aspects of the image constitute any improvement upon the distinction of the wider-narrower aspects of the image in any case. Both distinctions are equally "dangerous" and for the same reason. The idea of the formal aspects of the image is calculated to present the indestructible *humanum* of man. But this idea of the indestructibility of man as the *humanum* is frequently spoken of as though it were a sort of platonic essence. Used as such it becomes an abstract principle of rationality in which God and man together participate.

Correlative to this notion of man's indestructible *humanum* expressed by the notion of the formal is the idea of the material aspect of the image as wholly lost. Used as such it easily stands for the notion of man's pure freedom or contingency.

When taken together the formal aspect as abstract rationality and the material aspect as abstract irrationality today express the modern dialectical view of man's relation to God.

If then the terms *formal* and *material* are to be used at all by an orthodox theologian, they ought to be taken as correlative to one another on the presupposition of the presence of God's direct rev-

---

37. See chapter 7, footnote 17.
38. "Pickwickian" in that "historical" sense must be understood in an uncustomary way.

elation to man. When the concepts *formal* and *material* are applied to the image idea, but the image idea itself is part and parcel of a dialectical scheme of reality, as it is with such men as Brunner and Barth, then these concepts are destructive of the orthodox view of God as well as man.

All in all then, Hoeksema did not succeed in advancing the cause of biblical and Reformed theology at the points of the "remnants," the "proofs" and the image of God. At all these points he is regressive rather than progressive, and the reason in each instance is that he fails to think of man's *humanum* as at every point confronted by the direct revelation of God.

A similar point of regression must be noted with respect to Hoeksema's devotion to supralapsarianism. One could wish that he had dealt with Bavinck's magnificent discussion on the subject of supra and infra. Bavinck points out that unless they are taken as supplementative of one another, i.e., unless they are taken as limiting conceptions, of one another, they lead us out of the bounds of Christian thinking.

This way lies progress. Instead of following and developing the lead of Bavinck, Hoeksema reverts to the either/or idea. By doing so he explains too much.

His thinking on this point resembles his thinking on the question of common grace. In His eternal love God has chosen the elect to be His own. Therefore, God *cannot*, in any sense, have an attitude of favor to any man who is not one of His elect.

Hoeksema never answered adequately the charge that on his view the elect can never in any sense have been under the wrath of God and Christ need not have died for them in history. Hoeksema took no note.

His contemporary, Karl Barth, also holds to supralapsarianism. Hoeksema does not trouble to distinguish his own position from that of Barth. Barth says that he has modified supralapsarianism first by removing the orthodox presupposition of direct revelation. This enables him to say that election does not pertain to persons. No person in distinction from another person is either elect or reprobate. Secondly, on Barth's view reprobation is never the last word for any man. God's *yes* ultimately prevails over His *no*. The *humanum* is said to exist in the fact that when a man is really a man he is this as fellowman with Christ.

Here the idea that only the believer receives the revelation of God turns into the idea that man's manhood consists of his participation in the being of God. Here is the neo-Protestant version of the scholastic notion of the analogy of being.[39]

Hoeksema does, to be sure, in his discussion of eschatology, condemn the universalism of Barth and his school.[40] But nowhere does Hoeksema enter upon a discussion of Barth's basic theological principles. True, the *Dogmatics* does not pretend to deal with apologetics. Yet, Hoeksema has always found it important to distinguish his position sharply from orthodox Reformed theologians who believe in common grace, Why, then, did he not distinguish his position clearly and at every major point of doctrine from neo-orthodox theologians such as Barth?

There is, of course, much else in Hoeksema's work that could be discussed with profit. There is, indeed, much very valuable material in his work. We have, however, used our space to deal with what was most important to him.

With all our great admiration for Hoeksema as a preacher and as a, teacher of theology we must, nonetheless, maintain that however true he was to the idea of the sovereignty of the grace of God, he did not advance its proper form of expression in his works on theology.

39. This is a particularly devastating critique of Barthian neoorthodoxy, in that Barth was adamantly (and rightly) opposed to the analogy of being, but then argued for an "analogy of faith" that denied the basic truths of orthodox theology.

40. Hoeksema, *Reformed Dogmatics*, 730, 766.

CHAPTER 9

TERMINAL CONSIDERATIONS

S ince the first chapter of the present book appeared under separate cover about twenty-five years ago a very great change has taken place in the thinking of many Reformed scholars. A great number of Reformed scholars are now employing neo-orthodox terminology in order by means of it to express the doctrine of God's sovereign grace to sinful men. Dr. G. C. Berkouwer, the leading dogmatic theologian of the Free University of Amsterdam, the university founded by Abraham Kuyper, finds that the Synod of Dordt did not have the necessary categories of thought with which to express the biblical teaching of the grace of God. The Synod of Dordt had to resort to the notion of God's all-controlling causality in order to defend the idea of free grace. But the notion of causality is impersonal and mechanical. It cannot do justice to the sovereign freedom of the grace of God.[1]

Dr. Berkouwer has not told us how he expects to escape the universalism that inevitably accompanies the neo-orthodox doctrine of the *freedom* of God's grace. The freedom or sovereignty of God's grace is, according to neo-orthodoxy, the freedom or sovereignty of a God who has no character of his own. This God has not created

---

1. Cf. Cornelius Van Til, *The Sovereignty of Grace* (Philadelphia: Presbyterian and Reformed, 1969).

man or the world. He has therefore not ordained any ordinances for it. He could not work redemptively in it. To come into it "he" would have to turn into the opposite of himself, if he had any self. When he has come into the world he is *wholly* revealed in it and *wholly* hidden in it. All this by order of the noumenal-phenomenal scheme of Immanuel Kant's thinking.[2]

On such a view there is no common grace problem. There is no God who by His counsel or purpose through Christ creates and redeems the world. Man is not a creature made in the image of the God of Scripture. Accordingly there is no problem as to how God's comprehensive plan and man's responsible action in relation to that plan may be brought into coherence with one another. All orthodox theologians are asked to give up all the theological disputes they have ever had between one another. All grace is now sovereign and all grace is now universal. All churches may now retain their confessions for "historic" reasons while they all join in one grand new confession of the "dialectical" relation of "freedom" and "necessity" controlling both God and man. Together all may now proclaim the doctrine of sovereign, universal grace.

If you are an adherent of this new theology you may, on occasion, read the words of Christ on the cross: "My God, my God, why hast thou forsaken me?" Formerly you asked yourself the question how the eternal Father who loves His Son with unquenchable love could, at the same time, pour out His wrath upon His only begotten and well-beloved Son. This problem then brought to a focus all your theological problems. How can God in any sense and in any degree show love or favor to those whom He "passes by" when He saves His own. Again, how can God in any sense and in any degree show disfavor or wrath toward those whom He has from eternity loved in Christ.

---

2. Van Til spent much of his career opposing Barth and neoorthodox theology. This paragraph cuts to the conclusion of much of his other work in that area. In brief, since the *freedom* of God is essential to him, it determines his *character* and *everything* that he will be (including his triunity). As "wholly other," because absolutely free, he is only who he is in his revelation. Thus, the wholly other freely determines to be who he is *only* in Christ, and determines that man is who he is *only* in Christ. For more elaboration of this, see Van Til, *Christianity and Barthianism* (Philadelphia: Presbyterian and Reformed, 1962). For a contemporary and sympathetic Barthian view that reaches many of the same conclusions as Van Til, see Bruce McCormack, "Election and Trinity: Theses in Response to George Hunsinger," in *Trinity and Election in Contemporary Theology*, ed. Michael T. Dempsey (Grand Rapids: Eerdmans, 2011).

Now all such problems are seen to be pseudo-problems. You now know that there is no God who exists in eternity prior to His revelation in time. There is therefore no plan of God according to which the course of history takes its shape. God is identical with His revelation. And God is grace. He is what He is in His relation to man through Christ, and man is what he is in his relation to God as the one true man and therefore as the one true grace-receiver. All grace is therefore saving grace and all saving grace is common grace. All grace is sovereign, universal grace.

An additional advantage that comes to you if you accept this neo-orthodox view of grace, is that it is in accord with the principles of modern science and philosophy. Modern science and modern philosophy assume that ultimate reality is on the one hand purely contingent. It is in line with this idea that modern theology thinks of its "God" as indeterminate, i.e., free to turn into the opposite of himself. Modern science and modern philosophy assume, on the other hand, that ultimate reality is wholly determined and therefore wholly penetrable by the intellect of man. These two notions, that of pure contingency and that of pure determinism, are thought of as correlative to one another. It is on this notion of the correlativity of pure determinism and pure indeterminism that neo-orthodox theology builds its notion of God as on the one hand wholly hidden and as on the other hand wholly revealed. God's grace is wholly "arbitrary" or free and at the same time wholly determined. There is no man that is not lost, and there is no man that is not saved. And, what is all-important, grace is always the last word of God for man as man.

The great difficulty with this neo-orthodox view of sovereign-universal grace is that the view of reality and of knowledge on which it builds is inherently unintelligible. The idea of pure contingency and pure determinism, and with it the idea of pure ignorance and exhaustive knowledge, cancel each other out. There is no self-contained point of reference for human predication except in the self-contained triune God of historic Christianity.

One can understand why Roman Catholic and Arminian thinkers should find the neo-orthodox view of God's sovereign universal grace attractive. Their own thinking has, for centuries, entertained both the idea of pure contingency and the idea of pure determinism. Romanism and Arminianism have rejected the biblical view of God and of the grace of God, first because their view of the human will was based on the notion of pure contingency, and second because their view of rationality was based on the abstract notion of pure determinism. The first point is obvious. The second point is less obvious but no less true. The Romanist and the Arminian think they know that reality *cannot* be such that human responsibility operates within the plan of God.

Romanism and Arminianism begin all their reasoning about any subject, whether biblical or non-biblical, from the presupposition that man, though a creature of God, is none the less in some measure able to initiate action that is not subject to the all-controlling plan of God.

It is in accordance with this starting point that Romanism and Arminianism think of logic as an abstract impersonal principle, and of space-time facts as contingent. Such being the case, Romanism and Arminianism think of logic and fact as correlative to one another in much the same way that apostate philosophy thinks of them as correlative to one another.

Of course Romanism and Arminianism are seeking to be true to Christ and His word. But they cannot be true to Christ and His word so long as they *also* want to be true to what is the basic starting point and method of those who oppose Christ and His word.

It is obvious that Romanism and Arminianism are unable and unwilling to set the theology of Christ and His word squarely over against neo-orthodoxy. There is too much that they have in common with neo-orthodoxy for them to oppose it squarely. Neo-orthodoxy has built its theology on the modern scientific and modern philosophical view of man, of logic, and of fact. Only a theology that is unapologetically based upon the revelation of the self-attesting Christ of Scripture can challenge unbelief in general and Christ-denying as well as Christ-compromising forms of theology.

J. DOUMA—*ALGEMENE GENADE*[3]

We are therefore happy to terminate our discussion of the problem of common grace in relation to the presentation of the gospel of the sovereign grace of God in Christ to lost men,

3. Jochem Douma (1931–) is a Dutch theologian and part of the Reformed Churches, Liberated (Vrijgemaakt). He studied at the University of Kampen and the University of

with a consideration of Dr. Jochem Douma's book on *Common Grace*.[4]

Dr. Douma's book contains a very thorough comparison of the teachings of Abraham Kuyper, Klaas Schilder, and John Calvin on the question of common grace.

Douma sets forth the views of these three men in great detail. Having done this, he makes a comparison among their views and in his last chapter gives his evaluation. We shall limit ourselves to a consideration of his evaluation.

1. Double Predestination

The first point Douma discusses is that of double predestination. He says: "We maintain on this point, on the basis of our discussion of Rom 9–11, what the doctrinal statements of the Synod of Dordt I, 6 and 15 say on this point."[5]

Douma's evaluation of the differences among the three men he discussed is based upon the assumption that they agree with one another and that he agrees with all three of them on *this* point.

Douma then gives a brief exegesis of Rom 9–11. He cannot accept the new exegesis of this passage of Scripture given by Karl Barth, to the effect that the ideas of election and reprobation as taught in Scripture do not pertain to individual persons and are not finally determinative of the destiny of every individual man.[6]

The entire question is whether, under the pressure of a basically mistaken exegesis of Scripture founded on a non-biblical view of reality and knowledge, Reformed theology will give up its basic contention with respect to the triune God of Scripture who, from the fallen race of men, chooses a people for Himself and passes others by. Is it the sovereign will of God that is back of the eternal destiny of all men?

At this point Douma opposes the new exegesis of 9–11 given by Herman Ridderbos and G. C. Berkouwer. They are apparently

---

Amsterdam. He was in pastoral ministry, and was for almost thirty years a professor of ethics at Kampen. The book Van Til mentions is a publication of his thesis.

4. Jochem Douma, *Algemene genade* (Goes: Oosterbaan & Le Cointre, 1966).

5. Ibid., 289.

6. Ibid., 290–91.

seeking to escape the charge of determinism lodged against the historic Reformed position as stated by the Synod of Dordt. Douma expresses agreement with Herman Bavinck, who shows that the philosophy of determinism "does not know what to do" with the biblical idea of the counsel of God.

We express hearty agreement with Douma on this first point. There has been a tendency among Reformed theologians to criticize many of their forebears for having interpreted the dynamic, historical truths of Scripture in terms of the "static" concepts of the Greeks. Dr. H. M. Kuitert's[7] doctoral dissertation on *De Mensvormigheid Gods* (*The Anthropomorphic God*) contains a comprehensive critique of the history of Reformed theology from this point of view.

What these critics seem not to realize is that so far as they join Karl Barth and neo-orthodoxy in general, in identifying the God of Scripture with His manifestation and work in history, they have lost the gospel of the grace of God in Christ altogether. When Barth says that there is no *God in Himself* and there *is no absolute decree of God*, he means that God is identical with Christ and that Christ is identical with his work of "saving" all men.[8] Men are, on this view, "saved" "in advance." There is on this view no transition from wrath to grace in history. When Jesus said, "My God, my God, why hast thou forsaken me," the "grace" of God was not satisfying but canceling out the wrath of God. On this view there is no grace at all in the biblical sense of the term; nor is there any need for grace. On this view *all* is grace; reality is such that man may think of his ideal self as his real self.

2. *Non eodem modo* (not in the same way)

In his comparison of the views of the three theologians, Douma finds that Schilder maintained a direct parallelism, or equal ultimacy, between election and reprobation. Schilder was, says Douma, in a large measure of agreement with Herman Hoeksema on this

---

7. H. M. Kuitert (1924–) studied at the Free University of Amsterdam. After some time in the pastorate, he was appointed in 1965 as an assistant to G. C. Berkouwer at the Free University. He was appointed as a professor there in 1967, and retired in 1989. The book to which Van Til refers was his doctoral thesis under Berkouwer.

8. See Bruce McCormack, "Christ and the Decree: An Unsettled Question for the Reformed Churches Today," in *Reformed Theology in Contemporary Perspective*, ed. Lynn Quigley (Edinburgh: Rutherford House, 2006).

point. Douma disagrees with Schilder. "We travel a safer way if, when we speak of double predestination, we, with Dordt, speak in infralapsarian fashion."[9]

On this point too Douma follows Bavinck as the present writer did in his book *The Theology of James Daane*. Christ came to save, not to condemn the world. Christ's *proper* work is to redeem His people (*opus proprium*), while His alien work is to pass by others whom He punishes for their sin eternally (*opus alienum*).

We would go beyond Douma and say—following the lead of Bavinck—that the distinction between infra- and supralapsarianism is a distinction we must no longer carry on.[10] For it we must substitute the notion of the Christian limiting concept. Reasoning by "good and necessary consequence" from the idea of equal ultimacy, would introduce into God an eternal dualism. We must do the opposite. We must presuppose unity in God as back of what may "appear" contradictory to us. Only if we presuppose unity in God do the words of Christ, "My God, my God . . . ," retain genuine meaning.

Neither infra- nor supralapsarianism can do full justice to the idea of unity in God as the presupposition of the genuine significance of history as a whole, and of the work of Christ in history in particular. We are still dealing in abstractions so long as we do not regard all the "concepts" of Scripture as supplementative of one another and so long as we do not think of the biblical "system" of truth as an "analogical" system. Douma is clearly thinking along these lines and his work therefore marks real progress in our understanding of God's relationship to His world.

3. The Breadth of Predestination

It was Abraham Kuyper who did more than anyone else, says Douma, to make the idea of predestination, and more particularly the idea of predestination in Christ, all-comprehensive. In and for Christ all things are created. Election of individual men is election within the redeemed cosmos, and the cosmos has been redeemed by Christ. Accordingly a Christian must not take an ascetic position. The world belongs to Christ.

9. Douma, *Algemene genade*, 295.
10. See Bavinck, *RD*, 2:388ff.

4. Speculation in the Idea of Development

Much as we must praise Kuyper for his inclusion of *all things* under the idea of predestination we cannot follow him when he speaks of an organic development of the world of creation. We have here Kuyper's idea that the development of the powers of nature by means of common grace is something independent of God's work of saving grace.

Here we have, says Douma, Kuyper the philosopher of culture, no longer depending on a careful exegesis of Scripture but giving free reign to his speculative imagination. Let us rather be satisfied with the words of Paul when, speaking of Christ, he says that "from him and through him and to him are all things." When we do this then we recognize and honor the mystery of God's revelation to man in Christ for the salvation of the world.[11]

On both of the last points we must agree with Douma.

5. Christ and the Covenant of Grace

Having accepted Kuyper's idea of including *all things* in the redemptive work of Christ, and having rejected his idea of God's work through common grace as a "Nebenzweck"[12] to His work of saving His people, we turn again to Schilder.

We join Schilder in rejecting Kuyper's distinction between Christ as the mediator of creation and as the mediator of redemption. We must unite the idea of creation in Christ with that of His redemption of all things.[13]

However, when, in rejecting Kuyper's idea of common grace as a means by which the created world is kept from falling into nothingness, Schilder introduces the notion of a *substratum*, we cannot follow him.

Schilder argues that God intends some men to be saved and others not to be saved. Both groups need the world and its culture in order to attain their destined end. Accordingly, there must be a development of this world through history as a *substratum* on the basis of which the struggle between the elect and the non-elect can be carried on.

11. Douma, *Algemene genade*, 305.
12. See chapter 3, footnote 10.
13. That is, as was stated in the foreword, Van Til rejects Kuyper's notion of Christ as mediator of two relatively independent spheres. Rather, his mediation of creation is for the purpose of redeeming all things in the end.

We shall walk more safely if we realize that Scripture views the pre-existence of Christ and His work of creation as the Son of God, from the point of view of His work of reconciliation.[14]

There is one all-inclusive covenant of grace. All history must be seen in the light of this one covenant of grace. "The phases of this history are phases of the covenant of grace, which envelops the ages from the time of paradise by way of Noah, Abraham, and Christ to his coming again."[15]

With all this we express hearty agreement. We regret only that at this point Douma speaks of the position of Kuyper and that of Barth as though they differed only by way of emphasis. Kuyper spoke too abstractly of Christ as Mediator of creation, and Barth has no eye for anything but the redemptive work of Christ.[16] But surely Barth has no eye for the redemptive work of Christ any more than he does for His creative work. Barth simply does not believe the Christ of the Scripture at all.

6. Common Grace by Kuyper—Directed Wrongly

Kuyper's view of common grace is to be criticized because it too, as already noted, tends to be a speculative philosophy of culture instead of a biblically based view of the stages of history as all together manifesting various phases of the one covenant of grace through Christ with man.

This point is similar to what was earlier discussed.

7. Grace—Also to the Reprobate

If we speak in truly Christological fashion then we deal with "the *one* grace of God in Christ."[17]

Schilder does not do justice to this point. His parallelism between God's favor to the elect and His disfavor to the reprobate does not permit him to do justice to the grace of God even to the reprobate. "The different *effect* of God's revelation toward the elect and the reprobate does not take away the common *grace* character of this revelation. Scripture speaks plainly of grace toward the reprobate within the covenant."[18]

14. Douma, *Algemene genade*, 307.
15. Ibid., 309.
16. Ibid.
17. Ibid., 317.
18. Ibid.

Calvin does better justice than Schilder to this point. Even Calvin, however, does not do full justice to the Christo-centric character of grace. At this point we may learn from S. G. de Graaf.[19]

The reader may have noted that the present writer has from time to time stressed the point here made. This was done chiefly for the apologetic purpose of indicating that so long as man lives and breathes on earth, God through Christ, indirectly or directly, in all earnestness pleads with him to repent and turn back to God.

8. Judgment and Wrath of God

For all our inability to follow Schilder on his idea of equal ultimacy between God's grace and God's wrath, we must be thankful to him for the fact that, following Calvin, he observes God's wrath revealed in history. In recent times Reformed theologians have tended to forget this fact.

9. God's Attitude—"Speaking with Two Words"

We must not separate the "facts" of history, i.e., the manifestation both of God's favor and of His wrath, from his *attitude* expressed in these facts. God is angry with those who are not yet but one day will be His people. To turn away His wrath from them He pours it out upon His own Son. God is angry with His people even when He loves them in Christ with an eternal love, to the extent that they continue to fail to live according to the principle of redemption within them. The same thing holds, *mutatis mutandis*, with respect to the reprobate.

We must therefore not *systematize* away these facts as revealed.

It is this point that the present writer has greatly stressed, especially in *Common Grace* against the tendency of Hoeksema's thinking.

The point is, apologetically speaking, of utmost importance. It is the biblical "system" containing the "apparently contradictory," but unreservedly based on the unity of God presupposed and expressed in Scripture, that alone can meet the futilities of modern thought. Apparently it is the failure to see this point that leads some recent Reformed theologians to seek for a point of contact with modern

19. In a master's thesis on the subject, "The Christological Basis of Common Grace" (Westminster Theological Seminary, 1966), Jelle Tuinenga also praises De Graaf for his placing of the idea of common grace on a proper Christological basis. Tuinenga praises H. Dooyeweerd for doing the same as De Graaf.

science, modern philosophy, and modern theology, by means of agreement with them in their principles of interpretation. In all humility the present writer would suggest that this way is not the way of Paul as he would triumph with Christ, because he, and his world, were saved by Christ. "My God, my God, why hast thou forsaken me?" *Das Wort sollen sie lassen stehen.*[20] Do not reduce its meaning by saying this is to speak phenomenologically and that all phenomenological speech is at best a pointer to something in the *noumenal* of which no man knows anything.[21] We cannot expect to penetrate the mystery of the unity of the triune God as it underlies the multiformity of expressions He uses in relation to men. History is real. History has genuine significance, not in spite of, but because of the fact that God realizes His purposes through Christ, in it.

It is at this point that Douma deals with and misinterprets the first of the three points of the Synod of Kalamazoo.[22] He thinks of Kalamazoo as largely following the cultural optimism of Kuyper and as therefore dealing with abstractions. This is not the way the present writer understands Kalamazoo. Granted there was an influence of Kuyper present at Kalamazoo, it remains true that it was dealing simply and "naively" rather than scholastically with the fact that we *must not* follow Hoeksema in his logical deductions from the principle of reprobation any more than we must follow the Arminians in their logical deduction from the principle of human autonomy.

Douma speaks of Kalamazoo as speaking of God's favorable attitude "without context." Douma speaks of Kalamazoo as, therefore, making certain "optimistic noises" about the natural man.

Douma has misunderstood the main intent of Kalamazoo. He has similarly misunderstood the main intent of what the present writer, some time after Kalamazoo, presented on the question of common grace. He thinks that my purpose was to present a philosophy of history in an organic, speculative fashion. The exact opposite was the case. The whole argument to the effect that we must have an "analogical" system in which seemingly contradictory teachings

20. This is a quote attributed to Martin Luther. It means, in effect, "Do not tamper with the Word [of God]."
21. Cf. Douma, *Algemene genade*, 333.
22. Ibid., 388.

of Scripture have justice done them is, in essence, the same thing that Douma is doing.

He complains that my position is not clear to him (*Helder wordt het ons niet*). No doubt there is a grave lack of clarity in my exposition. But the basic reason for "lack of clarity" in the "biblical system" is for me due to the fact that God's unity of purpose cannot be exhaustively understood and expressed by the believer. It is the mystery of God in Christ before which we should bow. But his main criticism is that my position is "too schematic" (*te schematisch*). But that was just the point I sought to escape.

10. Grace and Necessity

As I was too schematic for Douma, so Kuyper sought to "look behind the scenes" in his view of predestination. Similarly Schilder indulged in speculation about the counsel of God. But we must reject every form of reasoning from and toward the philosophically speculative. We find our rest in the *faithfulness* of God expressed in Scripture. Man is never a finished product. God continues to deal with him in favor to the last as Jesus did with Judas.

11. Culture and Pilgrimage

The Christian knows that the world has been redeemed by Christ. "All things are yours and ye are Christ's" (1 Cor. 3:22–23). Kuyper and Schilder were both deeply interested in a true, a biblically founded philosophy of culture. Kuyper was more speculative than Schilder. What needs to be done is to give careful scriptural support of our philosophy of culture.

12. Common Grace?

Can we then, in view of all this discussion, asks Douma, maintain the "theologoumenon" (the theological teaching) of common grace? Yes, we can and we must. We must start again with Calvin. To be sure, Kuyper and Schilder were as anxious as was Calvin to confess Christ. Their interest in a Christian culture was for the purpose of showing modern man that the message of the gospel of Christ is all-comprehensive. Men are without excuse if they do not see both the grace and the wrath of God manifested in nature and in history. Romanism and Arminianism, we may add, have no truly biblical view of human depravity; accordingly they do not appreciate the depth of the grace of God. Romanism and Arminianism have no truly biblical view of the fact that *all things* are redeemed by Christ; accordingly they do not appreciate the breadth of the grace of God.

Today neo-orthodoxy must be signalized as not only lacking appreciation for the depth and the breadth of the grace of God but as virtually denying it altogether.

This takes us back to the beginning of this work. Its purpose was apologetic throughout. The gospel of God's sovereign grace to men can be presented to men for what it is in all its saving power only and alone if it is presented as being a challenge to repentance to the natural man at *every point* of his interest. If he does not repent and turn to Christ he will be lost and his culture with him. Only if the idea of common grace is Christ-centered and therefore biblically constructed can it help the Christian apologist as he pleads with men to forsake the wisdom of this world and accept the "foolishness" of the gospel of Christ, through which it pleases God to save those that believe.

BIBLIOGRAPHY

Adamson, Robert. *The Development of Greek Philosophy.* Edited by W. R. Sorley and R. P. Hardie. Edinburgh: W. Blackwood and Sons, 1908.

Aquinas, Thomas. *Summa Theologiae: Questions on God.* Edited by Brian Leftow and Brian Davies. Cambridge Texts in the History of Philosophy. Cambridge: Cambridge University Press, 2006.

Aristotle. *The Basic Works of Aristotle.* Edited by Richard McKeon. New York: Random House, 1968.

Audi, Robert, ed. *The Cambridge Dictionary of Philosophy.* Cambridge: Cambridge University Press, 1995.

Baugh, Steven M. " 'Savior of All People': 1 Timothy 4:10 in Context." *Westminster Theological Journal* 54 (1992): 331–40.

Bavinck, Herman. *The Certainty of Faith.* Translated by Harry der Nederlanden. St. Catharines, Ontario: Paideia Press, 1980.

———. *Reformed Dogmatics.* Edited by John Bolt. Translated by John Vriend. 4 vols. Grand Rapids: Baker Academic, 2004.

Berkouwer, G. C. *Man: The Image of God.* Grand Rapids: Eerdmans, 1962.

———. *The Providence of God.* Grand Rapids: Eerdmans, 1952.

Calvin, John. *Institutes of the Christian Religion.* Edited by John T. McNeill. Translated by Ford Lewis Battles. Library of Christian Classics, 20–21. 2 vols. London: SCM Press, 1960.

———. *Institutes of the Christian Religion.* Edited and translated by Henry Beveridge. 2 vols. Grand Rapids: Eerdmans, 1957.

———. *A Treatise on the Eternal Predestination of God.* In *Calvin's Calvinism,* translated by Henry Cole. Grand Rapids: Eerdmans, 1950.

Clowney, Edmund P. "Preaching the Word of the Lord: Cornelius Van Til, V.D.M." *Westminster Theological Journal* 46 (1984): 233–53.

De Graaf, S. G. *Promise and Deliverance*, vol. 1: *From Creation to the Conquest of Canaan*. Translated by H. Evan Runner. St. Catharines, Ontario: Paideia Press, 1979.

Hodge, Charles. *Systematic Theology*. 3 vols. London: James Clarke, 1960.

Kuyper, Abraham. *Encyclopaedie der heilige godgeleerdheid*. 3 vols. Amsterdam: J. A. Wormser, 1894.

————. *Principles of Sacred Theology*. Grand Rapids: Baker Book House, 1980.

McCormack, Bruce. "Christ and the Decree: An Unsettled Question for the Reformed Churches Today." In *Reformed Theology in Contemporary Perspective*, edited by Lynn Quigley, 124–42. Edinburgh, Scotland: Rutherford House, 2006.

————. "Election and Trinity: Theses in Response to George Hunsinger." In *Trinity and Election in Contemporary Theology*, edited by Michael T. Dempsey, 115–37. Grand Rapids: Eerdmans, 2011.

Muether, John R. *Cornelius Van Til: Reformed Apologist and Churchman*. Phillipsburg, NJ: P&R Publishing, 2008.

Oliphint, K. Scott. "Bavinck's Realism, the Logos Principle, and *Sola Scriptura*." *Westminster Theological Journal* 72 (2010): 359–90.

————. "The Consistency of Van Til's Methodology." *Westminster Theological Journal* 52 (1990): 27–49.

————. *Covenantal Apologetics: Principles and Practice in Defense of Our Faith*. Wheaton, IL: Crossway Books, 2013.

————. *God with Us: Divine Condescension and the Attributes of God*. Wheaton, IL: Crossway Books, 2012.

————. "A Primal and Simple Knowledge." In *A Theological Guide to Calvin's Institutes: Essays and Analysis*, edited by David Hall and Peter A. Lillback, 16–33. Philipsburg, NJ: P&R Publishing, 2008.

————. *Reasons for Faith: Philosophy in the Service of Theology*. Phillipsburg, NJ: P&R Publishing, 2006.

Poythress, Vern Sheridan. *Logic: A God-Centered Approach to the Foundation of Western Thought*. Wheaton, IL: Crossway Books, 2013.

Stoker, H. G. "On the Contingent and Present-Day Western Man." In *The Idea of a Christian Philosophy: Essays in Honour of D. H. Th. Vollenhoven*, edited by K. A. Bril, H. Hart, and J. Klapwijk, 144–66. Toronto: Wedge Publishing Foundation, 1973.

Van Til, Cornelius. *Christianity and Barthianism*. Philadelphia: Presbyterian and Reformed, 1962.

————. *The Defense of the Faith*. Edited by K. Scott Oliphint. Phillipsburg, NJ: P&R Publishing, 2008.

————. *Essays on Christian Education*. Phillipsburg, NJ: Presbyterian and Reformed, 1979.

————. *The Great Debate Today*. Philadelphia: Presbyterian and Reformed, 1970.

————. *An Introduction to Systematic Theology: Prolegomena and the Doctrines of Revelation, Scripture, and God*. Edited by William Edgar. Phillipsburg, NJ: P&R Publishing, 2007.

————. *The New Modernism: An Appraisal of the Theology of Barth and Brunner*. 2nd ed. Philadelphia: Presbyterian and Reformed, 1947.

————. *A Survey of Christian Epistemology*, vol. 2: *In Defense of the Faith*. Philadelphia: Presbyterian and Reformed, 1969.

Warfield, Benjamin B. *Faith and Life*. Bellingham, WA: Logos Research Systems, 2008.

————. "Inspiration of Scripture." In *The Works of Benjamin B. Warfield*, vol. 5: *Calvin and Calvinism*. Bellingham, WA: Logos Research Systems, 2008.

————. *The Works of Benjamin B. Warfield*, vol. 9: *Studies in Theology*. Bellingham, WA: Logos Research Systems, 2008.

INDEX OF PERSONS

Ursinus, Zacharias, 29, 240n4

van Mastricht, Petrus, 27, 28,
    29–30
Veenhof, Cornelis, 45–46
Volbeda, Samuel, 211
Vollenhoven, D. H. Th., 32, 45, 45n45,
    170–71

Vos, Geerhardus, xxiin16, xxivnn17–18,
    85, 243n13

Warfield, Benjamin B., 51, 99, 149, 170,
    177–78, 180, 197, 212, 214n125,
    243n13

Zwier, Daniel, 34–36, 44

Cornelius Van Til (1895–1987) was born in Grootegast, the Netherlands, and emigrated with his family to America in 1905. He attended Calvin College and Calvin Seminary before completing his studies at Princeton Theological Seminary and Princeton University with the Th.M. and Ph.D. degrees.

Drawn to the pastorate, Van Til spent one year in the ministry before taking a leave of absence to teach apologetics at Princeton Seminary. When the seminary reorganized, he was persuaded to join the faculty of the newly founded Westminster Theological Seminary. He remained there as professor of apologetics until his retirement in 1975.

Van Til wrote more than twenty books, in addition to more than thirty syllabi. Among his best-known titles are *The Defense of the Faith, Christian Apologetics, An Introduction to Systematic Theology,* and *Christianity and Barthianism.*

K. Scott Oliphint (M.A.R., Th.M., Ph.D., Westminster Theological Seminary) is professor of apologetics and systematic theology at Westminster Seminary, Philadelphia. He is the author of *Reasons for Faith* and *The Battle Belongs to the Lord,* and is coeditor of *Revelation and Reason: New Essays in Reformed Apologetics.*

ALSO BY CORNELIUS VAN TIL

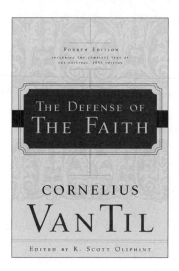

This new, annotated edition restores the full text of the original work in a form that is more easily understood. Newly edited and retypeset, this unabridged edition features a foreword and explanatory notes by K. Scott Oliphint, which help us to grasp a method of apologetics consistent with the nature of Christianity itself and continually relevant to our time.

"As an assigned text in my introductory systematics course, *The Defense of the Faith* typically meets with a combination of frustration and delight. Frustrating because Van Til often engages ideas, terms, and conversation partners unknown to contemporary (especially non-Reformed) readers, this work also has a cumulatively delightful effect in exposing the pretensions of human autonomy and the grandeur of God's sovereign grace. In his careful, thorough, and sympathetic notes, Professor Oliphint has done us all a tremendous service: turning down the frustration and turning up the delight!"
—**Michael S. Horton**

ALSO BY CORNELIUS VAN TIL

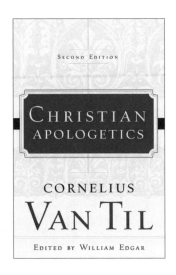

Here Van Til presents the underpinnings of his uniquely biblical approach to apologetics. He shows how Christian apologetics is rooted in a unified system of scriptural truth, a worldview that encompasses all spheres of knowledge. Noting the ultimate conflict between Christian and non-Christian systems, Van Til sets forth a method of argument that centers on an all-important, biblically defined point of contact with the unbeliever.

In this first typeset edition, William Edgar sheds light on Van Til's approach by adding a new introduction and explanatory notes.

"The appearance of this edition is most welcome. Its value is only enhanced by the editor's comments, which are invariably helpful, never intrusive."
   —**Richard B. Gaffin Jr.**

ALSO BY CORNELIUS VAN TIL

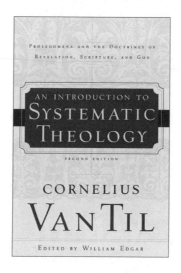

The theological foundations of Van Til's defense of the faith are set forth here as the unified system of truth to which believers are committed and with which nonbelievers need to be confronted.

Van Til explores the implications of Christian theology, particularly for philosophy, as he discusses epistemology, general and special revelation, and the knowledge and attributes of God. This newly edited and typeset edition features an introduction and explanatory notes by William Edgar.

"One of Van Til's two or three most important books, this is certainly a must-read for anyone who is trying to understand Van Til today. He challenges Christians to *think* in a distinctively biblical way. That biblical way opposes and challenges all religions and secular philosophies, all ideologies that place the ultimate source of truth and value in human beings rather than in God. Thoroughly re-edited, with an excellent introduction by William Edgar."
   —**John M. Frame**

MORE ON CORNELIUS VAN TIL
FROM P&R PUBLISHING

This work contributes to an understanding of Van Til and his apologetic insights by placing him within the context of twentieth-century developments in North American Reformed theology, including the formation of Westminster Seminary and the Orthodox Presbyterian Church, the rise of neo-evangelicalism, and the American reception of Karl Barth.

"Read and be persuaded by the powerful impact of Van Til's gentle yet confrontational blend of vigorous thought, gracious service, and Presbyterian churchmanship. This is essential reading for understanding Van Til's unique and creative integration of the best of the Dutch Reformed tradition with the strengths of American Presbyterianism, which gave birth to presuppositionalism and continues to energize interest in worldview analysis."
—**Peter A. Lillback**